TRADEMARK LAW

An Open-Source Casebook

Version 7 (2020)

Volume II

Barton Beebe

John M. Desmarais Professor of Intellectual Property Law

New York University School of Law

Volume II

539-5?0

74-80

III. Defenses to Trademark Infringement and Related Limitations on Trademark Rights

A. Descriptive Fair Use

In a typical descriptive fair use situation, the plaintiff uses a term as a trademark (e.g., SWEETARTS for candy) that the defendant also uses merely to describe its own goods (e.g., "sweet-tart" to describe the taste of OCEAN SPRAY cranberry juice). *See Sunmark, Inc. v. Ocean Spray Cranberries, Inc.*, 64 F.3d 1055 (7th Cir. 1995) (finding defendant's descriptive, non-trademark use of the term "sweet-tart" to be a descriptive fair use). The affirmative defense of descriptive fair use (sometimes called "classic" fair use) is based on Lanham Act §§ 33(b)(4), 15 U.S.C. § 1115(b)(4), which establishes a defense to trademark infringement on the ground:

> (4) That the use of the name, term, or device charged to be an infringement is a use, otherwise than as a mark, of the party's individual name in his own business, or of the individual name of anyone in privity with such party, or of a term or device which is descriptive of and used fairly and in good faith only to describe the goods or services of such party, or their geographic origin;

We begin our review of descriptive fair use in Part III.A.1 with *KP Permanent Make-Up, Inc. v. Lasting Impression I, Inc.*, 543 U.S. 111 (2004). *KP Permanent* does not apparently set forth any specific test that the circuits should apply to adjudicate a descriptive fair use claim. The opinion is included here primarily because of the importance of the Court's clear holding that in analyzing descriptive fair use, a court may find the defendant's conduct to be a descriptive fair use even if that conduct causes some degree of consumer confusion as to source.

We then turn in Part III.A.2 to the basic three-step test that most courts apply to evaluate a claim of descriptive fair use.

1. Descriptive Fair Use and Consumer Confusion

In *KP Permanent*, the declaratory plaintiff KP Permanent Make-Up, Inc. used the term "microcolor" in advertisements for its "permanent makeup" (shown below on the left). The defendant had previously registered the trademark MICRO COLORS at the PTO (on the right). In the excerpt that follows, the Supreme Court finally overruled the Ninth Circuit's bizarre doctrine that any likelihood of consumer confusion defeats a defense of descriptive fair use.

V7.0/2020-07-14

KP Permanent Make-Up, Inc. v. Lasting Impression I, Inc.
543 U.S. 111 (2004)

SOUTER, J., delivered the opinion of the Court, in which REHNQUIST, C.J., and STEVENS, O'CONNOR, KENNEDY, THOMAS, and GINSBURG, JJ., joined, in which SCALIA, J., joined as to all but footnotes 4 and 5, and in which BREYER, J., joined as to all but footnote 6.

. . . .

[1] On appeal, 328 F.3d 1061 (2003), the Court of Appeals for the Ninth Circuit thought it was error for the District Court to have addressed the fair use defense without delving into the matter of possible confusion on the part of consumers about the origin of KP's goods. The reviewing court took the view that no use could be recognized as fair where any consumer confusion was probable, and although the court did not pointedly address the burden of proof, it appears to have placed it on KP to show absence of consumer confusion. *Id.*, at 1072 ("Therefore, KP can only benefit from the fair use defense if there is no likelihood of confusion between KP's use of the term 'micro color' and Lasting's mark"). Since it found there were disputed material facts relevant under the Circuit's eight-factor test for assessing the likelihood of confusion, it reversed the summary judgment and remanded the case.

[2] We granted KP's petition for certiorari, 540 U.S. 1099 (2004), to address a disagreement among the Courts of Appeals on the significance of likely confusion for a fair use defense to a trademark infringement claim, and the obligation of a party defending on that ground to show that its

540

use is unlikely to cause consumer confusion. Compare 328 F.3d, at 1072 (likelihood of confusion bars the fair use defense); *PACCAR Inc. v. TeleScan Technologies, L.L.C.*, 319 F.3d 243, 256 (C.A.6 2003) ("[A] finding of a likelihood of confusion forecloses a fair use defense"); and *Zatarains, Inc. v. Oak Grove Smokehouse, Inc.*, 698 F.2d 786, 796 (C.A.5 1983) (alleged infringers were free to use words contained in a trademark "in their ordinary, descriptive sense, so long as such use [did] not tend to confuse customers as to the source of the goods"), with *Cosmetically Sealed Industries, Inc. v. Chesebrough-Pond's USA Co.*, 125 F.3d 28, 30–31 (C.A.2 1997) (the fair use defense may succeed even if there is likelihood of confusion); *Shakespeare Co. v. Silstar Corp. of Am., Inc.*, 110 F.3d 234, 243 (C.A.4 1997) ("[A] determination of likely confusion [does not] preclud[e] considering the fairness of use"); *Sunmark, Inc. v. Ocean Spray Cranberries, Inc.*, 64 F.3d 1055, 1059 (C.A.7 1995) (finding that likelihood of confusion did not preclude the fair use defense). We now vacate the judgment of the Court of Appeals.

II

A.

. . . .

[3] Two points are evident {from this review of the relevant statutory sections}. Section 1115(b) places a burden of proving likelihood of confusion (that is, infringement) on the party charging infringement even when relying on an incontestable registration. And Congress said nothing about likelihood of confusion in setting out the elements of the fair use defense in § 1115(b)(4).

[4] Starting from these textual fixed points, it takes a long stretch to claim that a defense of fair use entails any burden to negate confusion. It is just not plausible that Congress would have used the descriptive phrase "likely to cause confusion, or to cause mistake, or to deceive" in § 1114 to describe the requirement that a markholder show likelihood of consumer confusion, but would have relied on the phrase "used fairly" in § 1115(b)(4) in a fit of terse drafting meant to place a defendant under a burden to negate confusion. "'[W]here Congress includes particular language in one section of a statute but omits it in another section of the same Act, it is generally presumed that Congress acts intentionally and purposely in the disparate inclusion or exclusion.'" *Russello v. United States*, 464 U.S. 16, 23 (1983) (quoting *United States v. Wong Kim Bo*, 472 F.2d 720, 722 (C.A.5 1972); alteration in original).[4]

[5] Nor do we find much force in Lasting's suggestion that "used fairly" in § 1115(b)(4) is an oblique incorporation of a likelihood-of-confusion test developed in the common law of unfair competition. Lasting is certainly correct that some unfair competition cases would stress that use of a term by another in conducting its trade went too far in sowing confusion, and would either enjoin the use or order the defendant to include a disclaimer. See, *e.g., Baglin v. Cusenier Co.*, 221 U.S. 580, 602 (1911) ("[W]e are unable to escape the conclusion that such use, in the manner shown, was to serve the purpose of simulation . . ."); *Herring–Hall–Marvin Safe Co. v. Hall's Safe Co.*, 208 U.S. 554, 559 (1908) ("[T]he rights of the two parties have been reconciled by allowing the use, provided that an explanation is attached"). But the common law of unfair competition also tolerated some degree of confusion from a descriptive use of words contained in another person's trademark. See, *e.g., William R. Warner & Co. v. Eli Lilly & Co.*, 265 U.S. 526, 528 (1924) (as to plaintiff's trademark claim, "[t]he use of a similar name by another to truthfully describe his own product does not constitute a legal or moral

---

[4] Not only that, but the failure to say anything about a defendant's burden on this point was almost certainly not an oversight, not after the House Subcommittee on Trademarks declined to forward a proposal to provide expressly as an element of the defense that a descriptive use be "'[un]likely to deceive the public.'" Hearings on H.R. 102 et al. before the Subcommittee on Trade-Marks of the House Committee on Patents, 77th Cong., 1st Sess., 167–168 (1941) (hereinafter Hearings) (testimony of Prof. Milton Handler).

wrong, even if its effect be to cause the public to mistake the origin or ownership of the product"); *Canal Co. v. Clark,* 13 Wall. 311, 327, 20 L.Ed. 581 (1872) ("Purchasers may be mistaken, but they are not deceived by false representations, and equity will not enjoin against telling the truth"); see also 3 L. Altman, Callmann on Unfair Competition, Trademarks and Monopolies § 18:2, pp. 18–8 to 18–9, n. 1 (4th ed. 2004) (citing cases). While these cases are consistent with taking account of the likelihood of consumer confusion as one consideration in deciding whether a use is fair, see Part II–B, *infra,* they do not stand for the proposition that an assessment of confusion alone may be dispositive. Certainly one cannot get out of them any defense burden to negate it entirely.

[6] Finally, a look at the typical course of litigation in an infringement action points up the incoherence of placing a burden to show nonconfusion on a defendant. If a plaintiff succeeds in making out a prima facie case of trademark infringement, including the element of likelihood of consumer confusion, the defendant may offer rebutting evidence to undercut the force of the plaintiff's evidence on this (or any) element, or raise an affirmative defense to bar relief even if the prima facie case is sound, or do both. But it would make no sense to give the defendant a defense of showing affirmatively that the plaintiff cannot succeed in proving some element (like confusion); all the defendant needs to do is to leave the factfinder unpersuaded that the plaintiff has carried its own burden on that point. A defendant has no need of a court's true belief when agnosticism will do. Put another way, it is only when a plaintiff has shown likely confusion by a preponderance of the evidence that a defendant could have any need of an affirmative defense, but under Lasting's theory the defense would be foreclosed in such a case. "[I]t defies logic to argue that a defense may not be asserted in the only situation where it even becomes relevant." *Shakespeare Co. v. Silstar Corp.,* 110 F.3d, at 243. Nor would it make sense to provide an affirmative defense of no confusion plus good faith, when merely rebutting the plaintiff's case on confusion would entitle the defendant to judgment, good faith or not.

. . . .

B

[7] Since the burden of proving likelihood of confusion rests with the plaintiff, and the fair use defendant has no free-standing need to show confusion unlikely, it follows (contrary to the Court of Appeals's view) that some possibility of consumer confusion must be compatible with fair use, and so it is. The common law's tolerance of a certain degree of confusion on the part of consumers followed from the very fact that in cases like this one an originally descriptive term was selected to be used as a mark, not to mention the undesirability of allowing anyone to obtain a complete monopoly on use of a descriptive term simply by grabbing it first. *Canal Co. v. Clark,* 13 Wall., at 323–324, 327. The Lanham Act adopts a similar leniency, there being no indication that the statute was meant to deprive commercial speakers of the ordinary utility of descriptive words. "If any confusion results, that is a risk the plaintiff accepted when it decided to identify its product with a mark that uses a well known descriptive phrase." *Cosmetically Sealed Industries, Inc. v. Chesebrough–Pond's USA Co.,* 125 F.3d, at 30. See also *Park 'N Fly, Inc. v. Dollar Park and Fly, Inc.,* 469 U.S. 189, 201 (1985) (noting safeguards in Lanham Act to prevent commercial monopolization of language); *Car–Freshner Corp. v. S.C. Johnson & Son, Inc.,* 70 F.3d 267, 269 (C.A.2 1995) (noting importance of "protect[ing] the right of society at large to use words or images in their primary descriptive sense").[5] This right to describe is the reason that descriptive terms qualify for registration as trademarks only after taking on secondary meaning as "distinctive of the applicant's goods," 15 U.S.C. § 1052(f), with the registrant getting an exclusive right not in the original, descriptive sense, but only in the secondary one associated with the markholder's goods, 2 McCarthy, *supra,* § 11:45, p. 11–90 ("The only aspect of the mark which is given legal

---

[5] See also Hearings 72 (testimony of Wallace Martin, Chairman, American Bar Association Committee on Trade–Mark Legislation) ("Everybody has got a right to the use of the English language and has got a right to assume that nobody is going to take that English language away from him").

protection is that penumbra or fringe of secondary meaning which surrounds the old descriptive word").

[8] While we thus recognize that mere risk of confusion will not rule out fair use, we think it would be improvident to go further in this case, for deciding anything more would take us beyond the Ninth Circuit's consideration of the subject. It suffices to realize that our holding that fair use can occur along with some degree of confusion does not foreclose the relevance of the extent of any likely consumer confusion in assessing whether a defendant's use is objectively fair. Two Courts of Appeals have found it relevant to consider such scope, and commentators and *amici* here have urged us to say that the degree of likely consumer confusion bears not only on the fairness of using a term, but even on the further question whether an originally descriptive term has become so identified as a mark that a defendant's use of it cannot realistically be called descriptive. See *Shakespeare Co. v. Silstar Corp.*, 110 F.3d, at 243 ("[T]o the degree that confusion is likely, a use is less likely to be found fair ..." (emphasis deleted)); *Sunmark, Inc. v. Ocean Spray Cranberries, Inc.*, 64 F.3d, at 1059; Restatement § 28; Brief for American Intellectual Property Law Association as *Amicus Curiae* 13–18; Brief for Private Label Manufacturers Association as *Amicus Curiae* 16–17; Brief for Society of Permanent Cosmetic Professionals et al. as *Amici Curiae* 8–11.

[9] Since we do not rule out the pertinence of the degree of consumer confusion under the fair use defense, we likewise do not pass upon the position of the United States, as *amicus,* that the "used fairly" requirement in § 1115(b)(4) demands only that the descriptive term describe the goods accurately. Tr. of Oral Arg. 17. Accuracy of course has to be a consideration in assessing fair use, but the proceedings in this case so far raise no occasion to evaluate some other concerns that courts might pick as relevant, quite apart from attention to confusion. The Restatement raises possibilities like commercial justification and the strength of the plaintiff's mark. Restatement § 28. As to them, it is enough to say here that the door is not closed.

III

[10] In sum, a plaintiff claiming infringement of an incontestable mark must show likelihood of consumer confusion as part of the prima facie case, 15 U.S.C. § 1115(b), while the defendant has no independent burden to negate the likelihood of any confusion in raising the affirmative defense that a term is used descriptively, not as a mark, fairly, and in good faith, § 1115(b)(4).

[11] Because we read the Court of Appeals as requiring KP to shoulder a burden on the issue of confusion, we vacate the judgment and remand the case for further proceedings consistent with this opinion.[6]

2. The Three-Step Test for Descriptive Fair Use

The first case presented here, *Dessert Beauty, Inc. v. Fox*, is not a leading descriptive fair use case. It is presented here because it offers a clear example of a straightforward application of the descriptive

---

[6] The record indicates that on remand the courts should direct their attention in particular to certain factual issues bearing on the fair use defense, properly applied. The District Court said that Lasting's motion for summary adjudication conceded that KP used "microcolor" descriptively and not as a mark. Case No. SA CV 00–276–GLT (EEx), at 8, App. to Pet. for Cert. 29a. We think it is arguable that Lasting made those concessions only as to KP's use of "microcolor" on bottles and flyers in the early 1990's, not as to the stylized version of "microcolor" that appeared in KP's 1999 brochure. See Opposition to Motion for Summary Judgment/Adjudication in Case No. SA CV 00–276–GLT (EEx) (CD Cal.), pp. 18–19; Appellants' Opening Brief in No. 01–56055(CA9), pp. 31–32. We also note that the fair use analysis of KP's employment of the stylized version of "microcolor" on its brochure may differ from that of its use of the term on the bottles and flyers.

fair use test. Its facts are also bizarre. The second case, *Sorensen v. WD-40 Company*, is more complicated and somewhat more influential.

Dessert Beauty, Inc. v. Fox
568 F.Supp.2d 416 (S.D.N.Y. 2008)

CHIN, District Judge:

[1] At the heart of this litigation are two words: "love potion." Defendant and third-party plaintiff Mara Fox registered the trademark LOVE POTION for perfumed essential oils in 1995 and filed a declaration of incontestability for the LOVE POTION mark in 2001. In 2004, plaintiff Dessert Beauty, Inc. ("DBI") launched a line of beauty products that included two fragrance products described as "love potion fragrance" and "belly button love potion fragrance." At issue is whether DBI's use of the words "love potion" infringed Fox's LOVE POTION trademark, or whether the use was fair use, immune from liability.

[2] DBI seeks a declaratory judgment that it did not violate Fox's trademark; it also seeks to cancel the LOVE POTION trademark registration on the ground that it is generic . . . .

[3] The parties cross-move for summary judgment. For the reasons that follow, I conclude that DBI's use of "love potion" constituted fair use. Thus, DBI's motion is granted to the extent that judgment will be entered declaring that DBI did not engage in trademark infringement . . . .

BACKGROUND

A. The Facts

[4] The following facts are drawn from affidavits, attached exhibits, and deposition testimony submitted by the parties. For purposes of these cross-motions, the facts are construed in the light most favorable to Fox, except with respect to DBI's intentional interference with business relations claim.

1. Fox's Love Potion Perfume

[5] Fox created the "Love Potion Perfume" in 1990. In 1995, she registered the words "love potion" for "perfumed essential oils for personal use" with the U.S. Patent and Trademark Office ("USPTO"). In 2001, Fox filed a declaration of incontestability with the USPTO for the mark LOVE POTION.

[6] Fox concocted the Love Potion Perfume for a friend who "was having no luck in finding a relationship." According to Fox's website www.lovepotionperfume.com, entitled "Love Potion: Magickal Perfumerie & Gift Shoppe," her Love Potion Perfume is the "first Magical, Mystical, Wearable Love Potion," "[c]omprised from Ancient Aphrodisiac Recipes." Fox claims that she uses "the strongest ingredients known to inspire feelings of Love, Lust, Passion and Desire" and that her Love Potion Perfume "REALLY IS A *Love Potion*."

[7] The Love Potion Perfumes are sold in a clear bottle and packaged in a clear plastic bag and an organza[1] pouch:

---

[1] "Organza" is a "sheer, stiff fabric of silk or synthetic material." *The American Heritage Dictionary* 876 (2d College Ed.1991).

544

A label with the words "Love Potion Perfume" is affixed to the bottle.

2. DBI's Beauty Products

[8] In 2004, DBI launched a line of beauty products that were endorsed by celebrity Jessica Simpson. As part of DBI's advertising and marketing campaign, Simpson told the story that "every time [her then husband] would kiss [her] lips or skin, he would taste [her] lipstick, body lotion, and perfume—and hate it." Thus, the DBI products were created to "smell and taste good" and were advertised as "lickable, tasteable, and . . . kissable." Products such as the "Whipped Body Cream with Candy Sprinkles," "Chocolicious Body Gloss," and "Powdered Sugar Body Shimmer" were named after ingredients used to make desserts to suggest their "edible nature."

[9] In a catalogue entitled "Menu," DBI listed its products available in the Dessert Beauty line, such as "Bath Bubbles" and "Sugar Scrub." Two fragrance products are included. The "Love Potion Fragrance" was offered in three varieties: "Creamy, Juicy & Dreamy." The "Belly Button Love Potion Fragrance," offered in "Creamy" and "Juicy," was intended to be applied to the navel and sold in a "roll-on" container. The packages and bottles referred to the fragrance products as the "deliciously kissable love potion fragrance" or the "deliciously kissable belly button love potion."

---

* {This is the image as-is from the federal opinion.}

[10] DBI's trademark was DESSERT, which was indicated as such by the trademark symbol "TM" next to the word "Dessert" on all of its packaging and advertising materials. Its logo consisted of a pink lipstick stain and the mark DESSERT inside a black circle. Beneath the circle was the phrase "Sexy Girls Have Dessert" in script. The DESSERT trademark, in conjunction with the lipstick stain logo and catch phrase (the DBI "indicia"), was displayed prominently on every DBI product and used in all advertising materials.

3. Fox's Actions to Protect Her Trademark

[11] Fox's lawyer routinely issued cease and desist letters to manufacturers and retailers that sold perfume products containing the term "love potion." The record contains approximately 80 such letters sent to different vendors between 2000 and 2006.

[12] After learning in April 2004 that DBI was using the words "love potion" for its fragrance products, Fox's lawyer demanded that Randi Schinder, co-creator of the Dessert Beauty products, and David Suliteanu, president of Sephora USA LLC, "[c]ease and desist from any further use of the [LOVE POTION] mark" and "[p]rovide an accounting of any and all sales made to date." DBI's lawyer, on behalf of both DBI and Sephora, responded in a letter dated April 23, 2004, stating that DBI's "use of the term 'love potion' is fair use within § 33(b)(4) of the Lanham Act." After exchanging several letters regarding whether DBI's use of "love potion" was fair use, DBI voluntarily agreed to "cease and desist from the use of the term 'love potion,'" "change its website as soon as possible," and "delete the term 'love potion' from all bottles, packaging and advertising." DBI steadfastly maintained, however, that its "use of 'love potion' in phrases like 'deliciously kissable love potion fragrance' [was] merely descr[i]ptive." Despite DBI's agreement not to use "love potion," the parties continued to dispute the sufficiency of DBI's actions in removing the words "love potion" from its fragrance products.

546

[13] In addition to direct communication with DBI and Sephora, Fox filed a report with eBay's Verified Rights Owner ("VeRO") Program, which allows intellectual property owners to flag listings on eBay that purportedly infringe their trademark rights.

[14] Fox also waged a public campaign on her website, which contained the following message:

WE ARE A SMALL COMPANY DEFENDING OUR RIGHTFUL INCONTESTABLE TRADEMARKS AGAINST A CORPORATION THAT THINKS THEY CAN BULLY U.S. BECAUSE THEY CAN AFFORD IT. IF YOU FEEL YOU MUST SEND AN ANGRY LETTER, PLEASE DIRECT IT TO THEM FOR THEIR ILLEGAL, IMMORAL, UNETHICAL BUSINESS PRACTICE.

She hired a public relations company, which issued a press release in January 2006 about this lawsuit and DBI's alleged infringement of Fox's trademark. The press release, quoting Fox's third-party complaint, stated that DBI "willfully and maliciously initiate[d] a campaign to flood the major internet search engines with key word spamming to direct any inquiries of LOVE POTION to their retailers." Fox was quoted, stating that "in the first month following [DBI]'s launch, her sales were reduced by 96%. The following month, they were down 97%." (*Id.*). The press release also indicated that DBI "reported sales exceeding $120 million dollars." This press release was reported by numerous media publications, including the New York Post, which wrote that "the bimbonic blonde and her business partners ripped off [Fox's] trademarked cosmetics brand."

B. Procedural History

[15] DBI commenced this action against Fox and Love Potion LLC for: (1) a judgment declaring that DBI did not infringe Fox's trademark, (2) cancellation of Fox's LOVE POTION registration . . . . Fox filed counterclaims against DBI . . . asserting: (1) trademark infringement under the Lanham Act and state law, (2) false designation of origin under the Lanham Act . . . .

[16] Both parties now cross-move for summary judgment. DBI and Sephora move again to dismiss Fox's remaining claims on the ground that there is no trademark infringement or, in the alternative, that DBI's use of the term "love potion" is fair use. Fox moves to dismiss DBI's complaint in its entirety. I heard argument on July 15, 2008 and reserved decision.

DISCUSSION

[17] For the following reasons, I conclude that DBI's use of the term "love potion" is fair use within the meaning of section 33(b)(4) of the Lanham Act.[5] Accordingly, I do not address the parties' cross-motions with respect to the trademark infringement claims and proceed directly to the fair use analysis . . . .

B. Fair Use

[18] The fair use doctrine permits the use of protected marks to describe certain aspects of goods, but not as marks to identify the goods. Even if a party's conduct would otherwise constitute infringement of another's trademark, fair use provides an absolute defense to liability. *See* 15 U.S.C. § 1115(b)(4); *see also Cosmetically Sealed Indus., Inc. v. Chesebrough–Pond's USA Co.*, 125 F.3d 28, 30 (2d Cir. 1997); *Something Old, Something New, Inc. v. QVC, Inc.*, No. 98 Civ. 7450(SAS), 1999 WL 1125063, at *6 (S.D.N.Y. Dec.8, 1999). Section 33(b)(4) of the Lanham Act defines fair use as "a use, otherwise than as a mark, . . . of a term or device which is descriptive of and used fairly and in good faith only to describe the goods or services of [a] party." § 1115(b)(4). Accordingly, to avail itself of the

---

[5] There is "substantial congruence in California trademark law and the Lanham Act," and the fair use analysis for claims under the Lanham Act applies to claims under California law as well. *Bell v. Harley Davidson Motor Co.*, 539 F.Supp.2d 1249, 1261 (S.D.Cal.2008). Accordingly, I address only the federal claim.

fair use defense, DBI must have made use of Fox's LOVE POTION mark "(1) other than as a mark, (2) in a descriptive sense, and (3) in good faith." *EMI Catalogue P'ship v. Hill, Holliday, Connors, Cosmopulos Inc.,* 228 F.3d 56, 64 (2d Cir. 2000). I address these elements in turn.

1. Non–Trademark Use

[19] A trademark use occurs when a mark indicates the source or origin of consumer products. *See Tommy Hilfiger Licensing, Inc. v. Nature Labs, LLC,* 221 F.Supp.2d 410, 414 (S.D.N.Y.2002) (defining non-trademark use in the context of trademark parody). Here, DBI did not use "love potion" as a trademark because the source of its fragrance products was not identified by that term. Instead, the source was indicated by its own trademark DESSERT in conjunction with the lip stain logo and catch phrase "Sexy Girls Have Dessert," which were prominently displayed on all DBI products. Words on a product's packaging generally do not serve as a trademark where there is also a conspicuously visible trademark that clearly serves that function. *See Cosmetically Sealed,* 125 F.3d at 30–31 (the "non-trademark use of the challenged phrase [is] evidenced by the fact that the source of [plaintiffs'] product is clearly identified by the prominent display of [their] own trademarks"). Moreover, DBI placed a TM symbol only next to the word "Dessert," highlighting the non-trademark use of "love potion." The TM symbol was not placed next to the words "love potion."

[20] Moreover, DBI used the words "love potion" within the phrase "Love Potion Fragrance" or "Belly Button Love Potion Fragrance" to identify particular products within the DBI line. These names are listed in the "Menu" of beauty products along with the descriptive or generic names of other products such as "Bath Bubbles" and "Sugar Scrub." The product names served to distinguish the love potion fragrance products from other DBI products rather than to distinguish them from non-DBI products.

[21] Fox argues that a product name can constitute trademark use. Product names, however, generally do not amount to trademark use because such names, as a "common descriptive name of a product," are generic, *San Francisco Arts & Athletics, Inc. v. U.S. Olympic Comm.,* 483 U.S. 522, 532 n. 7 (1987), and generic terms cannot be trademarked under the Lanham Act, *see, e.g., PaperCutter, Inc. v. Fay's Drug Co.,* 900 F.2d 558, 562 (2d Cir. 1990). Product names identify a category or class of goods, but do not indicate the source of the goods. For instance, "perfume" is a product name that indicates that the product emits a fragrant scent when sprayed, but the word "perfume" does not indicate who manufactured the particular product. Accordingly, at least two courts in this Circuit have held that "regardless of whether or not a person knows that [a given word] is a trade-mark, if he uses the trade-mark word as the name of the product, it is used in a descriptive sense and is therefore generic." *Am. Thermos Prods. Co. v. Aladdin Indus., Inc.,* 207 F.Supp. 9, 20 (D.C.Conn.1962); *see also W.R. Grace & Co. v. Union Carbide Corp.,* 581 F.Supp. 148, 154–55 (S.D.N.Y.1983) (holding that a product name is not a trademark use, but is generic). Hence, because DBI used the words "love potion" not to describe the source of the product but as a product name in a generic, descriptive sense, the use was not trademark use.

2. Descriptive Use

[22] Fox argues that "love potion" can never be used in a descriptive sense when referring to perfume products because "love potion" is "a liquid consumable that is drunk" and "has not been used in its common parlance to describe [or] refer to a fragrance." Fox thus raises the question whether the term "love potion" can describe a product that is not, in actuality, a love potion. I conclude that it may for purposes of the fair use defense.

[23] A use of a mark is descriptive if "the words were used to describe the 'ingredients, quality or composition' of a product, not the source of the product." *JA Apparel Corp. v. Abboud,* No. 07 Civ. 7787(THK), 2008 WL 2329533, at *19 (S.D.N.Y. Jun.5, 2008) (citing *In Re Colonial Stores Inc.,* 55 C.C.P.A. 1049, 394 F.2d 549, 551 (C.C.P.A.1968)). Though the Lanham Act recognizes the fair use defense where the name or term is used "to describe the goods," § 1115(b)(4), the Second Circuit has explained that

548

the statute "has not been narrowly confined to words that describe a characteristic of the goods, such as size or quality. Instead, [the Second Circuit has] recognized that the phrase permits use of words or images that are used, in Judge Leval's helpful expression, in their 'descriptive sense.'" *Cosmetically Sealed*, 125 F.3d at 30 (citing *Car–Freshner Corp. v. S.C. Johnson & Son, Inc.*, 70 F.3d 267, 269 (2d Cir. 1995)).

[24] For instance, the Second Circuit has held the fair use defense applicable to a clothing manufacturer's use of the phrase "Come on Strong" as "describing a presumably desirable effect" of its menswear, even though articles of clothing do not literally "come on strong." *B & L Sales Assocs. v. H. Daroff & Sons, Inc.*, 421 F.2d 352, 354 (2d Cir. 1970). The Second Circuit has also held that even though "the words 'Seal it with a Kiss' do not describe a characteristic of the defendants' [lipstick], they surely are used in their 'descriptive sense'—to describe an action that the sellers hope consumers will take, using their product." *Cosmetically Sealed*, 125 F.3d at 30. In *Jean Patou, Inc. v. Jacqueline Cochran, Inc.*, 201 F.Supp. 861 (S.D.N.Y.1962), *aff'd*, 312 F.2d 125 (2d Cir. 1963), the plaintiff was the owner of the registered trademark JOY for use on perfumes and sought to enjoin the defendant from using the phrase "Joy of Bathing" on its bath products. But the court concluded that the challenged phrase was "designed to suggest the pleasure which will accompany the use of defendant's product in one's bath, and thus performs a descriptive function." *Jean Patou*, 201 F.Supp. at 865. Accordingly, when determining whether a use is descriptive, courts in the Second Circuit consider not only "whether the mark used describes certain aspects of the alleged infringer's own goods," but also "whether the mark as used describes an action the alleged infringer hopes consumers will make of its product." *EMI Catalogue*, 228 F.3d at 64–65.

[25] Viewed in this broad sense, it is clear that DBI used "love potion" descriptively. First, the words, by themselves, are descriptive. Dictionary.com defines "love potion" as a product "believed to arouse love or sexual passion toward a specified person." *See Radio Channel Networks, Inc. v. Broadcast.Com, Inc.*, No. 98 Civ. 4799(RPP), 1999 WL 124455, at *3 (S.D.N.Y. Mar.8, 1999) (consulting dictionary definitions when determining whether term "radio channel" was used in the descriptive sense). Although the words "love potion" do not describe an actual quality of DBI's fragrance products, they are used to describe the effects that the products may have on whoever "kisses" or "tastes" the products worn by the wearer, or at least to describe the purpose with which consumers will use the product.

[26] Second, the term "love potion" is a common term in the English language. The very fact that "love potion" is defined in several dictionaries as a product used for the purpose of attracting the opposite sex reflects the ordinary usage of the term to describe products used for those purposes. Moreover, the record contains approximately 80 cease and desist letters that were sent by Fox, indicating that "love potion" was commonly used by many sellers in the cosmetics industry to describe a product's purported effect on others.

[27] Third, that many merchants received warning letters from Fox for using "love potion" demonstrates that there is no other reasonably available word to describe the meaning captured by the term "love potion," namely, that the opposite sex will be attracted to the wearer of the product. Descriptive use is evident in such situations "[w]here a mark incorporates a term that is the only reasonably available means of describing a characteristic of another's goods." *EMI Catalogue*, 228 F.3d at 65; *see also New Kids on the Block v. News Am. Publ'g, Inc.*, 971 F.2d 302, 308 (9th Cir. 1992); 2 McCarthy on Trademarks and Unfair Competition § 10:14 (4th Ed.1999) ("Since the use of a descriptive title cannot serve to prevent others from using the title in a descriptive, non-trademark sense, others may be able to use the title as the only term available."). "To expect [plaintiffs] to use unwieldy or long terms would be contrary to the purpose of the fair use defense, [and Fox] cannot monopolize words and images that are used descriptively." *Something Old*, 1999 WL 1125063, at *7.

[28] Finally, descriptive use is often evident in the manner of use, such as the "physical nature of the use in terms of size, location, and other characteristics in comparison with the appearance of other

descriptive matter or other trademarks," *EMI Catalogue*, 228 F.3d at 65 (quoting Restatement (Third) of Unfair Competition § 28 cmt. c. (1995)), as well as "the presence of the defendant's own trademark in conjunction with the descriptive term," § 28 cmt. c; *see also Something Old*, 1999 WL 1125063, at *6 ("In determining descriptive use, the total context of the allegedly infringing term is considered, including lettering, type style, size and placement."). The factors noted above that indicated non-trademark usage—such as the prominent use of the DESSERT brand name—also demonstrate DBI's descriptive use of "love potion." For instance, the presence of a TM symbol next to DESSERT, contrasted with the absence of the symbol next to the words "love potion," suggests not only that "love potion" on the DBI products was a non-trademark use, but also that it constituted descriptive use. Moreover, on all the packaging, the words "love potion" were placed off-center and printed in a smaller font size than the trademark DESSERT. Most indicative of descriptive use is that "love potion" was used with other words to form a phrase describing the products.

3. Good Faith

[29] Fair use analysis also requires a finding that defendants used the protected mark in good faith. A "lack of good faith [is equated] with the subsequent user's intent to trade on the good will of the trademark holder by creating confusion as to source or sponsorship." *EMI Catalogue*, 228 F.3d at 66. In analyzing the good faith element, "the focus of the inquiry is … whether defendant in adopting its mark intended to capitalize on plaintiff's good will." *Id.* Furthermore, "[b]ecause the good faith inquiry in a fair use analysis necessarily concerns the question whether the user of a mark intended to create consumer confusion as to source or sponsorship, … the same contextual considerations [evaluated in a likelihood of confusion analysis for a trademark infringement claim] apply to a court's analysis of good faith in the fair use defense." *Id.* at 66–67. Thus, "a court must take into account the overall context in which the marks appear and the totality of factors that could cause consumer confusion" just as it would "[w]hen considering the likelihood of confusion and assessing the similarity of two marks." *Id.* at 66. In addition, the court, on a motion for summary judgment, must consider all evidence in the record pointing to the alleged infringer's both good and bad faith. *Id.* at 76.

[30] Turning to the evidence in the record, Fox argues that the following facts raise a material issue for trial concerning plaintiffs' alleged bad faith: first, DBI did not conduct a trademark search prior to the launch of its beauty products; and second,… DBI … failed to take necessary action to discontinue the sale of allegedly infringing products after receiving Fox's cease and desist letters.

[31] With respect to DBI's failure to conduct a trademark search, it is well established that "failure to perform an official trademark search … does not, standing alone, prove … bad faith." *Savin Corp. v. Savin Group*, 391 F.3d 439, 460 (2d Cir. 2004) (citing *Streetwise Maps, Inc. v. VanDam, Inc.*, 159 F.3d 739, 746 (2d Cir. 1998)) (internal citations omitted); *see also EMI Catalogue*, 228 F.3d at 67; *Car–Freshner*, 70 F.3d at 270. Even if plaintiffs had prior knowledge of Fox's trademark, that fact would not demonstrate lack of good faith without additional evidence supporting an inference of bad faith. *See, e.g., Savin Corp.*, 391 F.3d at 460; *Arrow Fastener Co. v. Stanley Works*, 59 F.3d 384, 397 (2d Cir. 1995); *EMI Catalogue*, 228 F.3d at 67; *Car–Freshner*, 70 F.3d at 270. Thus, as a matter of law, DBI's failure to conduct a trademark search prior to using "love potion," standing alone, does not demonstrate bad faith.

[32] Fox also points to DBI's alleged failure to discontinue the sale of products with the words "love potion" after she provided notice of the alleged trademark infringement. But the "failure to completely abandon the use after receiving a cease and desist letter is insufficient to support an allegation of bad faith" as a matter of law. *Something Old*, 1999 WL 1125063, at *7; *see also Wonder Labs, Inc. v. Procter & Gamble Co.*, 728 F.Supp. 1058, 1064 (S.D.N.Y.1990) (failure to abort advertising campaign upon receipt of cease and desist letter "is absolutely no proof that the defendant acted in bad faith to capitalize on the plaintiff's trademark"). Notice of Fox's trademark rights—either by her trademark registration or the cease and desist letters—"does not preclude use of the words contained in [Fox's] registered mark in their primary [, descriptive] sense," *Wonder Labs*, 728 F.Supp. at 1064,

especially where DBI believed that its use was descriptive, *see Something Old,* 1999 WL 1125063, at *7. Indeed, the numerous letters exchanged between the parties indicate that DBI had maintained the position that its use of "love potion" was fair use. (*See, e.g.,* 4/23/04 Letter ("our client's use of the term 'love potion' is fair use"); 5/24/04 Letter (same)). In its June 4, 2004 letter to Fox, DBI "for business reasons, [agreed] to cease and desist from the use of the term 'love potion,'" but nevertheless maintained that its "use of 'love potion' in phrases like 'deliciously kissable love potion fragrance' [was] merely descr[i]ptive." (6/4/04 Letter). These letters show that DBI believed that its use of "love potion" was descriptive.

[33] On the record before the Court, no reasonable jury could find bad faith; to the contrary, a reasonable jury could only conclude that DBI acted in good faith. An indication of good faith is "the display of defendant's own name or trademark in conjunction with the mark it allegedly infringes." *EMI Catalogue,* 228 F.3d at 67, citing *Cosmetically Sealed,* 125 F.3d at 30. This is so because the use of a distinct trademark minimizes any likelihood of confusion as to the source or sponsorship of a product. *See W.W.W. Pharmaceutical Co., Inc. v. Gillette Co.,* 984 F.2d 567, 573 (2d Cir. 1993) ("Where a similar mark is used in conjunction with a company name, the likelihood of confusion may be lessened."). As discussed above, all DBI products had the DESSERT trademark and indicia, reflecting DBI's efforts to differentiate its products in the marketplace rather than to trade on Fox's, or any other seller's, good will.

[34] Furthermore, in light of "the overall context in which the marks appear and the totality of factors that could cause consumer confusion," *EMI Catalogue,* 228 F.3d at 66–67, the dissimilarities between the products are patently obvious as to dispel any inference that DBI was trying to pass its products as one of Fox's Love Potion Perfumes or to confuse consumers as to source or sponsorship. The only similarity is the term "love potion," which alone is insufficient to establish a likelihood of confusion. *See Clairol, Inc. v. Cosmair, Inc.,* 592 F.Supp. 811, 815 (S.D.N.Y.1984) ("the mere fact that two marks may share words in common is not determinative" in assessing likelihood of confusion).

[35] The differences between the products and their marks, however, are manifest—a fact that Fox herself concedes. "Love potion" is written in different fonts on the parties' products; on the DBI labels, "deliciously kissable love potion fragrance" is written in sans serif font, but "Love Potion Perfume" is written in cursive. In addition, "Love Potion Perfume" is written on a white label strung to the perfume bottle. In contrast, the DBI product names and trademark are emblazoned directly on the bottles and packaging. Moreover, Fox's Love Potion Perfumes are sold in a diamond-shaped bottle and packaged in a clear plastic bag and organza pouch. On the other hand, DBI's love potion fragrance is packaged in a long, cylindrical tube with a pumping device; its belly button love potion fragrance is sold in a roll-on container and packaged in a rectangular box.

[36] Notwithstanding both parties' usage of the words "love potion," a reasonable jury could only find that it was not likely that consumers would be confused. In short, no reasonable jury could conclude that plaintiff acted in bad faith to capitalize on Fox's trademark. Indeed, the evidence only shows plaintiff's good faith. Because there is no material issue warranting trial with respect to the fair use defense, plaintiff's motion for summary judgment on the trademark claims is granted and Fox's cross motion is denied.

. . . .

SportFuel, Inc. v. Pepsico, Inc.
932 F.3d 589 (7th Cir. 2019)

Kanne, Circuit Judge.

[1] SportFuel appeals the district court's grant of summary judgment for Gatorade and its parent company, PepsiCo. SportFuel brought this suit against Gatorade alleging violations of its trademark after Gatorade rebranded itself with the slogan, "Gatorade The Sports Fuel Company." The district court deemed Gatorade's slogan a fair use protected by the Lanham Act. We affirm.

BACKGROUND

[2] SportFuel is a Chicago-based sports nutrition and wellness consulting firm whose clients include several of Chicago's prominent professional sports teams and their athletes. The company provides personalized nutrition consulting services to professional and amateur athletes, but also sells SportFuel-branded dietary supplements. SportFuel holds two registered trademarks for "SportFuel." It registered the first for "food nutrition consultation, nutrition counseling, and providing information about dietary supplements and nutrition." After several years of use, SportFuel's trademark became "incontestable" in 2013 under 15 U.S.C. § 1065. SportFuel also registered a trademark in 2015 for "goods and services related to dietary supplements and sports drinks enhanced with vitamins."

[3] Gatorade was created in 1965 at the University of Florida College of Medicine and public sales began several years later. Undoubtedly, Gatorade is more widely known. It is the official sports drink of the NBA, PGA, MLB, MLS, and many other professional and collegiate organizations. Whether by television imagery of victorious athletes drenching their coaches or teammates with a Gatorade shower from a distinctive cooler, or through aggressive national media marketing campaigns, Gatorade became a household name.

[4] In addition to its traditional sports drinks, Gatorade now customizes its sports drink line by selling formulas that are tailored to the nutritional needs of individual professional athletes. The company also sells numerous other sports nutrition products beyond sports drinks. It began to publicly describe its products as sports fuels in 2013. Seeking to broaden its public image to reflect its expanded variety of products, Gatorade began a rebranding effort. In 2016 it registered the trademark "Gatorade The Sports Fuel Company" with the United States Patent and Trademark Office ("PTO"). Notably, Gatorade disclaimed the exclusive use of "The Sports Fuel Company" after the PTO advised the company that the phrase was merely descriptive of its products.

[5] The only link between SportFuel and Gatorade is a nutritionist and dietician named Julie Burns, who founded SportFuel in 1993. Burns had a history of working with Gatorade: she served as a nutritionist on the Gatorade Sports Science Institute's Sports Nutrition Advisory Board from 1995 until 2003. Burns became aware of Gatorade's rebranding efforts and the alleged trademark infringement when she saw a Gatorade commercial featuring the new slogan. SportFuel filed suit against Gatorade and PepsiCo in August 2016. Its complaint alleged trademark infringement (15 U.S.C. § 1051), unfair competition, and false designation of origin in violation of the Lanham Act (15 U.S.C. § 1125(a)). Similarly, SportFuel asserted claims of trademark infringement and unfair competition in violation of Illinois law. *See* 815 Ill. Comp. Stat. §§ 505/1, 510/1. Gatorade raised counterclaims for a cancellation of SportFuel's trademark.

. . . .

[6] On June 14, 2018, the district court granted Gatorade's motion for summary judgment after finding that SportFuel failed to produce evidence that demonstrated a factual dispute on any of the three elements of Gatorade's fair use defense. The court also determined that because it found that Gatorade successfully raised the Act's fair use defense, it need not conduct a risk of confusion analysis for SportFuel's claims. Similarly, because the court determined that SportFuel's claims under Illinois law were subject to the same analysis as its federal claims, it did not separately consider those claims. SportFuel appeals.

II. ANALYSIS

. . . .

[7]... [T]o raise the fair use defense successfully, Gatorade must show that (1) it did not use "Sports Fuel" as a trademark, (2) the use is descriptive of its goods, and (3) it used the mark fairly and in good faith. *Sorensen v. WD-40 Co.*, 792 F.3d 712, 722 (7th Cir. 2015); *Packman v. Chi. Tribune Co.*, 267 F.3d 628, 639 (7th Cir. 2001). The district court determined that Gatorade met all three prongs.

. . . .

A. Gatorade Did Not Use "Sports Fuel" As a Trademark.

[8] SportFuel claims that the district court erred in finding that Gatorade did not use the term "Sports Fuel" as a trademark. SportFuel supports its argument with three factors: Gatorade uses the slogan as an "attention getting symbol," it placed a trademark indication after the slogan, and it sought to trademark the slogan.

. . . .

[9] As here, *Sands, Taylor & Wood Co. v. Quaker Oats Co.*, 978 F.2d 947, 953 (7th Cir. 1992), involved a suit over Gatorade's use of a slogan in an advertising campaign. 978 F.2d at 953–54. That campaign used the trademarked phrase "Thirst Aid" in the slogan "Gatorade is THIRST AID."[1] *Id.* There, the district court determined that although Gatorade used its house mark in addition to the slogan, the term "Thirst Aid" also served as a source indicator. *Id.* at 953. The district court emphasized that Gatorade featured the term "Thirst Aid" prominently on its product packaging—even more prominently than the Gatorade house mark. Gatorade appealed summary judgment in the plaintiff's favor, arguing that it used the term "Thirst Aid" descriptively and not as a trademark. *Id.*

[10] We affirmed and explained that although Gatorade used "Thirst Aid" in tandem with its house mark, it used the term as an "attention-getting symbol." *Id.* at 954. We observed that the "Gatorade is Thirst Aid" phrase employed a rhyming play-on-words and that Gatorade featured the slogan in larger, more noticeable font than the house mark. *Id.* We consequently determined that Gatorade's use of the slogan would likely lead consumers to associate the terms "Thirst Aid" and "Gatorade," and that such a use of "Thirst Aid" was meant to help consumers identify the source of the product. *Id.* These factors supported the district court's conclusion that Gatorade used the phrase as a trademark. *Id.*

[11] In this case, however, the record does not support the notion that Gatorade used the term "Sports Fuel" as a source indicator. Because visuals help considerably in trademark cases, we include the following photographs included in the parties' briefs of Gatorade's use of the slogan:

---

[1] Although the full slogan declared, "Gatorade is THIRST AID for That Deep Down Body Thirst," Gatorade's advertisements and the ensuing litigation focused on the first portion. 978 F.2d at 950.

[12] As in *Quaker Oats*, here Gatorade used the term "Sports Fuel" in conjunction with its house mark. But the similarities end there. The products' individual packaging and displays feature Gatorade's house mark and G Bolt logo more prominently. Gatorade rarely uses the term "Sports Fuel" directly on product packaging, except for where the company labeled a "Sports Fuel Drink" with the

554

term. Instead, it primarily features the slogan on in-store displays and other advertisements—appearing almost as a subtitle to the house mark. Additionally, the "Sports Fuel" slogan lacks the catchy, rhyming play-on-words at issue in *Quaker Oats*. Nothing about Gatorade's use in this context suggests that consumers would view "Sports Fuel" as a source indicator.

[13] SportFuel emphasizes that Gatorade employed a "TM" symbol with the slogan and obtained a trademark for the slogan. But these facts fail to support SportFuel's desired conclusion. The slogan notably included Gatorade's trademark-protected house mark. Additionally, Gatorade specifically disclaimed exclusive use of the phrase "The Sports Fuel Company" in its trademark application for "Gatorade The Sports Fuel Company." *Sunmark*, 64 F.3d at 1059 (noting that Ocean Spray disclaimed exclusive use of a contested, descriptive phrase). During the application process for Gatorade's slogan, the PTO specifically advised Gatorade that it viewed the term "Sports Fuel" as descriptive and therefore inappropriate for trademark use. And as the district court pointed out, Gatorade's chief marketing officer stated in his deposition that he viewed the whole phrase—including the protected house mark—as a trademark.

[14] Thus, even construing the record in SportFuel's favor on summary judgment, insufficient evidence supports SportFuel's claim. Accordingly, we do not believe the district court erred in determining that Gatorade never employed the term "Sports Fuel" as a trademark in its "Gatorade The Sports Fuel Company" slogan.

B. Gatorade Used "Sports Fuel" Descriptively.

[15] The district court also found that Gatorade used "Sports Fuel" descriptively, rather than suggestively, and therefore not as a trademark. SportFuel maintains that the district court erred in this determination. We review the district court's classification *de novo*. *Quaker Oats*, 978 F.2d at 952.

[16] Suggestive marks . . . do not "directly and immediately describe an aspect of the goods," rather they "require[ ] an observer or listener to use imagination and perception to determine the nature of the goods." *Uncommon, LLC v. Spigen, Inc.*, 926 F.3d 409, 421 (7th Cir. 2019) (quotations omitted). However, just because a phrase is unfamiliar and "requires a hearer to think about its meaning" does not necessarily mean it is suggestive. *Quaker Oats*, 978 F.2d at 953. Courts look to a variety of factors to distinguish between descriptive and suggestive terminology, but we find two factors particularly helpful in this instance.[2] "First, we can look to how, and how often, the relevant market uses the word [or phrase] in question." *Uncommon*, 926 F.3d at 421. Second, we employ the "imagination test," where we ask whether the word or phrase imparts information about the product or service directly or rather requires "some operation of the imagination to connect it with the goods." *Id.* at 422 (quoting *Platinum Home Mortg.*, 149 F.3d at 727). Both factors lead us to characterize the slogan here as descriptive.

[17] First, producers of nutritional products for athletes regularly invoke the "Sports Fuel" terminology to describe the products they sell. Gatorade provided numerous examples of this widespread industry use to the district court, including, for example, Twin Laboratories' "SPORT FUEL" and Trident Sports' "SPORTS FUEL." Similarly, the PTO recognized this point when it processed Gatorade's trademark application stating, "[a]s SPORTS FUEL is commonly used in reference to sports nutrition, consumers encountering the wording THE SPORTS FUEL COMPANY in the proposed mark would readily understand it to mean that the goods are provided by a company that provides sports nutrition." This widespread industry use, coupled with Gatorade's disclaimer of exclusive use of "The Sports Fuel Company," supports Gatorade's argument it used "Sports Fuel" descriptively.

---

[2] Courts also occasionally find dictionary definitions and third-party patent registrations probative of whether a term or phrase is descriptive. *See Uncommon*, 926 F.3d at 422-23.

[18] Second, SportFuel argues that Gatorade's use of "Sports Fuel" is suggestive—and not descriptive—of Gatorade's products because the term requires a mental leap to deduce that the company is really selling athletic nutrition products. To support this notion, SportFuel also points out that Gatorade's consumers, by and large, are not high-performance athletes. We find these arguments unpersuasive. The use of "Sports Fuel" in "Gatorade The Sports Fuel Company" clearly describes the category of goods that Gatorade produces. It requires no imaginative leap to understand that a company selling "Sports Fuel" is selling a variety of food products designed for athletes. That non-athletes regularly consume Gatorade's products has no bearing whether the term is descriptive. Just as the pervasive use of yoga pants and other activewear as casual clothing does not change the athletic characteristics of those products, the fact that Gatorade sells more sports drinks to average joes who limit their rigorous exercise to lawn mowing does not change the athletic characteristics of Gatorade's products.

[19] We conclude that Gatorade's slogan uses "Sports Fuel" in a descriptive sense.

C. Gatorade Uses "Sports Fuel" Fairly and in Good Faith.

[20] A party raising a fair use defense "must show that it used the plaintiff's mark fairly and in good faith." *Sorensen*, 792 F.3d at 725. Courts determine defendants' good faith by looking to their subjective purpose in using a slogan. *Packman*, 267 F.3d at 642. As an initial matter, we note that although the district court's analysis implicitly confirmed that Gatorade used "Sport Fuel" in good faith, it never stated its conclusion explicitly. Nonetheless, as we explain, we believe Gatorade produced sufficient evidence to show that it descriptively used the term "Sports Fuel" in its slogan fairly and in good faith. SportFuel insisted during summary judgment that the evidence, construed in its favor, demonstrated that Gatorade acted unfairly and in bad faith by using its slogan. But the district court rejected SportFuel's argument and explained why SportFuel failed to show that Gatorade acted in bad faith.

[21] On appeal, SportFuel challenges the district court's conclusion for three reasons. First, SportFuel claims that evidence produced during discovery justified inferring bad faith on Gatorade's part. Second, the district court purportedly erred in concluding that Gatorade used "Sports Fuel" fairly given the risk that reverse confusion posed to SportFuel. Third, Gatorade uses "Sports Fuel" in a trademark manner, *beyond* describing its goods or services.

1. SportFuel Provides Insufficient Evidence of Gatorade's Bad Faith.

[22] SportFuel alleges that the district court erred because it never properly considered evidence of Gatorade's bad faith. It provides four main examples to support this argument. First, it argues that Gatorade was aware of SportFuel's mark by virtue of Gatorade's previous working relationship with Julie Burns. Second, it suggests that Gatorade's continued use of "Sports Fuel" after SportFuel filed suit betrays its bad faith. Third, SportFuel points to a dearth of evidence concerning Gatorade's adoption of its new slogan. Fourth, SportFuel alludes to a falling out between Gatorade and Burns, suggesting that Gatorade adopted the new slogan to settle an old score.

[23] SportFuel alleges that Gatorade's bad faith is demonstrated by the fact that it began to use "Sports Fuel" even though it knew of SportFuel's mark. But the defendant's "mere knowledge" of the plaintiff's mark, without other evidence of subjective bad faith, is insufficient. *Sorensen*, 792 F.3d at 725. Accordingly, "[t]o survive summary judgment, a plaintiff must point to something more that suggests subjective bad faith." *Id.* Therefore, without other, substantial evidence, this factor provides no support for the claim that Gatorade used "Sports Fuel" in bad faith.

[24] SportFuel also points to Gatorade's continued use of "Sports Fuel," even after SportFuel filed this suit. But "it is lawful to use a mark that does not infringe some other; intentional infringement creates problems, but [a defendant's] intentional use of a mark that [it] had every right to use is not itself a ground on which to draw an adverse inference." *M-F-G Corp. v. EMRA Corp.*, 817 F.2d 410, 412

(7th Cir. 1987). Gatorade believed it had every right to use "Sports Fuel" in a descriptive sense, so its continued use after SportFuel filed suit also fails to justify an inference of bad faith.

[25] Third, SportFuel suggests that Gatorade failed to produce evidence in discovery that must have existed. Specifically, Gatorade's production included no documentation related to its approval of the slogan "Gatorade The Sports Fuel Company." SportFuel argues that a company as large as Gatorade certainly required high-level approval before adopting a nation-wide rebranding campaign. And presumably Gatorade would possess documentation of that approval. Yet, "[s]peculation will not suffice" to defeat summary judgment. *Borcky v. Maytag Corp.*, 248 F.3d 691, 695 (7th Cir. 2001); *Amadio v. Ford Motor Co.*, 238 F.3d 919, 927 (7th Cir. 2001) ("It is well-settled that speculation may not be used to manufacture a genuine issue of fact."); *Gorbitz v. Corvilla*, Inc., 196 F.3d 879, 882 (7th Cir.1999). SportFuel's argument relies on the assumption that something must have existed. But the time to pursue this idea was during discovery. SportFuel did not, and it cannot now avoid summary judgment with assumption or speculation. The record neither provides evidence to support the claim that Gatorade adopted the slogan in bad faith, nor indicates that Gatorade purposefully failed to produce such evidence.

[26] Fourth, SportFuel suggests that Gatorade's adoption of the slogan relates to a falling out between Burns and Gatorade. The problem with this claim—much like the last argument—is that SportFuel provides no relevant evidence as support. It relies on Burns's deposition testimony, where she stated that her relationship with Gatorade ended after she refused to endorse one of Gatorade's new sugary sports bar products. However, Burns's relationship with Gatorade ended more than a decade before the alleged infringement began. And the idea that a new slogan for a nation-wide rebranding campaign and stale antipathy towards Burns are connected is facially incredible when otherwise unsupported by the record.

[27] We accordingly find none of these factors significant enough—individually or in the aggregate—to create an inference of Gatorade's bad faith.

2. The Risk of Reverse Confusion Does Not Demonstrate Gatorade's Bad Faith.

[28] Second, SportFuel claims that the district court conducted an insufficient analysis of Gatorade's intent in using "Sports Fuel" because its alleged infringement creates reverse confusion.... In this case, the alleged reverse confusion would occur when Gatorade used its house mark alongside the term "Sports Fuel," which would effectively coopt SportFuel's trademark and confuse consumers by leading them to believe the companies were related.

[29] We cannot agree that the district court erred because it declined to examine Gatorade's intent in using "Sports Fuel." In *Quaker Oats*, we explained that intent is largely irrelevant in reverse confusion cases because "the defendant by definition is *not* palming off or otherwise attempting to create confusion as to the source of his product." *Id.* at 961 (emphasis in original); *but see Marketquest Grp., Inc. v. BIC Corp.*, 862 F.3d 927, 937 (9th Cir. 2017) (applying the Ninth Circuit's test that analyzes intent).

[30] But even if it were appropriate to examine Gatorade's intent in using "Sports Fuel" in its slogan, SportFuel's argument would fail. Gatorade provided evidence showing that it adopted the slogan to reflect its various types of sports fuel products. At the same time, SportFuel neither provides nor identifies substantive evidence to support the notion that Gatorade adopted its slogan in any spirit other than good faith.

3. Gatorade Uses "Sports Fuel" Descriptively.

[31] SportFuel lastly urges that Gatorade views the slogan as a trademark and therefore used "Sports Fuel" unfairly and in bad faith. As mentioned above, SportFuel supports this argument by pointing out that Gatorade adorns its slogan with a "TM." SportFuel also relies on testimony by Gatorade's chief marketing officer, in which he stated that he viewed the entire slogan, "Gatorade The Sports Fuel Company" as a trademark. For the reasons mentioned earlier in this opinion, we believe

Gatorade employed the term "Sports Fuel" descriptively and not as a trademark. We therefore do not accept that Gatorade used the slogan unfairly or in bad faith.

[32] Further, it is clear from the record that Gatorade provided sufficient evidence that it used the term "Sports Fuel" fairly and in good faith. Gatorade's stated purpose in adopting the challenged slogan was to help the company better describe its business and the products it sells. Nothing in the record actually contradicts this purpose. Gatorade produced evidence demonstrating that the company and its employees view themselves as producers of sports fuels. Moreover, Gatorade both specifically disclaimed exclusive use of the phrase "The Sports Fuel Company" and prominently used its house mark and G Bolt logo in a manner distinct from the slogan.

III. CONCLUSION

[33] For the foregoing reasons, the judgment of the district court is AFFIRMED.

3. Further Examples of Descriptive Fair Use Analyses

International Stamp Art v. U.S. Postal Service
456 F.3d 1270 (11th Cir. 2006)

In *International Stamp Art*, ISA produced cards, posters, and prints depicting postage stamps enclosed in a flat-edged perforated border design meant to invoke classic postage stamps. In 1996, it managed to get a trademark registration for this design:

Int. Cl.: 16

Prior U.S. Cls.: 2, 5, 22, 23, 29, 37, 38 and 50

Reg. No. 1,985,056

United States Patent and Trademark Office Registered July 9, 1996

TRADEMARK
PRINCIPAL REGISTER

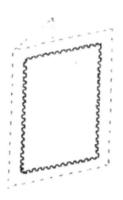

INTERNATIONAL STAMP ART, INC. (SOUTH CAROLINA CORPORATION)
ART CRAFT & FRAME BUILDING
PINEWOOD SHOPPING CENTER1009 NORTH PINE STREET
SPARTANBURG, SC 29303

FOR: PRINTED NOTE CARDS AND GREETING CARDS, IN CLASS 16 (U.S. CLS. 2, 5, 22, 23, 29, 37, 38 AND 50).

FIRST USE 3-4-1987; IN COMMERCE 3-4-1987.

THE MARK CONSISTS OF A PERFORATION DESIGN, PLACED ALONG THE EDGE OF PRINTED NOTE CARDS AND GREETING CARDS. THE MATTER SHOWN BY DOTTED LINES IS NOT PART OF THE MARK AND SERVES MERELY TO INDICATE THE POSITION OF THE MARK ON THE GOODS.
SEC. 2(F).

SER. NO. 74-583,278, FILED 10-7-1994.

KATHLEEN COONEY-PORTER, EXAMINING ATTORNEY

USPS licensed ISA among others to create merchandise incorporating USPS's images. "Stamp images were transmitted to licensees in the form of transparencies, each marked as copyright protected and depicting the entire stamp including any perforated edges." *Id.* at 1272. USPS eventually began to

558

produce its own line of stamp art cards, some of which incorporated the flat-edged perforated border design. ISA sued for trademark infringement. USPS claimed descriptive fair use.

Affirming the district court's grant of summary judgment, the Eleventh Circuit found descriptive fair use. The court devoted the bulk of its analysis to the third step, whether USPS's use was in good faith, i.e., "whether the alleged infringer intended to trade on the good will of the trademark owner by creating confusion as to the source of the goods or services." *Id.* at 1275. The court noted that "the overwhelming majority of stamps the Postal Service produces include perforated edges and have long done so," *id.*; that USPS "prominently places its own familiar Eagle trademark on the backs of its stamp art products thereby identifying them as Postal Service products," *id.*; and that "ISA has not identified any evidence that the Postal Service sought to mislead or confuse consumers into thinking that the source of the cards it produced was actually International Stamp Art," *id.*

ISA claimed that USPS had a "non-infringing, commercially viable alternative" in the form of "cards depicting the art upon which its stamp designs was based, rather than the stamps themselves." *Id.* at 1276. The Eleventh Circuit recognized that "[f]ailure to employ a non-infringing, commercially viable alternative can raise a genuine issue of material fact," *id.*, but was ultimately unpersuaded: "This, however, is not an alternative manner of depicting the stamps, but rather a choice not to depict stamps." *Id.*

Bell v. Harley Davidson Motor Co.
539 F.Supp.2d 1249 (S.D. Cal. 2008)

In *Bell v. Harley Davidson Motor Co.*, 539 F.Supp.2d 1249 (S.D. Cal. 2008), plaintiff Craig Bell owned three trademark registrations in the phrase RIDE HARD in connection with apparel, decals, and various merchandise (an example of which from Bell's complaint is provided below on the left). Defendant Harley Davidson uses the phrase ride hard in advertising and various merchandise, always accompanied by a Harley Davidson trademark (an example of which is below on the right). Bell sued for trademark infringement.

On cross motions for summary judgment, the court first applied the *Sleekcraft* multifactor test for the likelihood of consumer confusion to find no likelihood of confusion. The court then further found descriptive fair use. It cited *KP Permanent* for the proposition that "some possibility of consumer confusion must be compatible with fair use[.]" *KP Permanent*, at 121. It then applied the three-step test to find that Harley Davidson does not use the phrase as a trademark, "i.e., to identify the source of its products," *Bell*, at 1258, and uses the phrase only descriptively. The Court explained: "Although Bell protests that such a use does not describe a specific characteristic of Harley's products or goods, courts do not interpret the Lanham Act's fair use language so narrowly. To the contrary, courts have applied the fair use doctrine in situations where the defendant's use of the trademarked phrase described a feeling inherently associated with the phrase or typically experienced by the consumer upon using defendant's product." *Id.* The court further found good faith. "Harley–Davidson demonstrated its intent not to create confusion by including the Harley–Davidson name or bar-&-shield logo on every advertisement and piece of merchandise bearing the 'Ride Hard' phrase." *Id.* at 1259. Though Bell pointed out that Wrangler Clothing Company abandoned "Ride Hard" and substituted "Ride Rough" in response to Bell's 1999 lawsuit, Harley Davidson was not obligated to use an alternative phrase under these facts.

T-Shirt Front Detail

Fortune Dynamic, Inc. v. Victoria's Secret
618 F.3d 1025 (9th Cir. 2010)

In *Fortune Dynamic, Inc. v. Victoria's Secret*, 618 F.3d 1025 (9th Cir. 2010), Fortune Dynamic sold women's shoes under the registered mark DELICIOUS in the font shown below on the left. To market a new line of products under the trademark BEAUTY RUSH, Victoria's Secret launched a promotion in which anyone who purchased more than $35 worth of BEAUTY RUSH products would receive, among other things, a pink tank top across the chest of which, in silver typescript, was written the word "Delicious" as shown below on the right. "On the back, in much smaller lettering, there appeared the word "yum," and the phrase "beauty rush" was written in the back collar." *Id.* at 1025. Victoria's Secret distributed 602,723 such tank top shirts. Fortune Dynamic sued for trademark infringement.

In a lengthy opinion reversing the lower court's grant of summary judgment to Victoria's Secret and remanding for trial, the Ninth Circuit first considered the *Sleekcraft* factors for the likelihood of consumer confusion and found that a jury could reasonably find confusion. With respect to Victoria's Secret's fair use defense, the court concluded that a reasonable jury could find that Victoria's Secret was using the term "Delicious" as a trademark given the term's prominent placement on the front of the shirt, similar to where Victoria's Secret had placed two of its own trademarks PINK and VERY SEXY. The court also found issues of material fact on the question of whether Victoria's Secret was using the term "delicious" descriptively:

> Victoria's Secret says that it used "Delicious" merely to "describe the flavorful attributes of Victoria's Secret's BEAUTY RUSH lip gloss and other products that feature the same popular fruit flavors." A jury, however, could reasonably conclude otherwise. For one thing, in its advertisements, Victoria's Secret described its BEAUTY RUSH lip gloss as "deliciously sexy," not delicious. For another, Victoria's Secret's executives testified that they wanted "Delicious" to serve as a "playful self-descriptor," as if the wearer of the pink tank top is saying, "I'm delicious." These examples suggest that a jury could reasonably decide that Victoria's Secret did not use "Delicious" "only to describe its goods." 15 U.S.C. § 1115(b)(4) . . . . [A]lthough we accept some flexibility in what counts as descriptive, we reiterate that the scope of the fair use defense varies with the level of descriptive purity. Thus, as a defendant's use of a term becomes less and less purely descriptive, its chances of prevailing on the fair use defense become less and less likely.

560

Id. at 1041-42. The court also noted Victoria's Secret's lack of "precautionary measures" to dispel confusion and the "abundance of alternative words" that it could have used. *Id.* at 1042. On good faith, the court found that Victoria's Secret's failure to investigate whether anyone held a "delicious" trademark, combined with other evidence, suggested that a jury could reasonably find no good faith.

B. Nominative Fair Use

1. The Three-Step Test for Nominative Fair Use

In *New Kids on the Block v. News Am. Publ'g, Inc.*, 971 F.2d 302 (9th Cir. 1992), the Ninth Circuit first developed the concept of nominative fair use The defendants, two newspapers, conducted separate polls asking readers to call a 900 number to vote for their favorite member of the boy band New Kids on the Block. As *The Star* put it: "Which of the New Kids on the Block would you most like to move next door?" *Id.* at 305. The band sued for, among other things, trademark infringement. Affirming the district court's grant of summary judgment to the defendants, Judge Kozinski held that a "*nominative use* of a mark—where the only word reasonably available to describe a particular thing is pressed into service—lies outside the strictures of trademark law," *id.* at 308 (emphasis in original), and set out three "requirements" that a defendant's use must meet to qualify as nominative fair use:

> First, the product or service in question must be one not readily identifiable without use
> of the trademark; second, only so much of the mark or marks may be used as is

---

* From briefcase8.com via seattletrademarklawyer.com.

reasonably necessary to identify the product or service;[7] and third, the user must do nothing that would, in conjunction with the mark, suggest sponsorship or endorsement by the trademark holder.

Id. at 307. The Lanham Act did not then explicitly include any basis for the defense of nominative fair use and even now it arguably only references nominative fair use in connection with dilution, see § 43(c)(3)(A), 15 U.S.C. § 1125(c)(3)(A). On the issue of confusion, the defense remains essentially judge-made law.

Note the conceptual distinction between descriptive (or "classic") fair use and nominative fair use:

> The nominative fair use analysis is appropriate where a defendant has used the plaintiff's mark to describe the plaintiff's product, even if the defendant's ultimate goal is to describe his own product. Conversely, the classic fair use analysis is appropriate where a defendant has used the plaintiff's mark only to describe his own product, and not at all to describe the plaintiff's product.

Cairns v. Franklin Mint Co., 292 F.3d 1139, 1151 (9th Cir. 2002).

In the opinion below, Judge Kozinski returned to the concept of nominative fair use, this time in connection with domain names – and in light of *KP Permanent*. In reading through the opinion, consider the following questions:

- Why should the *New Kids* factors *replace* the *Sleekcraft* multifactor test for the likelihood of consumer confusion? Why shouldn't a court first work through the *Sleekcraft* test to determine if plaintiff has even made out its case and, if it has, then turn to the defendant's affirmative defense?

- What sense do you make of the final excerpted paragraphs of Judge Kozinski's opinion? How exactly should a Ninth Circuit court now proceed to evaluate a nominative fair use "defense"?

- Do you find the concurrence's concerns valid?

Toyota Motor Sales, U.S.A., Inc. v. Tabari
610 F.3d 1171 (2010)

KOZINSKI, Chief Judge:

[1] In this trademark infringement case, we consider the application of the nominative fair use doctrine to internet domain names.

Facts

[2] Farzad and Lisa Tabari are auto brokers—the personal shoppers of the automotive world. They contact authorized dealers, solicit bids and arrange for customers to buy from the dealer offering the best combination of location, availability and price. Consumers like this service, as it increases competition among dealers, resulting in greater selection at lower prices. For many of the same reasons, auto manufacturers and dealers aren't so keen on it, as it undermines dealers' territorial exclusivity and lowers profit margins. Until recently, the Tabaris offered this service at buy-a-lexus.com and buyorleaselexus.com.

---

[7] Thus, a soft drink competitor would be entitled to compare its product to Coca–Cola or Coke, but would not be entitled to use Coca–Cola's distinctive lettering. *See Volkswagenwerk Aktiengesellschaft v. Church*, 411 F.2d 350, 352 (9th Cir. 1969) ("{In advertising that he specialized in Volkswagen repair,} Church did not use Volkswagen's distinctive lettering style or color scheme, nor did he display the encircled 'VW' emblem" {and was therefore not infringing})....

V7.0/2020-07-14

[3] Toyota Motor Sales U.S.A. ("Toyota") is the exclusive distributor of Lexus vehicles in the United States, and jealous guardian of the Lexus mark. A Toyota marketing executive testified at trial that Toyota spends over $250 million every year promoting the Lexus brand. In the executive's estimation, "Lexus is a very prestigious luxury brand and it is an indication of an exclusive luxury experience." No doubt true.

[4] Toyota objected to the Tabaris' use on their website of copyrighted photography of Lexus vehicles and the circular "L Symbol Design mark." Toyota also took umbrage at the Tabaris' use of the string "lexus" in their domain names, which it believed was "likely to cause confusion as to the source of [the Tabaris'] web site." The Tabaris removed Toyota's photography and logo from their site and added a disclaimer in large font at the top. But they refused to give up their domain names. Toyota sued, and the district court found infringement after a bench trial. It ordered the Tabaris to cease using their domain names and enjoined them from using the Lexus mark in any other domain name. Pro se as they were at trial, the Tabaris appeal.

Nominative Fair Use

[5] When customers purchase a Lexus through the Tabaris, they receive a genuine Lexus car sold by an authorized Lexus dealer, and a portion of the proceeds ends up in Toyota's bank account. Toyota doesn't claim the business of brokering Lexus cars is illegal or that it has contracted with its dealers to prohibit selling through a broker. Instead, Toyota is using this trademark lawsuit to make it more difficult for consumers to use the Tabaris to buy a Lexus.

[6] The district court applied the eight-factor test for likelihood of confusion articulated in *AMF Inc. v. Sleekcraft Boats,* 599 F.2d 341, 348–49 (9th Cir. 1979), and found that the Tabaris' domain names—buy-a-lexus.com and buyorleaselexus.com—infringed the Lexus trademark. But we've held that the *Sleekcraft* analysis doesn't apply where a defendant uses the mark to refer to the trademarked good itself. *See Playboy Enters., Inc. v. Welles,* 279 F.3d 796, 801 (9th Cir. 2002); *New Kids on the Block v. News Am. Publ'g, Inc.,* 971 F.2d 302, 308 (9th Cir. 1992).[1] The Tabaris are using the term Lexus to describe their business of brokering Lexus automobiles; when they say Lexus, they mean Lexus. We've long held that such use of the trademark is a fair use, namely nominative fair use. And fair use is, by definition, not infringement. The Tabaris did in fact present a nominative fair use defense to the district court.

[7] In cases where a nominative fair use defense is raised, we ask whether (1) the product was "readily identifiable" without use of the mark; (2) defendant used more of the mark than necessary; or (3) defendant falsely suggested he was sponsored or endorsed by the trademark holder. *Welles,* 279 F.3d at 801 (quoting *New Kids,* 971 F.2d at 308–09). This test "evaluates the likelihood of confusion in nominative use cases." *Id.* It's designed to address the risk that nominative use of the mark will inspire a mistaken belief on the part of consumers that the speaker is sponsored or endorsed by the trademark holder. The third factor speaks directly to the risk of such confusion, and the others do so indirectly: Consumers may reasonably infer sponsorship or endorsement if a company uses an unnecessary trademark or "more" of a mark than necessary. But if the nominative use satisfies the three-factor *New Kids* test, it doesn't infringe. If the nominative use does not satisfy all the *New Kids*

---

[1] This is no less true where, as here, "the defendant's ultimate goal is to describe his own product." *Cairns v. Franklin Mint Co.,* 292 F.3d 1139, 1151 (9th Cir. 2002) (emphasis omitted). In *Welles,* for instance, we applied our nominative fair use analysis to a former playmate's use of the Playboy mark to describe herself and her website. 279 F.3d at 801. We observed that, in those circumstances, "application of the *Sleekcraft* test, which focuses on the similarity of the mark used by the plaintiff and the defendant, would lead to the incorrect conclusion that virtually all nominative uses are confusing." *Id.*

factors, the district court may order defendants to modify their use of the mark so that all three factors are satisfied; it may not enjoin nominative use of the mark altogether.[2]

A.

[8] The district court enjoined the Tabaris from using "any … domain name, service mark, trademark, trade name, meta tag or other commercial indication of origin that includes the mark LEXUS." A trademark injunction, particularly one involving nominative fair use, can raise serious First Amendment concerns because it can interfere with truthful communication between buyers and sellers in the marketplace. *See Va. State Bd. of Pharmacy v. Va. Citizens Consumer Council, Inc.*, 425 U.S. 748, 763–64 (1976). Accordingly, "we must [e]nsure that [the injunction] is tailored to eliminate only the specific harm alleged." *E. & J. Gallo Winery v. Gallo Cattle Co.*, 967 F.2d 1280, 1297 (9th Cir. 1992). To uphold the broad injunction entered in this case, we would have to be convinced that consumers are likely to believe a site is sponsored or endorsed by a trademark holder whenever the domain name contains the string of letters that make up the trademark.

[9] In performing this analysis, our focus must be on the "'reasonably prudent consumer' in the marketplace." *Cf. Dreamwerks Prod. Grp., Inc. v. SKG Studio,* 142 F.3d 1127, 1129 (9th Cir. 1998) (describing the test for likelihood of confusion in analogous *Sleekcraft* context). The relevant marketplace is the online marketplace, and the relevant consumer is a reasonably prudent consumer accustomed to shopping online; the kind of consumer who is likely to visit the Tabaris' website when shopping for an expensive product like a luxury car. *See, e.g., Interstellar Starship Servs., Ltd. v. Epix, Inc.,* 304 F.3d 936, 946 (9th Cir. 2002). Unreasonable, imprudent and inexperienced web-shoppers are not relevant.

[10] The injunction here is plainly overbroad—as even Toyota's counsel grudgingly conceded at oral argument—because it prohibits domain names that on their face dispel any confusion as to sponsorship or endorsement. The Tabaris are prohibited from doing business at sites like independent-lexus-broker.com and we-are-definitely-not-lexus.com, although a reasonable consumer wouldn't believe Toyota sponsors the websites using those domains. Prohibition of such truthful and non-misleading speech does not advance the Lanham Act's purpose of protecting consumers and preventing unfair competition; in fact, it undermines that rationale by frustrating honest communication between the Tabaris and their customers.

[11] Even if we were to modify the injunction to exclude domain names that expressly disclaim sponsorship or endorsement (like the examples above), the injunction would still be too broad. The Tabaris may not do business at lexusbroker.com, even though that's the most straightforward, obvious and truthful way to describe their business. The nominative fair use doctrine allows such truthful use of a mark, even if the speaker fails to expressly disavow association with the trademark holder, so long as it's unlikely to cause confusion as to sponsorship or endorsement. *See Welles,* 279 F.3d at 803 n.26. In *New Kids,* for instance, we found that use of the "New Kids on the Block" mark in a newspaper survey did not infringe, even absent a disclaimer, because the survey said "nothing that expressly or by fair implication connotes endorsement or joint sponsorship." 971 F.2d at 309. Speakers are under no obligation to provide a disclaimer as a condition for engaging in truthful, non-misleading speech.

[12] Although our opinion in *Volkswagenwerk Aktiengesellschaft v. Church* remarked on that defendant's "prominent use of the word 'Independent' whenever the terms 'Volkswagen' or 'VW' appeared in his advertising," 411 F.2d 350, 352 (9th Cir. 1969), it isn't to the contrary. The inclusion of such words will usually negate any hint of sponsorship or endorsement, which is why we mentioned

---

[2] If defendants are unable or unwilling to modify their use of the mark to comply with *New Kids,* then the district court's order to modify may effectively enjoin defendants from using the mark at all.

them in concluding that there was no infringement in *Volkswagenwerk*. *Id.* But that doesn't mean such words are required, and *Volkswagenwerk* doesn't say they are. Our subsequent cases make clear they're not. *See Welles*, 279 F.3d at 803 n.26; *New Kids*, 971 F.2d at 309.[3]

[13] The district court reasoned that the fact that an internet domain contains a trademark will "generally" suggest sponsorship or endorsement by the trademark holder. When a domain name consists *only* of the trademark followed by .com, or some other suffix like .org or .net, it will typically suggest sponsorship or endorsement by the trademark holder. *Cf. Panavision Int'l, L.P. v. Toeppen*, 141 F.3d 1316, 1327 (9th Cir. 1998).[4] This is because "[a] customer who is unsure about a company's domain name will often guess that the domain name is also the company's name." *Id.* (quoting *Cardservice Int'l v. McGee*, 950 F.Supp. 737, 741 (E.D.Va. 1997)) (internal quotation marks omitted); *see also Brookfield Commc'ns, Inc. v. W. Coast Entm't Corp.*, 174 F.3d 1036, 1045 (9th Cir. 1999). If customers type in trademark.com and find the site occupied by someone other than the trademark holder, they may well believe it *is* the trademark holder, despite contrary evidence on the website itself. Alternatively, they may become discouraged and give up looking for the trademark holder's official site, believing perhaps that such a website doesn't exist. *Panavision*, 141 F.3d at 1327.

[14] But the case where the URL consists of nothing but a trademark followed by a suffix like .com or .org is a special one indeed. *See Brookfield*, 174 F.3d at 1057. The importance ascribed to trademark.com in fact suggests that far less confusion will result when a domain making nominative use of a trademark includes characters in addition to those making up the mark. *Cf. Entrepreneur Media, Inc. v. Smith*, 279 F.3d 1135, 1146–47 (9th Cir. 2002). Because the official Lexus site is almost certain to be found at lexus.com (as, in fact, it is), it's far less likely to be found at other sites containing the word Lexus. On the other hand, a number of sites make nominative use of trademarks in their domains but are not sponsored or endorsed by the trademark holder: You can preen about your Mercedes at mercedesforum.com and mercedestalk.net, read the latest about your double-skim-no-whip latte at starbucksgossip.com and find out what goodies the world's greatest electronics store has on sale this week at fryselectronics-ads.com. Consumers who use the internet for shopping are generally quite sophisticated about such matters and won't be fooled into thinking that the prestigious German car manufacturer sells boots at mercedesboots.com, or homes at mercedeshomes.com, or that

---

[3] The Sixth Circuit enjoined a domain name in part because it did "not include words like 'independent' or 'unaffiliated,'" but in that case there were additional factors indicating sponsorship or endorsement, including the use of stylized versions of the plaintiff's marks on the site. *PACCAR Inc. v. TeleScan Techs., L.L.C.*, 319 F.3d 243, 256–57 (6th Cir. 2003). Where these or other factors suggest that nominative use is likely to cause confusion, a disclaimer may well be necessary. But a disclaimer is not required every time a URL contains a mark.

[4] Of course, not every trademark.com domain name is likely to cause consumer confusion. *See Interstellar Starship*, 304 F.3d at 944–46. For instance, we observed in *Interstellar Starship* that an apple orchard could operate at the website apple.com without risking confusion with Apple Computers, in light of the vast difference between their products. *Id.* at 944. "If, however, the apple grower ... competed directly with Apple Computer by selling computers, initial interest confusion probably would result," as the apple grower would be using the apple.com domain to appropriate the goodwill Apple Computer had developed in its trademark. *Id.*

When a website deals in goods or services related to a trademarked brand, as in this case, it is much closer to the second example, where apple.com competes with Apple Computers. If a company that repaired iPods, iPads and iPhones were to set up at apple.com, for instance, consumers would naturally assume that the company was sponsored or endorsed by Apple (or, more likely, that it *was* Apple). Where a site is used to sell goods or services related to the trademarked brand, a trademark.com domain will therefore suggest sponsorship or endorsement and will not generally be nominative fair use.

comcastsucks.org is sponsored or endorsed by the TV cable company just because the string of letters making up its trademark appears in the domain.

[15] When people go shopping online, they don't start out by typing random URLs containing trademarked words hoping to get a lucky hit. They may start out by typing trademark.com, but then they'll rely on a search engine or word of mouth.[6] If word of mouth, confusion is unlikely because the consumer will usually be aware of who runs the site before typing in the URL. And, if the site is located through a search engine, the consumer will click on the link for a likely-relevant site without paying much attention to the URL. Use of a trademark in the site's domain name isn't materially different from use in its text or metatags in this context; a search engine can find a trademark in a site regardless of where exactly it appears. In *Welles*, we upheld a claim that use of a mark in a site's metatags constituted nominative fair use; we reasoned that "[s]earchers would have a much more difficult time locating relevant websites" if the law outlawed such truthful, non-misleading use of a mark. 279 F.3d at 804. The same logic applies to nominative use of a mark in a domain name.

[16] Of course a domain name containing a mark cannot be nominative fair use if it suggests sponsorship or endorsement by the trademark holder. We've already explained why trademark.com domains have that effect. *See* pp. 1177–78 *supra.* Sites like trademark-USA.com, trademark-of-glendale.com or e-trademark.com will also generally suggest sponsorship or endorsement by the trademark holder; the addition of "e" merely indicates the electronic version of a brand, and a location modifier following a trademark indicates that consumers can expect to find the brand's local subsidiary, franchise or affiliate. *See Visa Int'l Serv. Ass'n v. JSL Corp.,* No. 08–15206, 2010 WL 2559003, 610 F.3d 1088 (9th Cir. June 28, 2010). For even more obvious reasons, domains like official-trademark-site.com or we-are-trademark.com affirmatively suggest sponsorship or endorsement by the trademark holder and are not nominative fair use.[7] But the district court's injunction is not limited to this narrow class of cases and, indeed, the Tabaris' domain names do not fall within it.

[17] When a domain name making nominative use of a mark does not actively suggest sponsorship or endorsement, the worst that can happen is that some consumers may arrive at the site uncertain as to what they will find. But in the age of FIOS, cable modems, DSL and T1 lines, reasonable, prudent and experienced internet consumers are accustomed to such exploration by trial and error. *Cf. Interstellar Starship,* 304 F.3d at 946. They skip from site to site, ready to hit the back button whenever they're not satisfied with a site's contents. They fully expect to find some sites that aren't what they imagine based on a glance at the domain name or search engine summary. Outside the special case of trademark.com, or domains that actively claim affiliation with the trademark holder, consumers don't form any firm expectations about the sponsorship of a website until they've seen the landing page—if then. This is sensible agnosticism, not consumer confusion. *See* Jennifer E. Rothman, *Initial Interest Confusion: Standing at the Crossroads of Trademark Law,* 27 Cardozo L.Rev. 105, 122–24, 140, 158 (2005). So long as the site as a whole does not suggest sponsorship or endorsement by the trademark holder, such momentary uncertainty does not preclude a finding of nominative fair use.

---

[6] By "word of mouth" we, of course, refer not merely to spoken recommendations from friends and acquaintances, but to the whole range of information available to online shoppers, including chat rooms, discussion forums, feedback and evaluation websites, and the like.

[7] Domain names containing trademarks may also be prohibited because they dilute the value of those marks—for instance, by creating negative associations with the brand. *Cf. Playboy Enters., Inc. v. Netscape Commc'ns Corp.,* 354 F.3d 1020, 1033 (9th Cir. 2004). For example, the website People of Walmart, which publishes rude photos of Walmart shoppers at peopleofwalmart.com, might dilute the Walmart trademark by associating it with violations of customers' privacy and the idea that a visitor to Walmart stores risks being photographed and ridiculed on the internet. *See* Jeffrey Zaslow, *Surviving the Age of Humiliation,* Wall St. J., May 5, 2010, at D1. But Toyota does not allege that the Tabaris' site has any such effect.

[18] Toyota argues it is entitled to exclusive use of the string "lexus" in domain names because it spends hundreds of millions of dollars every year making sure everyone recognizes and understands the word "Lexus." But "[a] large expenditure of money does not in itself create legally protectable rights." *Smith v. Chanel, Inc.*, 402 F.2d 562, 568 (9th Cir. 1968); *see also Ty Inc. v. Perryman*, 306 F.3d 509, 513 (7th Cir. 2002); Mark A. Lemley, *The Modern Lanham Act and the Death of Common Sense*, 108 Yale L.J. 1687, 1714–15 (1999). Indeed, it is precisely because of Toyota's investment in the Lexus mark that "[m]uch useful social and commercial discourse would be all but impossible if speakers were under threat of an infringement lawsuit every time they made reference to [Lexus] by using its trademark." *New Kids*, 971 F.2d at 307.[8]

[19] It is the wholesale prohibition of nominative use in domain names that would be unfair. It would be unfair to merchants seeking to communicate the nature of the service or product offered at their sites. And it would be unfair to consumers, who would be deprived of an increasingly important means of receiving such information. As noted, this would have serious First Amendment implications. The only winners would be companies like Toyota, which would acquire greater control over the markets for goods and services related to their trademarked brands, to the detriment of competition and consumers. The nominative fair use doctrine is designed to prevent this type of abuse of the rights granted by the Lanham Act.

B.

[20] Toyota asserts that, even if the district court's injunction is overbroad, it can be upheld if limited to the Tabaris' actual domain names: buyorleaselexus.com and buy-a-lexus.com. We therefore apply the three-part *New Kids* test to the domain names, and we start by asking whether the Tabaris' use of the mark was "necessary" to describe their business. Toyota claims it was not, because the Tabaris could have used a domain name that did not contain the Lexus mark. It's true they could have used some other domain name like autobroker.com or fastimports.com, or have used the text of their website to explain their business. But it's enough to satisfy our test for necessity that the Tabaris needed to communicate that they specialize in Lexus vehicles, and using the Lexus mark in their domain names accomplished this goal. While using Lexus in their domain names wasn't the only way to communicate the nature of their business, the same could be said of virtually any choice the Tabaris made about how to convey their message: Rather than using the internet, they could publish advertisements in print; or, instead of taking out print ads, they could rely on word of mouth. We've never adopted such a draconian definition of necessity, and we decline to do so here. In *Volkswagenwerk*, for instance, we affirmed the right of a mechanic to put up a sign advertising that he specialized in repairing Volkswagen cars, although he could have used a sandwich board, distributed leaflets or shouted through a megaphone. 411 F.2d at 352.[9] One way or the other, the Tabaris need to let consumers know that they are brokers of Lexus cars, and that's nearly impossible to do without mentioning Lexus, *cf. Monte Carlo Shirt, Inc. v. Daewoo Int'l (Am.) Corp.*, 707 F.2d 1054, 1058 (9th Cir. 1983), be it via domain name, metatag, radio jingle, telephone solicitation or blimp.

---

[8] "Words . . . do not worm their way into our discourse by accident." Alex Kozinski, *Trademarks Unplugged*, 68 N.Y.U. L. Rev. 960, 975 (1993). Trademark holders engage in "well-orchestrated campaigns intended to burn them into our collective consciousness." *Id.* Although trademark holders gain something by pushing their trademark into the lexicon, they also inevitably lose a measure of control over their mark.

[9] The Seventh Circuit has similarly upheld the right of a seller of Beanie Babies to operate at "bargainbeanies.com" on the grounds that "[y]ou can't sell a branded product without using its brand name." *Ty Inc.*, 306 F.3d at 512. In a prophetic choice of examples, Judge Posner remarked that prohibiting such a domain name "would amount to saying that if a used car dealer truthfully advertised that it sold Toyotas, or if a muffler manufacturer truthfully advertised that it specialized in making mufflers for installation in Toyotas, Toyota would have a claim of trademark infringement." *Id.*

[21] The fact that the Tabaris also broker other types of cars does not render their use of the Lexus mark unnecessary.[10] Lisa Tabari testified: "I in my conviction and great respect for the company always try to convince the consumer to first purchase a Lexus or Toyota product." If customers decide to buy some other type of car, the Tabaris may help with that, but their specialty is Lexus. The Tabaris are entitled to decide what automotive brands to emphasize in their business, and the district court found that the Tabaris do in fact specialize in Lexus vehicles. Potential customers would naturally be interested in that fact, and it was entirely appropriate for the Tabaris to use the Lexus mark to let them know it.

[22] Nor are we convinced by Toyota's argument that the Tabaris unnecessarily used domain names containing the Lexus trademark as their trade name. *See Volkswagenwerk,* 411 F.2d at 352. The Tabaris' business name is not buyorleaselexus.com or buy-a-lexus.com; it's Fast Imports. Toyota points out that the Tabaris' domain names featured prominently in their advertising, but that by no means proves the domain names were synonymous with the Tabaris' business. The Tabaris may have featured their domain names in their advertisements in order to tell consumers where to find their website, as well as to communicate the fact that they can help buy or lease a Lexus. Toyota would have to show significantly more than "prominent" advertisement to establish the contrary. We therefore conclude that the Tabaris easily satisfy the first *New Kids* factor.

[23] As for the second and third steps of our nominative fair use analysis, Toyota suggests that use of the stylized Lexus mark and "Lexus L" logo was more use of the mark than necessary and suggested sponsorship or endorsement by Toyota. This is true: The Tabaris could adequately communicate their message without using the visual trappings of the Lexus brand. *New Kids,* 971 F.2d at 308 n.7. Moreover, those visual cues might lead some consumers to believe they were dealing with an authorized Toyota affiliate. Imagery, logos and other visual markers may be particularly significant in cyberspace, where anyone can convincingly recreate the look and feel of a luxury brand at minimal expense. It's hard to duplicate a Lexus showroom, but it's easy enough to ape the Lexus site.

[24] But the Tabaris submitted images of an entirely changed site at the time of trial: The stylized mark and "L" logo were gone, and a disclaimer appeared in their place. The disclaimer stated, prominently and in large font, "We are not an authorized Lexus dealer or affiliated in any way with Lexus. We are an Independent Auto Broker." While not required, such a disclaimer is relevant to the nominative fair use analysis. *See Welles,* 279 F.3d at 803. Toyota claims the Tabaris' disclaimer came too late to protect against confusion caused by their domain names, as such confusion would occur before consumers saw the site or the disclaimer. *See Brookfield,* 174 F.3d at 1057. But nothing about the Tabaris' domains would give rise to such confusion; the Tabaris did not run their business at lexus.com, and their domain names did not contain words like "authorized" or "official." *See* pp. 1178–79 *supra.* Reasonable consumers would arrive at the Tabaris' site agnostic as to what they would find. Once there, they would immediately see the disclaimer and would promptly be disabused of any notion that the Tabaris' website is sponsored by Toyota. Because there was no risk of confusion as to sponsorship or endorsement, the Tabaris' use of the Lexus mark was fair.

[25] This makeover of the Tabaris' site is relevant because Toyota seeks only forward-looking relief. In *Volkswagenwerk,* we declined to order an injunction where the defendant had likewise stopped all infringing activities by the time of trial, 411 F.2d at 352, although we've said that an injunction may be proper if there's a risk that infringing conduct will recur, *Polo Fashions, Inc. v. Dick*

---

[10] Toyota doesn't suggest that the Tabaris used the Lexus mark to refer to those other cars, or that the Tabaris used the Lexus mark in order to redirect customers to those cars. *See, e.g., Nissan Motor Co. v. Nissan Computer Corp.,* 378 F.3d 1002, 1019 (9th Cir. 2004). Everyone seems to concede the Tabaris are bona fide Lexus brokers. We therefore do not consider whether the Tabaris used the Lexus mark in conjunction with brokering vehicles other than Lexus, or whether such use would be infringing.

Bruhn, Inc., 793 F.2d 1132, 1135–36 (9th Cir. 1986). Even assuming some form of an injunction is required to prevent relapse in this case, the proper remedy for infringing use of a mark on a site generally falls short of entirely prohibiting use of the site's domain name, as the district court did here. *See Interstellar Starship,* 304 F.3d at 948. "[O]nly upon proving the rigorous elements of cyber-squatting . . . have plaintiffs successfully forced the transfer of an infringing domain name." *Id.* Forced relinquishment of a domain is no less extraordinary.

[26] The district court is in a better position to assess in the first instance the timing and extent of any infringing conduct, as well as the scope of the remedy, if any remedy should prove to be required. We therefore vacate the injunction and remand for reconsideration. The important principle to bear in mind on remand is that a trademark injunction should be tailored to prevent ongoing violations, not punish past conduct. Speakers do not lose the right to engage in permissible speech simply because they may have infringed a trademark in the past.

C.

[27] When considering the scope and timing of any infringement on remand, the district court must eschew application of *Sleekcraft* and analyze the case solely under the rubric of nominative fair use. *Cairns,* 292 F.3d at 1151. The district court treated nominative fair use as an affirmative defense to be established by the Tabaris only after Toyota showed a likelihood of confusion under *Sleekcraft.* This was error; nominative fair use "replaces" *Sleekcraft* as the proper test for likely consumer confusion whenever defendant asserts to have referred to the trademarked good itself. *Id.* (emphasis omitted); *see also Welles,* 279 F.3d at 801.

[28] On remand, Toyota must bear the burden of establishing that the Tabaris' use of the Lexus mark was *not* nominative fair use. A finding of nominative fair use is a finding that the plaintiff has failed to show a likelihood of confusion as to sponsorship or endorsement. *See Welles,* 279 F.3d at 801; *New Kids,* 971 F.2d at 308 ("Because [nominative fair use] does not implicate the source-identification function that is the purpose of trademark, it does not constitute unfair competition.").[11] And, as the Supreme Court has unambiguously instructed, the Lanham Act always places the "burden of proving likelihood of confusion . . . on the party charging infringement." *KP Permanent Make–Up, Inc. v. Lasting Impression I, Inc.,* 543 U.S. 111, 118 (2004); *see also id.* at 120–21. In this case, that party is Toyota. "[A]ll the [Tabaris] need[ ] to do is to leave the factfinder unpersuaded." *Id.* at 120.

[29] We have previously said the opposite: "[T]he nominative fair use defense shifts to the defendant the burden of proving no likelihood of confusion." *Brother Records, Inc.,* 318 F.3d at 909 n.5. But that rule is plainly inconsistent with *Lasting Impression* and has been "effectively overruled." *Miller v. Gammie,* 335 F.3d 889, 893 (9th Cir. 2003) (en banc); *see also* 4 *McCarthy on Trademarks and Unfair Competition* § 23:11 at 82 n.5 (4th ed. 2010). A defendant seeking to assert nominative fair use as a defense need only show that it used the mark to refer to the trademarked good, as the Tabaris undoubtedly have here. The burden then reverts to the plaintiff to show a likelihood of confusion.

. . . .

VACATED AND REMANDED

---

[11] This is necessarily so because, unlike classic fair use, nominative fair use is not specifically provided for by statute. A court may find classic fair use despite "proof of infringement" because the Lanham Act authorizes that result. *See* 15 U.S.C. § 1115(b)(4). Nominative fair use, on the other hand, represents a finding of no liability under that statute's basic prohibition of infringing use. *See id.* § 1114.

569

FERNANDEZ, Circuit Judge, concurring:

[1] I concur in the majority's conclusion that the district court erred in its handling of the nominative fair use defense. I write separately, however, because I cannot concur in all that is said by the majority.

[2] First, and principally, I feel compelled to disassociate myself from statements by the majority which are not supported by the evidence or by the district court's findings. I simply cannot concur in essentially factual statements whose provenance is our musings rather than the record and determinations by trier of fact. For example, on this record I do not see the basis for the majority's assertion that the "relevant consumer is . . . accustomed to shopping online"; or that "[c]onsumers who use the internet for shopping are generally quite sophisticated" so that they are not likely to be misled; or that "the worst that can happen is that some consumers may arrive at [a] site uncertain as to what they will find"; or that, in fact, consumers are agnostic and, again, not likely to be misled; or that "[r]easonable consumers would arrive at the Tabaris' site agnostic as to what they would find."

. . . .

[3] Thus, I respectfully concur in the result.

We have long awaited some statement from the Second Circuit as to whether the circuit recognizes the nominative fair use defense, and if it does, how courts should evaluate it. That statement finally came in the following opinion. Does Judge Pooler's approach in the Second Circuit strike you as more sensible than Judge Kozinski's in the Ninth?

Int'l Info. Sys. Sec. Certification Consortium, Inc. v. Sec. Univ., LLC
823 F.3d 153 (2d Cir. 2016)

POOLER, Circuit Judge:

{The plaintiff developed a certification program and the certification mark CISSP to denote a "Certified Information Systems Security Professional" who has passed the plaintiff's certification exam. The defendant offered various courses to prepare individuals for the plaintiff's exam. It was undisputed that the defendant could use the plaintiff's mark to indicate that these courses were directed towards preparing students to take the plaintiff's exam. However, the defendant advertised its courses as taught by "Master CISSP Clement Dupuis", allegedly suggesting that Mr. Dupuis had obtained some higher, "Master" level of certification from the plaintiff. On cross-motions for summary judgment, the district court applied the *New Kids* factors in place of the *Polaroid* factors and found, among other things, that the defendant's use was a nominative fair use. The plaintiff appealed.}

II. Infringement Claims

C. Likelihood of Confusion in Nominative Use Cases

[1] [W]e turn to the question of how the district court should assess likelihood of confusion on remand.

[2] As discussed above, our Court's test for assessing likelihood of confusion is the *Polaroid* test . . . . This Court has repeatedly urged district courts to apply the *Polaroid* factors even "where a factor is irrelevant to the facts at hand." *Arrow Fastener Co.,* 59 F.3d at 400 ("[I]t is incumbent upon the district judge to engage in a deliberate review of each factor, and, if a factor is inapplicable to a case, to explain why.").

[3] The district court, rather than applying the *Polaroid* factors, applied the Ninth Circuit's test which applies in cases of nominative use of marks. Nominative use is a "use of another's trademark to

570

identify, not the defendant's goods or services, but the plaintiff's goods or services." McCarthy § 23:11. It is called "nominative" use "because it 'names' the real owner of the mark." *Id.* "The doctrine of nominative fair use allows a defendant to use a plaintiff's trademark to identify the plaintiff's goods so long as there is no likelihood of confusion about the source of the defendant's product or the mark-holder's sponsorship or affiliation." *Tiffany (NJ) Inc. v. eBay Inc.,* 600 F.3d 93, 102 (2d Cir. 2010) (alterations and internal quotation marks omitted). Because the *Polaroid* factors—or their analogues in other circuits—are not easily applied in cases of nominative use, various courts have created new tests to apply in such circumstances. The Ninth Circuit's nominative fair use doctrine stems from its decision in *New Kids on the Block v. News America Publishing, Inc.,* 971 F.2d 302 (9th Cir. 1992) . . . . Other circuits have adopted variations of this test. *See, e.g., Universal Commc'n Sys., Inc. v. Lycos, Inc.,* 478 F.3d 413, 424 (1st Cir. 2007); *Century 21 Real Estate Corp. v. Lendingtree, Inc.,* 425 F.3d 211, 220–22 (3d Cir. 2005); *Pebble Beach Co. v. Tour 18 I Ltd.,* 155 F.3d 526, 546–47 (5th Cir. 1998).

[4] In the Ninth Circuit, nominative fair use is not an affirmative defense because it does not protect a defendant from liability if there is, in fact, a likelihood of consumer confusion. Rather, the nominative fair use test replaces the multi-factor test that the Ninth Circuit typically employs to determine consumer confusion, i.e., it replaces the Ninth Circuit's analogue to the *Polaroid* test. *See Cairns v. Franklin Mint Co.,* 292 F.3d 1139, 1150–51 (9th Cir. 2002); *accord Toyota Motor Sales, U.S.A., Inc. v. Tabari,* 610 F.3d 1171, 1175 (9th Cir. 2010); *see also* McCarthy § 23:11 ("The Ninth Circuit, in crafting a separate category of a 'nominative fair use' analysis, created a specialized tool to analyze a certain class of cases of alleged infringement . . . . The Ninth Circuit did not intend nominative fair use to constitute an affirmative defense.").

[5] By contrast, the Third Circuit, another court to have developed a nominative fair use doctrine, affords defendants broader protection. The Third Circuit treats nominative fair use as an affirmative defense that may be asserted by the defendant despite a likelihood of consumer confusion. To be entitled to protection based on the affirmative defense, a defendant must show

> (1) that the use of plaintiff's mark is necessary to describe both the plaintiff's product or service and the defendant's product or service; (2) that the defendant uses only so much of the plaintiff's mark as is necessary to describe plaintiff's product; and (3) that the defendant's conduct or language reflect the true and accurate relationship between plaintiff and defendant's products or services.

Century 21 Real Estate Corp., 425 F.3d at 222.

[6] To this point, this Court has not adopted either the Ninth Circuit or the Third Circuit's rule on nominative fair use. Nonetheless, district courts within our Circuit frequently use the Ninth Circuit's formulation. *See, e.g., Car–Freshner Corp. v. Getty Images, Inc.,* 822 F.Supp.2d 167, 177–78 (N.D.N.Y. 2011); *Audi AG v. Shokan Coachworks, Inc.,* 592 F.Supp.2d 246, 269–70 (N.D.N.Y. 2008) (collecting cases). Further, as discussed below we have endorsed the principles underlying the nominative fair use doctrine. *See Tiffany (NJ) Inc.,* 600 F.3d at 102–03; *Dow Jones & Co. v. Int'l Sec. Exch., Inc.,* 451 F.3d 295, 308 (2d Cir. 2006).

[7] Having considered the case law, as well as the positions of the United States Patent and Trademark Office, we reject the Third Circuit's treatment of nominative fair use as an affirmative defense. The Lanham Act sets forth numerous affirmative defenses to infringement claims that can be asserted even if the plaintiff has established likelihood of confusion. *See* 15 U.S.C. § 1115(b). The Third Circuit's basis for treating nominative fair use as an affirmative defense is that the Supreme Court has treated classic, or descriptive, fair use as an affirmative defense. *See Century 21 Real Estate Corp.,* 425 F.3d at 222 (citing *KP Permanent Make–Up, Inc. v. Lasting Impression I, Inc.,* 543 U.S. 111, 118–20, 125 S.Ct. 542, 160 L.Ed.2d 440 (2004)). But in treating descriptive fair use as an affirmative defense, the Supreme Court was interpreting a provision of the Lanham Act which provided that claims of infringement are subject to various defenses, including

> That the use of the name, term, or device charged to be an infringement is a use, otherwise than as a mark, of the party's individual name in his own business, or of the individual name of anyone in privity with such party, or of a term or device which is descriptive of and used fairly and in good faith only to describe the goods or services of such party, or their geographic origin . . . .

15 U.S.C. § 1115(b)(4); *see KP Permanent Make–Up, Inc.*, 543 U.S. at 118–20, 125 S.Ct. 542 (analyzing 15 U.S.C. § 1115(b)(4) and ultimately concluding that Congress intended descriptive fair use to be an affirmative defense). That is, under the Supreme Court's interpretation, the Lanham Act explicitly provides that descriptive fair use is an affirmative defense. And nominative fair use cannot fall within § 1115(b)(4)'s language, as nominative fair use is not the use of a name, term, or device otherwise than as a mark which is descriptive of and used merely to describe the goods or services of the alleged infringer. *See Cosmetically Sealed Indus., Inc. v. Chesebrough–Pond's USA Co.*, 125 F.3d 28, 30 (2d Cir. 1997) (finding descriptive fair use when the alleged infringer engaged in a "non-trademark use of words in their descriptive sense"). Nominative use involves using the mark at issue *as a mark* to specifically invoke the mark-holder's mark, rather than its use, other than as a mark, to describe the alleged infringer's goods or services. If Congress had wanted nominative fair use to constitute an additional affirmative defense, it would have provided as such. We therefore hold that nominative fair use is not an affirmative defense to an infringement claim.

[8] We turn next to the question of whether we should adopt a nominative fair use test, either to supplant or to replace the *Polaroid* test. Although we see no reason to replace the *Polaroid* test in this context, we also recognize that many of the *Polaroid* factors are a bad fit here and that we have repeatedly emphasized that the *Polaroid* factors are non-exclusive. And although we have not expressly rejected or accepted other circuits' nominative fair use tests, we "have recognized that a defendant may lawfully use a plaintiff's trademark where doing so is necessary to describe the plaintiff's product and does not imply a false affiliation or endorsement by the plaintiff of the defendant." *Tiffany (NJ) Inc.*, 600 F.3d at 102–03 . . . .

[9] Because we believe that the nominative fair use factors will be helpful to a district court's analysis, we hold that, in nominative use cases, district courts are to consider the Ninth Circuit and Third Circuit's nominative fair use factors, in addition to the *Polaroid* factors. When considering a likelihood of confusion in nominative fair use cases, *in addition to* discussing each of the *Polaroid* factors, courts are to consider: (1) whether the use of the plaintiff's mark is necessary to describe both the plaintiff's product or service and the defendant's product or service, that is, whether the product or service is not readily identifiable without use of the mark; (2) whether the defendant uses only so much of the plaintiff's mark as is necessary to identify the product or service; and (3) whether the defendant did anything that would, in conjunction with the mark, suggest sponsorship or endorsement by the plaintiff holder, that is, whether the defendant's conduct or language reflects the true or accurate relationship between plaintiff's and defendant's products or services.

[10] When assessing the second nominative fair use factor, courts are to consider whether the alleged infringer "step[ped] over the line into a likelihood of confusion by using the senior user's mark too prominently or too often, in terms of size, emphasis, or repetition." McCarthy § 23:11; *see, e.g., PACCAR Inc. v. TeleScan Technologies, L.L.C.*, 319 F.3d 243, 256 (6th Cir. 2003) ("Using [the plaintiff's] trademarks in its domain names, repeating the marks in the main titles of the web sites and in the wallpaper underlying the web sites, and mimicking the distinctive fonts of the marks go beyond using the marks 'as is reasonably necessary to identify' [the plaintiff's] trucks, parts, and dealers."), *abrogated on other grounds by KP Permanent Make–Up, Inc.*, 543 U.S. at 116–17; *Brother Records, Inc. v. Jardine*, 318 F.3d 900, 908 (9th Cir. 2003) (considering the fact that the defendant used the mark "'The Beach Boys' more prominently and boldly" than the rest of its name "The Beach Boys Family and Friends" such that event organizers and members of the audience were confused about who was performing); *Playboy Enters., Inc. v. Welles*, 279 F.3d 796, 804 (9th Cir. 2002) (holding that defendant's

repeated use of the abbreviation "PMOY '81" meaning "Playmate of the Year 1981" on the background/wallpaper of her website failed to establish nominative fair use because "[t]he repeated depiction of "PMOY '81" is not necessary to describe [the defendant]"), *abrogated on other grounds by Miller v. Gammie*, 335 F.3d 889 (9th Cir. 2003); *cf. Swarovski Aktiengesellschaft v. Building No. 19, Inc.*, 704 F.3d 44, 51–52 (1st Cir. 2013) (reversing preliminary injunction restricting discount retailer from using large size font in advertising sale of "Swarovski" crystal figurines because lower court erred by assuming that retailer used "more of the mark than necessary" without determining if large size font was likely to cause consumer confusion).

[11] Additionally, when considering the third nominative fair use factor, courts must not, as the district court did here, consider only source confusion, but rather must consider confusion regarding affiliation, sponsorship, or endorsement by the mark holder. *See Courtenay Commc'ns Corp. v. Hall*, 334 F.3d 210, 213 n. 1 (2d Cir. 2003) (vacating dismissal of Lanham Act claims and holding nominative fair use did not supply alternative grounds for dismissal because defendant's "hyperlink connection to a page of endorsements suggests affiliation, sponsorship, or endorsement by" the plaintiff (internal quotation marks omitted)).

[12] We therefore remand for reconsideration of the *Polaroid* factors in addition to the nominative fair use factors . . . .

Questions and Comments

1. *The Ninth Circuit's Burden Shifting Approach*. McCarthy has parsed the burden-shifting language of *Tabari* as follows: "The Ninth Circuit has made it clear that a defendant who raises the nominative fair use issue need only show that it uses the mark to refer to the plaintiff's trademarked goods or services. The burden then reverts to the plaintiff to show a likelihood of confusion under the nominative fair use analysis . . . . In the Ninth Circuit and in other circuits that follow its approach, the 'nominative fair use' analysis is a 'defense' only in the sense that an accused infringer in certain cases can use the analysis to argue that there will be no infringement because there will be no likelihood of confusion." McCARTHY § 23:11 (footnote omitted). Does this clarify the approach of the Ninth Circuit and other circuits that follow it?

2. *The Third Circuit's Hybrid Approach in* Century 21. In *Century 21 Real Estate Corp. v. Lendingtree, Inc.*, 425 F.3d 211 (3d Cir. 2005), the Third Circuit rejected the Ninth Circuit's approach in which the *New Kids* factors replace the multifactor test for the likelihood of consumer confusion. Instead, seeking properly to cast the nominative fair use "defense" as a true affirmative defense, the *Century 21* court set forth four factors Third Circuit courts should consider in the nominative fair use context to determine if there was a likelihood of confusion: "(1) the price of the goods and other factors indicative of the care and attention expected of consumers when making a purchase; (2) the length of time the defendant has used the mark without evidence of actual confusion; (3) the intent of the defendant in adopting the mark; and (4) the evidence of actual confusion." *Id.* at 225-26. If the plaintiff meets its burden of proving a likelihood of confusion under these factors, then the defendant bears the burden of winning each of the following factors to make out the defense of nominative fair use: "1. Is the use of plaintiff's mark necessary to describe (1) plaintiff's product or service and (2) defendant's product or service? 2. Is only so much of the plaintiff's mark used as is necessary to describe plaintiff's products or services? 3. Does the defendant's conduct or language reflect the true and accurate relationship between plaintiff and defendant's products or services?" *Id.* at 228. Dissenting, Judge Fisher was highly critical of this new approach. *See id.* at 232 (Fisher, J., dissenting).

2. Further Examples of Nominative Fair Use Analyses

Liquid Glass Enterprises, Inc. v. Dr. Ing. h.c.F. Porsche AG
8 F. Supp. 2d 398 (D.N.J. 1998)

In *Liquid Glass Enterprises, Inc. v. Dr. Ing. h.c.F. Porsche AG*, 8 F. Supp. 2d 398 (D.N.J. 1998), the declaratory plaintiff Liquid Glass ran numerous advertisements incorporating Porsche automobiles. The court focused on two. The first was "an ad appearing in the May 1997 issue of a national car magazine, *Motor Trend*, which portrays a provocatively-dressed woman applying Liquid Glass car polish to a Porsche 911 with the trademark 'PORSCHE' prominently displayed on the car." *Id.* at 399. The second was a ten-minute video for use at trade shows that

> opens with a Porsche 911 (with the Porsche crest plainly visible) accelerating down a highway. Immediately following, the video cuts to a woman who is undressing and taking a shower. Thereafter, the video cuts alternately between a car (not a Porsche) being washed and polished and a woman showering, putting on her makeup and getting dressed. The video then illustrates Liquid Glass's uses on numerous expensive cars and ends with a shot of the Porsche 911 speeding down the road.

Id. at 400.

Applying *New Kids*, the court found no nominative fair use and ultimately granted the declaratory defendant's preliminary injunction motion. As to the first factor, "Liquid Glass has asserted no reason why the Porsche trademark or trade dress is necessary in its promotion of Liquid Glass products." *Id.* at 402. As to the second factor, "[n]either does Liquid Glass use only so much of Porsche's trademarks and trade dress as is reasonably necessary. *See, e.g., Volkswagenwerk Aktiengesellschaft v. Church*, 411 F.2d 350, 352 (9th Cir. 1969) (repair shop can only use the word 'Volkswagen' but cannot use the distinctive lettering or the encircled 'VW' emblem)". *Id.* at 402-403. As to the third *New Kids* factor, the court then proceeded through the Third Circuit's *Scott Paper* multifactor test for consumer confusion to find that "Liquid Glass's advertisements could mislead the public into believing that Porsche endorsed Liquid Glass's products or at least approved of their use on Porsche automobiles." *Id.* at 403. The court also found dilution by blurring.

Toho Co., Ltd. v. William Morrow & Co., Inc.
33 F. Supp. 2d 1206 (C.D. Cal. 1998)

In *Toho Co., Ltd. v. William Morrow & Co., Inc.*, 33 F. Supp. 2d 1206 (C.D. Cal. 1998), Toho was the producer of and intellectual property rights holder in the Godzilla motion pictures. The defendant planned to release a 227-page Godzilla compendium book entitled "Godzilla!", the title of which was "written in the distinctive lettering style used by Toho and its licensees in their merchandising activities." *Id.* at 1209. Toho moved for a preliminary injunction.

Applying *New Kids*, the court found, on factor one, that "[t]he product (the Godzilla character) is one not readily identifiable without the use of the trademark. A 'giant sized pre-historic dragon-like monster' may be an adequate description of Plaintiff's product, but use of the 'Godzilla' mark is required to readily identify Plaintiff's product." *Id.* at 1211. However, on factor two, "the cover of the Morrow Book contains Toho's trademark in bold orange lettering prominently displayed. This prong of the test does not appear to be satisfied because Morrow's use exceeds its legitimate referential purpose." *Id.* On the third New Kids factor, the court proceeded through the Ninth Circuit's *Sleekcraft* test for the likelihood of consumer confusion to find that "consumer confusion is likely." *Id.* at 1215.

In a separate discussion (placed after its analysis of the first and second New Kids Factors but before its *Sleekcraft* analysis), the court found that the defendant's disclaimers on the front and back of the book were ineffective. The court described the disclaimers:

> On the front cover, the word "UNAUTHORIZED" appears at the very top of the page, in relatively small lettering, surrounded by an orange bordering. On the back cover the following disclaimer appears, highlighted by its appearance against a blue background: "THIS BOOK WAS NOT PREPARED, APPROVED, LICENSED OR ENDORSED BY ANY ENTITY INVOLVED IN CREATING OR PRODUCING ANY GODZILLA MOVIE, INCLUDING COLUMBIA/TRISTAR AND TOHO CO. LTD."

Id. at 1212. The court concluded:

> This Court finds that the disclaimers do not alleviate the potential for consumer confusion. The word "UNAUTHORIZED" on the front cover only conveys a limited amount of information. It is not necessarily clear that alerting the average consumer to the word "UNAUTHORIZED" would negate consumer confusion as to Toho's sponsorship or endorsement of the Morrow Book. As the court in T*win Peaks Productions v. Publications Intern.*, 996 F.2d 1366, 1379 (2nd Cir. 1993) stated, the disclaimer would have been far more effective had it simply stated "that the publication has not been prepared, approved, or licensed by any entity that created or produced the" original Toho Godzilla films. That this information is conveyed on the back cover does not suffice. This Court is of the belief that most consumers look primarily at the front cover of a book prior to purchase. Moreover, the color of the disclaimer on the front cover does not effectively draw the attention of the average consumer as its bordering is in the same shade as the title. Further, the word is placed at the top of the page where most consumers' eyes are not likely to dwell. Perhaps if the information contained on the back cover were placed on the front cover, consumer confusion could be negated. The disclaimer is also not placed on the spine of the Morrow Book, a place where many consumers are likely to view before seeing the cover. Toho also asserts that the advertisement for the Morrow Book placed on the Internet at sites such as "Amazon.com" does not even contain the disclaimer. In summary, this Court finds that the disclaimers are ineffective.

Id. at 1213.

Consider, by contrast, the approach taken by the following book:

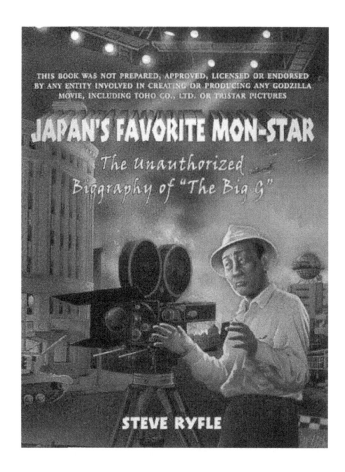

Tom Forsythe, *Barbie Enchiladas* (1997)

See www.tomforsythe.com

Tom Forsythe, *Malted Barbie* (1997)

See www.tomforsythe.com

Mattel, Inc. v. Walking Mountain Productions
353 F.3d 792 (9th Cir. 2003)

Pregerson, Judge:

[1] In the action before us, Plaintiff Mattel Corporation asks us to prohibit Defendant artist Thomas Forsythe from producing and selling photographs containing Mattel's "Barbie" doll. Most of Forsythe's photos portray a nude Barbie in danger of being attacked by vintage household appliances. Mattel argues that his photos infringe on their copyrights, trademarks, and trade dress. We . . . affirm the district court's grant of summary judgment to Forsythe.

{The court applied the four copyright fair use factors established in 17 U.S.C. § 107 and found fair use of Mattel's copyrighted Barbie doll. It then turned to the trademark claims.}

[2] We now address whether the district court erred in granting summary judgment in favor of Forsythe on Mattel's claims of trademark and trade dress infringement and dilution . . . .

A. Trademark

{The court applied the *Rogers v. Grimaldi* test, reviewed below in Section III.C, to find that Forsythe's references to Barbie in the titles of his photographs were not infringing.}

B. Trade dress

[3] Mattel also claims that Forsythe misappropriated its trade dress in Barbie's appearance, in violation of the Lanham Act, 15 U.S.C. § 1125. Mattel claims that it possesses a trade dress in the Superstar Barbie head and the doll's overall appearance. The district court concluded that there was no likelihood that the public would be misled into believing that Mattel endorsed Forsythe's photographs despite Forsythe's use of the Barbie figure.

577

[4] Arguably, the Barbie trade dress also plays a role in our culture similar to the role played by the Barbie trademark—namely, symbolization of an unattainable ideal of femininity for some women. Forsythe's use of the Barbie trade dress, therefore, presumably would present First Amendment concerns similar to those that made us reluctant to apply the Lanham Act as a bar to the artistic uses of Mattel's Barbie trademark in both *MCA* and this case. But we need not decide how the *MCA/Rogers* First Amendment balancing might apply to Forsythe's use of the Barbie trade dress because we find, on a narrower ground, that it qualifies as nominative fair use.

. . . .

[5] Forsythe's use of the Barbie trade dress is nominative. Forsythe used Mattel's Barbie figure and head in his works to conjure up associations of Mattel, while at the same time to identify his own work, which is a criticism and parody of Barbie. *See Cairns,* 292 F.3d at 1151. Where use of the trade dress or mark is grounded in the defendant's desire to refer to the plaintiff's product as a point of reference for defendant's own work, a use is nominative.

[6] Fair use may be either nominative or classic. *Id.* at 1150. We recognize a fair use defense in claims brought under § 1125 where the use of the trademark "does not imply sponsorship or endorsement of the product because the mark is used only to describe the thing, rather than to identify its source." *New Kids on the Block,* 971 F.2d at 306. Thus, we recently reiterated that, in the trademark context, nominative use becomes nominative *fair use* when a defendant proves three elements:

> First, the plaintiff's product or service in question must be one not readily identifiable without use of the trademark; second, only so much of the mark or marks may be used as is reasonably necessary to identify the plaintiff's product or service; and third, the user must do nothing that would, in conjunction with the mark, suggest sponsorship or endorsement by the trademark holder.

Cairns, 292 F.3d at 1151 (quoting *New Kids on the Block,* 971 F.2d at 308).

Forsythe's use easily satisfies the first element; his use of the Barbie figure and head are reasonably necessary in order to conjure up the Barbie product in a photographic medium. *See id.* at 1153 ("[T]here is no substitute for Franklin Mint's use of Princess Diana's likeness on its Diana-related products . . . ."). It would have been extremely difficult for Forsythe to create a photographic parody of Barbie without actually using the doll.

[7] Forsythe also satisfies the second element, which requires that a defendant only use so much of a trademark or trade dress as is reasonably necessary. As we recognized in *Cairns,* "[w]hat is 'reasonably necessary to identify the plaintiff's product' differs from case to case." *Id.* at 1154. Where identification "of the defendant's product depends on the description [or identification] of the plaintiff's product, more use of the plaintiff's trademark" or trade dress is reasonably necessary. *Id.* Given the photographic medium and Forsythe's goal of representing the social implications of Barbie, including issues of sexuality and body image, Forsythe's use of the Barbie torso and head is both reasonable and necessary. It would be very difficult for him to represent and describe his photographic parodies of Barbie without using the Barbie likeness.

[8] Though a "closer call than the first two elements" of the nominative fair use analysis, *id.* at 1155, the final element—that the user do nothing that would, in conjunction with use of the mark or dress, suggest sponsorship or endorsement by the trademark or trade dress holder—is satisfied here and weighs in Forsythe's favor. This element does not require that the defendant make an affirmative statement that their product is not sponsored by the plaintiff. *Id.*

[9] Mattel attempts to argue that Forsythe suggested sponsorship by asserting to potential consumers that one of his photographs "hangs on the wall of the office of Mattel's President of Production," to whom Forsythe referred as "Joe Mattel."

[10] One of the purchasers of Forsythe's work apparently told Forsythe that he had given the work to this Mattel senior executive as a gift. Forsythe repeated this fact in certain letters to galleries

578

and friends. Forsythe claims that he had no intention of suggesting sponsorship and that he meant the statement humorously. In virtually every promotional packet in which Forsythe mentioned "Joe Mattel," he also included a copy of his biography in which he identified himself as "someone criticizing Mattel's Barbie and the values for which it stands." The letters in the packets asserted that Forsythe was attempting to "deglamourize[ ] Barbie," "skewer[ ] the Barbie myth," and expose an "undercurrent of dissatisfaction with consumer culture." A similar mission statement was prominently featured on his website.

[11] The rest of the materials in these promotional packets sent to galleries reduce the likelihood of any consumer confusion as to Mattel's endorsement of Forsythe's work. Any reasonable consumer would realize the critical nature of this work and its lack of affiliation with Mattel. Critical works are much less likely to have a perceived affiliation with the original work. *New Kids on the Block,* 971 F.2d at 309 (finding no suggested sponsorship in part because a poll in a magazine regarding the popularity of the New Kids asked if the New Kids had become a "turn off"). Moreover, even if "Joe Mattel" existed, we question whether possession by a third-party passive recipient of an allegedly infringing work can suggest sponsorship.

. . . .

C. Dilution

[12] Mattel also appeals the district court's grant of summary judgment on its trademark and dress dilution claims. The district court found that Forsythe was entitled to summary judgment because his use of the Barbie mark and trade dress was parody and thus "his expression is a non-commercial use."

[13] Dilution may occur where use of a trademark "whittle[s] away . . . the value of a trademark" by "blurring their uniqueness and singularity" or by "tarnishing them with negative associations." *MCA,* 296 F.3d at 903(internal citations omitted). However, "[t]arnishment caused merely by an editorial or artistic parody which satirizes plaintiff's product or its image is not actionable under an anti-dilution statute because of the free speech protections of the First Amendment . . . ." 4 McCarthy, *supra,* § 24:105, at 24–225. A dilution action only applies to purely commercial speech. *MCA,* 296 F.3d at 904. Parody is a form of noncommercial expression if it does more than propose a commercial transaction. *See id.* at 906. Under *MCA,* Forsythe's artistic and parodic work is considered noncommercial speech and, therefore, not subject to a trademark dilution claim.

[14] We reject Mattel's Lanham Act claims and affirm the district court's grant of summary judgment in favor of Forsythe. Mattel cannot use "trademark laws to . . . censor all parodies or satires which use [its] name" or dress. *New Kids on the Block,* 971 F.2d at 309.

{The district court eventually ordered Mattel to pay Forsythe's legal fees in the amount of $1.9 million. See *Mattel, Inc. v. Walking Mountain Productions*, 2004 WL 1454100 (C.D.Cal., June 21, 2004). This was in addition to the Ninth Circuit's determination that Mattel should pay the costs of the appeal. See *Mattel, Inc. v. Walking Mountain Productions*, 353 F.3d 792, 816 (9th Cir. 2003).}

You may recall the *Smack Apparel* case excerpted above in Parts I.A.1.b and II.B.5. Why weren't Smack Apparel's uses nominative uses? Excerpted here is the core of the Fifth Circuit's analysis.

Board of Supervisors for Louisiana State University Agricultural & Mechanical College v. Smack Apparel Co.
550 F.3d 465, 489 (5th Cir. 2008)

REAVLEY, Circuit Judge:

. . . .

D. Nominative fair use

[1] Smack used the Universities' colors and indicia in more than a nominative sense. It did not incorporate the colors and other indicia to describe or compare its shirts with shirts licensed by the Universities, nor did it do so to tell the public what it had copied. Smack did incorporate the marks to identify the Universities as the subject of the shirts, but it did so in a way that improperly suggested affiliation, sponsorship, or endorsement.

[2] To take a simple example, two shirt designs targeted toward the fans of OSU and USC refer to the number of national championships those universities have won and ask, respectively, "got seven?" and "got eight?" Both shirts proclaim "WE DO!" and contain other specific indicia identifying the schools. Smack did not win any national championships—the respective Universities did. The use of the inclusive first-person personal pronoun "we" easily permits the inference that the schools are the speakers in the shirts and therefore endorsed the message.

[3] As noted by the district court, Smack copied the mark with "an intent to rely upon the drawing power in enticing fans of the particular universities to purchase their shirts." Such an attempt to capitalize on consumer confusion is not a nominative fair use.[122] We conclude that the district court correctly granted summary judgment to the Universities on this issue.

. . . .

C.   Expressive Uses of Trademarks

We use the term "expressive" to denote the great variety of unauthorized uses of marks for purposes such as parody, criticism, or social commentary, be they for-profit or entirely non-commercial in nature. Unlike copyright law and its doctrine of copyright fair use, trademark law has no one-size-fits-all doctrine to address the permissibility of such expressive uses. Further complicating matters is that any particular expressive use must be analyzed both for the likelihood that it will cause consumer confusion and for the likelihood that it will cause trademark dilution.

In Part III.C.1, we turn first to a leading example of a court's analysis of a for-profit parodic use both under the multifactor test for the likelihood of consumer confusion and the test under Lanham Act § 43(c), 15 U.S.C. § 1125(c), for the likelihood of trademark blurring and trademark tarnishment. *Louis Vuitton Malletier S.A. v. Haute Diggity Dog, LLC*, 507 F.3d 252 (4th Cir. 2007), is a lengthy opinion that is presented here almost in full, but it will reward a thorough reading. Not all courts follow the example of the *Haute Diggity Dog* analysis, however. Indeed, the case law on expressive uses and the likelihood of consumer confusion can be quite diverse. Part III.C.1 also offers a brief summary of a minor case, *MPS Entm't, LLC v. Abercrombie & Fitch Stores, Inc.*, No. 11 Civ. 24110, 2013 WL 3288039 (S.D. Fla. June 28, 2013), in which the court engaged in a routine use of the multifactor test for the likelihood of confusion (without any special attention to the issue of parody) and simply found no likelihood of confusion.

We then turn in Part III.C.2 to the *Rogers v. Grimaldi* test for artistically relevant uses of trademarks. In recent years, this test has become increasingly influential as a replacement for the likelihood of confusion test in expressive use situations. Note importantly, however, that the *Rogers v. Grimaldi* test limits itself only to the question of consumer confusion. It does not address the additional question of whether the expressive use blurs or tarnishes the targeted mark. On that issue, a typical defendant may seek to avail itself of the "Exclusions" from antidilution protection provided by Lanham Act § 43(c)(3), 15 U.S.C. 1125(c)(3).

---

[122] *See New Kids on the Block v. News Am. Publ'g, Inc.*, 971 F.2d 302, 308 (9th Cir.1992).

Accordingly, Part III.C.3 focuses on expressive uses and trademark dilution and considers further aspects of the Lanham Act § 43(c)(3) exclusions.

One final preliminary comment, going to the limits of the reading in this subpart: for all of the elaborate doctrine that is meant to limit plaintiffs' trademark rights and allow defendants' expressive uses, the fact is that defendants often cannot afford to avail themselves of these limits. They often settle rather than bankrupt themselves through litigation. Consider one example of this sad reality:

> Seal Press, a small book publisher that specializes in non-fiction and fiction by women writers, published a book, "Adios, Barbie," that examined body image from a feminist perspective {image of first edition book cover shown below on left}. Seal was sued by Mattel for dilution. Commenting on the suit, the Seal Press publisher said "[w]e thought the First Amendment provided us with every right to evoke the outrageousness of tall, thin, and white being the only widely accepted body type." But Mattel overwhelmed the small press. In a settlement, Seal agreed to remove Barbie's name from the book's title and to remove images of the doll's clothing and accoutrements from its cover. "We are a small publisher," said the publisher. "We're not insured for the costs associated with this type of lawsuit."

Julie Zando-Denis, *Not Playing Around: The Chilling Power of the Federal Trademark Dilution Act of 1995*, 11 CARDOZO WOMEN'S L.J. 599, 614 (2005) (footnotes omitted).

There is simply no question that if Seal Press had had the resources to litigate the matter, it would have prevailed with respect to both confusion and dilution against Mattel — whose reputation for scorched-earth litigation tactics is matched only by its reputation for almost always losing in court against those who stand up to its bullying. *See, e.g., Mattel Inc. v. Walking Mountain Productions*, 353 F.3d 792 (9th Cir. 2003); *Mattel, Inc. v. Pitt*, 229 F. Supp. 2d 315, 318 (S.D.N.Y. 2002). For more on the degree to which the mere threat of litigation can produce very strong "chilling effects" on expressive uses of trademarks, see Leah Chan Grinvald, *Shaming Trademark Bullies*, 2011 WISC. L. REV. 625 (2011).

1. **Expressive Uses and the Tests for Confusion and Dilution**

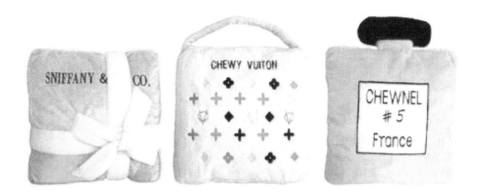

Louis Vuitton Malletier S.A. v. Haute Diggity Dog, LLC
507 F.3d 252 (4th Cir. 2007)

NIEMEYER, Circuit Judge:

[1] Louis Vuitton Malletier S.A., a French corporation located in Paris, that manufactures luxury luggage, handbags, and accessories, commenced this action against Haute Diggity Dog, LLC, a Nevada corporation that manufactures and sells pet products nationally, alleging trademark infringement under 15 U.S.C. § 1114(1)(a), trademark dilution under 15 U.S.C. § 1125(c), copyright infringement under 17 U.S.C. § 501, and related statutory and common law violations. Haute Diggity Dog manufactures, among other things, plush toys on which dogs can chew, which, it claims, parody famous trademarks on luxury products, including those of Louis Vuitton Malletier. The particular Haute Diggity Dog chew toys in question here are small imitations of handbags that are labeled "Chewy Vuiton" and that mimic Louis Vuitton Malletier's LOUIS VUITTON handbags.

[2] On cross-motions for summary judgment, the district court concluded that Haute Diggity Dog's "Chewy Vuiton" dog toys were successful parodies of Louis Vuitton Malletier's trademarks, designs, and products, and on that basis, entered judgment in favor of Haute Diggity Dog on all of Louis Vuitton Malletier's claims.

[3] On appeal, we agree with the district court that Haute Diggity Dog's products are not likely to cause confusion with those of Louis Vuitton Malletier and that Louis Vuitton Malletier's copyright was not infringed. On the trademark dilution claim, however, we reject the district court's reasoning but reach the same conclusion through a different analysis. Accordingly, we affirm.

I

[4] Louis Vuitton Malletier S.A. ("LVM") is a well known manufacturer of luxury luggage, leather goods, handbags, and accessories, which it markets and sells worldwide. In connection with the sale of its products, LVM has adopted trademarks and trade dress that are well recognized and have become famous and distinct. Indeed, in 2006, *BusinessWeek* ranked LOUIS VUITTON as the 17th "best brand" of all corporations in the world and the first "best brand" for any fashion business.

[5] LVM has registered trademarks for "LOUIS VUITTON," in connection with luggage and ladies' handbags (the "LOUIS VUITTON mark"); for a stylized monogram of "LV," in connection with traveling bags and other goods (the "LV mark"); and for a monogram canvas design consisting of a canvas with repetitions of the LV mark along with four-pointed stars, four-pointed stars inset in curved diamonds, and four-pointed flowers inset in circles, in connection with traveling bags and other products (the "Monogram Canvas mark"). In 2002, LVM adopted a brightly-colored version of the Monogram Canvas mark in which the LV mark and the designs were of various colors and the background was white (the "Multicolor design"), created in collaboration with Japanese artist Takashi Murakami. For the Multicolor design, LVM obtained a copyright in 2004. In 2005, LVM adopted another design consisting of a canvas with repetitions of the LV mark and smiling cherries on a brown background (the "Cherry design").

[6] The original LOUIS VUITTON, LV, and Monogram Canvas marks, however, have been used as identifiers of LVM products continuously since 1896.

[7] During the period 2003–2005, LVM spent more than $48 million advertising products using its marks and designs .... It sells its products exclusively in LVM stores and in its own in-store boutiques that are contained within department stores such as Saks Fifth Avenue, Bloomingdale's, Neiman Marcus, and Macy's. LVM also advertises its products on the Internet through the specific websites www.louisvuitton.com and www. eluxury. com.

[8] Although better known for its handbags and luggage, LVM also markets a limited selection of luxury pet accessories—collars, leashes, and dog carriers—which bear the Monogram Canvas mark and the Multicolor design. These items range in price from approximately $200 to $1600. LVM does not make dog toys.

[9] Haute Diggity Dog, LLC, which is a relatively small and relatively new business located in Nevada, manufactures and sells nationally—primarily through pet stores—a line of pet chew toys and beds whose names parody elegant high-end brands of products such as perfume, cars, shoes, sparkling wine, and handbags. These include—in addition to Chewy Vuiton (LOUIS VUITTON)—Chewnel No. 5 (Chanel No. 5), Furcedes (Mercedes), Jimmy Chew (Jimmy Choo), Dog Perignonn (Dom Perignon), Sniffany & Co. (Tiffany & Co.), and Dogior (Dior). The chew toys and pet beds are plush, made of polyester, and have a shape and design that loosely imitate the signature product of the targeted brand. They are mostly distributed and sold through pet stores, although one or two Macy's stores carries Haute Diggity Dog's products. The dog toys are generally sold for less than $20, although larger versions of some of Haute Diggity Dog's plush dog beds sell for more than $100.

[10] Haute Diggity Dog's "Chewy Vuiton" dog toys, in particular, loosely resemble miniature handbags and undisputedly evoke LVM handbags of similar shape, design, and color. In lieu of the

LOUIS VUITTON mark, the dog toy uses "Chewy Vuiton"; in lieu of the LV mark, it uses "CV"; and the other symbols and colors employed are imitations, but not exact ones, of those used in the LVM Multicolor and Cherry designs.

[11] In 2002, LVM commenced this action, naming as defendants Haute Diggity Dog; Victoria D.N. Dauernheim, the principal owner of Haute Diggity Dog; and Woofies, LLC, a retailer of Haute Diggity Dog's products, located in Asburn, Virginia, for trademark, trade dress, and copyright infringement. Its complaint includes counts for trademark counterfeiting, under 15 U.S.C. § 1114(1)(a); trademark infringement, under 15 U.S.C. § 1114(1)(a); trade dress infringement, under 15 U.S.C. § 1125(a)(1); unfair competition, under 15 U.S.C. § 1125(a)(1); trademark dilution, under 15 U.S.C. § 1125(c); trademark infringement, under Virginia common law; trade dress infringement, under Virginia common law; unfair competition, under Virginia common law; copyright infringement of the Multicolor design, under 17 U.S.C. § 501; and violation of the Virginia Consumer Protection Act, under Virginia Code § 59.1–200. On cross-motions for summary judgment, the district court granted Haute Diggity Dog's motion and denied LVM's motion, entering judgment in favor of Haute Diggity Dog on all of the claims. It rested its analysis on each count principally on the conclusion that Haute Diggity Dog's products amounted to a successful parody of LVM's marks, trade dress, and copyright. See *Louis Vuitton Malletier S.A. v. Haute Diggity Dog, LLC,* 464 F.Supp.2d 495 (E.D.Va.2006).

[12] LVM appealed and now challenges, as a matter of law, virtually every ruling made by the district court.

II

[13] LVM contends first that Haute Diggity Dog's marketing and sale of its "Chewy Vuiton" dog toys infringe its trademarks because the advertising and sale of the "Chewy Vuiton" dog toys is likely to cause confusion. *See* 15 U.S.C. § 1114(1)(a). LVM argues:

> The defendants in this case are using almost an exact imitation of the house mark VUITTON (merely omitting a second "T"), and they painstakingly copied Vuitton's Monogram design mark, right down to the exact arrangement and sequence of geometric symbols. They also used the same design marks, trade dress, and color combinations embodied in Vuitton's Monogram Multicolor and Monogram Cerises [Cherry] handbag collections. Moreover, HDD did not add any language to distinguish its products from Vuitton's, and its products are not "widely recognized."[1]

[14] Haute Diggity Dog contends that there is no evidence of confusion, nor could a reasonable factfinder conclude that there is a likelihood of confusion, because it successfully markets its products as parodies of famous marks such as those of LVM. It asserts that "precisely because of the [famous] mark's fame and popularity ... confusion is avoided, and it is this lack of confusion that a parodist depends upon to achieve the parody." Thus, responding to LVM's claims of trademark infringement, Haute Diggity Dog argues:

> The marks are undeniably similar in certain respects. There are visual and phonetic similarities. [Haute Diggity Dog] admits that the product name and design mimics LVM's and is based on the LVM marks. It is necessary for the pet products to conjure up the

---

[1] We take this argument to be that Haute Diggity Dog is copying too closely the marks and trade dress of LVM. But we reject the statement that LVM has a trademark consisting of the one word VUITTON. At oral argument, counsel for LVM conceded that the trademark is "LOUIS VUITTON," and it is always used in that manner rather than simply as "VUITTON." It appears that LVM has employed this technique to provide a more narrow, but irrelevant, comparison between its VUITTON and Haute Diggity Dog's "Vuiton." In resolving this case, however, we take LVM's arguments to compare "LOUIS VUITTON" with Haute Diggity Dog's "Chewy Vuiton."

original designer mark for there to be a parody at all. However, a parody also relies on "equally obvious dissimilarit[ies] between the marks" to produce its desired effect.

Concluding that Haute Diggity Dog did not create any likelihood of confusion as a matter of law, the district court granted summary judgment to Haute Diggity Dog. *Louis Vuitton Malletier*, 464 F.Supp.2d at 503, 508. We review its order *de novo. See CareFirst of Md., Inc. v. First Care, P.C.*, 434 F.3d 263, 267 (4th Cir. 2006).

[15] To prove trademark infringement, LVM must show (1) that it owns a valid and protectable mark; (2) that Haute Diggity Dog uses a "re-production, counterfeit, copy, or colorable imitation" of that mark in commerce and without LVM's consent; and (3) that Haute Diggity Dog's use is likely to cause confusion. 15 U.S.C. § 1114(1)(a); *CareFirst*, 434 F.3d at 267. The validity and protectability of LVM's marks are not at issue in this case, nor is the fact that Haute Diggity Dog uses a colorable imitation of LVM's mark. Therefore, we give the first two elements no further attention. To determine whether the "Chewy Vuiton" product line creates a likelihood of confusion, we have identified several nonexclusive factors to consider: (1) the strength or distinctiveness of the plaintiff's mark; (2) the similarity of the two marks; (3) the similarity of the goods or services the marks identify; (4) the similarity of the facilities the two parties use in their businesses; (5) the similarity of the advertising used by the two parties; (6) the defendant's intent; and (7) actual confusion. *See Pizzeria Uno Corp. v. Temple*, 747 F.2d 1522, 1527 (4th Cir. 1984). These *Pizzeria Uno* factors are not always weighted equally, and not all factors are relevant in every case. *See CareFirst*, 434 F.3d at 268.

[16] Because Haute Diggity Dog's arguments with respect to the *Pizzeria Uno* factors depend to a great extent on whether its products and marks are successful parodies, we consider first whether Haute Diggity Dog's products, marks, and trade dress are indeed successful parodies of LVM's marks and trade dress.

[17] For trademark purposes, "[a] 'parody' is defined as a simple form of entertainment conveyed by juxtaposing the irreverent representation of the trademark with the idealized image created by the mark's owner." *People for the Ethical Treatment of Animals v. Doughney* ("*PETA* "), 263 F.3d 359, 366 (4th Cir. 2001) (internal quotation marks omitted). "A parody must convey two simultaneous—and contradictory—messages: that it is the original, but also that it is *not* the original and is instead a parody." *Id.* (internal quotation marks and citation omitted). This second message must not only differentiate the alleged parody from the original but must also communicate some articulable element of satire, ridicule, joking, or amusement. Thus, "[a] parody relies upon a difference from the original mark, presumably a humorous difference, in order to produce its desired effect." *Jordache Enterprises, Inc. v. Hogg Wyld, Ltd.*, 828 F.2d 1482, 1486 (10th Cir. 1987) (finding the use of "Lardashe" jeans for larger women to be a successful and permissible parody of "Jordache" jeans).

[18] When applying the *PETA* criteria to the facts of this case, we agree with the district court that the "Chewy Vuiton" dog toys are successful parodies of LVM handbags and the LVM marks and trade dress used in connection with the marketing and sale of those handbags. First, the pet chew toy is obviously an irreverent, and indeed intentional, representation of an LVM handbag, albeit much smaller and coarser. The dog toy is shaped roughly like a handbag; its name "Chewy Vuiton" sounds like and rhymes with LOUIS VUITTON; its monogram CV mimics LVM's LV mark; the repetitious design clearly imitates the design on the LVM handbag; and the coloring is similar. In short, the dog toy is a small, plush imitation of an LVM handbag carried by women, which invokes the marks and design of the handbag, albeit irreverently and incompletely. No one can doubt that LVM handbags are the target of the imitation by Haute Diggity Dog's "Chewy Vuiton" dog toys.

[19] At the same time, no one can doubt also that the "Chewy Vuiton" dog toy is not the "idealized image" of the mark created by LVM. The differences are immediate, beginning with the fact that the "Chewy Vuiton" product is a dog toy, not an expensive, luxury LOUIS VUITTON handbag. The toy is smaller, it is plush, and virtually all of its designs differ. Thus, "Chewy Vuiton" is not LOUIS VUITTON

("Chewy" is not "LOUIS" and "Vuiton" is not "VUITTON," with its two Ts); CV is not LV; the designs on the dog toy are simplified and crude, not detailed and distinguished. The toys are inexpensive; the handbags are expensive and marketed to be expensive. And, of course, as a dog toy, one must buy it with pet supplies and cannot buy it at an exclusive LVM store or boutique within a department store. In short, the Haute Diggity Dog "Chewy Vuiton" dog toy undoubtedly and deliberately conjures up the famous LVM marks and trade dress, but at the same time, it communicates that it is not the LVM product.

[20] Finally, the juxtaposition of the similar and dissimilar—the irreverent representation and the idealized image of an LVM handbag—immediately conveys a joking and amusing parody. The furry little "Chewy Vuiton" imitation, as something to be *chewed by a dog*, pokes fun at the elegance and expensiveness of a LOUIS VUITTON handbag, which must *not* be chewed by a dog. The LVM handbag is provided for the most elegant and well-to-do celebrity, to proudly display to the public and the press, whereas the imitation "Chewy Vuiton" "handbag" is designed to mock the celebrity and be used by a dog. The dog toy irreverently presents haute couture as an object for casual canine destruction. The satire is unmistakable. The dog toy is a comment on the rich and famous, on the LOUIS VUITTON name and related marks, and on conspicuous consumption in general. This parody is enhanced by the fact that "Chewy Vuiton" dog toys are sold with similar parodies of other famous and expensive brands— "Chewnel No. 5" targeting "Chanel No. 5"; "Dog Perignonn" targeting "Dom Perignon"; and "Sniffany & Co." targeting "Tiffany & Co."

[21] We conclude that the *PETA* criteria are amply satisfied in this case and that the "Chewy Vuiton" dog toys convey "just enough of the original design to allow the consumer to appreciate the point of parody," but stop well short of appropriating the entire marks that LVM claims. *PETA*, 263 F.3d at 366 (quoting *Jordache*, 828 F.2d at 1486).

[22] Finding that Haute Diggity Dog's parody is successful, however, does not end the inquiry into whether Haute Diggity Dog's "Chewy Vuiton" products create a likelihood of confusion. *See* 6 J. Thomas McCarthy, *Trademarks and Unfair Competition* § 31:153, at 262 (4th ed. 2007) ("There are confusing parodies and non-confusing parodies. All they have in common is an attempt at humor through the use of someone else's trademark"). The finding of a successful parody only influences the way in which the *Pizzeria Uno* factors are applied. *See, e.g., Anheuser–Busch, Inc. v. L & L Wings, Inc.*, 962 F.2d 316, 321 (4th Cir. 1992) (observing that parody alters the likelihood-of-confusion analysis). Indeed, it becomes apparent that an effective parody will actually diminish the likelihood of confusion, while an ineffective parody does not. We now turn to the *Pizzeria Uno* factors.

A

[23] As to the first *Pizzeria Uno* factor, the parties agree that LVM's marks are strong and widely recognized. They do not agree, however, as to the consequences of this fact. LVM maintains that a strong, famous mark is entitled, as a matter of law, to broad protection. While it is true that finding a mark to be strong and famous usually favors the plaintiff in a trademark infringement case, the opposite may be true when a legitimate claim of parody is involved. As the district court observed, "In cases of parody, a strong mark's fame and popularity is precisely the mechanism by which likelihood of confusion is avoided." *Louis Vuitton Malletier*, 464 F.Supp.2d at 499 (citing *Hormel Foods Corp. v. Jim Henson Prods., Inc.*, 73 F.3d 497, 503–04 (2d Cir. 1996); *Schieffelin & Co. v. Jack Co. of Boca, Inc.*, 850 F.Supp. 232, 248 (S.D.N.Y.1994)). "An intent to parody is not an intent to confuse the public." *Jordache*, 828 F.2d at 1486.

[24] We agree with the district court. It is a matter of common sense that the strength of a famous mark allows consumers immediately to perceive the target of the parody, while simultaneously allowing them to recognize the changes to the mark that make the parody funny or biting. *See Tommy Hilfiger Licensing, Inc. v. Nature Labs, LLC*, 221 F.Supp.2d 410, 416 (S.D.N.Y.2002) (noting that the strength of the "TOMMY HILFIGER" fashion mark did not favor the mark's owner in an infringement

case against "TIMMY HOLEDIGGER" novelty pet perfume). In this case, precisely because LOUIS VUITTON is so strong a mark and so well recognized as a luxury handbag brand from LVM, consumers readily recognize that when they see a "Chewy Vuiton" pet toy, they see a parody. Thus, the strength of LVM's marks in this case does not help LVM establish a likelihood of confusion.

B

[25] With respect to the second *Pizzeria Uno* factor, the similarities between the marks, the usage by Haute Diggity Dog again converts what might be a problem for Haute Diggity Dog into a disfavored conclusion for LVM.

[26] Haute Diggity Dog concedes that its marks are and were designed to be somewhat similar to LVM's marks. But that is the essence of a parody—the invocation of a famous mark in the consumer's mind, so long as the distinction between the marks is also readily recognized. While a trademark parody necessarily copies enough of the original design to bring it to mind as a target, a successful parody also distinguishes itself and, because of the implicit message communicated by the parody, allows the consumer to appreciate it. *See PETA*, 263 F.3d at 366 (citing *Jordache*, 828 F.2d at 1486); *Anheuser–Busch*, 962 F.2d at 321.

[27] In concluding that Haute Diggity Dog has a successful parody, we have impliedly concluded that Haute Diggity Dog appropriately mimicked a part of the LVM marks, but at the same time sufficiently distinguished its own product to communicate the satire. The differences are sufficiently obvious and the parody sufficiently blatant that a consumer encountering a "Chewy Vuiton" dog toy would not mistake its source or sponsorship on the basis of mark similarity.

[28] This conclusion is reinforced when we consider how the parties actually use their marks in the marketplace. *See CareFirst*, 434 F.3d at 267 (citing *What–A–Burger of Va., Inc. v. Whataburger, Inc.*, 357 F.3d 441, 450 (4th Cir. 2004)); *Lamparello v. Falwell*, 420 F.3d 309, 316 (4th Cir. 2005); *Hormel Foods*, 73 F.3d at 503. The record amply supports Haute Diggity Dog's contention that its "Chewy Vuiton" toys for dogs are generally sold alongside other pet products, as well as toys that parody other luxury brands, whereas LVM markets its handbags as a top-end luxury item to be purchased only in its own stores or in its own boutiques within department stores. These marketing channels further emphasize that "Chewy Vuiton" dog toys are not, in fact, LOUIS VUITTON products.

C

[29] Nor does LVM find support from the third *Pizzeria Uno* factor, the similarity of the products themselves. It is obvious that a "Chewy Vuiton" plush imitation handbag, which does not open and is manufactured as a dog toy, is not a LOUIS VUITTON handbag sold by LVM. Even LVM's most proximate products—dog collars, leashes, and pet carriers—are fashion accessories, not dog toys. As Haute Diggity Dog points out, LVM does not make pet chew toys and likely does not intend to do so in the future. Even if LVM were to make dog toys in the future, the fact remains that the products at issue are not similar in any relevant respect, and this factor does not favor LVM.

D

[30] The fourth and fifth *Pizzeria Uno* factors, relating to the similarity of facilities and advertising channels, have already been mentioned. LVM products are sold exclusively through its own stores or its own boutiques within department stores. It also sells its products on the Internet through an LVM-authorized website. In contrast, "Chewy Vuiton" products are sold primarily through traditional and Internet pet stores, although they might also be sold in some department stores. The record demonstrates that both LVM handbags and "Chewy Vuiton" dog toys are sold at a Macy's department store in New York. As a general matter, however, there is little overlap in the individual retail stores selling the brands.

[31] Likewise with respect to advertising, there is little or no overlap. LVM markets LOUIS VUITTON handbags through high-end fashion magazines, while "Chewy Vuiton" products are advertised primarily through pet-supply channels.

[32] The overlap in facilities and advertising demonstrated by the record is so minimal as to be practically nonexistent. "Chewy Vuiton" toys and LOUIS VUITTON products are neither sold nor advertised in the same way, and the *de minimis* overlap lends insignificant support to LVM on this factor.

E

[33] The sixth factor, relating to Haute Diggity Dog's intent, again is neutralized by the fact that Haute Diggity Dog markets a parody of LVM products. As other courts have recognized, "An intent to parody is not an intent to confuse the public." *Jordache*, 828 F.2d at 1486. Despite Haute Diggity Dog's obvious intent to profit from its use of parodies, this action does not amount to a bad faith intent to create consumer confusion. To the contrary, the intent is to do just the opposite—to evoke a humorous, satirical association that *distinguishes* the products. This factor does not favor LVM.

F

[34] On the actual confusion factor, it is well established that no actual confusion is required to prove a case of trademark infringement, although the presence of actual confusion can be persuasive evidence relating to a likelihood of confusion. *See CareFirst*, 434 F.3d at 268.

[35] While LVM conceded in the district court that there was no evidence of actual confusion, on appeal it points to incidents where retailers misspelled "Chewy Vuiton" on invoices or order forms, using two Ts instead of one. Many of these invoices also reflect simultaneous orders for multiple types of Haute Diggity Dog parody products, which belies the notion that any actual confusion existed as to the source of "Chewy Vuiton" plush toys. The misspellings pointed out by LVM are far more likely in this context to indicate confusion over how to spell the product name than any confusion over the source or sponsorship of the "Chewy Vuiton" dog toys. We conclude that this factor favors Haute Diggity Dog.

[36] In sum, the likelihood-of-confusion factors substantially favor Haute Diggity Dog. But consideration of these factors is only a proxy for the ultimate statutory test of whether Haute Diggity Dog's marketing, sale, and distribution of "Chewy Vuiton" dog toys is likely to cause confusion. Recognizing that "Chewy Vuiton" is an obvious parody and applying the *Pizzeria Uno* factors, we conclude that LVM has failed to demonstrate any likelihood of confusion. Accordingly, we affirm the district court's grant of summary judgment in favor of Haute Diggity Dog on the issue of trademark infringement.

III

[37] LVM also contends that Haute Diggity Dog's advertising, sale, and distribution of the "Chewy Vuiton" dog toys dilutes its LOUIS VUITTON, LV, and Monogram Canvas marks, which are famous and distinctive, in violation of the Trademark Dilution Revision Act of 2006 ("TDRA"), 15 U.S.C.A. § 1125(c) (West Supp.2007). It argues, "Before the district court's decision, Vuitton's famous marks were unblurred by any third party trademark use." "Allowing defendants to become the first to use similar marks will obviously blur and dilute the Vuitton Marks." It also contends that "Chewy Vuiton" dog toys are likely to tarnish LVM's marks because they "pose a choking hazard for some dogs."

[38] Haute Diggity Dog urges that, in applying the TDRA to the circumstances before us, we reject LVM's suggestion that a parody "automatically" gives rise to "actionable dilution." Haute Diggity Dog contends that only marks that are "identical or substantially similar" can give rise to actionable dilution, and its "Chewy Vuiton" marks are not identical or sufficiently similar to LVM's marks. It also argues that "[its] spoof, like other obvious parodies," "'tends to increase public identification' of [LVM's] mark with [LVM]," quoting *Jordache*, 828 F.2d at 1490, rather than impairing its distinctiveness, as the TDRA requires. As for LVM's tarnishment claim, Haute Diggity Dog argues that LVM's position is at best based on speculation and that LVM has made no showing of a likelihood of dilution by tarnishment.

. . . .

[39] Thus, to state a dilution claim under the TDRA, a plaintiff must show:

(1) that the plaintiff owns a famous mark that is distinctive;

(2) that the defendant has commenced using a mark in commerce that allegedly is diluting the famous mark;

(3) that a similarity between the defendant's mark and the famous mark gives rise to an association between the marks; and

(4) that the association is likely to impair the distinctiveness of the famous mark or likely to harm the reputation of the famous mark.

[40] In the context of blurring, distinctiveness refers to the ability of the famous mark uniquely to identify a single source and thus maintain its selling power. *See N.Y. Stock Exch. v. N.Y., N.Y. Hotel LLC,* 293 F.3d 550, 558 (2d Cir. 2002) (observing that blurring occurs where the defendant's use creates "the possibility that the [famous] mark will lose its ability to serve as a unique identifier of the plaintiff's product") (*quoting Deere & Co. v. MTD Prods., Inc.,* 41 F.3d 39, 43 (2d Cir. 1994)); *Playboy Enterprises, Inc. v. Welles,* 279 F.3d 796, 805 (9th Cir. 2002) (same). In proving a dilution claim under the TDRA, the plaintiff need not show actual or likely confusion, the presence of competition, or actual economic injury. *See* 15 U.S.C.A. § 1125(c)(1).

[41] The TDRA creates three defenses based on the defendant's (1) "fair use" (with exceptions); (2) "news reporting and news commentary"; and (3) "noncommercial use." *Id.* § 1125(c)(3).

A

[42] We address first LVM's claim for dilution by blurring.

[43] The first three elements of a trademark dilution claim are not at issue in this case. LVM owns famous marks that are distinctive; Haute Diggity Dog has commenced using "Chewy Vuiton," "CV," and designs and colors that are allegedly diluting LVM's marks; and the similarity between Haute Diggity Dog's marks and LVM's marks gives rise to an association between the marks, albeit a parody. The issue for resolution is whether the association between Haute Diggity Dog's marks and LVM's marks is likely to impair the distinctiveness of LVM's famous marks.

[44] In deciding this issue, the district court correctly outlined the six factors to be considered in determining whether dilution by blurring has been shown. *See* 15 U.S.C.A. § 1125(c)(2)(B). But in evaluating the facts of the case, the court did not directly apply those factors it enumerated. It held simply:

> [The famous mark's] strength is not likely to be blurred by a parody dog toy product. Instead of blurring Plaintiff's mark, the success of the parodic use depends upon the continued association with LOUIS VUITTON.

Louis Vuitton Malletier, 464 F.Supp.2d at 505. The amicus supporting LVM's position in this case contends that the district court, by not applying the statutory factors, misapplied the TDRA to conclude that simply because Haute Diggity Dog's product was a parody meant that "there can be no *association* with the famous mark as a matter of law." Moreover, the amicus points out correctly that to rule in favor of Haute Diggity Dog, the district court was required to find that the "association" did not impair the distinctiveness of LVM's famous mark.

LVM goes further in its own brief, however, and contends:

> When a defendant uses an imitation of a famous mark in connection with related goods, a claim of parody cannot preclude liability for dilution.

> * * *

> The district court's opinion utterly ignores the substantial goodwill VUITTON has established in its famous marks through more than a century of *exclusive* use. Disregarding the clear Congressional mandate to protect such famous marks against

dilution, the district court has granted [Haute Diggity Dog] permission to become the first company other than VUITTON to use imitations of the famous VUITTON Marks.

[45] In short, LVM suggests that any use by a third person of an imitation of its famous marks dilutes the famous marks as a matter of law. This contention misconstrues the TDRA.

[46] The TDRA prohibits a person from using a junior mark that is likely to dilute (by blurring) the famous mark, and blurring is defined to be an impairment to the famous mark's distinctiveness. "Distinctiveness" in turn refers to the public's recognition that the famous mark identifies a single source of the product using the famous mark.

[47] To determine whether a junior mark is likely to dilute a famous mark through blurring, the TDRA directs the court to consider all factors relevant to the issue, including six factors that are enumerated in the statute . . . . Not every factor will be relevant in every case, and not every blurring claim will require extensive discussion of the factors. But a trial court must offer a sufficient indication of which factors it has found persuasive and explain why they are persuasive so that the court's decision can be reviewed. The district court did not do this adequately in this case. Nonetheless, after we apply the factors as a matter of law, we reach the same conclusion reached by the district court.

[48] We begin by noting that parody is not automatically a complete *defense* to a claim of dilution by blurring where the defendant uses the parody as its own designation of source, i.e., *as a trademark*. Although the TDRA does provide that fair use is a complete defense and allows that a parody can be considered fair use, it does not extend the fair use defense to parodies used as a trademark. As the statute provides:

> The following shall not be actionable as dilution by blurring or dilution by tarnishment under this subsection:
>
> (A) Any fair use . . . other than as a designation of source for the person's own goods or services, including use in connection with . . . parodying . . . .

15 U.S.C.A. § 1125(c)(3)(A)(ii) (emphasis added). Under the statute's plain language, parodying a famous mark is protected by the fair use defense only if the parody is *not* "a designation of source for the person's own goods or services."[*]

[49] The TDRA, however, does not require a court to ignore the existence of a parody that is used as a trademark, and it does not preclude a court from considering parody as part of the circumstances to be considered for determining whether the plaintiff has made out a claim for dilution by blurring. Indeed, the statute permits a court to consider "all relevant factors," including the six factors supplied in § 1125(c)(2)(B).

[50] Thus, it would appear that a defendant's use of a mark as a parody is relevant to the overall question of whether the defendant's use is likely to impair the famous mark's distinctiveness. Moreover, the fact that the defendant uses its marks as a parody is specifically relevant to several of the listed factors. For example, factor (v) (whether the defendant intended to create an association with the famous mark) and factor (vi) (whether there exists an actual association between the defendant's mark and the famous mark) directly invite inquiries into the defendant's intent in using the parody, the defendant's actual use of the parody, and the effect that its use has on the famous mark. While a parody intentionally creates an association with the famous mark in order to be a parody, it also intentionally communicates, if it is successful, that it is *not* the famous mark, but rather a satire of

---

[*] {What may not be clear from the opinion is that Haute Diggity Dog applied in 2005 to register CHEWY VUITON as its own trademark. *See* US Serial No. 78546019, Jan. 12, 2005, and US Serial No. 78724751, Oct. 1, 2005. Haute Diggity Dog expressly abandoned both applications in 2006, but the damage to its litigation position had apparently already been done.}

590

the famous mark. *See PETA,* 263 F.3d at 366. That the defendant is using its mark as a parody is therefore relevant in the consideration of these statutory factors.

[51] Similarly, factors (i), (ii), and (iv)—the degree of similarity between the two marks, the degree of distinctiveness of the famous mark, and its recognizability—are directly implicated by consideration of the fact that the defendant's mark is a successful parody. Indeed, by making the famous mark an object of the parody, a successful parody might actually enhance the famous mark's distinctiveness by making it an icon. The brunt of the joke becomes yet more famous. *See Hormel Foods,* 73 F.3d at 506 (observing that a successful parody "tends to increase public identification" of the famous mark with its source); *see also Yankee Publ'g Inc. v. News Am. Publ'g Inc.,* 809 F.Supp. 267, 272–82 (S.D.N.Y.1992) (suggesting that a sufficiently obvious parody is unlikely to blur the targeted famous mark).

[52] In sum, while a defendant's use of a parody as a mark does not support a "fair use" defense, it may be considered in determining whether the plaintiff-owner of a famous mark has proved its claim that the defendant's use of a parody mark is likely to impair the distinctiveness of the famous mark.

[53] In the case before us, when considering factors (ii), (iii), and (iv), it is readily apparent, indeed conceded by Haute Diggity Dog, that LVM's marks are distinctive, famous, and strong. The LOUIS VUITTON mark is well known and is commonly identified as a brand of the great Parisian fashion house, Louis Vuitton Malletier. So too are its other marks and designs, which are invariably used with the LOUIS VUITTON mark. It may not be too strong to refer to these famous marks as icons of high fashion.

[54] While the establishment of these facts satisfies essential elements of LVM's dilution claim, *see* 15 U.S.C.A. § 1125(c)(1), the facts impose on LVM an increased burden to demonstrate that the distinctiveness of its famous marks is likely to be impaired by a successful parody. Even as Haute Diggity Dog's parody mimics the famous mark, it communicates simultaneously that it is not the famous mark, but is only satirizing it. *See PETA,* 263 F.3d at 366. And because the famous mark is particularly strong and distinctive, it becomes more likely that a parody will not impair the distinctiveness of the mark. In short, as Haute Diggity Dog's "Chewy Vuiton" marks are a successful parody, we conclude that they will not blur the distinctiveness of the famous mark as a unique identifier of its source.

[55] It is important to note, however, that this might not be true if the parody is so similar to the famous mark that it likely could be construed as actual use of the famous mark itself. Factor (i) directs an inquiry into the "degree of similarity between the junior mark and the famous mark." If Haute Diggity Dog used the actual marks of LVM (as a parody or otherwise), it could dilute LVM's marks by blurring, regardless of whether Haute Diggity Dog's use was confusingly similar, whether it was in competition with LVM, or whether LVM sustained actual injury. *See* 15 U.S.C.A. § 1125(c)(1). Thus, "the use of DUPONT shoes, BUICK aspirin, and KODAK pianos would be actionable" under the TDRA because the unauthorized use of the famous marks *themselves* on unrelated goods might diminish the capacity of these trademarks to distinctively identify a single source. *Moseley,* 537 U.S. at 431 (quoting H.R.Rep. No. 104–374, at 3 (1995), *as reprinted in* 1995 U.S.C.C.A.N. 1029, 1030). This is true even though a consumer would be unlikely to confuse the manufacturer of KODAK film with the hypothetical producer of KODAK pianos.

[56] But in this case, Haute Diggity Dog mimicked the famous marks; it did not come so close to them as to destroy the success of its parody and, more importantly, to diminish the LVM marks' capacity to identify a single source. Haute Diggity Dog designed a pet chew toy to imitate and suggest, but not *use,* the marks of a high-fashion LOUIS VUITTON handbag. It used "Chewy Vuiton" to mimic "LOUIS VUITTON"; it used "CV" to mimic "LV"; and it adopted *imperfectly* the items of LVM's designs. We conclude that these uses by Haute Diggity Dog were not so similar as to be likely to impair the distinctiveness of LVM's famous marks.

[57] In a similar vein, when considering factors (v) and (vi), it becomes apparent that Haute Diggity Dog intentionally associated its marks, but only partially and certainly imperfectly, so as to convey the simultaneous message that it was not in fact a source of LVM products. Rather, as a parody, it separated itself from the LVM marks in order to make fun of them.

[58] In sum, when considering the relevant factors to determine whether blurring is likely to occur in this case, we readily come to the conclusion, as did the district court, that LVM has failed to make out a case of trademark dilution by blurring by failing to establish that the distinctiveness of its marks was likely to be impaired by Haute Diggity Dog's marketing and sale of its "Chewy Vuiton" products.

B

[59] LVM's claim for dilution by tarnishment does not require an extended discussion. To establish its claim for dilution by tarnishment, LVM must show, in lieu of blurring, that Haute Diggity Dog's use of the "Chewy Vuiton" mark on dog toys harms the reputation of the LOUIS VUITTON mark and LVM's other marks. LVM argues that the possibility that a dog could choke on a "Chewy Vuiton" toy causes this harm. LVM has, however, provided no record support for its assertion. It relies only on speculation about whether a dog could choke on the chew toys and a logical concession that a $10 dog toy made in China was of "inferior quality" to the $1190 LOUIS VUITTON handbag. The speculation begins with LVM's assertion in its brief that "defendant Woofie's admitted that 'Chewy Vuiton' products pose a choking hazard for some dogs. Having prejudged the defendant's mark to be a parody, the district court made light of this admission in its opinion, and utterly failed to give it the weight it deserved," citing to a page in the district court's opinion where the court states:

> At oral argument, plaintiff provided only a flimsy theory that a pet may some day choke on a Chewy Vuiton squeak toy and incite the wrath of a confused consumer against LOUIS VUITTON.

Louis Vuitton Malletier, 464 F.Supp.2d at 505. The court was referring to counsel's statement during oral argument that the owner of Woofie's stated that "she would not sell this product to certain types of dogs because there is a danger they would tear it open and choke on it." There is no record support, however, that any dog has choked on a pet chew toy, such as a "Chewy Vuiton" toy, or that there is any basis from which to conclude that a dog would likely choke on such a toy.

[60] We agree with the district court that LVM failed to demonstrate a claim for dilution by tarnishment. *See Hormel Foods,* 73 F.3d at 507.

. . . .

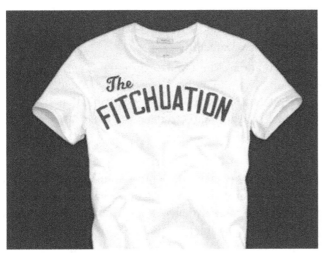 

MPS Entm't, LLC v. Abercrombie & Fitch Stores, Inc.
No. 11 Civ. 24110, 2013 WL 3288039 (S.D. Fla. June 28, 2013)

MPS Entm't, LLC v. Abercrombie & Fitch Stores, Inc., No. 11 Civ. 24110, 2013 WL 3288039 (S.D. Fla. June 28, 2013), offers a good, quick, and perhaps memorable example of an expressive use case where the court did not trouble itself with any extended analysis of whether the parody at issue was successful. Instead, the court simply applied the multifactor test for the likelihood of consumer confusion and found no likelihood of confusion.

In *MPS*, the defendant clothing store began selling a t-shirt (shown above on the left) bearing the phrase "The Fitchuation" in February 2010. "The Fitchuation" referred to Michael Sorrentino, one of the stars of the reality television show *The Jersey Shore*, which ran on MTV from 2009 to 2012 (above on right). In October 2010, Sorrentino, through the plaintiff, filed an application at the PTO to register the mark THE SITUATION for entertainment services. At the time of the opinion, Sorrentino was selling t-shirts on his website containing the words "The Situation" and "Official Situation Nation."

In 2011, after Sorrentino appeared in the show wearing various of the defendant's trademarks, the defendant sent a letter to MTV offering to pay up to $10,000 to cast members <u>not</u> to wear any clothing bearing Abercrombie & Fitch trademarks. The letter stated:

> A & F obviously has not sought product placement on the show, and we believe that, since the character portrayed by Mr. Sorrentino is not brand appropriate, his display of A & F clothing could be misconstrued as an endorsement by him of our clothing or—worse—an endorsement by A & F of his wearing our clothing.

> We have no interest at this point in pursuing any sort of legal action against MTV or the producers of "Jersey Shore." In fact, we would be willing to pay MTV or Mr. Sorrentino or other characters up to $10,000 NOT to wear any clothing bearing the "ABERCROMBIE & FITCH," "A & F," "FITCH," "MOOSE" or related trademarks. For additional episodes aired this season, we would appreciate it if you would ensure that our brands are pixilated or otherwise appropriately masked.

Id. at *2. Defendant also issued a press release announcing its offer to the cast members of Jersey Shore and singled out Sorrentino by name: "We have therefore offered a substantial payment to Michael 'The Situation' Sorrentino and the producers of MTV's *The Jersey Shore* to have the character wear an alternate brand." *Id*.

Plaintiff sued on the ground that the t-shirt bearing the term "The Fitchuation" and the press release violated his trademark rights.

Granting the defendant's motion for summary judgment, the court applied the Eleventh Circuit's multifactor test for the likelihood of consumer confusion to find that the t-shirt did not create a likelihood of confusion. As to the similarity of the marks factor,

> The target of A & F's parody is "The Situation." The t-shirt expresses "The Fitchuation" visually and phonetically different than "The Situation." There is no evidence of A & F "palming off" its t-shirt as that of the plaintiffs where, as here, the t-shirt has the A & F inside label and prominently uses A & F's own famous trademark "Fitch" as part of the parody.

Id. at *7. On the proximity of the goods or services,

> A & F's apparel goods are dissimilar to the plaintiffs' entertainment services. The plaintiffs concede that they did not offer apparel under a "Situation" mark until after A & F introduced "The Fitchuation" t-shirt. There is no evidence that the public attributes the parties' respective goods and services to the same single source.

Id. The court found in favor of the defendant on the intent and actual confusion factors as well.

As to the press release, the court found nominative fair use:

> The Court finds that the use of Michael Sorrentino's name and nickname in the press release was a non-actionable fair use under trademark law. A & F used only so much of the plaintiff's name as was reasonably necessary to respond to his wearing A & F's brand on The Jersey Shore, and did not do anything that would suggest Sorrentino's sponsorship or endorsement. A & F's press release expressly disassociated Sorrentino from A & F, and the plaintiffs have conceded that no third party has expressed any confusion that the press release rejecting Sorrentino's image somehow suggested sponsorship or endorsement by Sorrentino.

Id. at *13.

2. The *Rogers v. Grimaldi* Test for Unauthorized "Artistic" Uses

In *Rogers v. Grimaldi*, 875 F.2d 994 (2d Cir. 1989), Ginger Rogers (of the dance duo with Fred Astaire) sued the producers of the Federico Fellini film *Ginger and Fred* for using her name in the film's title. "The film tells the story of two fictional Italian cabaret performers, Pippo and Amelia, who, in their heyday, imitated Rogers and Astaire and became known in Italy as 'Ginger and Fred.' The film focuses on a televised reunion of Pippo and Amelia, many years after their retirement. Appellees describe the film as the bittersweet story of these two fictional dancers and as a satire of contemporary television variety shows." *Id.* at 996-97. In finding no violation of Rogers' Lanham Act § 43(a) rights, the Second Circuit sought to strike a balance between two competing policy objectives and in the process gave birth to the *Rogers v. Grimaldi* test:

> We believe that in general the {Lanham} Act should be construed to apply to artistic works only where the public interest in avoiding consumer confusion outweighs the public interest in free expression. In the context of allegedly misleading titles using a celebrity's name, that balance will normally not support application of the Act unless the title has no artistic relevance to the underlying work whatsoever, or, if it has some artistic relevance, unless the title explicitly misleads as to the source or the content of the work.

Id. at 999.

In the opinion that follows, *Gordon v. Drape Creative*, 909 F.3d 257 (9th Cir. Nov. 20, 2018), we consider a controversial application of the *Rogers* test involving the meme "Honey Badger Don't Care." The Ninth Circuit had initially issued its opinion in *Gordon* in July 2018, but largely in response to an amicus brief filed by a group of intellectual property law professors, the court withdrew that opinion four months later and issued the opinion below, which represents a slight modification (too slight, some would say) of the previous opinion.

Note that most previous applications of the *Rogers* test that are reviewed in *Gordon* (and were excerpted in previous versions of this casebook) were basically easy cases in which the defendant clearly should have prevailed. *Gordon* is significant because it is the first case applying the *Rogers* test in which the test, if unthinkingly applied, seemed to lead to the wrong result (i.e., to the bad faith defendant prevailing).

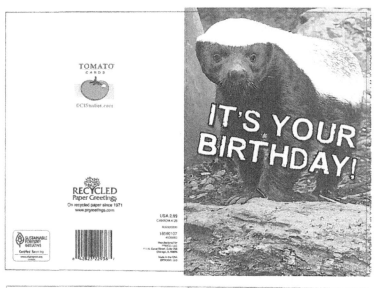

An example of the defendant's greeting cards

Gordon v. Drape Creative, Inc.
909 F.3d 257 (9th Cir. Nov. 20, 2018), *superseding* **897 F.3d 1185 (9th Cir. July 30, 2018)**

BYBEE, Circuit Judge

[1] Plaintiff Christopher Gordon is the creator of a popular YouTube video known for its catchphrases "Honey Badger Don't Care" and "Honey Badger Don't Give a S---." Gordon has

trademarked the former phrase for various classes of goods, including greeting cards. Defendants Drape Creative, Inc. ("DCI"), and Papyrus-Recycled Greetings, Inc. ("PRG"), designed and produced greeting cards using both phrases with slight variations. Gordon brought this suit for trademark infringement, and the district court granted summary judgment for defendants, holding that Gordon's claims were barred by the test set forth in *Rogers v. Grimaldi*, 875 F.2d 994 (2d Cir. 1989).

[2] We use the *Rogers* test to balance the competing interests at stake when a trademark owner claims that an expressive work infringes on its trademark rights. The test construes the Lanham Act to apply to expressive works "only where the public interest in avoiding consumer confusion outweighs the public interest in free expression." *Id.* at 999. "[T]hat balance will normally not support application of the Act, unless the [use of the mark] has no artistic relevance to the underlying work whatsoever, or . . . explicitly misleads [consumers] as to the source or the content of the work." *Id.*

[3] The *Rogers* test is not an automatic safe harbor for any minimally expressive work that copies someone else's mark. Although on every prior occasion in which we have applied the test, we have found that it barred an infringement claim as a matter of law, this case presents a triable issue of fact. Defendants have not used Gordon's mark in the creation of a song, photograph, video game, or television show, but have largely just pasted Gordon's mark into their greeting cards. A jury could determine that this use of Gordon's mark is explicitly misleading as to the source or content of the cards. We therefore reverse the district court's grant of summary judgment and remand for further proceedings on Gordon's claims.

I

[4] Plaintiff Christopher Gordon is a comedian, writer, and actor, who commonly uses the name "Randall" as an alias on social media. Defendant DCI is a greeting-card design studio. DCI works exclusively with American Greetings Corporation and its subsidiaries, which include the other defendant in this case, PRG. PRG is a greeting-card manufacturer and distributor.

A

[5] In January 2011, under the name Randall, Gordon posted a video on YouTube titled *The Crazy Nastyass Honey Badger*, featuring National Geographic footage of a honey badger overlaid with Gordon's narration. In the video, Gordon repeats variations of the phrases "Honey Badger Don't Care" and "Honey Badger Don't Give a S---," as a honey badger hunts and eats its prey. The parties refer to these phrases as "HBDC" and "HBDGS," and we adopt their convention.

[6] Gordon's video quickly generated millions of views on YouTube and became the subject of numerous pop-culture references in television shows, magazines, and social media. As early as February 2011, Gordon began producing and selling goods with the HBDC or HBDGS phrases, such as books, wall calendars, t-shirts, costumes, plush toys, mouse pads, mugs, and decals. Some of the items were sold online; others were sold through national retailers such as Wal-Mart, Target, Urban Outfitters, and Hot Topic. In June 2011, Gordon copyrighted his video's narration under the title *Honey Badger Don't Care*, and in October 2011, he began filing trademark applications for the HBDC phrase for various classes of goods. The Patent and Trademark Office ("PTO") eventually registered "Honey Badger Don't Care" for International Classes 9 (audio books, etc.), 16 (greeting cards, etc.), 21 (mugs), 25 (clothing), and 28 (Christmas decorations, dolls, etc.). However, Gordon never registered the HBDGS phrase for any class of goods.

[7] At the peak of his popularity, Gordon promoted his brand on television and radio shows and in interviews with national publications such as *Forbes*, *The Wall Street Journal*, and *The Huffington Post*. His brand was further boosted by celebrities like Taylor Swift and Anderson Cooper quoting his video and by LSU football players tagging their teammate, Heisman Trophy finalist Tyrann Mathieu, with the moniker "Honey Badger" for his aggressive defensive play. In November 2011, *Advertising Age* referred

to Gordon's brand as one of "America's Hottest Brands" in an article titled "Hot Brand? Honey Badger Don't Care."

B

[8] In January 2012, Gordon hired Paul Leonhardt to serve as his licensing agent. Soon thereafter, Leonhardt contacted Janice Ross at American Greetings—the parent company of defendant PRG—to discuss licensing honey-badger themed greeting cards. Leonhardt and Ross had multiple email exchanges and conversations over several weeks. Ross at one point expressed some interest in a licensing agreement, stating: "I think it's a really fun and irreverent property and would love to see if there's an opportunity on one of our distribution platforms. But in order to do that, I need to get some key colleagues of mine on board the Crazy Honey Badger Bandwagon." Nevertheless, neither American Greetings nor defendants ever signed a licensing agreement with Gordon.

[9] Leonhardt did eventually secure several licensing deals for Gordon. Between May and October 2012, Gordon's company—Randall's Honey Badger, LLC ("RHB")—entered into licensing agreements with Zazzle, Inc., and The Duck Company for various honey-badger themed products, including greeting cards. RHB also entered into licensing agreements with other companies for honey-badger costumes, toys, t-shirts, sweatshirts, posters, and decals, among other things. HBDC and HBDGS were the two most common phrases used on these licensed products. For example, two of Zazzle's best-selling honey-badger greeting cards stated on their front covers "Honey Badger Don't Care About Your Birthday."

[10] At the same time that Gordon was negotiating licensing agreements with Zazzle and Duck, defendants began developing their own line of unlicensed honey-badger greeting cards. Beginning in June 2012, defendants sold seven different greeting cards using the HBDC or HBDGS phrases with small variations:

- The fronts of two "Election Cards" showed a picture of a honey badger wearing a patriotic hat and stated "The Election's Coming." The inside of one card said "Me and Honey Badger don't give a $#%@! Happy Birthday," and the inside of the other said "Honey Badger and me just don't care. Happy Birthday."

- The fronts of two "Birthday Cards" featured different pictures of a honey badger and stated either "It's Your Birthday!" or "Honey Badger Heard It's Your Birthday." The inside of both cards said "Honey Badger Don't Give a S---."

- The fronts of two "Halloween Cards" showed a picture of a honey badger next to a jack-o-lantern and stated "Halloween is Here." The inside of the cards said either "Honey Badger don't give a $#*%!" or "Honey Badger don't give a s---."

- A "Critter Card" employed a Twitter-style format showing a series of messages from "Honey Badger@don'tgiveas---." The front stated "Just killed a cobra. Don't give a s---"; "Just ate a scorpion. Don't give a s---"; and "Rolling in fire ants. Don't give a s---."[3] The inside said "Your Birthday's here. . . I give a s---."

[11] The back cover of each card displayed the mark for "Recycled Paper Greetings" and listed the websites www.DCIStudios.com and www.prgreetings.com. DCI's President testified that he drafted all of the cards in question but could not recall what inspired the cards' designs. He claimed to have never heard of a video involving a honey badger.

---

[3] Gordon's video refers to a honey badger getting stung by bees and eating a cobra—e.g., "Now look, here's a house full of bees. You think the honey badger cares? It doesn't give a s--- . . . . But look the honey badger doesn't care, it's getting stung like a thousand times. It doesn't give a s--- . . . . Look! Here comes a fierce battle between a king cobra and a honey badger. . . . And of course, what does a honey badger have to eat for the next few weeks? Cobra."

597

[12] In June 2015, Gordon filed this suit against DCI and PRG, alleging trademark infringement under the Lanham Act, among other claims. The district court granted summary judgment for defendants, holding that defendants' greeting cards were expressive works, and applying the *Rogers* test to bar all of Gordon's claims. Gordon timely appealed.

II

. . . .[5]

[13] In general, we apply a "likelihood-of-confusion test" to claims brought under the Lanham Act. *Twentieth Century Fox Television v. Empire Distrib., Inc.*, 875 F.3d 1192, 1196 (9th Cir. 2017); *Mattel, Inc. v. Walking Mountain Prods.*, 353 F.3d 792, 806–07 (9th Cir. 2003). The likelihood-of-confusion test requires the plaintiff to prove two elements: (1) that "it has a valid, protectable trademark" and (2) that "the defendant's use of the mark is likely to cause confusion." *S. Cal. Darts Ass'n v. Zaffina*, 762 F.3d 921, 929 (9th Cir. 2014) (alteration omitted). Ordinarily, this test "strikes a comfortable balance" between the Lanham Act and the First Amendment. *Mattel, Inc. v. MCA Records, Inc.*, 296 F.3d 894, 900 (9th Cir. 2002).

[14] That said, where artistic expression is at issue, we have expressed concern that "the traditional test fails to account for the full weight of the public's interest in free expression." *Id.* The owner of a trademark "does not have the right to control public discourse" by enforcing his mark. *Id.* We have adopted the Second Circuit's *Rogers* test to strike an appropriate balance between First Amendment interests in protecting artistic expression and the Lanham Act's purposes to secure trademarks rights. Under *Rogers*, we read the Act "to apply to artistic works only where the public interest in avoiding consumer confusion outweighs the public interest in free expression." *Id.* at 901 (quoting *Rogers*, 875 F.2d at 999). More concretely, we apply the Act to an expressive work only if the defendant's use of the mark is (1) not artistically relevant to the work or (2) explicitly misleads consumers as to the source or the content of the work. *See id.* at 902. Effectively, *Rogers* employs the First Amendment as a rule of construction to avoid conflict between the Constitution and the Lanham Act.

[15] We pause here to clarify the burden of proof under the *Rogers* test. The *Rogers* test requires the defendant to make a threshold legal showing that its allegedly infringing use is part of an expressive work protected by the First Amendment. If the defendant successfully makes that threshold showing, then the plaintiff claiming trademark infringement bears a heightened burden—the plaintiff must satisfy not only the likelihood-of-confusion test but also at least one of *Rogers*'s two prongs. *Cf. Makaeff v. Trump Univ., LLC*, 715 F.3d 254, 261 (9th Cir. 2013) (if a defendant meets its "initial burden" of showing a First Amendment interest, then a public-figure plaintiff claiming defamation must meet a "heightened standard of proof" requiring a showing of "actual malice"). That is, when the defendant demonstrates that First Amendment interests are at stake, the plaintiff claiming infringement must show (1) that it has a valid, protectable trademark, and (2) that the mark is either not artistically relevant to the underlying work *or* explicitly misleading consumers as to the source or content of the

---

[5] The district court declined to distinguish between HBDC, which is a registered trademark, and HBDGS, which is not. We assume for purposes of this decision that HBDC and HBDGS are both protected marks, even if HBDGS is not registered. *See Matal v. Tam*, ––– U.S. ––––, 137 S.Ct. 1744, 1752 (2017) (explaining that "an unregistered trademark can be enforced against would-be infringers" under 15 U.S.C. § 1125(a)); *Brown v. Elec. Arts, Inc.*, 724 F.3d 1235, 1241 (9th Cir. 2013) (noting that the *Rogers* test applies "in [§ 1125(a)] cases involving expressive works"). Gordon claimed infringement under § 1125(a) in his complaint, and defendants challenged Gordon's ownership of HBDGS as a protected mark in their motion for summary judgment. The district court is free to revisit this issue on remand.

work. If the plaintiff satisfies both elements, it still must prove that its trademark has been infringed by showing that the defendant's use of the mark is likely to cause confusion.[7]

[16] .... When, as here, the defendant moves for summary judgment and has demonstrated that its use of the plaintiff's mark is part of an expressive work, the burden shifts to the plaintiff to raise a genuine dispute as to at least one of *Rogers*'s two prongs. In other words, to evade summary judgment, the plaintiff must show a triable issue of fact as to whether the mark is artistically relevant to the underlying work or explicitly misleads consumers as to the source or content of the work.

III

[17] Before applying the *Rogers* test to the instant case, we briefly review the test's origin in the Second Circuit and development in our court.[8] We have applied the *Rogers* test on five separate occasions, and each time we have concluded that it barred the trademark infringement-claim as a matter of law. Three of those cases, like *Rogers*, involved the use of a trademark in the title of an expressive work. Two cases involved trademarks in video games and extended the *Rogers* test to the use of a trademark in the body of an expressive work.

A

[18] The *Rogers* case concerned the movie *Ginger and Fred*, a story of two fictional Italian cabaret performers who imitated the famed Hollywood duo of Ginger Rogers and Fred Astaire. 875 F.2d at 996–97. Rogers sued the film's producers under the Lanham Act, alleging that the film's title gave the false impression that the film—created and directed by well-known filmmaker Federico Fellini—was about her or sponsored by her. *Id.* at 997. The district court, however, granted summary judgment for the defendant film producers. *Id.*

[19] On appeal, the Second Circuit recognized that, "[t]hough First Amendment concerns do not insulate titles of artistic works from all Lanham Act claims, such concerns must nonetheless inform our consideration of the scope of the Act as applied to claims involving such titles." *Id.* at 998. The court said it would construe the Lanham Act "to apply to artistic works only where the public interest in avoiding consumer confusion outweighs the public interest in free expression." *Id.* at 999. Refining its inquiry, the court further held that, "[i]n the context of allegedly misleading titles using a celebrity's name, that balance will normally not support application of the Act unless [1] the title has no artistic relevance to the underlying work whatsoever, or, [2] if it has some artistic relevance, unless the title explicitly misleads as to the source or the content of the work." *Id.*

[20] With respect to artistic relevance, the Second Circuit found that the names "Ginger" and "Fred" were "not arbitrarily chosen just to exploit the publicity value of their real life counterparts" but had "genuine relevance to the film's story." *Id.* at 1001. The film's title was "truthful as to its content" and conveyed "an ironic meaning that [was] relevant to the film's content." *Id.* On the second prong of its inquiry, the court held that the title was not explicitly misleading because it "contain[ed] no explicit indication that Rogers endorsed the film or had a role in producing it." *Id.* Any risk that the title would

---

[7] We have been careful not to "conflate[ ] the ['explicitly misleading'] prong of the *Rogers* test with the general *Sleekcraft* likelihood-of-confusion test," *Twentieth Century Fox*, 875 F.3d at 1199, but it bears noting that *Twentieth Century Fox* made this distinction to ensure that the likelihood-of-confusion test did not dilute *Rogers*'s explicitly misleading prong. Other circuits have noted that *Rogers*'s second prong is essentially a more exacting version of the likelihood-of-confusion test. *See Westchester Media v. PRL USA Holdings, Inc.*, 214 F.3d 658, 665 (5th Cir. 2000); *Twin Peaks Prods., Inc. v. Publ'ns Int'l, Ltd.*, 996 F.2d 1366, 1379 (2d Cir. 1993). A plaintiff who satisfies the "explicitly misleading" portion of *Rogers* should therefore have little difficulty showing a likelihood of confusion.

[8] The *Rogers* test has been adopted in other circuits as well. *See Univ. of Ala. Bd. of Trs. v. New Life Art, Inc.*, 683 F.3d 1266, 1278 (11th Cir. 2012); *Parks v. LaFace Records*, 329 F.3d 437, 452 (6th Cir. 2003); *Westchester Media v. PRL USA Holdings, Inc.*, 214 F.3d 658, 665 (5th Cir. 2000).

mislead consumers was "outweighed by the danger that suppressing an artistically relevant though ambiguous title will unduly restrict expression." *Id.* The Second Circuit therefore affirmed summary judgment for the defendant film producers. *Id.* at 1005.

B

[21] We first employed the *Rogers* test in *MCA Records*, 296 F.3d 894, which concerned the song "Barbie Girl" by the Danish band Aqua. The song—which lampooned the values and lifestyle that the songwriter associated with Barbie dolls—involved one band-member impersonating Barbie and singing in a high-pitched, doll-like voice. *Id.* at 899. Mattel, the manufacturer of Barbie dolls, sued the producers and distributors of "Barbie Girl" for infringement under the Lanham Act, and the district court granted summary judgment for the defendants. *Id.* Applying the *Rogers* test, we affirmed. *Id.* at 902. We held that the use of the Barbie mark in the song's title was artistically relevant to the underlying work because the song was "about Barbie and the values Aqua claims she represents." *Id.* In addition, the song "d[id] not, explicitly or otherwise, suggest that it was produced by Mattel." *Id.* "The *only* indication that Mattel might be associated with the song [was] the use of Barbie in the title," and if the use of the mark alone were enough to satisfy *Rogers*'s second prong, "it would render *Rogers* a nullity." *Id.* Because the Barbie mark was artistically relevant to the song and not explicitly misleading, we concluded that the band could not be held liable for infringement.

[22] We applied the *Rogers* test to another suit involving Barbie in *Walking Mountain Prods.*, 353 F.3d 792. There, photographer Thomas Forsythe developed a series of photographs titled "Food Chain Barbie" depicting Barbie dolls or parts of Barbie dolls in absurd positions, often involving kitchen appliances. *Id.* at 796. Forsythe described the photographs as critiquing "the objectification of women associated with [Barbie]." *Id.* Mattel claimed that the photos infringed its trademark and trade dress, but we affirmed summary judgment for Forsythe because "[a]pplication of the *Rogers* test here leads to the same result as it did in *MCA*." *Id.* at 807. Forsythe's use of the Barbie mark was artistically relevant to his work because his photographs depicted Barbie and targeted the doll with a parodic message. *Id.* Moreover, apart from Forsythe's use of the mark, there was no indication that Mattel in any way created or sponsored the photographs. *Id.*

[23] Most recently, we applied the *Rogers* test in *Twentieth Century Fox Television*, 875 F.3d 1192. Twentieth Century Fox produced the television show *Empire*, which revolved around a fictional hip-hop record label named "Empire Enterprises." *Id.* at 1195. Empire Distribution, an actual hip-hop record label, sent Twentieth Century Fox a cease-and-desist letter, and Twentieth Century Fox sued for a declaratory judgment that its show did not violate Empire's trademark rights. *Id.* In affirming summary judgment for Twentieth Century Fox, we rejected Empire's argument that "the *Rogers* test includes a threshold requirement that a mark have attained a meaning beyond its source-identifying function."[9] *Id.* at 1197. Whether a mark conveys a meaning beyond identifying a product's source is not a threshold requirement but only a relevant consideration: "trademarks that transcend their identifying purpose are more likely to be used in artistically relevant ways," but such transcendence is not necessary to trigger First Amendment protection. *Id.* at 1198 (quotation marks and citation omitted).

[24] We concluded that Empire could not satisfy *Rogers*'s first prong because Twentieth Century Fox "used the common English word 'Empire' for artistically relevant reasons," namely, that the show's setting was New York (the Empire State) and its subject matter was an entertainment conglomerate (a figurative empire). *Id.* Finally, we resisted Empire's efforts to conflate the likelihood-of-confusion test

---

[9] We explained in *MCA Records* that trademarks sometimes "transcend their identifying purpose" and "become an integral part of our vocabulary." 296 F.3d at 900. Examples include "Rolls Royce" as proof of quality or "Band-Aid" for any quick fix.

with *Rogers*'s second prong. To satisfy that prong, it is not enough to show that "the defendant's use of the mark would confuse consumers as to the source, sponsorship or content of the work;" rather, the plaintiff must show that the defendant's use "*explicitly* misl[ed] consumers." *Id.* at 1199. Because Twentieth Century Fox's *Empire* show contained "no overt claims or explicit references to Empire Distribution," we found that Empire could not satisfy *Rogers*'s second prong. *Id.* Empire's inability to satisfy either of *Rogers*'s two prongs meant that it could not prevail on its infringement claim.

C

[25] We first extended the *Rogers* test beyond a title in *E.S.S. Ent'mt 2000, Inc. v. Rock Star Videos, Inc.*, 547 F.3d 1095, 1099 (9th Cir. 2008). In that case, defendant Rockstar Games manufactured and distributed the video game *Grand Theft Auto: San Andreas*, which took place in a fictionalized version of Los Angeles. *Id.* at 1096–97. One of the game's neighborhoods—East Los Santos—"lampooned the seedy underbelly" of East Los Angeles by mimicking its businesses and architecture. *Id.* at 1097. The fictional East Los Santos included a virtual strip club called the "Pig Pen." *Id.* ESS Entertainment 2000, which operates the Play Pen Gentlemen's Club in the real East Los Angeles, claimed that Rockstar's depiction of the Pig Pen infringed its trademark and trade dress. *Id.*

[26] We recognized that the *Rogers* test was developed in a case involving a title, and adopted by our court in a similar case, but we could find "no principled reason why it ought not also apply to the use of a trademark in the body of the work." *Id.* at 1099. With respect to *Rogers*'s first prong, we explained that "[t]he level of relevance merely must be above zero" and the Pig Pen met this threshold by being relevant to Rockstar's artistic goal of creating "a cartoon-style parody of East Los Angeles." *Id.* at 1100. On the second prong, we concluded that the game did not explicitly mislead as to the source of the mark and would not "confuse its players into thinking that the Play Pen is somehow behind the Pig Pen or that it sponsors Rockstar's product. . . . A reasonable consumer would not think a company that owns one strip club in East Los Angeles . . . also produces a technologically sophisticated video game." *Id.* at 1100–01. Because ESS Entertainment 2000 could not demonstrate either of *Rogers*'s two prongs, we affirmed summary judgment for Rockstar.

[27] Another video-game case dealt with the *Madden NFL* series produced by Electronic Arts, Inc. ("EA"). *Brown v. Elec. Arts, Inc.*, 724 F.3d 1235 (9th Cir. 2013). Legendary football player Jim Brown alleged that EA violated § 43(a) of the Lanham Act by using his likeness in its games. *Id.* at 1238–39. The district court granted EA's motion to dismiss, and we affirmed. *Id.* at 1239. We reiterated *E.S.S.*'s holding that the level of artistic relevance under *Rogers*'s first prong need only exceed zero and found it was "obvious that Brown's likeness ha[d] at least some artistic relevance to EA's work." *Id.* at 1243. We also found that Brown had not alleged facts that would satisfy *Rogers*'s second prong: "EA did not produce a game called *Jim Brown Presents Pinball* with no relation to Jim Brown or football beyond the title; it produced a football game featuring likenesses of thousands of current and former NFL players, including Brown." *Id.* at 1244. We asked "whether the use of Brown's likeness would confuse *Madden NFL* players into thinking that Brown is somehow behind the games or that he sponsors EA's product," and held that it would not. *Id.* at 1245–47 (alterations omitted). As in *E.S.S.*, the plaintiff could not satisfy either of *Rogers*'s two prongs, and judgment for the defendant was proper.

IV

[28] In each of the cases coming before our court, the evidence was such that no reasonable jury could have found for the plaintiff on either prong of the *Rogers* test, and we therefore concluded that the plaintiff's Lanham Act claim failed as a matter of law. This case, however, demonstrates *Rogers*'s outer limits. Although defendants' greeting cards are expressive works to which *Rogers* applies, there remains a genuine issue of material fact as to *Rogers*'s second prong—i.e., whether defendants' use of Gordon's mark in their greeting cards is explicitly misleading.

A

[29] As a threshold matter, we have little difficulty determining that defendants have met their initial burden of demonstrating that their greeting cards are expressive works protected under the First Amendment. As we have previously observed, "[a greeting] card certainly evinces '[a]n intent to convey a particularized message . . . , and in the surrounding circumstances the likelihood was great that the message would be understood by those who viewed it.' " *Hilton v. Hallmark Cards*, 599 F.3d 894, 904 (9th Cir. 2010) (quoting *Spence v. Washington*, 418 U.S. 405, 410–11, 94 S.Ct. 2727, 41 L.Ed.2d 842 (1974) (per curiam)); *see also Roth Greeting Cards v. United Card Co.*, 429 F.2d 1106, 1110 (9th Cir. 1970) (plaintiff's greeting cards, considered as a whole, "represent[ed] a tangible expression of an idea" and hence were copyrightable). Each of defendants' cards relies on graphics and text to convey a humorous message through the juxtaposition of an event of some significance—a birthday, Halloween, an election—with the honey badger's aggressive assertion of apathy. Although the cards may not share the creative artistry of Charles Schulz or Sandra Boynton, the First Amendment protects expressive works "[e]ven if [they are] not the expressive equal of *Anna Karenina* or *Citizen Kane*." *Brown*, 724 F.3d at 1241. Because defendants have met their initial burden, the burden shifts to Gordon to raise a triable issue of fact as to at least one of *Rogers*'s two prongs.

B

[30] *Rogers*'s first prong requires proof that defendants' use of Gordon's mark was not "artistically relevant" to defendants' greeting cards. We have said that "the level of artistic relevance of the trademark or other identifying material to the work merely must be above zero." *Id.* at 1243 (internal alterations omitted) (quoting *E.S.S.*, 547 F.3d at 1100). Indeed, "even the slightest artistic relevance" will suffice; courts and juries should not have to engage in extensive "artistic analysis." *Id.* at 1243, 1245; *see Bleistein v. Donaldson Lithographing Co.*, 188 U.S. 239, 251, 23 S.Ct. 298, 47 L.Ed. 460 (1903) ("It would be a dangerous undertaking for persons trained only to the law to constitute themselves final judges of the worth of pictorial illustrations, outside of the narrowest and most obvious limits.").

Gordon's mark is certainly relevant to defendants' greeting cards; the phrase is the punchline on which the cards' humor turns. In six of the seven cards, the front cover sets up an expectation that an event will be treated as important, and the inside of the card dispels that expectation with either the HBDC or HBDGS phrase. The last card, the "Critter Card," operates in reverse: the front cover uses variations of the HBDGS phrase to establish an apathetic tone, while the inside conveys that the card's sender actually cares about the recipient's birthday. We thus conclude that Gordon has not raised a triable issue of fact with respect to *Rogers*'s "artistic relevance" prong.

C

[31] Even if the use of the mark is artistically relevant to the work, the creator of the work can be liable under the Lanham Act if the creator's use of the mark is "explicitly misleading as to source or content." *Rogers*, 875 F.2d at 999. "This second prong of the *Rogers* test 'points directly at the purpose of trademark law, namely to avoid confusion in the marketplace by allowing a trademark owner to prevent others from duping consumers into buying a product they mistakenly believe is sponsored [or created] by the trademark owner.' " *Brown*, 724 F.3d at 1245 (quoting *E.S.S.*, 547 F.3d at 1100). The "key here [is] that the creator must *explicitly* mislead consumers," and we accordingly focus on "the nature of the [junior user's] behavior" rather than on "the impact of the use." *Id.* at 1245–46.

[32] In applying this prong, however, we must remain mindful of the purpose of the *Rogers* test, which is to balance "the public interest in avoiding consumer confusion" against "the public interest in free expression." *Rogers*, 875 F.2d at 999. This is not a mechanical test—"all of the relevant facts and circumstances" must be considered. *Id.* at 1000 n.6. We therefore reject the district court's rigid requirement that, to be explicitly misleading, the defendant must make an "affirmative statement of the plaintiff's sponsorship or endorsement." Such a statement may be sufficient to show that the use of a mark is explicitly misleading, but it is not a prerequisite. *See* 2 MCCARTHY § 10:17.10 (noting that

Rogers's second prong does not hinge on the junior user "falsely assert[ing] that there is an affiliation"). In some instances, the use of a mark alone may explicitly mislead consumers about a product's source if consumers would ordinarily identify the source by the mark itself. If an artist pastes Disney's trademark at the bottom corner of a painting that depicts Mickey Mouse, the use of Disney's mark, while arguably relevant to the subject of the painting, could explicitly mislead consumers that Disney created or authorized the painting, even if those words do not appear alongside the mark itself.

[33] To be sure, we have repeatedly observed that "the mere use of a trademark alone cannot suffice to make such use explicitly misleading." *E.S.S.*, 547 F.3d at 1100 (citing *MCA Records*, 296 F.3d at 902). But each time we have made this observation, it was clear that consumers would not view the mark alone as identifying the source of the artistic work. No one would think that a song or a photograph titled "Barbie" was created by Mattel, because consumers "do not expect [titles] to identify" the "origin" of the work. *MCA Records*, 296 F.3d at 902. Nor would anyone "think a company that owns one strip club in East Los Angeles ... also produces a technologically sophisticated video game." *E.S.S.*, 547 F.3d at 1100–01. But this reasoning does not extend to instances in which consumers *would* expect the use of a mark alone to identify the source.

[34] A more relevant consideration is the degree to which the junior user uses the mark in the same way as the senior user. In the cases in which we have applied the *Rogers* test, the junior user has employed the mark in a different context—often in an entirely different market—than the senior user. In *MCA Records* and *Walking Mountain*, for example, Mattel's Barbie mark was used in a song and a series of photos. In *E.S.S.*, the mark of a strip club was used in a video game. And in *Twentieth Century Fox*, the mark of a record label was used in a television show. In each of these cases, the senior user and junior user used the mark in different ways. This disparate use of the mark was at most "only suggestive" of the product's source and therefore did not outweigh the junior user's First Amendment interests. *Rogers*, 875 F.2d at 1000.

[35] But had the junior user in these cases used the mark in the same way as the senior user—had Twentieth Century Fox titled its new show *Law & Order: Special Hip-Hop Unit*[10]—such identical usage could reflect the type of "explicitly misleading description" of source that *Rogers* condemns. 875 F.2d at 999–1000. *Rogers* itself makes this point by noting that "misleading titles that are confusingly similar *to other titles*" can be explicitly misleading, regardless of artistic relevance. *Id.* at 999 n.5 (emphasis added). Indeed, the potential for explicitly misleading usage is especially strong when the senior user and the junior user both use the mark in similar artistic expressions. Were we to reflexively apply *Rogers*'s second prong in this circumstance, an artist who uses a trademark to identify the source of his or her product would be at a significant disadvantage in warding off infringement by another artist, merely because the product being created by the other artist is also "art." That would turn trademark law on its head.

[36] A second consideration relevant to the "explicitly misleading" inquiry is the extent to which the junior user has added his or her own expressive content to the work beyond the mark itself. As *Rogers* explains, the concern that consumers will not be "misled as to the source of [a] product" is generally allayed when the mark is used as only one component of a junior user's larger expressive creation, such that the use of the mark at most "implicitly suggest[s]" that the product is associated with the mark's owner. *Id.* at 998–99; *see* 6 MCCARTHY § 31:144.50 ("[T]he deception or confusion must be relatively obvious and express, not subtle and implied."). But using a mark as the centerpiece of an expressive work itself, unadorned with any artistic contribution by the junior user, may reflect nothing more than an effort to "induce the sale of goods or services" by confusion or "lessen[ ] the distinctiveness and thus the commercial value of" a competitor's mark. *S.F. Arts & Athletics, Inc. v. U.S. Olympic Comm.*, 483 U.S. 522, 539, 107 S.Ct. 2971, 97 L.Ed.2d 427 (1987).

---

[10] *Cf. Law & Order: Special Victims Unit* (NBC Universal).

[37] Our cases support this approach. In cases involving the use of a mark in the title of an expressive work—such as the title of a movie (*Rogers*), a song (*MCA Records*), a photograph (*Walking Mountain*), or a television show (*Twentieth Century Fox*)—the mark obviously served as only one "element of the [work] and the [junior user's] artistic expressions." *Rogers*, 875 F.2d at 1001. Likewise, in the cases extending *Rogers* to instances in which a mark was incorporated into the body of an expressive work, we made clear that the mark served as only one component of the larger expressive work. In *E.S.S.*, the use of the Pig Pen strip club was "quite incidental to the overall story" of the video game, such that it was not the game's "main selling point." 547 F.3d at 1100–01. And in *Brown*, Jim Brown was one of "thousands of current and former NFL players" appearing in the game, and nothing on the face of the game explicitly engendered consumer misunderstanding. 724 F.3d at 1244–46. Indeed, EA altered Brown's likeness in certain versions of the game, an artistic spin that "made consumers *less* likely to believe that Brown was involved." *Id.* at 1246–47.

[38] In this case, we cannot decide as a matter of law that defendants' use of Gordon's mark was not explicitly misleading. There is at least a triable issue of fact as to whether defendants simply used Gordon's mark with minimal artistic expression of their own, and used it in the same way that Gordon was using it—to identify the source of humorous greeting cards in which the bottom line is "Honey Badger don't care." Gordon has introduced evidence that he sold greeting cards and other merchandise with his mark; that in at least some of defendants' cards, Gordon's mark was used without any other text; and that defendants used the mark knowing that consumers rely on marks on the inside of cards to identify their source. Gordon's evidence is not bulletproof; for example, defendants' cards generally use a slight variation of the HBDGS phrase, and they list defendants' website on the back cover. But a jury could conclude that defendants' use of Gordon's mark on one or more of their cards is "explicitly misleading as to [their] source." *Rogers*, 875 F.2d at 999.

[39] Because we resolve the first *Rogers* prong against Gordon as a matter of law, a jury may find for Gordon only if he proves by a preponderance of the evidence that defendants' use of his mark is explicitly misleading as to the source or content of the cards.[11]

V

[40] For the foregoing reasons, we REVERSE and REMAND to the district court for further proceedings consistent with this opinion.

Questions and Comments

1. Rogers' *second prong*. Much of the controversy surrounding the *Gordon* opinion is focused on its treatment of the second prong of the *Rogers* test, going to whether the defendant's conduct "explicitly misleads as to the source . . . of the work." Previous case law had adopted an exceedingly defendant-friendly approach to this prong. For example, in *Brown v. Electronic Arts*, 724 F.3d 1235 (9th Cir. 2013), the case involving the video game maker's use of Jim Brown's likeness, the Ninth Circuit explained that even persuasive survey evidence showing consumer confusion would not be enough to satisfy the prong:

> The test requires that the use be *explicitly* misleading to consumers. To be relevant, evidence must relate to the nature of the behavior of the identifying material's user, not the impact of the use. Even if Brown could offer a survey demonstrating that consumers of the Madden NFL series believed that Brown endorsed the game, that would not support the claim that the use was explicitly misleading to consumers.

---

[11] We note that the district court has not yet addressed defendants' abandonment defense. We express no opinion on that issue and leave it for the district court to address in the first instance.

Id. at 1245-46 (emphasis in original). *Gordon* significantly modifies *Rogers*' second prong by adding two "consideration[s]", first, whether "the junior user uses the mark in the same way as the senior user," and second, "the extent to which the junior user has added his or her own expressive content to the work beyond the mark itself." If persuasive survey evidence showing consumer confusion is not enough to satisfy the "explicitly misleading" standard, then why would the defendant's use "in the same way" or in a non-additive manner satisfy the standard? Do these considerations address the question of whether the defendant's conduct explicitly misleads or are they ultimately concerned with other goals? Keep in mind that the *Rogers*' test was originally designed as a balancing test intended to determine when "the public interest in avoiding consumer confusion outweighs the public interest in free expression." *Rogers v. Grimaldi*, 875 F.2d 994, 999 (2d Cir. 1989).

2. *The* Rogers *test and merchandising uses by the defendant.* In *Twentieth Century Fox Television v. Empire Distrib., Inc.*, 875 F.3d 1192 (9th Cir. 2017), the plaintiff Empire Distribution was a "well-known and respected record label that records and releases albums in the urban music genre." *Id.* at 1195. Not mentioned in *Gordon*'s review of *Empire* was the fact that "Fox has also promoted the *Empire* show and its associated music through live musical performances, radio play, and consumer goods such as shirts and champagne glasses bearing the show's "Empire" brand." *Id.* Empire Distribution asserted that this conduct should not be protected by *Rogers*. The Ninth Circuit disagreed:

> Although it is true that these promotional efforts technically fall outside the title or body of an expressive work, it requires only a minor logical extension of the reasoning of *Rogers* to hold that works protected under its test may be advertised and marketed by name, and we so hold. Indeed, the *Rogers* case itself concerned both a movie with an allegedly infringing title and its advertising and promotion, although the majority opinion did not deal separately with the latter aspect. *See Rogers*, 875 F.2d at 1005 (Griesa, J., concurring in the judgment). The balance of First Amendment interests struck in *Rogers* and *Mattel* could be destabilized if the titles of expressive works were protected but could not be used to promote those works. In response, Empire Distribution raises the specter of a pretextual expressive work meant only to disguise a business profiting from another's trademark, but the record in this case makes clear that the *Empire* show is no such thing. Fox's promotional activities, including those that generate revenue, are auxiliary to the television show and music releases, which lie at the heart of its "Empire" brand.

Empire Distrib., 875 F.3d at 1196-97.

Is this reasoning persuasive? Should Fox be allowed to sell music from its show under "its 'Empire' brand"?

3. *Expressive works and commercial speech under* Rogers. In *Facenda v. N.F.L. Films, Inc.*, 542 F.3d 1007 (3d Cir. 2008), NFL Films had produced "The Making of Madden NFL 06," a 22-minute infomercial broadcast on the NFL Network eight times over three days in 2005 to promote the soon-to-be released video game. Thirteen seconds of the program consisted of sound recordings of the well-known (to NFL fans) voice of the sports announcer John Facenda making various grandiose statements about the heroic wonder of NFL football. His estate sued on grounds of false endorsement under Lanham Act § 43(a) and violation of Pennsylvania state right of publicity law. The Third Circuit declined to apply the *Rogers* analysis to Facenda's § 43(a) claim "[b]ecause we hold that 'The Making of Madden NFL 06' is commercial speech rather than artistic expression," and thus the infomercial would not even satisfy *Rogers*' threshold requirement that the work at issue be an expressive work. *Facenda*, 542 F.3d at 1018. Does this strike you as a reasonable distinction, in which a work is either "commercial speech" or "artistic expression"? Regardless, do you think the Third Circuit reached the right result in declining to apply *Rogers* to an informercial that merely "aims to promote another creative work, the video game[,]" and "consist[ed] of mere praise for the product"? *Facenda*, 542 F.3d at 1018.

605

4. *Virtual reality and trademark rights.* Game designers seeking accurately to simulate non-virtual reality face significant challenges as this reality consists more and more of valuable intellectual properties, whether they take the form of public advertisements incorporating trademarks, distinctive product designs, well-known human personalities, or other embodiments. A number of trademark cases have sought, not always consistently, to determine when the unauthorized simulation of a trademark—or purported trademark—constitutes infringement. The two most significant, both referenced in *Gordon*, are *E.S.S. Entertainment 2000, Inc. v. Rock Star Videos, Inc.*, 547 F.3d 1095 (9th Cir. 2008), and *Brown v. Electronic Arts*, 724 F.3d 1235 (9th Cir. 2013). *See also VIRAG, S.R.L. v. Sony Computer Entm't Am. LLC*, No. 15 Civ. 01729, 2015 WL 5000102 (N.D. Cal. Aug. 21, 2015), aff'd, 699 F. App'x 667 (9th Cir. 2017) (dismissing plaintiff's trademark infringement claim on ground that defendant's *Gran Turismo* racing simulation games' depiction of plaintiff's racetrack advertising was permissible under *Rogers*); *Mil-Spec Monkey, Inc. v. Activision Blizzard, Inc.*, No. 14 Civ. 02361, 2014 WL 6655844 (N.D. Cal. Nov. 24, 2014) (finding to be non-infringing defendant's use of plaintiff's "angry monkey" trademark in defendant's combat simulation *Call of Duty: Ghosts*); *Electronic Arts, Inc. v. Textron Inc.*, 12 Civ. 00118, 2012 WL 3042668 (N.D. Cal. July 25, 2012) (denying declaratory plaintiff's motion to dismiss in dispute over plaintiff's depiction of defendant's helicopter designs in plaintiff's combat simulation *Battlefield 3*); *Dillinger, LLC v. Electronic Arts, Inc.*, 09 Civ. 1236, 2011 WL 2457678 (S.D. Ind. June 16, 2011) (finding to be non-infringing defendant's use of term "Dillinger" in reference to weapons in organized crime simulations *The Godfather* and *The Godfather II*). *Cf. In re NCAA Student–Athlete Name & Likeness Licensing Litigation*, 724 F.3d 1268 (9th Cir. 2013).

3. Further Aspects of Expressive Uses and Trademark Dilution

Lanham Act § 43(c)(3), 15 U.S.C. § 1125(c)(3)

> (3) Exclusions. The following shall not be actionable as dilution by blurring or dilution by tarnishment under this subsection:
>
> > (A) Any fair use, including a nominative or descriptive fair use, or facilitation of such fair use, of a famous mark by another person other than as a designation of source for the person's own goods or services, including use in connection with—
> >
> > > (i) advertising or promotion that permits consumers to compare goods or services; or
> > >
> > > (ii) identifying and parodying, criticizing, or commenting upon the famous mark owner or the goods or services of the famous mark owner.
> >
> > (B) All forms of news reporting and news commentary.
> >
> > (C) Any noncommercial use of a mark.

We focus here on two of the exclusions listed in § 43(c)(3): the exclusion for "[a]ny noncommercial use of a mark" and the exclusion for uses "in connection with . . . identifying and parodying, criticizing, or commenting upon the famous mark owner or the goods or services of the famous mark owner."

a. Noncommercial Expressive Uses

The noncommercial use exception has proven, where it applies, to be an extraordinarily powerful limitation on trademark dilution liability. The two brief case overviews below show why.

Mattel, Inc. v. MCA Records, Inc.
296 F.3d 894 (9th Cir. 2002)

As recounted above in *Gordon*, the basic facts of *Mattel v. MCA* are not complicated. In 1997, the Europop group Aqua released the song "Barbie Girl," which eventually achieved 11th place on Rolling Stone's list of the 20 most annoying songs ever[*], and which included lyrics such as

I'm a Barbie girl, in the Barbie world

Life in plastic, it's fantastic!

You can brush my hair, undress me everywhere

Imagination, life is your creation

Come on Barbie, let's go party!

Mattel, Inc., the manufacturers of the Barbie doll, sued for trademark infringement, including trademark blurring and tarnishment.

The Ninth Circuit affirmed the district court's grant of summary judgment to the defendant. On the issue of consumer confusion, Judge Kozinski applied the *Rogers v. Grimaldi* test and found:

The song title does not explicitly mislead as to the source of the work; it does not, explicitly or otherwise, suggest that it was produced by Mattel. The only indication that Mattel might be associated with the song is the use of Barbie in the title; if this were enough to satisfy this prong of the *Rogers* test, it would render *Rogers* a nullity.

Id. at 902.

As to blurring and tarnishment, Judge Kozinski determined that Aqua's conduct qualified under the "noncommercial use" exemption from liability in then § 43(c)(4)(B), 15 U.S.C. § 1125(c)(4)(B), which has been retained in the new § 43(c) as § 43(c)(3)(C), 15 U.S.C. § 1125(c)(3)(C). After reviewing the legislative history of the old Federal Trademark Dilution Act, Judge Kozinksi reasoned:

To determine whether Barbie Girl falls within this exemption, we look to our definition of commercial speech under our First Amendment caselaw. *See* H.R.Rep. No. 104–374, at 8, *reprinted in* 1995 U.S.C.C.A.N. 1029, 1035 (the exemption "expressly incorporates the concept of 'commercial' speech from the 'commercial speech' doctrine"); 141 Cong. Rec. S19306–10, S19311 (daily ed. Dec. 29, 1995) (the exemption "is consistent with existing [First Amendment] case law"). "Although the boundary between commercial and noncommercial speech has yet to be clearly delineated, the 'core notion of commercial speech' is that it 'does no more than propose a commercial transaction.'" *Hoffman v.*

---

[*] http://www.rollingstone.com/music/blogs/staff-blog/the-20-most-annoying-songs-20070702

Capital Cities/ABC, Inc., 255 F.3d 1180, 1184 (9th Cir. 2001) (quoting *Bolger v. Youngs Drug Prod's Corp.,* 463 U.S. 60, 66, 103 S.Ct. 2875, 77 L.Ed.2d 469 (1983)). If speech is not "purely commercial"—that is, if it does more than propose a commercial transaction—then it is entitled to full First Amendment protection. *Id.* at 1185–86 (internal quotation marks omitted).

. . . .

{ } Barbie Girl is not purely commercial speech, and is therefore fully protected. To be sure, MCA used Barbie's name to sell copies of the song. However, as we've already observed, the song also lampoons the Barbie image and comments humorously on the cultural values Aqua claims she represents. Use of the Barbie mark in the song Barbie Girl therefore falls within the noncommercial use exemption to the FTDA. For precisely the same reasons, use of the mark in the song's title is also exempted.

Mattel v. MCA Records, 296 F.3d at 906-907.

VIP Products LLC v. Jack Daniel's Properties, Inc.
953 F.3d 1170 (9th Cir. 2020)

In *VIP Products LLC v. Jack Daniel's Properties, Inc.*, 953 F.3d 1170 (9th Cir. 2020), the basic facts were as follows:

> VIP designs, markets, and sells "Silly Squeakers," rubber dog toys that resemble the bottles of various well-known beverages, but with dog-related twists. One Silly Squeaker, for example, resembles a Mountain Dew bottle, but is labeled "Mountain Drool." VIP's purported goal in creating Silly Squeakers was to "reflect" "on the humanization of the dog in our lives," and to comment on "corporations [that] take themselves very seriously." Over a million Silly Squeakers were sold from 2007 to 2017.

> In July of 2013, VIP introduced the Bad Spaniels squeaker toy. The toy is roughly in the shape of a Jack Daniel's bottle and has an image of a spaniel over the words "Bad Spaniels." The Jack Daniel's label says, "Old No. 7 Brand Tennessee Sour Mash Whiskey;" the label on the Bad Spaniels toy instead has the phrase "the Old No. 2, on your Tennessee Carpet." A tag affixed to the Bad Spaniels toy states that the "product is not affiliated with Jack Daniel Distillery."

Id. at 1172. After a bench trial, the district court ruled in favor of Jack Daniel's on its confusion and dilution claims. Id.

On the issue of consumer confusion, the Ninth Circuit remanded because the district court failed to apply (or even mention) the *Rogers* test. *See id.* at 1175 ("Like the greeting cards in *Gordon*, the Bad Spaniels dog toy, although surely not the equivalent of the *Mona Lisa*, is an expressive work.").

On the issue of dilution by tarnishment (Jack Daniel's having not argued blurring), the Ninth Circuit reversed the district court's finding of tarnishment outright. Here is the entirety of the Ninth Circuit's abrupt discussion of the tarnishment issue:

> When the use of a mark is "noncommercial," there can be no dilution by tarnishment. 15 U.S.C. § 1125(c)(3)(C); *see* A.R.S. § 44-1448.01(C)(2). Speech is noncommercial "if it does more than propose a commercial transaction," *Nissan Motor Co. v. Nissan Comput. Corp.*, 378 F.3d 1002, 1017 (9th Cir. 2004) (quoting *MCA Records*, 296 F.3d at 906), and contains some "protected expression," *MCA Records*, 296 F.3d at 906. Thus, use of a mark may be "noncommercial" even if used to "sell" a product. *See Nissan Motor Co.*, 378 F.3d at 1017; *MCA Records*, 296 F.3d at 906.

Although VIP used JDPI's trade dress and bottle design to sell Bad Spaniels, they were also used to convey a humorous message. That message, as set forth { } above, is protected by the First Amendment. VIP therefore was entitled to judgment in its favor on the federal and state law dilution claims. *See Nissan Motor Co.*, 378 F.3d at 1017; *MCA Records*, 296 F.3d at 906.

VIP Products, 953 F.3d at 1176.

Questions and Comments

1. *An alternative approach to the question of noncommercial uses.* For a significantly more subtle (but less defendant-friendly) approach to the question of whether a use qualifies as non-commercial, see *Jordan v. Jewel Food Stores, Inc.*, 743 F.3d 509 (7th Cir. 2014).

b. What Qualifies as Parody under § 43(c)(3)(A)(ii)?

The following two opinions count as relatively minor opinions in the case law on trademark dilution and parody. But together they provide a good means of exploring the question of what constitutes parody under Lanham Act § 43(c)(3)(A)(ii). Do the opinions adopt differing approaches to the definition of parody under that subsection or were the facts (or quality of the lawyering) in the two cases sufficiently different to explain the differing outcomes?

Louis Vuitton Malletier, S.A. v. Hyundai Motor Am.
No. 10 Civ. 1611, 2012 WL 1022247 (S.D.N.Y. Mar. 22, 2012)

P. KEVIN CASTEL, District Judge.

[1] During the post-game show of the 2010 Super Bowl, defendant Hyundai Motor America ("Hyundai") debuted a commercial that its counsel describes as "a humorous, socio-economic commentary on luxury defined by a premium price tag, rather than by the value to the consumer." The ad, which would eventually air five times over the course of a month, included a one-second shot of a basketball decorated with a distinctive pattern resembling the famous trademarks of plaintiff Louis Vuitton Malletier, S.A. ("Louis Vuitton").

[2] Louis Vuitton has asserted trademark and unfair competition claims under New York and federal law, alleging that the commercial diluted and infringed its marks. . . . Louis Vuitton moves for summary judgment on its trademark dilution claims as to liability only, and Hyundai has moved for summary judgment in its favor on all claims.

[3] For the reasons explained, Louis Vuitton's motion is granted and Hyundai's motion is denied.

BACKGROUND

A. *Hyundai's Use of Louis Vuitton Markings in the "Luxury" Ad.*

[4] Hyundai's thirty-second commercial goes by the name "Luxury." It consists of brief vignettes that show "policemen eating caviar in a patrol car; large yachts parked beside modest homes; blue-collar workers eating lobster during their lunch break; a four-second scene of an inner-city basketball game played on a lavish marble court with a gold hoop; and a ten-second scene of the Sonata driving down a street lined with chandeliers and red-carpet crosswalks."

[5] The commercial's "scene of an inner-city basketball game" features "a basketball bearing marks similar, but not identical," to the Louis Vuitton marks. Louis Vuitton characterizes the vignette as "a street-yard basketball scene in which it would use a basketball with markings copied from the design and colors of the [Louis Vuitton] Marks, altering them only slightly."

[6] The Louis Vuitton marks are known as the "toile monogram." As described by Hyundai, it "consists of a repeating pattern design of the letters 'LV and flower-like symbols on a chestnut-brown background." In the cease-and-desist letter that it would send to Hyundai after the ad's initial broadcast, Louis Vuitton described the marks as having "three distinctive elemental designs—a pinwheel design, a diamond with an inset pinwheel design, and a circle with an inset flower design ...." Louis Vuitton first registered this mark with the United States Patent and Trademark Office in 1932, and subsequently registered the mark's individual elements. The most prominent alteration in the "Luxury" ad was the substitution of the letters "LZ" for "LV," although Hyundai made small modifications to the other elements of the mark, including slight alterations to their proportions.

[7] According to Hyundai, the commercial sought to "emphasize" the "style, quality and amenities" of the 2011 Sonata, "a mid-sized Sedan priced at approximately $20,000." As described by Hyundai, the "Luxury" ad sought to redefine the concept of luxury by communicating to consumers that Sonata offered "luxury for all." The Commercial attempted to accomplish this goal by poking fun at the silliness of luxury-as-exclusivity by juxtaposing symbols of luxury with everyday life (for example, large yachts parked beside modest homes).

[8] As further explained by Hyundai, "The symbols of 'old' luxury, including the [Louis Vuitton] Marks, were used as part of the Commercial's humorous social commentary on the need to redefine luxury during a recession .... The commercial poked fun at these symbols of 'old' luxury to distinguish them from [Hyundai] in an effort to challenge consumers to rethink what it means for a product to be luxurious." In Hyundai's view, the ad sought "to distinguish [Louis Vuitton] from the common-sense Sonata."

[9] Hyundai does not dispute that the Louis Vuitton marks "are famous and distinctive" as "widely recognized luxury marks," and are "viewed by some as the most valuable luxury brand in the world." While the parties set forth slight and immaterial differences in their characterizations of the basketball's design, they agree that the ball was intended to evoke "the original Louis Vuitton Toile Monogram ...."

[10] Christopher J. Perry, a former marketing executive at Hyundai, confirmed in a Rule 30(b)(6) deposition that Hyundai worked to "genericize[ ] the Louis Vuitton marks" so "that they remained very similar" to the brown-and-gold marks of Louis Vuitton. Perry said that "the brown and gold of [Louis Vuitton]" were intended to give the basketball a "more stylized and luxurious look to it," and that these colors were "a distinctive special reference" that was "tied to Louis Vuitton." ....

....

[11] The "Luxury" ad was motivated in part by a desire on the part of Hyundai to change its brand image among consumers. As described by Hyundai, "among those who highly considered but did not purchase an earlier model of the Sonata, brand reputation and resale value were the main reasons for

rejection." . . . Ewanick, who had been at Hyundai at the time the ad was developed, testified that it was "[c]orrect" to say that Hyundai "used the Louis Vuitton[-]like marks in order to raise the image of the Hyundai brand in the mind of the consumer[.]" (Pl. 56.1 ¶ 69; Def. 56.1 Resp. ¶ 69.)

[12] Elsewhere, Hyundai states that it "objects to [Louis Vuitton's] implication that the sole and immediate purpose of the campaign was to sell cars. Rather, the admissible evidence demonstrates [Hyundai's] goal to build consideration and awareness and try to change the brand perception long term." (Def. 56.1 Resp. ¶ 3; quotation marks and alteration omitted.)

B. *Hyundai Previously Sought, But Did Not Receive, Permission to Display Several Luxury Marks in Its Commercial.*

[13] Before going forward with the final version of "Luxury," Hyundai requested permission from numerous companies to display their luxury marks in a commercial. Hyundai's outside advertising firm contacted thirteen companies to see whether they would permit Hyundai to use their brands free of charge. In a never-broadcast vignette, Hyundai displayed "a vending machine that dispensed luxury handbags ....." Six brands (Chanel, Prada, Coach, Yves Saint Laurent, Chloe, Gucci and Ferragamo) expressly declined consent. Others (Fendi, Chloe, Dolce & Gabbana, Marc Jacobs, Burberry and Louis Vuitton) never responded to the request. As described by Hyundai's counsel, "it does not appear" that its outside advertising firm "ever spoke with anyone at [Louis Vuitton] about this Commercial." An e-mail of November 19, 2009 sent within Hyundai's outside advertising firm states that as to permission from Louis Vuitton: "have not been able to get a return phone call-email has not been sent." A separate e-mail in the chain states: "Unfortunately we have not found one who would be open to participating yet."

C. *Hyundai's Continued Airing of "Luxury."*

[14] The "Luxury" ad first ran during the Superbowl post-game show of February 7, 2010, following the New Orleans Saints' 31–17 victory over the Indianapolis Colts. On February 12, 2010, Louis Vuitton sent Hyundai a cease-and-desist letter objecting to the inclusion of Louis Vuitton imagery in the "Luxury" ad. By then, Hyundai had already arranged for "Luxury" to air three times during the NBA All–Star Game weekend, over February 12–14, 2010. Hyundai executives decided to wait for an opinion from legal counsel before taking action on the ad, and went forward with the plan to run the ad during the NBA programming.

[15] Louis Vuitton commenced this litigation on March 1, 2010. Hyundai executives "took the complaint under advisement," and again aired the commercial during the 9 p.m. hour of the Academy Awards on March 7, 2010.

. . . .

{The court found a likelihood of dilution by blurring and then turned to Hyundai's claim that its use qualified as a parodic fair use under Lanham Act § 43(c)(3)(A)(ii).}

. . . .

2. *The Record Includes Express Evidence that Hyundai Intended No Parody, Criticism or Comment Upon Louis Vuitton.*

[16] Through deposition testimony and in submissions by counsel, Hyundai has disclaimed any intention to parody, criticize or comment upon Louis Vuitton. Rather, it contends that the basketball design in the "Luxury" ad reflects a broader social comment, one that embodies "an effort to challenge consumers to rethink what it means for a product to be luxurious."

[17] The text of the TDRA expressly states that fair use applies if dilution has arisen due to "use in connection with ... identifying and parodying, criticizing, or commenting upon the famous mark owner or the goods or services of the famous mark owner." 15 U.S.C. § 1125(c)(3)(A)(ii) (emphasis added) {*sic*}. Because Hyundai has disclaimed any comment, criticism or parody of Louis Vuitton, the "Luxury" ad does not, as a matter of law, qualify for fair use under the TDRA.

[18] Louis Vuitton has directed the Court to deposition testimony in which individuals involved in the ad's creation state that the ad contains no comment on Louis Vuitton. In the Rule 30(b)(6) deposition, Perry testified as follows:

Q. Okay. Why didn't you just use the [un-altered] Louis Vuitton marks?

A. I don't recall the – Innocean came back to us and suggested adjustments.

Q. Well, why didn't you say, gee, to make the association even stronger, let's just use the Louis Vuitton marks?

A. The intent of the spot wasn't to – was to portray these over-the-top overwhelming luxury ideas.

Q. Right. And, in fact, you weren't commenting in any way or giving any commentary on Louis Vuitton, were you?

[Defense counsel]: Objection to the form. You may answer.

A. No.

Q. And the point here was not to actually make fun of Louis Vuitton or criticize Louis Vuitton, was it?

[Defense counsel]: Objection to the form.

A. That is correct.

Q. So why not use the Louis Vuitton marks themselves?

[Defense counsel]: Asked and answered. You may answer.

A. I suppose we could have. We opted not to. It wasn't the intent to try to – the intent wasn't specific to – the same reason why we didn't use specific brands on any of the other things we did. It was just to convey luxury. And to your point that the brown and gold conveyed luxury.

Q. The intent wasn't to say anything about Louis Vuitton, was it?

[Defense counsel]: Asked and answered.

A. Correct

Similarly, Perry testified that any commentary in the "Luxury" ad was of a broad, societal nature, and not directed to any item or brand. He stated:

Q. Well, were you trying to provide commentary on the specific things that are shown in the course of the commercial?

A. No.

Q. No. You were—you were trying to give a kind of general social comment, correct?

A. That's correct.

Q. And am I correct that the individual scenes that you used within the course of the commercial, you could use one, you could use another. It's just a matter of sort of decisions of which ones you liked best, right?

[Defense counsel]: Objection to the form of the question. You may answer.

A. Yes.

* * *

Q. In fact, you could have—had you wanted to, you could have continued to do the ad and have it make sense without any additional basketball scene at all; isn't that true?

A. Yes.

[19] Boone, an account executive at the advertising firm that oversaw the "Luxury" ad, also testified that the ad contained no comment directed toward Louis Vuitton or its marks:

Q. So what other than Louis Vuitton were you attempting to have consumers take away from the basketball with these markings on it?

A. That was just one teeny, tiny piece of the commercial that was meant to signify luxury.... It was a 30-second commercial that in its totality at the end of watching that commercial they would say, oh, this commercial is about communicating that Hyundai is a vehicle that provides luxury to all, that we're bringing luxury – you don't have to spend gazillions of dollars to have luxury, that this car – it was about the car, about communicating the Hyundai product. We weren't trying to at all promote Louis Vuitton. That was not our objective. We wanted to sell Hyundais through this over-arching communication about that you can get luxury at an affordable price, that was what we were trying to do.

Q. You weren't commenting on Louis Vuitton in any way, were you?

[Defense counsel]: Object to the form of the question.

A. Can you be more specific with your question?

Q. I'm just asking you were you attempting through the commercial to comment on Louis Vuitton?

A. No.

Q. I'm sorry?

A. No.

Q. Were you in some ways trying to criticize Louis Vuitton?

A. No.

Q. Were you in some ways trying to make fun of Louis Vuitton?

A. No.

Q. Were you in any way trying to compare the Hyundai with Louis Vuitton?

A. No.

Q. And it's your position that this wasn't about Louis Vuitton at all, this basketball, is that correct?

A. Correct.

[20] In opposition to Louis Vuitton's motion, Hyundai does not direct the Court to evidence that contradicts this testimony. It does not, for example, cite to testimony or other evidence in which other persons involved in the process explained an intention to parody or comment upon Louis Vuitton. Indeed, in its memorandum of law, Hyundai does not even address this evidence. Its opposition instead turns on discussion of legal authorities that do not apply the TDRA, with little engagement of the record cited by Louis Vuitton and minimal discussion of the statutory text.

[21] Moreover, Hyundai's counsel states that the "Luxury" ad makes no comment on Louis Vuitton: "The symbols of 'old' luxury, including the [Louis Vuitton] Marks, were used as part of the Commercial's humorous social commentary on the need to redefine luxury during a recession, *even though the Commercial's overall intent was not to comment directly on [Louis Vuitton] or the other luxury symbols.*" (Def. Supplemental 56.1 ¶ 17; emphasis added.) It also states that "[a]lthough the Commercial was *not intended as a direct attack on any of the luxury products shown,* [Hyundai] used these items as part of a humorous social commentary on the current definition of luxury itself, which was a contrast to the 'luxury for all' offered by the Sonata." (Def. Supplemental 56 .1 ¶ 2; emphasis added.)

[22] In its opposition brief, Hyundai's counsel also states:

> Surely the Commercial could have been made by evoking a different designer's marks on the basketball (*e.g.,* Gucci, Fendi, etc.). Yet, *some* symbol of luxury had to be chosen to make the basketball an integral part of the basketball vignette; for commentary purposes, HMA chose LVM, the number one luxury brand in 2010.

Yet Hyundai does not suggest that Louis Vuitton or these other marks were the object of parody, comment or criticism, but instead that these brands were proxies for its broader observation about an "old" luxury that stands in contrast with the Sonata line. They were not comment, criticism or parody "upon the famous mark owner or the goods or services of the famous mark owner." 15 U.S.C. § 1125(c)(3)(A)(ii).

[23] Louis Vuitton has come forward with evidence that the "Luxury" ad is not a comment, criticism or parody of Louis Vuitton. Hyundai has cited no evidence to the contrary. In addition, even Hyundai's counsel states that "the Commercial's overall intent was not to comment directly on [Louis Vuitton] or the other luxury symbols," but rather, to make a generalized statement that contrasts the Sonata with "old" luxury.

[24] Based on this record, I conclude that no reasonable trier of fact could conclude that the Louis Vuitton-style marks shown in the "Luxury" ad could constitute "use in connection with ... identifying and parodying, criticizing, or commenting upon the famous mark owner or the goods or services of the famous mark owner." 15 U.S.C. § 1125(c)(3)(A)(ii).

From the appendix to *My Other Bag*

Louis Vuitton Malletier v. My Other Bag, Inc.
156 F.Supp.3d 425 (SDNY 2016), aff'd, 674 F. App'x 16 (2d Cir. 2016)

JESSE M. FURMAN, United States District Judge:

[1] Defendant My Other Bag, Inc. ("MOB") sells simple canvas tote bags with the text "My Other Bag ..." on one side and drawings meant to evoke iconic handbags by luxury designers, such as Louis Vuitton, Chanel, and Fendi, on the other. MOB's totes—indeed, its very name—are a play on the classic "my other car ..." novelty bumper stickers, which can be seen on inexpensive, beat up cars across the

country informing passersby—with tongue firmly in cheek—that the driver's "other car" is a Mercedes (or some other luxury car brand). The "my other car" bumper stickers are, of course, a joke—a riff, if you will, on wealth, luxury brands, and the social expectations of who would be driving luxury and non-luxury cars. MOB's totes are just as obviously a joke, and one does not necessarily need to be familiar with the "my other car" trope to get the joke or to get the fact that the totes are meant to be taken in jest.

[2] Louis Vuitton Malletier, S.A. ("Louis Vuitton"), the maker of Louis Vuitton bags, is perhaps unfamiliar with the "my other car" trope. Or maybe it just cannot take a joke. In either case, it brings claims against MOB with respect to MOB totes that are concededly meant to evoke iconic Louis Vuitton bags. More specifically, Louis Vuitton brings claims against MOB for trademark dilution and infringement under the Lanham Act, 15 U.S.C. § 1125(c); a claim of trademark dilution under New York law; and a claim of copyright infringement. MOB now moves for summary judgment on all of Louis Vuitton's claims; Louis Vuitton cross moves for summary judgment on its trademark dilution claims and its copyright infringement claim, and moves also to exclude the testimony of MOB's expert and to strike the declarations (or portions thereof) of MOB's expert and MOB's founder and principal. For the reasons that follow, MOB's motion for summary judgment is granted and Louis Vuitton's motions are all denied.

BACKGROUND

[3] The relevant facts, taken from the Complaint and admissible materials submitted in connection with the pending motions, are either undisputed or described in the light most favorable to Louis Vuitton.... Louis Vuitton is a world-renowned luxury fashion house known for its high-quality handbags and other luxury goods. Louis Vuitton bags often sell for thousands of dollars, and the company invests substantial sums in creating and maintaining a sense of exclusivity and luxury. As a result, several of Louis Vuitton's designs and trademarks are famous and well-recognized icons of wealth and expensive taste. In particular, Louis Vuitton's Toile Monogram design—"a repeating pattern featuring the interlocking, stylized letters 'L' and 'V' and three stylized flower designs", depictions of which appear in an appendix to this Opinion—has become "the defining signature of the Louis Vuitton brand," (Louis Vuitton SOF ¶ 4). Louis Vuitton has registered trademarks in the Toile Monogram and in the component stylized flower designs. Two other iconic Louis Vuitton designs, the Monogram Multicolore and the Damier, have achieved comparable levels of recognition and are also registered as trademarks. By all accounts, and as the discussion below will make clear, Louis Vuitton aggressively enforces its trademark rights.

[4] MOB was founded by Tara Martin in 2011. As noted, the name "My Other Bag" was inspired by novelty bumper stickers, which can sometimes be seen on inexpensive cars claiming that the driver's "other car" is an expensive, luxury car, such as a Mercedes. MOB produces and sells canvas tote bags bearing caricatures of iconic designer handbags on one side and the text "My Other Bag . . ." on the other. Several of MOB's tote bags—one of which is depicted in the appendix to this Opinion—display images concededly designed to evoke classic Louis Vuitton bags. As the appendix illustrates, the drawings use simplified colors, graphic lines, and patterns that resemble Louis Vuitton's famous Toile Monogram, Monogram Multicolore, and Damier designs, but replace the interlocking "LV" and "Louis Vuitton" with an interlocking "MOB" or "My Other Bag." MOB markets its bags as "[e]co-friendly, sustainable tote bags playfully parodying the designer bags we love, but practical enough for everyday life." While Louis Vuitton sells its handbags for hundreds, if not thousands, of dollars apiece, MOB's totes sell at prices between thirty and fifty-five dollars. Its website and other marketing play up the idea that high-priced designer bags cannot be used to carry around, say, dirty gym clothes or messy groceries, while its casual canvas totes can....

....

DISCUSSION

. . . .

A. Trademark Dilution

. . . .

1. Fair Use

[5] {T}he Court concludes as a matter of law that MOB's bags are protected as fair use—in particular, that its use of Louis Vuitton's marks constitutes "parody." As noted, a successful parody communicates to a consumer that "an entity separate and distinct from the trademark owner is poking fun at a trademark or the policies of its owner." 6 J. Thomas McCarthy, McCarthy on Trademarks and Unfair Competition § 31:153 (4th ed., updated Dec. 2015) ("McCarthy"). In other words, a parody clearly indicates to the ordinary observer "that the defendant is not connected in any way with the owner of the target trademark." *Id.* That is precisely what MOB's bags communicate. Indeed, the whole point is to play on the well-known "my other car ..." joke by playfully suggesting that the carrier's "*other* bag"—that is, *not* the bag that he or she is carrying—is a Louis Vuitton bag. That joke— combined with the stylized, almost cartoonish renderings of Louis Vuitton's bags depicted on the totes—builds significant distance between MOB's inexpensive workhorse totes and the expensive handbags they are meant to evoke, and invites an amusing comparison between MOB and the luxury status of Louis Vuitton. Further, the image of exclusivity and refinery that Louis Vuitton has so carefully cultivated is, at least in part, the brunt of the joke: Whereas a Louis Vuitton handbag is something wealthy women may handle with reverent care and display to communicate a certain status, MOB's canvas totes are utilitarian bags "intended to be stuffed with produce at the supermarket, sweaty clothes at the gym, or towels at the beach." (Mem. Law Def. My Other Bag, Inc. Supp. Mot. Summ. J ("MOB's Mem.") 24).

[6] Louis Vuitton protests that, even if MOB's totes are a parody of *something*, they are not a parody of its handbags and, relatedly, that MOB's argument is a *post hoc* fabrication for purposes of this litigation. The company notes that MOB's Chief Executive Officer, Tara Martin, has referred to its bags as "iconic" and stated that she never intended to disparage Louis Vuitton. (*see* Calhoun Decl., Ex. 25, MOB website describing its bags as "an ode to handbags women love"). Thus, Louis Vuitton argues, the "My Other Bag ..." joke mocks only MOB itself or, to the extent it has a broader target, "any humor is merely part of a larger social commentary, not a parody directed towards Louis Vuitton or its products." (Louis Vuitton's Mem. at 19). In support of those arguments, Louis Vuitton relies heavily on its victory in an unpublished 2012 opinion from this District: *Louis Vuitton Malletier, S.A. v. Hyundai Motor Am.*, No. 10–CV–1611 (PKC), 2012 WL 1022247 (S.D.N.Y. Mar. 22, 2012). In that case, {t}he Court rejected Hyundai's parody defense based in large part on deposition testimony from Hyundai representatives that conclusively established that the car company had no intention for the commercial to make any statement about Louis Vuitton *at all*. *See id.* at *17–19 (excerpting deposition testimony establishing that Hyundai did not mean to "criticize" or "make fun of" Louis Vuitton, or even "compare the Hyundai with [Louis Vuitton]"). On the basis of that testimony, the Court concluded that Hyundai had "disclaimed any intention to parody, criticize or comment upon Louis Vuitton" and that the ad was only intended to make a "broader social comment" about "what it means for a product to be luxurious." *Id.* at *17 (internal quotation marks omitted).

[7] The *Hyundai* decision is not without its critics, *see, e.g.*, 4 McCarthy § 24:120, but, in any event, this case is easily distinguished on its facts. Here, unlike in *Hyundai*, it is self-evident that MOB did mean to say something about Louis Vuitton specifically. That is, Louis Vuitton's handbags are an integral part of the joke that gives MOB its name and features prominently on every tote bag that MOB sells. In arguing otherwise, Louis Vuitton takes too narrow a view of what can qualify as a parody. The quip "My Other Bag ... is a Louis Vuitton," printed on a workhorse canvas bag, derives its humor from a constellation of features—including the features of the canvas bag itself, society's larger obsession

617

with status symbols, *and* the meticulously promoted image of expensive taste (or showy status) that Louis Vuitton handbags have, to many, come to symbolize. The fact that MOB's totes convey a message about more than *just* Louis Vuitton bags is not fatal to a successful parody defense. *See Campbell v. Acuff–Rose Music, Inc.*, 510 U.S. 569, 580 (1994) (holding that a copyright parodist must show that his parody, "*at least in part*, comments on [the parodied] author's work" (emphasis added)); *Harley–Davidson, Inc. v. Grottanelli*, 164 F.3d 806, 813 (2d Cir.1999) (applying that standard to trademark parody). And the fact that Louis Vuitton at least does not find the comparison funny is immaterial; Louis Vuitton's sense of humor (or lack thereof) does not delineate the parameters of its rights (or MOB's rights) under trademark law. *See, e.g., Cliffs Notes*, 886 F.2d at 495–96 ("[T]he district court apparently thought that the parody here had to make an obvious joke out of the cover of the original in order to be regarded as a parody. We do not see why this is so. It is true that some of the covers of the parodies brought to our attention, unlike that of [the defendant], contain obvious visual gags. But parody may be sophisticated as well as slapstick; a literary work is a parody if, taken as a whole, it pokes fun at its subject." (footnote omitted)); *cf. Yankee Publ'g Inc. v. News Am. Publ'g Inc.*, 809 F.Supp. 267, 280 (S.D.N.Y.1992) ("Although [the defendant's] position would probably be stronger if its joke had been clearer, the obscurity of its joke does not deprive it of First Amendment support. First Amendment protections do not apply only to those who speak clearly, whose jokes are funny, and whose parodies succeed.").[4]

[8] In those regards, another decision from this District, *Tommy Hilfiger Licensing, Inc. v. Nature Labs, LLC*, 221 F.Supp.2d 410, 415 (S.D.N.Y.2002), is more on point. That case involved a line of parody perfume products for use on pets. In particular, the defendant had created a pet perfume called Tommy Holedigger, which resembled a Tommy Hilfiger fragrance in name, scent, and packaging. *See id.* at 412–413. Hilfiger, like Louis Vuitton here, argued (albeit in connection with a claim of trademark infringement rather than dilution) that the defendant was not entitled to protection as a parody because "its product admittedly makes no comment about Hilfiger." *Id.* at 415. In support of that argument, Hilfiger cited testimony from the defendant's general partner that his product was not intended to make any comment about Hilfiger or its products. *See id.* Noting that the general partner had also testified that "he was intending to create a 'parody ... target[ing] ... Tommy Hilfiger,' 'a fun play on words,' or 'spoof ... [t]o create enjoyment, a lighter side,' " Judge Mukasey rejected Hilfiger's argument as follows:

> Although [the general partner] had difficulty expressing the parodic content of his communicative message, courts have explained that:
>
> Trademark parodies ... do convey a message. The message may be simply that business and product images need not always be taken too seriously; a trademark parody reminds us that we are free to laugh at the images and associations linked with the mark. The message also may be a simple form of entertainment conveyed by juxtaposing the irreverent representation of the trademark with the idealized image created by the mark's owner.

---

[4] Even if *Hyundai* were not distinguishable, this Court would decline to follow it. In the Court's view, the *Hyundai* Court blurred the distinction between association and dilution. As discussed in more detail below, association is a necessary, but not sufficient, condition for a finding of dilution by blurring. *See, e.g., Moseley v. V Secret Catalogue, Inc.*, 537 U.S. 418, 433, 123 S.Ct. 1115, 155 L.Ed.2d 1 (2003) ("[T]he mere fact that consumers mentally associate the junior user's mark with a famous mark is not sufficient to establish actionable dilution. ... [S]uch mental association will not necessarily reduce the capacity of the famous mark to identify the goods of its owner.").

Id. (quoting *L.L. Bean, Inc. v. Drake Publishers, Inc.*, 811 F.2d 26, 34 (1st Cir.1987)). He added, in a comment that applies equally well here: "One can readily see why high-end fashion brands would be ripe targets for such mockery." *Id.*

[9] Alternatively, relying principally on *Dallas Cowboys Cheerleaders, Inc. v. Pussycat Cinema, Ltd.*, 604 F.2d 200 (2d Cir.1979), Louis Vuitton argues that MOB's totes cannot be a parody because they do not need to use Louis Vuitton's trademarks for the parody to make sense. Strictly speaking, that is true—to the extent that MOB could use any well-known luxury handbag brand to make its points. But, whereas the defendant in *Dallas Cowboys Cheerleaders*, a purveyor of a "gross and revolting sex film," 604 F.2d at 202, did not have to use anyone else's trademark—let alone the plaintiff's specific trademark—to make its point (allegedly, "comment[ing] on 'sexuality in athletics,' " *id.* at 206), the same cannot be said here. MOB's tote bags would not make their point, and certainly would not be funny, if the obverse of the tote merely depicted some generic handbag. Such a tote would confusingly communicate only that "my other bag . . . is some other bag." In other words, Louis Vuitton's argument distorts any "necessity" requirement beyond recognition, and myopically suggests that, where a parody must evoke at least one of a finite set of marks in order to make its point, it can evoke none of them because reference to any *particular* mark in the set is not absolutely necessary. The Court declines to create such an illogical rule.

. . . .

c. The Louis Vuitton / Penn Law School Controversy

Shown below is the poster at issue, Louis Vuitton's cease and desist letter, and Penn's response, to which LV did not reply. Given the arguments made in the two letters, which side has the better of the argument?

Penn Intellectual Property Group
Annual Symposium

Fashion Law

4:35   Panel 1
Trademark and the Fast Fashion Phenomenon

Moderator: Gideon Parchomovsky, Penn Law

Barton Beebe, NYU School of Law
Avery Fischer, G.C., Ralph Lauren
Young Kwon, G.C., Forever 21
Susan Scafidi, Fordham Law School
Suzanna White, Assoc. G.C., Coach. Inc.

5:40   Panel 2
Copyright for Fashion Design:
Evaluating the IDPPPA

Moderator: Shyamkrishna Balganesh, Penn Law

Johanna Blakley, Norman Lear Center, USC
David Faux, New York State Bar Association,
        Fashion Law Committee Chair
Barbara Kolsun, G.C., Stuart Weitzman
Michelle Marsh, Kenyon & Kenyon LLP
Staci Riordan, Fox Rothschild LLP

6:45   Keynote
"Copyright and the Fall Line"

David Nimmer
UCLA School of Law, Irell & Manella LLP

March 20, 2012

4:30 p.m. to 7:45 p.m.
Reception to follow.

Levy Conference Center
University of Pennsylvania Law School

Sponsored by

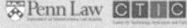

With donations from

COVINGTON

The program has been approved for 3 hours of substantive law credit
and 3 hours of ethics credit for Pennsylvania lawyers. Credit may be
available in other jurisdictions as well.

MAISON FONDÉE EN 1854

By Electronic and First Class Mail

February 29, 2012

Dean Michael A. Fitts
University of Pennsylvania Law School
3501 Sansom Street
Philadelphia, Pennsylvania 19104

     Re: <u>IP Issues in Fashion Law</u>

Dear Dean Fitts:

    I am the Director of Civil Enforcement, North America, for Louis Vuitton Malletier ("Louis Vuitton"). I write to express our concerns over the unauthorized use of our trademarks to promote the March 20, 2012 Penn Intellectual Property Group event, "IP Issues in Fashion Law."

    Louis Vuitton is the owner of world famous registered and common law trademarks, including the following trademarks as shown below (the "LV Trademarks"):

    Georges Vuitton, Louis Vuitton's son, created the "Toile Monogram" pattern, comprised of the initial LV and three distinctive design elements -- a circle with a four-leafed flower inset; a curved beige diamond with a four-point star inset; and its negative -- in the 1890's to protect the Louis Vuitton brand from unlawful imitators. Since that time, Louis Vuitton has manufactured and sold products bearing the Toile Monogram and secured numerous federal trademark registrations for the LV Trademarks, including the Toile Monogram and each of the elements of the pattern.

    Since its founding in 1854, Louis Vuitton has built up a worldwide reputation for its design, innovation, quality and style in women's and men's leather goods and fashion apparel and accessories. The LV Trademarks, including the Toile Monogram, are among the most famous trademarks in the luxury goods industry and the world. To help protect its valuable trademarks and to preserve the good will and exclusivity of Louis Vuitton designs, Louis Vuitton closely

LOUIS VUITTON NORTH AMERICA, INC.   1 EAST 57TH STREET NEW YORK, NEW YORK 10022

621

Dean Michael A. Fitts
February 29, 2012
Page 2

controls the sale of its products and the use of its trademarks, and has devoted and continues to devote substantial resources to protect the LV Trademarks.

While every day Louis Vuitton knowingly faces the stark reality of battling and interdicting the proliferation of infringements of the LV Trademarks, I was dismayed to learn that the University of Pennsylvania Law School's Penn Intellectual Property Group had misappropriated and modified the LV Trademarks and Toile Monogram as the background for its invitation and poster for the March 20, 2012 Annual Symposium on "IP Issues in Fashion Law." A copy of the invitation/poster is attached as Exhibit A.

This egregious action is not only a serious willful infringement and knowingly dilutes the LV Trademarks, but also may mislead others into thinking that this type of unlawful activity is somehow "legal" or constitutes "fair use" because the Penn Intellectual Property Group is sponsoring a seminar on fashion law and "must be experts." People seeing the invitation/poster may believe that Louis Vuitton either sponsored the seminar or was otherwise involved, and approved the misuse of its trademarks in this manner. I would have thought the Penn Intellectual Property Group, and its faculty advisors, would understand the basics of intellectual property law and know better than to infringe and dilute the famous trademarks of fashion brands, including the LV Trademarks, for a symposium on fashion law. (Louis Vuitton believes that education of the public about intellectual property issues is important and has sponsored such activities in the past. In fact, Louis Vuitton is a corporate sponsor of Fordham Law School's Fashion Law Institute).

Louis Vuitton is proud of its reputation for protecting intellectual property and creativity. We hope, and expect now that this action has been brought to your attention, that immediate steps will be taken to stop all use of this invitation/poster that violates the LV Trademarks. Please contact me within five days to assure me that steps have been taken to avoid confusion and dilution of the LV Trademarks. Your understanding and anticipated cooperation is appreciated.

Very truly yours,

Attachment

V7.0/2020-07-14

Robert F. Firestone, Esq.
Associate General Counsel
Direct Dial: 215.746.5266
Robert.firestone@ogc.upenn.edu

March 2, 2012

Via Email M.Pantalony@us.vuitton.com and First Class Mail

Michael Pantalony, Esq.
Director, Civil Enforcement, North America
Louis Vuitton Malletier
1 East 57th Street
New York, NY 10022

Dear Mr. Pantalony:

I represent the University of Pennsylvania, its Law School, and a student group at the Law School, the Pennsylvania Intellectual Property Group (PIPG), and Dean Michael Fitts forwarded your February 29, 2012 letter to me.

PIPG does not agree that the artwork on its poster and invitation infringes any of Louis Vuitton's trademarks, nor does it dilute any of those trademarks. In fact, 15 U.S.C. 1125(c)(3) expressly protects a noncommercial use of a mark and a parody from any claim for dilution. There also is no violation of 15 U.S.C. 1125(a) because there is no likelihood of confusion that Louis Vuitton sponsored or is associated with PIPG's annual educational symposium.

You assert that the clever artwork parody that appears on the poster and invitation is a "serious willful infringement." However, to constitute trademark infringement under the Lanham Act, PIPG has to be using a trademark in interstate commerce, which is substantially similar to Louis Vuitton's mark(s), and which is likely to cause confusion between Louis Vuitton's luxury apparel goods and PIPG's educational conference among the relevant audience. First, I don't believe that PIPG's artwork parody was adopted as, or is being used as, a trademark to identify any goods and services. It is artwork on a poster to supplement text, designed to evoke some of the very issues to be discussed at the conference, including the importance of intellectual property rights to fashion companies, the controversy over the proposed Innovative Design Protection and Piracy Prevention Act, and the exceptions in the law to liability for dilution, including parody. Second, although you don't cite the actual federal trademark registrations that you assert protect your marks, I doubt any of them are registered in Class 41 to cover educational symposia in intellectual property law issues. There is no substantial similarity between the goods identified by Louis Vuitton's marks and the PIPG educational symposium. Third, there is no likelihood of confusion possible here. The lawyers, law students, and fashion industry executives who will attend the symposium certainly are unlikely to think that Louis Vuitton is organizing the conference; the poster clearly says that PIPG has organized the event, with support from Penn Law and a number of nationally-known law firms. The artwork on the poster and invitation does not constitute trademark infringement.

Office of the General Counsel
133 South 36th Street, Suite 300   Philadelphia, PA 19104-3246
Tel 215-746-5200   Fax 215-746-5222

V7.0/2020-07-14

You also state that PIPG's use of its artwork parody knowingly dilutes the Louis Vuitton trademarks. I disagree. First, PIPG has not commenced use of the artwork as a mark or trade name, which is a prerequisite for any liability under 15 U.S.C. 1125(c)(1). More importantly, however, even if PIPG has used the artwork as a mark, there is an explicit exception to any liability for dilution by blurring or dilution by tarnishment for "any noncommercial use of a mark." 15 U.S.C. 1125(c)(3)(C). A law student group at a non-profit university promoting its annual educational symposium is a noncommercial use. Lastly, the artwork clearly is a fair use under 15 U.S.C. 1125(c)(3)(A), and a parody protected under 15 U.S.C. 1125(c)(3)(A)(ii). See also Louis Vuitton Malletier vs. Haute Diggity Dog, LLC, 507 F.3d 252 (4th Cir. 2007).

The poster and invitation are clear that Louis Vuitton is not a sponsor of the symposium, and no reasonable person would be confused or deceived as to sponsorship, affiliation, connection or association regarding Louis Vuitton and PIPG's conference, merely because of the clever artwork parody illustrating the invitation and poster. I do not think there is any liability under 15 U.S.C. 1125(a)(1), either.

Therefore, I will be advising PIPG that it may continue to use posters and invitations to its annual symposium that contain the artwork to which Louis Vuitton objects, without violating any of Louis Vuitton's legitimate trademark rights. I realize that Steven Barnes, the Associate Dean for Communications at the Law School, previously sent you an email stating that PIPG would stop using the posters and invitations. However, Mr. Barnes sent that email before seeking legal advice from our office and without sharing that legal advice with PIPG. Now that we have had the time to consider your letter and investigate the facts and the law, I will be advising the students otherwise.

If there is any need to discuss this further, please contact me directly. In addition, I encourage you to attend the symposium on March 20, 2012. Educating our students about both the rights of, and the defenses against, intellectual property owners, is a key goal of the symposium. The students have invited some of the in-house counsel from some of your peer fashion companies to speak on the panels, and I am sure the students would welcome your attendance as well. If you are able to come, please let me know, so I can introduce myself in person, and try to introduce you to some of the Penn Law faculty and students working to make their annual educational symposium about the unique and challenging intellectual property issues in the fashion industry a success.

Sincerely,

Robert F. Firestone

Cc: Dean Michael Fitts, University of Pennsylvania Law School

Office of the General Counsel
133 South 36th Street, Suite 300   Philadelphia, PA 19104-3246
Tel 215-746-5200   Fax 215-746-5222

D. Trademark Abandonment

A defendant may show that a mark has been abandoned and is thus unprotectable by showing either that (1) the plaintiff has ceased to use the mark with the intent not to resume use, or (2) the plaintiff has failed to control the use of the mark (for example, by licensing its use indiscriminately) with the result that the mark has lost its significance as a designation of a particular source. These two modes of abandonment are based on the definition of "abandoned" in Lanham Act § 45, 15 U.S.C. § 1127:

A mark shall be deemed to be "abandoned" if either of the following occurs:

(1) When its use has been discontinued with intent not to resume such use. Intent not to resume may be inferred from circumstances. Nonuse for 3 consecutive years shall be prima facie evidence of abandonment. "Use" of a mark means the bona fide use of such mark made in the ordinary course of trade, and not made merely to reserve a right in a mark.

(2) When any course of conduct of the owner, including acts of omission as well as commission, causes the mark to become the generic name for the goods or services on or in connection with which it is used or otherwise to lose its significance as a mark. Purchaser motivation shall not be a test for determining abandonment under this paragraph.

1. Abandonment Through Cessation of Use

The following excerpt is taken from *ITC Ltd. v. Punchgini, Inc.*, 482 F.3d 135 (2d Cir. 2007), parts of which we have already considered in Part I.E.3 in connection with the well-known marks doctrine. The reader will recall that, in 1986, the plaintiff ITC Ltd. opened a restaurant under the name Bukhara in New York City. In 1987, the plaintiff entered into a franchise agreement for a Bukhara restaurant in Chicago. Also in 1987, the plaintiff registered at the PTO the mark BUKHARA in connection with "restaurant services" (*See* U.S. Trademark Registration No. 1,461,445 (Oct. 13, 1987)). The New York City restaurant closed in 1991 and ITC cancelled its Chicago franchise in 1997. In 2000, the defendant Punchgini, Inc. opened the restaurant Bukhara Grill in New York City. In 2003, the plaintiff sued for trademark infringement. The district court had granted summary judgment in favor of the defendant.

In this case, the well-known marks issue related to the abandonment issue in the following respect. If ITC was found to have abandoned the BUKHARA mark in the United States, then the only good argument ITC had left was that even though it had ceased to use its mark in commerce in the United States, the mark's global reputation qualified it for protection as a "well-known mark" within the United States.

ITC Ltd. v. Punchgini, Inc.
482 F.3d 135, 145-53 (2d Cir. 2007)

Raggi, Circuit Judge:

. . . .

B. Trademark Infringement

[1] . . . Even if a plaintiff makes the showing required by federal and state [trademark] law, however, the alleged infringer may nevertheless prevail if it can establish the owner's prior abandonment of the mark. *See* 15 U.S.C. § 1115(b)(2); *Nercessian v. Homasian Carpet Enter., Inc.*, 60 N.Y.2d 875, 877, 470 N.Y.S.2d 363, 364, 458 N.E.2d 822 (1983) (holding that "rights in a trade name may be lost by abandonment"). Indeed, abandonment is not only an affirmative defense to an infringement action; it is a ground for cancelling a federally registered mark. *See* 15 U.S.C. § 1064(3).

[2] Relying on this principle, defendants submit that ITC's infringement claim is necessarily defeated as a matter of law by proof that, by the time they opened their Bukhara Grill restaurants in New York, ITC had effectively abandoned the Bukhara mark in the United States. Like the district court, we conclude that defendants successfully established abandonment as a matter of law, warranting both summary judgment in their favor and cancellation of ITC's registered mark.

1. The Doctrine of Abandonment

[3] The abandonment doctrine derives from the well-established principle that trademark rights are acquired and maintained through use of a particular mark. *See Pirone v. MacMillan, Inc.*, 894 F.2d 579, 581 (2d Cir. 1990) ("'There is no such thing as property in a trade-mark except as a right appurtenant to an established business or trade in connection with which the mark is employed.'" (quoting *United Drug Co. v. Theodore Rectanus Co.*, 248 U.S. 90, 97 (1918))). This is true even of marks that have been registered with the Patent and Trademark Office. *See Basile, S.p.A. v. Basile*, 899 F.2d 35, 37 n. 1 (D.C.Cir. 1990) ("Although [a mark's] registration is a predicate to its protection under [section 32(1)(a) of] the Lanham Act, the underlying right depends not on registration but rather on use."). Indeed, one of the fundamental premises underlying the registration provisions in the Lanham Act is that trademark rights flow from priority and that priority is acquired through use. *See, e.g.,* 15 U.S.C. § 1057(c) (stating that registration of mark "shall constitute constructive use of the mark, conferring a right of priority, nationwide in effect . . . against any other person except for a person whose mark has not been abandoned and who, prior to such filing[,] . . . has used the mark"). Thus, so long as a person is the first to use a particular mark to identify his goods or services in a given market, and so long as that owner continues to make use of the mark, he is "entitled to prevent others from using the mark to describe their own goods" in that market. *Defiance Button Mach. Co. v. C & C Metal Prods. Corp.*, 759 F.2d 1053, 1059 (2d Cir. 1985); *see also Sengoku Works v. RMC Int'l*, 96 F.3d 1217, 1219 (9th Cir. 1996) ("It is axiomatic in trademark law that the standard test of ownership is priority of use.").

[4] If, however, an owner ceases to use a mark without an intent to resume use in the reasonably foreseeable future, the mark is said to have been "abandoned." *See Silverman v. CBS, Inc.*, 870 F.2d 40, 45 (2d Cir. 1989); 2 J. Thomas McCarthy, McCarthy on Trademarks and Unfair Competition, § 17:5, at 17–8 (4th ed. 2002) (observing that "abandonment" refers to situations involving the "non-use of a mark, coupled with an express or implied intention to abandon or not to resume use"). Once abandoned, a mark returns to the public domain and may, in principle, be appropriated for use by other actors in the marketplace, *see Indianapolis Colts, Inc. v. Metro. Baltimore Football Club Ltd. P'ship,* 34 F.3d 410, 412 (7th Cir. 1994), in accordance with the basic rules of trademark priority, *see Manhattan Indus., Inc. v. Sweater Bee by Banff, Ltd.,* 627 F.2d 628, 630 (2d Cir. 1980).

2. Demonstrating Abandonment

[5] The party asserting abandonment bears the burden of persuasion with respect to two facts: (1) non-use of the mark by the legal owner, and (2) lack of intent by that owner to resume use of the mark in the reasonably foreseeable future. *See* 15 U.S.C. § 1127; *Stetson v. Howard D. Wolf & Assocs.,* 955 F.2d 847, 850 (2d Cir. 1992); *Silverman v. CBS, Inc.,* 870 F.2d at 45; *see also On–Line Careline, Inc. v. America Online, Inc.,* 229 F.3d 1080, 1087 (Fed.Cir. 2000) (placing burden of persuasion on party seeking cancellation on ground of abandonment); *Warner Bros. Inc. v. Gay Toys, Inc.,* 724 F.2d 327, 334 (2d Cir. 1983) (placing burden of persuasion on party asserting abandonment as defense).

[6] ITC concedes that defendants satisfied the first element through proof that ITC has not used the Bukhara mark for restaurant services in the United States since August 28, 1997. Nevertheless, ITC insists that a triable issue of fact exists with respect to its intent to resume use of the service mark in the United States. To the extent the district court concluded otherwise, ITC submits the court applied an incorrect legal standard. To explain why we are not persuaded by this argument, we begin by discussing the particular legal significance of non-use of a registered mark for a period of at least three years.

3. Prima Facie Evidence of Abandonment

[7] The Lanham Act expressly states that "[n]onuse" of a mark "for 3 consecutive years shall be prima facie evidence of abandonment." 15 U.S.C. § 1127. This court has explained that the term "prima facie evidence" in this context means "a rebuttable presumption of abandonment." *Saratoga Vichy Spring Co. v. Lehman,* 625 F.2d 1037, 1044 (2d Cir. 1980); *accord Silverman v. CBS, Inc.,* 870 F.2d at 45.

The role played by such a presumption is best understood by reference to Rule 301 of the Federal Rules of Evidence:

> In all civil actions and proceedings not otherwise provided for by Act of Congress or by these rules, a presumption imposes on the party against whom it is directed the burden of going forward with evidence to rebut or to meet the presumption, but does not shift to such party the burden of proof in the sense of the risk of non-persuasion, which remains throughout the trial upon the party on whom it was originally cast.

Fed.R.Evid. 301. Although the term "presumption" is not specifically defined in the Rules of Evidence, it is generally understood to mean "an assumption of fact resulting from a rule of law which requires such fact to be assumed from another fact or group of facts found or otherwise established in the action." 21B Charles Alan Wright & Kenneth W. Graham, Jr., Federal Practice and Procedure § 5124 (2d ed. 2005); *see also Texas Dep't of Cmty. Affairs v. Burdine,* 450 U.S. 248, 256 n. 10 (1981) (describing presumption as "legally mandatory inference"). The assumption ceases to operate, however, upon the proffer of contrary evidence. *See generally A.C. Aukerman Co. v. R.L. Chaides Constr. Co.,* 960 F.2d 1020, 1037 (Fed.Cir. 1992) (observing that under Rule 301, a "presumption is not merely rebuttable but completely vanishes upon the introduction of evidence sufficient to support a finding of the nonexistence of the presumed fact"); *Saratoga Vichy Spring Co. v. Lehman,* 625 F.2d at 1043 (suggesting that presumption of abandonment "disappears when rebutted by contrary evidence").

[8] Thus, in this case, the statutory presumption of abandonment requires that one fact, i.e., abandonment, be inferred from another fact, i.e., non-use of the mark for three years or more. The significance of a presumption of abandonment is to shift the burden of production to the mark owner to come forward with evidence indicating that, despite three years of non-use, it intended to resume use of the mark within a reasonably foreseeable time. *See Imperial Tobacco, Ltd. v. Philip Morris, Inc.,* 899 F.2d 1575, 1579 (Fed.Cir. 1990) (noting that triggering of presumption "eliminates the challenger's burden to establish the [lack of] intent [to resume use] element of abandonment as an initial part of its case"); *see also Cumulus Media, Inc. v. Clear Channel Commc'ns,* 304 F.3d 1167, 1176–77 (11th Cir. 2002); *On–Line Careline, Inc. v. America Online, Inc.,* 229 F.3d at 1087. The ultimate burden of persuasion on the issue of abandonment, however, remains at all times with the alleged infringer. *See Emergency One, Inc. v. American FireEagle, Ltd.,* 228 F.3d 531, 536 (4th Cir. 2000).

4. The Evidence Necessary to Defeat a Presumption of Abandonment

[9] This court has observed that "to overcome a presumption of abandonment after a sufficiently long period of non-use, a defendant need show only an intention to resume use 'within the reasonably foreseeable future.'" *Empresa Cubana del Tabaco v. Culbro Corp.,* 399 F.3d 462, 468 n. 2 (2d Cir. 2005) (quoting *Silverman v. CBS, Inc.,* 870 F.2d at 45). ITC submits that the district court erred in imposing a stricter standard, specifically requiring ITC to adduce "'objective, hard evidence of actual concrete plans to resume use in the reasonably foreseeable future when the conditions requiring suspension abate'" to defeat defendants' summary judgment motion. *ITC Ltd. v. Punchgini, Inc.,* 373 F.Supp.2d at 280 (quoting *Emmpresa Cubana Del Tabaco v. Culbro Corp.,* 213 F.Supp.2d 247, 268–69 (S.D.N.Y.2002)).

[10] This court has, in fact, criticized the particular language quoted by the district court, observing that such a "heavy burden" is not required by our precedent. *See Empresa Cubana del Tabaco v. Culbro Corp.,* 399 F.3d at 467 n. 2. Courts and commentators are in general agreement that proffered evidence is "sufficient" to rebut a presumption as long as the evidence could support a reasonable jury

finding of "the nonexistence of the presumed fact." *Wanlass v. Fedders Corp.,* 145 F.3d 1461, 1464 (Fed.Cir. 1998) . . . . In short, upon defendants' presentation of evidence establishing a *prima facie* case of abandonment under the Lanham Act, ITC was required to come forward only with such contrary evidence as, when viewed in the light most favorable to ITC, would permit a reasonable jury to infer that it had not abandoned the mark. Specifically, it needed to adduce sufficient evidence to permit a reasonable jury to conclude that, in the three-year period of non-use—from August 28, 1997, when ITC terminated the Chicago Bukhara franchise, to August 28, 2000—ITC nevertheless maintained an intent to resume use of its registered mark in the reasonably foreseeable future.[9] *See Silverman v. CBS, Inc.,* 870 F.2d at 47; *accord Empresa Cubana del Tabaco v. Culbro Corp.,* 399 F.3d at 467 n. 2. Hard evidence of concrete plans to resume use of the mark would certainly carry this burden. But we do not foreclose the possibility that other circumstances, viewed in the light most favorable to the non-movant, might also support the necessary jury inference of intent. *See, e.g., Geneva Pharms. Tech. Corp. v. Barr Labs., Inc.,* 386 F.3d 485, 506 (2d Cir. 2004) (looking to totality of circumstances to infer intent).

5. Defendants' Entitlement to Summary Judgment

. . . .

b. ITC's Failure to Adduce Evidence from Which a Reasonable Jury Could Infer Intent to Resume Use

[11] As this court has recognized, "intent is always a subjective matter of inference and thus rarely amenable to summary judgment." *Saratoga Vichy Spring Co. v. Lehman,* 625 F.2d at 1044. At the same time, however, "'[t]he summary judgment rule would be rendered sterile . . . if the mere incantation of intent or state of mind would operate as a talisman to defeat an otherwise valid motion.'" *Distasio v. Perkin Elmer Corp.,* 157 F.3d 55, 61–62 (2d Cir. 1998) (quoting *Meiri v. Dacon,* 759 F.2d 989, 997 (2d Cir. 1985)). The latter point is particularly relevant in the context of an abandonment dispute, because "[i]n every contested abandonment case, the respondent denies an intention to abandon its mark; otherwise there would be no contest." *Imperial Tobacco, Ltd. v. Philip Morris, Inc.,* 899 F.2d at 1581. Thus, courts have generally held that a trademark owner cannot rebut a presumption of abandonment merely by asserting a subjective intent to resume use of the mark at some later date. . . . *Emergency One, Inc. v. American FireEagle, Ltd.,* 228 F.3d at 537 ("[T]he owner of a trademark cannot defeat an abandonment claim . . . by simply asserting a vague, subjective intent to resume use of a mark at some unspecified future date.") . . . ; *see also Silverman v. CBS, Inc.,* 870 F.2d at 47 ("A bare assertion of possible future use is not enough."). Rather, to rebut a presumption of abandonment on a motion for summary judgment, the mark owner must come forward with evidence "with respect to . . . what outside events occurred from which an intent to resume use during the nonuse period may reasonably be inferred." *Imperial Tobacco, Ltd. v. Philip Morris, Inc.,* 899 F.2d at 1581; *accord Emergency One, Inc. v. American FireEagle, Ltd.,* 228 F.3d at 537–38; *see also Silverman v. CBS, Inc.,* 870 F.2d at 47 (noting that presumption of abandonment can be rebutted "by showing

---

[9] Although we have not previously stated specifically that a mark holder's intent to resume use of the mark must be formulated during the three-year period of non-use, we do so now, noting that two other circuit courts have also reached this conclusion. *See, e.g., Imperial Tobacco, Ltd. v. Philip Morris, Inc.,* 899 F.2d at 1580–81 [Fed. Cir.] (expressly recognizing that intent must be formulated during non-use period); *Emergency One, Inc. v. American FireEagle, Ltd.,* 228 F.3d at 537 [4th Cir.] (same). Indeed, we think this conclusion follows naturally from the fact that an abandoned mark may be appropriated for use by other actors in the marketplace. An intent to resume use of the mark formulated after more than three years of non-use cannot be invoked to dislodge the rights of another party who has commenced use of a mark—thereby acquiring priority rights in that mark—after three years of non-use. We do not, however, foreclose the use of evidence arising after the relevant three-year period to demonstrate an intent *within* that period to resume use.

reasonable grounds for the suspension and plans to resume use in the reasonably foreseeable future when the conditions requiring suspension abate"[10]).

[12] ITC argues that four facts would allow a reasonable factfinder to infer its intent to resume use of the Bukhara mark for restaurants in the United States: (1) the reasonable grounds for its suspension of use of the mark, (2) its efforts to develop and market a Dal Bukhara line of packaged food, (3) its attempts to identify potential United States restaurant franchisees, and (4) its continued use of the Bukhara mark for restaurants outside the United States. We are not persuaded.

(1) Grounds for Suspending Use

[13] ITC advances two reasons for suspending use of the Bukhara mark in the United States from 1997 to 2000: (a) Indian regulations requiring it to return profits earned abroad severely hindered its ability to open and operate profitable Bukhara restaurants in the United States, and (b) depressed market conditions in the hospitality industry from 1988 to 2003 inhibited its development of franchise partnerships in the United States. Because these reasons are unsupported by record evidence, they plainly cannot demonstrate the requisite intent.[11]

[14] As to the first point, the record indicates that many of the Indian regulations cited by ITC had been in effect since 1973. Clearly, these regulations did not prevent ITC from opening its Bukhara restaurant in New York in 1986 or from licensing a Bukhara restaurant in Chicago in 1987. Although ITC submits that the regulations were a significant factor in the failure of these two restaurants, no evidence was adduced to support this conclusory assertion. *See generally Bridgeway Corp. v. Citibank*, 201 F.3d 134, 142 (2d Cir. 2000) (holding that conclusory statements, conjecture, and inadmissible evidence are insufficient to defeat summary judgment). Indeed, the record is to the contrary. When, at deposition, an ITC corporate representative was asked why the New York Bukhara closed, he replied simply that the restaurant was highly leveraged and unable to meet its debt obligations. He made no mention of any Indian regulations. Similarly, the letter by which ITC terminated its Chicago license agreement referenced only the franchisee's failure to pay fees owed to ITC, making no mention of Indian regulations.

[15] Further, ITC fails to explain how Indian regulations, which ITC claims applied to any business operated outside India, hindered its use of the Bukhara mark for restaurants in the United States between 1997 and 2000 but permitted it to open a Bukhara restaurant in the United Arab Emirates in 1998. To the extent ITC argues that the regulations limited its options by effectively requiring it to partner exclusively with well-established hotels, it offers no evidence that hotels in the United States were unreceptive to such a partnership arrangement.

[16] With respect to ITC's argument that a market decline in the hospitality industry between 1988 and 2003 explains its non-use of the mark, the record indicates only a decline in India and the

---

[10] The two factors identified in *Silverman* are not distinct but intertwined. A mark owner's reason for suspending use of a mark is relevant to abandonment analysis only as circumstantial evidence shedding possible light on his intent to resume future use within a reasonable period of time. In short, not every "reasonable suspension" will necessarily rebut a presumption of abandonment. *See Silverman v. CBS, Inc.*, 870 F.2d at 47 (observing that "however laudable one might think CBS's motives to be, such motives cannot overcome the undisputed fact that CBS has not used its mark for more than 20 years and that, even now, it has no plans to resume [its] use in the reasonably foreseeable future," and further noting that "we see nothing in the statute that makes the consequence of an intent not to resume use turn on the worthiness of the motive for holding such intent").

[11] We do not decide whether such allegations, if supported by evidence, would permit any inference of ITC's intent to resume use of the Bukhara mark for restaurants in the foreseeable future. We note only that the conclusion is by no means obvious.

overseas market. ITC proffered no evidence demonstrating a decline in the United States hospitality market during the relevant 1997–2000 period of non-use.[12]

(2) Marketing Dal Bukhara Food Products

[17] ITC points to only one piece of evidence during the relevant 1997–2000 period indicating its intent to use the name Bukhara in connection with packaged foods: the minutes from a July 27, 2000 corporate management committee meeting in India, which approved an initiative to market food products under the name "Bukhara Dal." Significantly, the minutes nowhere indicate ITC's intent to market this product in the United States, much less ITC's intent to resume use of the Bukhara mark for restaurants in this country. Accordingly, we conclude that the minutes, by themselves, are insufficient to create a genuine issue of material fact as to ITC's intent to resume use of its registered service mark in the United States.

[18] The remaining evidence adduced by ITC all post-dates the relevant 1997–2000 period of non-use. Specifically, in 2001, ITC commissioned a study regarding the marketing of packaged food bearing the Bukhara mark in the United States. That same year, ITC filed trademark applications for several marks containing the word "Bukhara" in relation to packaged food products. Not until 2003 did ITC actually showcase its packaged food line at a New York trade show or sell these products to two United States distributors. These acts, all occurring well after 2000 and suggesting future use of the Bukhara mark for a product other than restaurants, are insufficient to support the necessary inference that, *in the non-use period*, ITC maintained an intent to resume use of the mark for restaurants in the United States in the reasonably foreseeable future.

(3) Identifying Bukhara Franchisees

[19] ITC argues that evidence of its discussions with various persons about expanding the Bukhara restaurant franchise to New York, California, and Texas creates a jury issue as to its intent to resume use of its registered mark within a reasonably foreseeable time. In fact, the only evidence of these so-called "discussions" is a few facsimiles, e-mails, and letters sent to ITC over a five-year period from 1998 to 2002. There is no evidence that ITC initiated any of these contacts. More to the point, no evidence indicates that ITC responded to or seriously considered these unsolicited proposals in a manner that would permit a reasonable jury to infer its intent to resume use of its Bukhara mark for restaurants. As such, these communications, even when viewed in the light most favorable to ITC, do not give rise to a material question of fact on the issue of ITC's intent to resume use of its registered mark.

[20] ITC submits that record evidence also reveals its negotiations to expand the Bukhara restaurant brand into Starwood hotels. The proffered evidence consists of (1) a 2002 letter from Starwood's Asia–Pacific headquarters indicating a general interest in operating Bukhara restaurants in some of its hotels outside India, and (2) a 2004 story from an Indian newspaper about ITC's intent to open Bukhara restaurants in London and Tokyo. Neither document references the possible opening of a Bukhara restaurant in the United States. Moreover, both the letter and the news story post-date the 1997–2000 period of non-use that gives rise to the presumption of abandonment, and they make no mention of any intent to resume use arising during this critical time frame. Accordingly, this evidence is insufficient to raise a material issue of fact.

---

[12] Indeed, there is no reason to think plaintiffs could make such a showing with respect to the New York hospitality market, which experienced considerable growth during the period 1997–2000. *See* John Holusha, "Commercial Property; An Up Cycle Just Keeps Rolling," *The New York Times* 11:1 (Sept. 24, 2000) (noting historically high occupancy rates in city hotels with 13% growth in first half of year); cf. Marian Burros, "Waiter, Hold the Foie Gras: Slump Hits New York Dining," *The New York Times* A:1 (Sept. 4, 2001) (noting, in 2001, first signs of decline in city's 10–year restaurant boom).

(4) Bukhara Restaurants Outside the United States

[21] Finally, ITC cites *La Societe Anonyme des Parfums le Galion v. Jean Patou, Inc.* to support its argument that the continued operation of its Bukhara restaurants outside the United States demonstrates "an ongoing program to exploit the mark commercially," giving rise to an inference of an intent to resume the mark's use in this country, 495 F.2d 1265, 1272 (2d Cir. 1974). In fact, ITC's reliance on *Societe Anonyme* is misplaced. In that case, this court ruled that a "meager trickle" of perfume sales within the United States—89 bottles sold over a period of 20 years—was insufficient to establish trademark rights in the United States. *Id.* Nothing in that case suggests that ongoing foreign use of a mark, by itself, supports an inference that the owner intends to re-employ a presumptively abandoned mark in the United States. Cf. *id.* at 1271 n. 4 (noting "well-settled" view "that foreign use is ineffectual to create trademark rights in the United States"). Indeed, we identify no authority supporting that conclusion.

[22] Accordingly, like the district court, we conclude that ITC's continued foreign use of the Bukhara mark for restaurants does not raise a material issue of fact regarding its intent to resume similar use of the mark in the United States. Because ITC plainly abandoned its right to the Bukhara mark for restaurant services in the United States, we affirm the award of summary judgment in favor of defendants on ITC's federal and state infringement claims.

Crash Dummy Movie, LLC v. Mattel, Inc.
601 F.3d 1387 (Fed. Cir. 2010)

RADER, Circuit Judge.

[1] The Trademark Trial and Appeal Board ("Board") sustained Mattel, Inc.'s ("Mattel") challenge to The Crash Dummy Movie, LLC's ("CDM") application to register the mark CRASH DUMMIES for a line

631

of games and playthings. The record leaves no doubt that CDM's proposed mark is likely to cause confusion with Mattel's previously used marks CRASH DUMMIES and THE INCREDIBLE CRASH DUMMIES (collectively, "CRASH DUMMIES marks") for action figures and playsets. CDM asserts, however, that these marks were abandoned. Because substantial evidence supports the Board's finding that Mattel overcame the statutory presumption of abandonment of its CRASH DUMMIES marks, this court affirms.

I.

[2] Mattel's predecessor-in-interest, Tyco Industries, Inc. ("Tyco"), first produced a line of toys under the CRASH DUMMIES marks in 1991. In 1993, Tyco obtained federal trademark registrations for the CRASH DUMMIES marks: CRASH DUMMIES (Registration No. 1809338) and THE INCREDIBLE CRASH DUMMIES (Registration No. 1773754). Tyco sold toys under the CRASH DUMMIES marks through at least 1994. In addition, Tyco entered into forty-nine licenses for use of the CRASH DUMMIES marks in connection with a variety of products. The licenses expired on December 31, 1995, with some licenses having a product sell-off period of four to six months following their expiration.

[3] On July 14, 1995, CDM entered into an option agreement with Tyco to produce a motion picture based on Tyco's line of toys sold under the CRASH DUMMIES marks. The option agreement expired on July 14, 1996. Although CDM attempted to renegotiate a license later that year, Tyco declined to enter into another option agreement with CDM.

[4] In the mid-1990's, Tyco experienced financial difficulties and began negotiating an acquisition with Mattel. On February 12, 1997, Tyco assigned its trademark portfolio, including the CRASH DUMMIES marks, to Mattel. Mattel officially purchased Tyco on December 31, 1997. Mattel later recorded Tyco's assignment with the United States Patent Trademark Office ("USPTO") on February 13, 1998. Due to the size of the acquisition, the two businesses did not fully integrate until late 2004 or early 2005.

[5] In 1998, KB Toys approached Mattel, hoping to become the exclusive retailer of toys sold under the CRASH DUMMIES marks. Mattel declined the offer. Mattel needed to retool Tyco's CRASH DUMMIES toys in order to meet Mattel's stringent safety standards. Mattel determined that the cost of retooling was too significant in light of KB Toys's sales projections at the time.

[6] From 2000 to 2003, Mattel worked on developing a new line of toys under the CRASH DUMMIES marks. In 2000, Mattel began brainstorming ideas for CRASH DUMMIES toys. Mattel researched, developed, and tested its new toys as early as 2001, and obtained concept approval by 2002. Mattel began manufacturing CRASH DUMMIES toys in October 2003, and ultimately reintroduced them into the market in December 2003. While Mattel was developing new toys, the USPTO cancelled the registrations for the CRASH DUMMIES marks on December 29, 2000, because Mattel did not file a section 8 declaration of use and/or excusable nonuse for the marks.

[7] On March 31, 2003, CDM filed an intent-to-use application for the mark CRASH DUMMIES for games and playthings. Mattel opposed CDM's application, claiming priority to Tyco's prior registration and use of the CRASH DUMMIES marks. Mattel and CDM agree that their respective marks are likely to cause confusion. The only disputed issue before the Board was whether Mattel was entitled to claim common law trademark rights to the CRASH DUMMIES marks predating CDM's March 2003 filing date. The Board found a prima facie abandonment of the CRASH DUMMIES marks based on three years of nonuse, beginning at the earliest on December 31, 1995, and ending at Mattel's actual shipment of CRASH DUMMIES toys in December 2003. However, the Board concluded that Mattel rebutted the presumption of abandonment of its common law trademark rights by showing "reasonable grounds for the suspension and plans to resume use in the reasonably foreseeable future when the conditions requiring suspension abate." CDM appeals the Board's decision sustaining Mattel's opposition. This court has jurisdiction under 28 U.S.C. § 1295(a)(4)(B).

II.

632

[8] Abandonment of a trademark is a question of fact, which this court reviews for substantial evidence. *On-Line Careline, Inc. v. Am. Online, Inc.*, 229 F.3d 1080, 1087 (Fed.Cir. 2000). The substantial evidence standard requires this court to ask whether a reasonable person might find that the evidentiary record supports the agency's conclusion. *Id.* at 1085. "[T]he possibility of drawing two inconsistent conclusions from the evidence does not prevent an administrative agency's finding from being supported by substantial evidence." *Consolo v. Fed. Maritime Comm'n*, 383 U.S. 607, 620 (1966).

[9] In addition, this court reviews evidentiary rulings for an abuse of discretion. *Chen v. Bouchard*, 347 F.3d 1299, 1307 (Fed.Cir. 2003) (citation omitted). This court reverses the Board's evidentiary rulings only if they: (1) were clearly unreasonable, arbitrary, or fanciful; (2) were based on an erroneous conclusions of law; (3) rest on clearly erroneous findings of fact; or (4) follow from a record that contains no evidence on which the Board could rationally base its decision. *Id.* (citation omitted).

III.

[10] A registered trademark is considered abandoned if its "use has been discontinued with intent not to resume such use." 15 U.S.C. § 1127 (2006). "Nonuse for 3 consecutive years shall be prima facie evidence of abandonment." *Id.* A showing of a prima facie case creates a rebuttable presumption that the trademark owner has abandoned the mark without intent to resume use. *On-Line Careline*, 229 F.3d at 1087. "The burden then shifts to the trademark owner to produce evidence that he either used the mark during the statutory period or intended to resume use." *Id.* "The burden of persuasion, however, always remains with the [challenger] to prove abandonment by a preponderance of the evidence." *Id.*

[11] As an initial matter, CDM does not challenge the Board's finding that Tyco did not abandon the CRASH DUMMIES marks before the 1997 assignment. CDM only challenges the Board's factual finding regarding Mattel's intent to resume use after it acquired the marks in February 1997 until it began selling CRASH DUMMIES toys in December 2003.

[12] Substantial evidence supports the Board's finding that Mattel intended to resume use of the CRASH DUMMIES marks during the contested time period. First, in 1998, Mattel entered into discussions with KB Toys about becoming the exclusive retailer of CRASH DUMMIES toys. Mattel considered the relative merits of exclusive sales through KB Toys and the high cost of retooling Tyco's product line to meet Mattel's stringent safety standards. Mattel's analysis shows that it contemplated manufacturing toys under the CRASH DUMMIES marks at the time the discussion took place. Although Mattel did not ultimately enter into the KB Toys agreement, no evidence suggests that Mattel rejected the business opportunity because it decided to abandon the marks.

[13] Second, common sense supports the conclusion that Mattel would not have recorded Tyco's trademark assignment with the USPTO in 1998 unless it intended to use the CRASH DUMMIES mark within the foreseeable future. Although Mattel later allowed its trademark registrations to lapse, cancellation of a trademark registration does not necessarily translate into abandonment of common law trademark rights. Nor does it establish its owner's lack of intent to use the mark. *See Miller Brewing Co. v. Oland's Breweries (1971), Ltd.*, 548 F.2d 349, 352 n. 4 (CCPA 1976) ("Although Oland & Son's registration was cancelled in January of 1968 for failure to file a continued use affidavit, this, in and of itself, does not show an intent to abandon.") (citation omitted). Therefore, Mattel's failure to file a timely Section 8 declaration of use and/or excusable nonuse for the marks does not negate Mattel's intent to resume use of the mark.

[14] Third, substantial evidence supports the Board's finding that Mattel's research and development efforts from 2000 to 2003 indicate its intent to resume use of the marks. Mattel relied on its internal documents and testimony by Peter Frank, Mattel's marketing manager, to describe its product development activities. Based on the documents, Frank testified that Mattel began brainstorming ideas for the CRASH DUMMIES toys in 2000, researched and tested them in 2001, and

633

obtained concept approval in 2002. He also explained that Mattel began manufacturing the CRASH DUMMIES toys in October 2003, culminating in actual shipment in December 2003.

[15] In addition, Mattel's shipment of CRASH DUMMIES toys in December 2003 supports Frank's testimony about Mattel's research and development efforts in the early 2000's. This court does not disregard this record evidence because it falls outside of the three-year statutory period of nonuse. The Board may consider evidence and testimony regarding Mattel's practices that occurred before or after the three-year statutory period to infer Mattel's intent to resume use during the three-year period. *See Miller Brewing Co. v. Oland's Breweries*, 548 F.2d 349, 352 (CCPA 1976) (considering evidence beyond a statutory period to affirm the Board's decision to sustain opposition to a trademark application). Therefore, substantial evidence shows that Mattel continuously worked on developing CRASH DUMMIES toys from 2000 to 2003.

. . . .

[16] Mattel needed sufficient time to research, develop, and market its retooled CRASH DUMMIES toys after acquiring Tyco's CRASH DUMMIES marks in 1997. Despite Mattel's delay in utilizing the marks for its toys, substantial evidence supports the Board's finding that Mattel rebutted the statutory presumption of abandonment of the marks. Accordingly, the Board correctly held that CDM may not register its proposed mark CRASH DUMMIES for a line of games and playthings.

IV.

[17] Because substantial evidence supports the Board's finding that Mattel intended to resume use of the CRASH DUMMIES marks during the period of non-use, this court affirms.

Questions and Comments

1. *Why might a firm deliberately and formally abandon a mark?* At least one reason is for tax write-off purposes. *See, e.g., California Cedar Prod. Co. v. Pine Mountain Corp.*, 724 F.2d 827, 829 (9th Cir. 1984) (describing previous owner of DURAFLAME mark's "objective of withdrawing from the artificial firelog market and writing off for accounting purposes" the mark's goodwill); *Manhattan Indus., Inc. v. Sweater Bee by Banff, Ltd.*, 627 F.2d 628, 630 n .2 (2d Cir. 1980) ("Although the record does not show General Mills' reason for abandoning the mark {KIMBERLY for women's apparel}, counsel suggested at oral argument, in answer to the court's question, that the abandonment might have been for tax purposes."). *Cf. id.* at 629 ("Upon the mark's abandonment, a free-for-all ensued" in which several different clothing manufacturers sought to claim rights in the mark).

2. *Badwill?* Trademark law enables firms to protect the goodwill they have developed in the various goods or services they provide. But what about trademarks that develop a reputation for severely defective goods and poor performance? It is apparently routine practice that after a commercial airliner crashes, airlines will rush to paint over any identifying trademarks appearing on the exterior of the wreckage if that wreckage is photographable. *See* Will Coldwell, *Thai Airways and that logo – just part of post-plane-crash etiquette?*, THE GUARDIAN, Sept. 9, 2013, https://www.theguardian.com/world/ 2013/sep/09/thai-airways-logo-crash-etiquette; Nick Squires, *Alitalia paints over crashed plane's markings*, THE TELEGRAPH, Feb. 4, 2013, https://www.telegraph.co.uk/news/worldnews/europe/ italy/9847651/Alitalia-paints-over-crashed-planes-markings.html (quoting a spokesman of Alitalia, after it painted over its trademark on wreckage, that "[t]his is something that is done by airline companies in many countries and we are surprised that such a fuss is being made. It is a matter of brand protection."). *Cf.* Reuters, *AIG to Revive AIG Name; Drop Chartis, SunAmerica Names: Reuters*, INSURANCE JOURNAL, June 28, 2012, https://www.insurancejournal.com/news/ national/2012/ 06/28/253571.htm (discussing AIG's efforts to rename itself, in part for the safety of its own employees, after the 2008 financial crisis and its subsequent decision to return to the AIG name). Should trademark law (or some neighboring body of law) require that firms continue to use marks that have developed badwill? *See* Note, *Badwill*, 116 HARV. L. REV. 1845 (2003).

2. *Is it enough if the plaintiff shows that it intended not to abandon the mark?* Strictly speaking, under Lanham Act § 45, 15 U.S.C. § 1127, the defendant bears the burden to persuade the court only that the plaintiff, after discontinuing use of the mark, did not intend to resume use of the mark. The defendant need not show that the plaintiff affirmatively intended to abandon the mark. In other words, even if the plaintiff can show that it intended not to abandon the mark, a showing that the plaintiff nevertheless did not intend to resume use of the mark is enough to trigger abandonment. This may seem like lawerly hair-splitting (and in most cases, it probably is), but plaintiffs can sometimes show that they intended not to abandon the mark even when they had no plans to resume use of the mark. *See generally Exxon Corp. v. Humble Expl. Co.*, 695 F.2d 96, 102 (5th Cir. 1983) ("There is a difference between intent not to abandon or relinquish and intent to resume use in that an owner may not wish to abandon its mark but may have no intent to resume its use."). *Accord Silverman v. CBS Inc.*, 870 F.2d 40, 46 (2d Cir. 1989) ("We think that Congress, by speaking of 'intent not to resume' rather than 'intent to abandon' in this section of the Act meant to avoid the implication that intent never to resume use must be shown.").

2. Abandonment Through Failure to Control Use

Reg. No. 4,215,095	THE FREECYCLE NETWORK (ARIZONA NON-PROFIT CORPORATION) PO BOX 294
Registered Sep. 25, 2012	TUCSON, AZ 85702
COLLECTIVE MEMBERSHIP	FOR: INDICATING MEMBERSHIP IN AN ORGANIZATION THAT PROMOTES THE RE-USE OF UNWANTED ITEMS, IN CLASS 200 (U.S. CL. 200)
PRINCIPAL REGISTER	FIRST USE 7-20-2012. IN COMMERCE 7-20-2012.
	THE MARK CONSISTS OF THE TERM "FREECYCLE.ORG" WITH A CURVED ARROW BELOW THE TERM AND A CURVED ARROW HAVING FIVE DROPLET-LIKE DESIGNS RADIATING THEREFROM ABOVE THE TERM.
	SN 85-357,555, FILED 6-27-2011
	JULIE GUTTADAURO, EXAMINING ATTORNEY

FreecycleSunnyvale v. Freecycle Network
626 F.3d 509 (9th Cir. 2010)

CALLAHAN, Circuit Judge:

[1] FreecycleSunnyvale ("FS") is a member group of The Freecycle Network ("TFN"), an organization devoted to facilitating the recycling of goods. FS filed a declaratory action against TFN arising from a trademark licensing dispute, alleging noninfringement of TFN's trademarks and tortious interference with FS's business relations. FS moved for partial summary judgment on the issue of whether its naked licensing defense to trademark infringement allowed it to avoid a finding of

infringement as a matter of law.[1] TFN argued that it had established adequate quality control standards over its licensees' services and use of the trademarks to avoid a finding of naked licensing and abandonment of its trademarks. The district court granted summary judgment to FS. We hold that TFN (1) did not retain express contractual control over FS's quality control measures, (2) did not have actual controls over FS's quality control measures, and (3) was unreasonable in relying on FS's quality control measures. Because we find that TFN engaged in naked licensing and thereby abandoned its trademarks, we affirm.

I

A

[2] In March 2003, Deron Beal ("Beal") founded TFN, an umbrella non-profit Arizona corporation dedicated to "freecycling." The term "freecycling" combines the words "free" and "recycling" and refers to the practice of giving an unwanted item to a stranger so that it can continue to be used for its intended purpose, rather than disposing of it.[2] As practiced by TFN, freecycling is primarily a local activity conducted by means of internet groups, which are created by volunteers through online service providers like Yahoo! Groups and Google Groups.[3] Although not required to do so, most TFN member groups use Yahoo! Groups as a forum for members to coordinate their freecycling activities. TFN also maintains its own website, www.freecycle.org, which provides a directory of member groups as well as resources for volunteers to create new groups. The website also includes a section devoted to etiquette guidelines.

[3] TFN asserts that it maintains a "Freecycle Ethos"—a democratic leadership structure, in which decisions are made through a process of surveys and discussions among volunteer moderators. Local volunteer moderators are responsible for enforcing TFN's rules and policies, but the moderators have flexibility in enforcement depending on the moderators' assessment of their local communities.

[4] Since May 2003, TFN has been using three trademarks, FREECYCLE, THE FREECYCLE NETWORK, and a logo (collectively "the trademarks") to identify TFN's services and to identify member groups' affiliation with TFN. Federal registration of the trademarks is currently pending in the United States, but the trademarks have been registered in other countries. TFN permits member groups to use the trademarks. When TFN first started, Beal personally regulated the use of the trademarks but, as TFN has grown, it has relied on local moderators to regulate member groups' use of the trademarks.

---

[1] Naked licensing occurs when a licensor does not exercise adequate quality control over its licensee's use of a licensed trademark such that the trademark may no longer represent the quality of the product or service the consumer has come to expect. *See Barcamerica Int'l USA Trust v. Tyfield Importers, Inc.,* 289 F.3d 589, 595–96 (9th Cir. 2002). By not enforcing the terms of the trademark's use, the licensor may forfeit his rights to enforce the exclusive nature of the trademark. The key question is therefore whether TFN produced any evidence to raise a material fact issue as to whether it: (1) retained contractual rights to control the quality of the use of its trademark; (2) actually controlled the quality of the trademark's use; or (3) reasonably relied on FS to maintain the quality. *Barcamerica,* 289 F.3d at 596–98 (upholding trademarks where a licensor is familiar with the licensee and reasonably relies on the licensee's own quality control efforts).

[2] Beal did not coin the word "freecycle" and TFN is not the first organization to promote freecycling.

[3] In general, online discussion groups such as Yahoo! Groups and Google Groups allow individuals with a shared common interest to communicate by means of posting messages to the particular group's online forum. Such groups may be subject to terms and conditions of the service provider. In addition, discussion groups often have volunteer group moderators who monitor the discussions, and each group may adopt and enforce rules and regulations (e.g., discussion etiquette) separate from whatever terms the online service provider imposes.

[5] Lisanne Abraham ("Abraham") founded FS on October 7, 2003, in Sunnyvale, California, without TFN's knowledge or involvement. She established the group by entering into a service contract with Yahoo! Groups and becoming the group's moderator. Upon establishing FS, Abraham adapted etiquette guidelines and instructions for how to use FS from either TFN's or one of TFN's member group's website. On October 7, 2003, Abraham emailed Beal directly asking for a logo for FS, and they spoke over the phone within days of the email communication. After the phone conversation, Beal emailed Abraham on October 9, 2003, stating: "You can get the neutral logo from www.freecycle.org, just don't use it for commercial purposes or you [sic] maybe Mark or Albert can help you to do your own fancy schmancy logo!"[4] This email is the only record of a direct communication between FS and TFN regarding the use of any of the trademarks.

[6] Between October 7, 2003, and October 9, 2003, FS was added to TFN's list of online freecycling groups displayed on TFN's website. Then, on October 9, 2003, Abraham received an email from Beal addressed to nineteen moderators of new freecycle Yahoo! Groups which, among other things, welcomed them to TFN. The email did not discuss or include any restrictions or guidance on the use of TFN's trademarks. On October 13, 2003, Abraham received another email from TFN, this time an invitation to join the "freecyclemodsquad" Yahoo! Group ("modsquad group"), an informal discussion forum exclusively for the moderators of freecycle Yahoo! Groups to share ideas.

[7] Before 2004, TFN had only a few suggested guidelines in the etiquette section of its website, including a "Keep it Free" rule. Then, on January 4, 2004, Beal sent an email to the modsquad group, asking whether TFN should also limit listed items to those that were legal. Ultimately, Beal proposed the adoption of a "Keep it Free, Legal & Appropriate for All Ages" rule and asked "that all moderators vote on whether they feel this is the one rule that should apply to ALL local groups or not." Between January 4 and January 11, 2004, a majority of the modsquad group voted to require all local groups to adopt the rule and, on January 11, Beal informed the group that "I'm glad to say ... we now have one true guiding principle." Although the moderators adopted the "Keep it Free, Legal & Appropriate for All Ages" rule, following its adoption, they frequently discussed what the actual meaning of the rule was and, ultimately, its definition and enforcement varied from group to group.

[8] Although the underlying reason is not evident from the record or the parties' briefs, on November 1 and November 14, 2005, TFN sent emails to FS ordering the group to cease and desist using the Freecycle name and logo and threatening to have Yahoo! terminate FS's Yahoo! Group if FS did not comply. On November 5, FS emailed Yahoo! and disputed TFN's ability to forbid the use of the trademarks by informing Yahoo! of the license that TFN allegedly had granted FS in October 2003 (i.e., Beal's October 9, 2003 email authorizing Abraham to use the logo). On November 21, Yahoo! terminated the FS Yahoo! Group at TFN's request, after receiving a claim from TFN that FS was infringing on TFN's trademark rights.

B

[9] On January 18, 2006, FS filed a declaratory judgment action against TFN in the U.S. District Court for the Northern District of California, alleging noninfringement of TFN's trademarks and tortious interference with FS's business relations. TFN brought counterclaims for trademark infringement and unfair competition under the Lanham Act and California Business and Professions Code section 17200.

[10] FS then moved for summary judgment on the issue of whether its naked licensing defense to trademark infringement allowed it to avoid a finding of infringement as a matter of law. FS argued that

---

[4] Mark Messinger is the moderator for the Olympia, Washington, freecycle group. He helped Abraham fashion a unique freecycle logo for Sunnyvale. Albert Kaufman apparently introduced Abraham to freecycling.

637

TFN had abandoned its trademarks because it engaged in naked licensing when it granted FS the right to use the trademarks without either (1) the right to control or (2) the exercise of actual control over FS's activities. On March 13, 2008, the district court granted summary judgment in favor of FS, holding that TFN engaged in naked licensing and therefore abandoned its rights to the trademarks. The parties stipulated to dismiss the remaining claims, and final judgment was entered on May 20, 2008. TFN thereafter timely filed its appeal.

II

. . . .

[11] In ruling on a motion for summary judgment, our inquiry "necessarily implicates the substantive evidentiary standard of proof that would apply at the trial on the merits." *Id.* at 252. We have held that the proponent of a naked license theory of trademark abandonment must meet a "stringent standard of proof." *Barcamerica*, 289 F.3d at 596 (internal quotation marks omitted); *see also Prudential Ins. Co. of Am. v. Gibraltar Fin. Corp. of Cal.*, 694 F.2d 1150, 1156 (9th Cir. 1982) ("Abandonment of a trademark, being in the nature of forfeiture, must be strictly proved."); *Edwin K. Williams & Co. v. Edwin K. Williams & Co. E.*, 542 F.2d 1053, 1059 (9th. Cir. 1976) ("[A] person who asserts insufficient control [of a trademark] must meet a high burden of proof.").

[12] We have yet to determine, however, whether this high standard of proof requires "clear and convincing" evidence or a "preponderance of the evidence." *See Electro Source, LLC v. Brandess–Kalt–Aetna Group, Inc.*, 458 F.3d 931, 935 n. 2 (9th Cir. 2006) (reserving the issue of the standard of proof to show trademark abandonment, but noting that at least one district court in the Ninth Circuit had required "clear and convincing" evidence). Indeed, in *Grocery Outlet Inc. v. Albertson's Inc.*, 497 F.3d 949, 952–54 (9th Cir. 2007) (per curiam), Judges Wallace and McKeown disagreed in separate concurrences as to which standard applies. Judge Wallace advocated the clear and convincing standard, while Judge McKeown argued that the preponderance of the evidence standard applied. *Id.*

[13] A review of our sister circuits' decisions reveals that only two circuits have considered which standard to apply, with one reserving the issue and the other adopting a preponderance of the evidence standard. *See Cumulus Media, Inc. v. Clear Channel Commcn's, Inc.*, 304 F.3d 1167, 1175 n. 12 (11th Cir. 2002) (declining to address the meaning of "strict burden" because the outcome of the case would be the same with either standard of proof); *Cerveceria Centroamericana, S.A. v. Cerveceria India, Inc.*, 892 F.2d 1021, 1024 (Fed.Cir. 1989) (adopting the preponderance of the evidence standard). Most published lower court decisions that have reached this issue appear to have interpreted the "strictly proven" standard to require "clear and convincing" evidence of naked licensing. *See* 3 J. Thomas McCarthy, *McCarthy on Trademarks and Unfair Competition* § 17:12 n.2 (4th ed. 2010).[5]

[14] Here, we need not decide which standard of proof applies because, even applying the higher standard of proof—clear and convincing—and viewing the evidence in the light most favorable to TFN as the non-moving party, FS has demonstrated that TFN engaged in naked licensing and consequently abandoned the trademarks.

III

---

[5] Citing, *inter alia, Mathy v. Republic Metalware Co.*, 35 App. D.C. 151, 1910 WL 20792 at *3, (1910) ("Abandonment being in the nature of a forfeiture, it is incumbent upon the person alleging it to prove by clear and convincing evidence that the right claimed has been relinquished."); *Dial–A–Mattress Operating Corp. v. Mattress Madness, Inc.*, 841 F.Supp. 1339, 1355 (E.D.N.Y.1994) ("[A]n affirmative defense alleging a break in plaintiff's chain of priority under the doctrine of abandonment must be proven by clear and convincing evidence."); *EH Yacht, LLC v. Egg Harbor, LLC*, 84 F.Supp.2d 556, 564–65 (D.N.J.2000) (noting that the majority of courts have held that the "strictly proven" standard requires proof by clear and convincing evidence.); *accord Cash Processing Servs. v. Ambient Entm't*, 418 F.Supp.2d 1227, 1232 (D.Nev.2006).

[15] An introduction to "naked licensing" of trademarks is in order, as this issue has seldom arisen in this circuit or in our sister circuits. Our only discussion of this subject is in *Barcamerica*, 289 F.3d at 598 (holding that Barcamerica, a vintner, engaged in naked licensing and abandoned its trademark by failing to retain or otherwise exercise adequate quality control over the trademark it had licensed to another company), and that decision informs and guides our discussion here.

[16] As a general matter, trademark owners have a duty to control the quality of their trademarks. McCarthy § 18:48. "It is well-established that '[a] trademark owner may grant a license and remain protected provided quality control of the goods and services sold under the trademark by the licensee is maintained.'" *Barcamerica*, 289 F.3d at 595–96 (quoting *Moore Bus. Forms, Inc. v. Ryu*, 960 F.2d 486, 489 (5th Cir. 1992)).

[17] "Naked licensing" occurs when the licensor "fails to exercise adequate quality control over the licensee." *Id.* at 596. Naked licensing may result in the trademark's ceasing to function as a symbol of quality and a controlled source. *Id.* (citing McCarthy § 18:48). We have previously declared that naked licensing is "*inherently deceptive* and constitutes abandonment of any rights to the trademark by the licensor." *Id.* at 598. "Consequently, where the licensor fails to exercise adequate quality control over the licensee, 'a court may find that the trademark owner has abandoned the trademark, in which case the owner would be estopped from asserting rights to the trademark.'" *Id.* at 596 (quoting *Moore,* 960 F.2d at 489).

A

[18] At issue here is whether there is clear and convincing evidence, viewed in the light most favorable to TFN, that TFN allowed FS to use the trademarks with so few restrictions as to compel a finding that TFN engaged in naked licensing and abandoned the trademarks. TFN contends that disputed issues of material fact remain as to whether TFN's quality control standards, during the relevant time period, were sufficient. Although TFN concedes that it did not have an express license agreement, it alleges that a reasonable jury could find that it had adequate quality control measures in place when FS was authorized to use the trademarks, making summary judgment inappropriate.

1

[19] When deciding summary judgment on claims of naked licensing, we first determine whether the license contained an express contractual right to inspect and supervise the licensee's operations. *See Barcamerica*, 289 F.3d at 596. The absence of an agreement with provisions restricting or monitoring the quality of goods or services produced under a trademark supports a finding of naked licensing. *Id.* at 597; *see also Stanfield v. Osborne Indus., Inc.*, 52 F.3d 867, 871 (10th Cir. 1995) (granting summary judgment where license agreement lacked right to inspect or supervise licensee's operations and gave the licensee sole discretion to design the trademark).

[20] TFN concedes that it did not have an express license agreement with FS regarding FS's use of the trademarks. Without an express license agreement, TFN necessarily lacks express contractual rights to inspect and supervise FS. However, TFN argues that the October 9, 2003 email, in which Beal advised Abraham that: "You can get the neutral logo from www.freecycle.org, *just don't use it for commercial purposes* ....", reflects an implied license. Emphasis added.

[21] Even assuming that Beal's emailed admonition to Abraham not to use the trademarks for commercial purposes constitutes an implied licensing agreement, it contained no express contractual right to inspect or supervise FS's services and no ability to terminate FS's license if FS used the trademarks for commercial purposes. *See Barcamerica*, 289 F.3d at 597 (determining that a license agreement lacking similar controls was insufficient). We therefore hold that, by TFN's own admission, there is no disputed issue of material fact as to whether TFN maintained an express contractual right to control quality.

2

[22] TFN next contends that, despite its lack of an express contractual *right to* control quality, a material issue of fact remains as to whether TFN maintained *actual* control over its member groups' services and use of the trademarks when FS was granted use of the trademarks in October 2003. "The lack of an express contract right to inspect and supervise a licensee's operations is not conclusive evidence of lack of control." *Barcamerica,* 289 F.3d at 596. However, where courts have excused the lack of a contractual right to control quality, they have still required that the licensor demonstrate *actual* control through inspection or supervision. *See, e.g., Stanfield,* 52 F.3d at 871 ("The absence of an express contractual right of control does not necessarily result in abandonment of a mark, as long as the licensor in fact exercised sufficient control over its licensee.").

[23] TFN asserts that it exercised actual control over the trademarks because it had several quality control standards in place, specifically: (1) the "Keep it Free, Legal, and Appropriate for all Ages" standard and TFN's incorporation of the Yahoo! Groups' service terms; (2) the non-commercial services requirement (expressed in Beal's October 9, 2003 email); (3) the etiquette guidelines listed on TFN's website; and (4) TFN's "Freecycle Ethos" which, TFN contends, establishes policies and procedures for member groups, even if local member groups are permitted flexibility in how to apply those policies and procedures. In addition, TFN cites *Birthright v. Birthright, Inc.,* 827 F.Supp. 1114 (D.N.J.1993) for the principle that loosely organized non-profits like TFN and FS that share "the common goals of a public service organization" are subject to less stringent quality control requirements.

[24] First, we disagree with TFN's contentions that the "Keep it Free, Legal, and Appropriate for all Ages" standard and its incorporation of the Yahoo! Groups' service terms constituted actual controls over its member groups.[6] The undisputed evidence showed that TFN's licensees were not required to adopt the "Keep it Free, Legal, and Appropriate for all Ages" standard, nor was it uniformly applied or interpreted by the local groups. Similarly, FS was not required to use Yahoo! Groups and was not asked to agree to the Yahoo! Groups' service terms as a condition of using TFN's trademarks. Moreover, the Yahoo! Groups' service terms, which regulate generic online activity like sending spam messages and prohibiting harassment, cannot be considered quality controls over TFN's member groups' services and use of the trademarks. The service terms apply to every Yahoo! Group, and do not control the quality of the freecycling services that TFN's member groups provide. Thus, the "Keep it Free, Legal and Appropriate for All Ages" standard and the Yahoo! Groups' service terms were not quality controls over FS's use of the trademarks.

[25] Second, we conclude that TFN's non-commercial requirement says nothing about the *quality* of the services provided by member groups and therefore does not establish a control requiring member groups to maintain consistent quality. Thus, it is not an actual control in the trademark context. Third, because member groups may freely adopt and adapt TFN's listed rules of etiquette and because of the voluntary and amorphous nature of these rules, they cannot be considered an actual control. For example, FS modified the etiquette that was listed on TFN's website and TFN never required FS to conform to TFN's rules of etiquette. Fourth, TFN admits that a central premise of its "Freecycle Ethos" is local enforcement with local variation. By definition, this standard does not maintain consistency across member groups, so it is not an actual control.

---

[6] Notably, Beal did not propose, and the modsquad did not adopt, this standard until January 2004, more than three months after Abraham founded FS in October 2003. The only standard listed in TFN's etiquette section on its website in 2003 was "Keep it Free," but there was no requirement that member groups adopt this standard. Similarly, TFN's incorporation of the Yahoo! Groups' service terms was not done until after FS was given use of the trademarks in October 2003. Because we hold that TFN did not exercise actual control no matter what time period is considered, we do not address whether actual supervision would be sufficient if it starts at some point after the granting of a license to use a trademark.

[26] Even assuming that TFN's asserted quality control standards actually relate to the quality of its member groups' services, they were not adequate quality controls because they were not enforced and were not effective in maintaining the consistency of the trademarks. Indeed, TFN's alleged quality controls fall short of the supervision and control deemed inadequate in other cases in which summary judgment on naked licensing has been granted to the licensee. *See, e.g., Barcamerica*, 289 F.3d at 596–97 (finding no express contractual right to inspect and supervise the use of the marks coupled with licensor's infrequent wine tastings and unconfirmed reliance on the winemaker's expertise was inadequate evidence of quality controls to survive summary judgment); *Stanfield*, 52 F.3d at 871 (granting summary judgment to the licensee where the license agreement lacked a right to inspect or supervise licensee's operations, and alleged actual controls were that the licensor examined one swine heating pad, looked at other pet pads, and occasionally reviewed promotional materials and advertising).

[27] Moreover, even if we were inclined to accept the premise allegedly set forth in *Birthright*, that loosely organized non-profits that share common goals are subject to less stringent quality control requirements for trademark purposes, the result would be the same. In *Birthright*, the court held that the license was not naked because the licensor "monitored and controlled" its licensees' use of the trademarks. 827 F.Supp. at 1139–40; *see also Barcamerica*, 289 F.3d at 596 (holding that a licensor may overcome the lack of a formal agreement if it exercises actual control over its licensees). Here, TFN exercised no actual control over its licensees, so even under a less stringent standard, TFN has not raised a material issue of fact as to whether it exercised actual control over FS's use of the trademarks. *See Barcamerica*, 289 F.3d at 598.

3

[28] TFN contends that even if it did not exercise actual control, it justifiably relied on its member groups' quality control measures. Although "courts have upheld licensing agreements where the licensor is familiar with and relies upon the licensee's own efforts to control quality," *Barcamerica*, 289 F.3d at 596 (internal quotation marks and brackets omitted), we, like the other circuits that have considered this issue, have required that the licensor and licensee be involved in a "close working relationship" to establish adequate quality control in the absence of a formal agreement, *id.* at 597; *accord Stanfield*, 52 F.3d at 872; *Taco Cabana Int'l, Inc. v. Two Pesos, Inc.*, 932 F.2d 1113, 1121 (5th Cir. 1991). In *Barcamerica*, we cited four examples of "close working relationships" that would allow the licensor to rely on the licensee's own quality control: (1) a close working relationship for eight years; (2) a licensor who manufactured ninety percent of the components sold by a licensee and with whom it had a ten year association and knew of the licensee's expertise; (3) siblings who were former business partners and enjoyed a seventeen-year business relationship; and (4) a licensor with a close working relationship with the licensee's employees, and the pertinent agreement provided that the license would terminate if certain employees ceased to be affiliated with the licensee. 289 F.3d at 597.

[29] Here, TFN and FS did not enjoy the type of close working relationship that would permit TFN to rely on FS's quality control measures. TFN had no long term relationship with Abraham or the FS group. In fact, the October 9, 2003 email between Beal and Abraham, which mentions using the TFN logo, was the parties' first and only written communication about the trademarks prior to TFN's requests to stop using them in November 2006. In addition, TFN had no experience with FS that might have supported its alleged confidence in FS's quality control measures. Thus, even considered in a light most favorable to TFN, no evidence showed the type of close working relationship necessary to overcome TFN's lack of quality controls over FS. *See id.*

[30] Furthermore, we have held that, while reliance on a licensee's own quality control efforts is a relevant factor, such reliance is *not alone sufficient* to show that a naked license has not been granted.[7] *See Transgo, Inc. v. Ajac Transmission Parts Corp.,* 768 F.2d 1001, 1017–18 (9th Cir. 1985) (noting that, although the licensor had worked closely with the licensee for ten years, the licensor did not rely solely on his confidence in the licensee, but exercised additional control by, *inter alia,* periodically inspecting those goods and was consulted regarding any changes in the product). Because sole reliance on a licensee's own control quality efforts is not enough to overcome a finding of naked licensing without other indicia of control, *see id.* at 1017–18, and because TFN lacked a close working relationship with FS and failed to show any other indicia of actual control, we conclude that TFN could not rely solely on FS's own quality control efforts.

B

[31] TFN's three remaining arguments also fail to raise a material issue of fact that precludes a grant summary of judgment for FS. First, TFN asserts that it should be subject to a lesser level of quality control standard because its services are not dangerous to the public and the public expects local variation in services so the probability of deception is low. We have stated that the "standard of quality control and the degree of necessary inspection and policing by the licensor will vary." *Barcamerica,* 289 F.3d at 598. The licensor need only exercise "control sufficient to meet the reasonable expectations of customers." McCarthy, § 18:55. However, because TFN did not establish *any* quality control requirements for its member groups, we do not need to decide what efforts to oversee a licensee's performance might meet a low standard of quality control.

[32] TFN's remaining two arguments—(1) that FS must show both naked licensing *and* a loss of trademark significance, and (2) that FS is estopped from supporting its naked licensing defense with evidence that demonstrates that TFN did not adequately control the services offered by FS when using the trademarks—are both raised for the first time on appeal, so we decline to reach them. *See United States v. Robertson,* 52 F.3d 789, 791 (9th Cir. 1994) ("Issues not presented to the district court cannot generally be raised for the first time on appeal.").

IV

[33] We determine, viewing the record in the light most favorable to TFN, that TFN (1) did not retain express contractual control over FS's quality control measures, (2) did not have actual control over FS's quality control measures, and (3) was unreasonable in relying on FS's quality control measures. Therefore, we conclude that TFN engaged in naked licensing and consequently abandoned the trademarks. The district court's grant of summary judgment in favor of FS and against TFN is AFFIRMED.

Questions and Comments

1. *Trademark rights and open innovation.* Linus Torvalds released the Linux operating system kernel in 1991 and has since overseen the development of Linux into one of the world's leading operating systems, particularly for servers, mainframes, supercomputers, and, through the Linux-derived Android mobile operating system, smartphones. Linux is open source software and Torvalds is an outspoken advocate for the open source movement. But Torvalds asserts tight control over the LINUX trademark. *See* https://www.linuxfoundation.org/about/linux-mark/. He does so in part to

---

[7] Other circuits have also relied on the licensor's confidence in the licensee only where there were additional indicia of control. *See, e.g., Stanfield,* 52 F.3d at 872 (holding summary judgment for the licensee appropriate where no special relationship between the parties existed and no evidence of actual control over the licensee existed); *Land O'Lakes Creameries, Inc. v. Oconomowoc Canning Co.,* 330 F.2d 667 (7th Cir. 1964) (upholding trademark where licensor's name appeared on trademark product label, and product was sold under license for forty years without complaints about quality).

642

ensure that the trademark not be deemed abandoned and in part to control the development of the Linux operating system itself. On the important role played by trademark rights (and moral rights) in open source software development, see Greg Vetter, *The Collaborative Integrity of Open-Source Software*, 2004 UTAH L. REV. 563 (2004).

2. *Reclaiming abandoned marks*. After a mark has been abandoned, anyone may establish rights in the mark by beginning to use the mark in commerce or filing an application to register the mark. In *California Cedar Prod. Co. v. Pine Mountain Corp.*, 724 F.2d 827 (9th Cir. 1984), the Clorox Corporation was the owner through a subsidiary of the DURAFLAME mark. Clorox withdrew from the artificial firelog market and published a notice in the Wall Street Journal announcing its abandonment of the mark. Clorox did so for tax purposes; by abandoning the mark, it could write off the value of the mark. On the same day as the Wall Street Journal announcement, California Cedar, which manufactured firelogs for Clorox under the DURAFLAME mark, began selling DURAFLAME-branded firelogs in packaging that identified California Cedar as their source. Two other entities asserted rights in the mark. The defendant Pine Mountain had hurriedly begun to sell DURAFLAME-branded firelogs two days before the Wall Street Journal announcement. Another entity began selling such firelogs two days after the announcement. Affirming the district court's granting of a preliminary injunction to California Cedar, the Ninth Circuit determined that Pine Mountain's sales were "both premature and in bad faith." *Id.* at 830. "[S]ince California Cedar was the first to use the 'Duraflame' trademark and trade dress after its abandonment, it was likely to prevail on the merits." *Id.* at 831. The facts of *California Cedar* transpired before the Trademark Law Revision Act of 1989. In a comparable present-day situation, how might a sophisticated claimant establish rights in an abandoned mark?

3. *Abandoned marks and "residual goodwill."* After a prior owner has abandoned a mark, the mark may possess "residual goodwill" that points towards the prior owner. In very rare cases, this residual goodwill may defeat a finding of abandonment. *See, e.g., Ferrari S.p.A. Esercizio Fabriche Automobili e Corse v. McBurnie*, 11 U.S.P.Q.2d 1843, 1989 WL 298658, at *8 (S.D. Cal. 1989) (finding no abandonment where due to continuing very strong associations between Ferrari and the exterior design of the Daytona Spyder and Ferrari's continuing manufacture of spare parts, "Ferrari has not only achieved a strong existing goodwill but continues to maintain a residual goodwill in the unique design of the DAYTONA SPYDER"). The new user of a mark that possesses "residual goodwill" may be required to take reasonable measures, such as the use of a disclaimer, to ensure that consumers do not mistakenly believe that the new user's products originate in the old user of the mark. *See* Jerome Gilson & Anne Gilson LaLonde, *The Zombie Trademark: A Windfall and a Pitfall*, 98 TRADEMARK REP. 1280 (2008).

E.   Assignment in Gross

An "assignment in gross" occurs when a trademark assignor assigns ownership of a mark (1) without also assigning the underlying business and goodwill and (2) the assignee produces goods or services sufficiently different from the assignor's that consumers would be deceived. When a trademark owner engages in an "assignment in gross" of its mark, the trademark assignor loses rights in its mark and the assignee essentially receives nothing. In most situations, as in the following case, the assignee may claim exclusive rights in the mark, but the basis of and the priority date for those rights stems only from the assignee's new use of the mark, not from any previous use by the assignor.

Sugar Busters LLC v Brennan
177 F.3d 258 (5th Cir. 1999)

KING, Chief Judge:

[1] This appeal challenges the district court's grant of a preliminary injunction prohibiting defendants-appellants from selling or distributing a book entitled "SUGAR BUST For Life!" as infringing plaintiff-appellee's federally registered service mark, "SUGARBUSTERS." Plaintiff-appellee is an assignee of a registered "SUGARBUSTERS" service mark and the author of a best-selling diet book entitled "SUGAR BUSTERS! Cut Sugar to Trim Fat." We determine that the assignment of the registered "SUGARBUSTERS" service mark to plaintiff-appellee was in gross and was therefore invalid, and we vacate the injunction . . . .

I. FACTUAL AND PROCEDURAL HISTORY

[2] Plaintiff-appellee Sugar Busters, L.L.C. (plaintiff) is a limited liability company organized by three doctors and H. Leighton Steward, a former chief executive officer of a large energy corporation, who co-authored and published a book entitled "SUGAR BUSTERS! Cut Sugar to Trim Fat" in 1995. In "SUGAR BUSTERS! Cut Sugar to Trim Fat," the authors recommend a diet plan based on the role of insulin in obesity and cardiovascular disease. The authors' premise is that reduced consumption of insulin-producing food, such as carbohydrates and other sugars, leads to weight loss and a more healthy lifestyle. The 1995 publication of "SUGAR BUSTERS! Cut Sugar to Trim Fat" sold over 210,000 copies, and in May 1998 a second edition was released. The second edition has sold over 800,000 copies and remains a bestseller.

[3] Defendant-appellant Ellen Brennan was an independent consultant employed by plaintiff to assist with the sales, publishing, and marketing of the 1995 edition. In addition, Ellen Brennan wrote a foreword in the 1995 edition endorsing the diet plan, stating that the plan "has proven to be an effective and easy means of weight loss" for herself and for her friends and family. During her

644

employment with plaintiff, Ellen Brennan and Steward agreed to co-author a cookbook based on the "SUGAR BUSTERS!" lifestyle. Steward had obtained plaintiff's permission to independently produce such a cookbook, which he proposed entitling "Sugar Busting is Easy." Plaintiff reconsidered its decision in December 1997, however, and determined that its partners should not engage in independent projects. Steward then encouraged Ellen Brennan to proceed with the cookbook on her own, and told her that she could "snuggle up next to our book, because you can rightly claim you were a consultant to Sugar Busters!"

[4] Ellen Brennan and defendant-appellant Theodore Brennan then co-authored "SUGAR BUST For Life!," which was published by defendant-appellant Shamrock Publishing, Inc. in May 1998. "SUGAR BUST For Life" states on its cover that it is a "cookbook and companion guide by the famous family of good food," and that Ellen Brennan was "Consultant, Editor, Publisher, [and] Sales and Marketing Director for the original, best-selling 'Sugar Busters!™ Cut Sugar to Trim Fat.'" The cover states that the book contains over 400 recipes for "weight loss, energy, diabetes and cholesterol control and an easy, healthful lifestyle." Approximately 110,000 copies of "SUGAR BUST For Life!" were sold between its release and September 1998.

[5] Plaintiff filed this suit in the United States District Court for the Eastern District of Louisiana on May 26, 1998 . . . .

[6] The mark that is the subject of plaintiff's infringement claim is a service mark that was registered in 1992 by Sugarbusters, Inc., an Indiana corporation operating a retail store named "Sugarbusters" in Indianapolis that provides products and information for diabetics. The "SUGARBUSTERS" service mark, registration number 1,684,769, is for "retail store services featuring products and supplies for diabetic people; namely, medical supplies, medical equipment, food products, informational literature and wearing apparel featuring a message regarding diabetes." Sugarbusters, Inc. sold "any and all rights to the mark" to Thornton–Sahoo, Inc. on December 19, 1997, and Thornton–Sahoo, Inc. sold these rights to Elliott Company, Inc. (Elliott) on January 9, 1998. Plaintiff obtained the service mark from Elliott pursuant to a "servicemark purchase agreement" dated January 26, 1998. Under the terms of that agreement, plaintiff purchased "all the interests [Elliott] owns" in the mark and "the goodwill of all business connected with the use of and symbolized by" the mark. Furthermore, Elliott agreed that it "will cease all use of the [m]ark, [n]ame and [t]rademark [i]nterests within one hundred eighty (180) days."

. . . .

[7] Defendants argued to the district court that plaintiff's service mark is invalid because: (1) it was purchased "in gross," . . . .

[8] . . . The district court found that the mark is valid and that the transfer of the mark to plaintiff was not "in gross" because

> [t]he plaintiff has used the trademark to disseminate information through its books, seminars, the Internet, and the cover of plaintiff's recent book, which reads "Help Treat Diabetes and Other Diseases." Moreover, the plaintiff is moving forward to market and sell its own products and services, which comport with the products and services sold by the Indiana corporation. There has been a full and complete transfer of the good will related to the mark, and the plaintiff has licensed the Indiana corporation to use the mark for only six months to enable it to wind down its operations.

Id.

II. DISCUSSION

. . . .

B. Plaintiff's Registered Service Mark

[9] A trademark is merely a symbol of goodwill and has no independent significance apart from the goodwill that it symbolizes. *See Marshak v. Green,* 746 F.2d 927, 929 (2d Cir. 1984); 2 J. THOMAS MCCARTHY, MCCARTHY ON TRADEMARKS AND UNFAIR COMPETITION § 18:2 (4th ed.1999) [hereinafter MCCARTHY]. "A trade mark only gives the right to prohibit the use of it so far as to protect the owner's good will . . . ." *Prestonettes, Inc. v. Coty,* 264 U.S. 359, 368, 44 S.Ct. 350, 68 L.Ed. 731 (1924) (Holmes, J.). Therefore, a trademark cannot be sold or assigned apart from the goodwill it symbolizes. *See* 15 U.S.C. § 1060 ("A registered mark or a mark for which application to register has been filed shall be assignable with the goodwill of the business in which the mark is used, or with that part of the goodwill of the business connected with the use of and symbolized by the mark."); *Marshak,* 746 F.2d at 929. The sale or assignment of a trademark without the goodwill that the mark represents is characterized as in gross and is invalid. *See PepsiCo, Inc. v. Grapette Co.,* 416 F.2d 285, 287 (8th Cir. 1969); 2 MCCARTHY § 18:3.

[10] The purpose of the rule prohibiting the sale or assignment of a trademark in gross is to prevent a consumer from being misled or confused as to the source and nature of the goods or services that he or she acquires. *See Visa, U.S.A., Inc. v. Birmingham Trust Nat'l Bank,* 696 F.2d 1371, 1375 (Fed.Cir. 1982). "Use of the mark by the assignee in connection with a different goodwill and different product would result in a fraud on the purchasing public who reasonably assume that the mark signifies the same thing, whether used by one person or another." *Marshak,* 746 F.2d at 929. Therefore, "'if consumers are not to be misled from established associations with the mark, [it must] continue to be associated with the same or similar products after the assignment.' *Visa, U.S.A.,* 696 F.2d at 1375 (quoting *Raufast S.A. v. Kicker's Pizzazz, Ltd.,* 208 U.S.P.Q. 699, 702 (E.D.N.Y.1980)).

[11] Plaintiff's purported service mark in "SUGARBUSTERS" is valid only if plaintiff also acquired the goodwill that accompanies the mark; that is, "the portion of the business or service with which the mark is associated." *Id.* Defendants claim that the transfer of the "SUGARBUSTERS" mark to plaintiff was in gross because "[n]one of the assignor's underlying business, including its inventory, customer lists, or other assets, were transferred to [plaintiff]." Defendants' view of goodwill, however, is too narrow. Plaintiff may obtain a valid trademark without purchasing any physical or tangible assets of the retail store in Indiana—"the transfer of goodwill requires only that the services be sufficiently similar to prevent consumers of the service offered under the mark from being misled from established associations with the mark." *Id.* at 1376 (internal quotation marks omitted); *see Marshak,* 746 F.2d at 930 ("The courts have upheld such assignments if they find that the assignee is producing a product or performing a service substantially similar to that of the assignor and that the consumers would not be deceived or harmed."); *PepsiCo,* 416 F.2d at 288 ("Basic to this concept [of protecting against consumer deception] is the proposition that any assignment of a trademark and its goodwill (with or without tangibles or intangibles assigned) requires the mark itself be used by the assignee on a product having substantially the same characteristics."); *cf. Money Store v. Harriscorp Fin., Inc.,* 689 F.2d 666, 678 (7th Cir. 1982) ("In the case of a service mark . . . confusion would result if an assignee offered a service different from that offered by the assignor of the mark.").

[12] The district court found, without expressly stating the applicable legal standard, that "[t]here has been a full and complete transfer of the good will related to the mark." *Sugar Busters,* 48 U.S.P.Q.2d at 1514. The proper standard, as discussed above, is whether plaintiff's book and the retail store in Indiana are sufficiently similar to prevent consumer confusion or deception when plaintiff uses the mark previously associated with the store as the title of its book. We conclude that even if the district court applied this standard, its finding that goodwill was transferred between Elliott and plaintiff is clearly erroneous.

[13] In concluding that goodwill was transferred, the district court relied in part on its finding that the mark at issue is registered in International Class 16, "information, literature, and books." However, the registration certificate issued by the United States Patent and Trademark Office states that the service mark is "in class 42" and is "for retail store services featuring products and supplies for diabetic people." *Id.* The district court also relied on its finding that "plaintiff is moving forward to market and sell its own products and services, which comport with the products and services sold by the Indiana corporation." *Id.* Steward testified, however, that plaintiff does not have any plans to operate a retail store, and plaintiff offered no evidence suggesting that it intends to market directly to consumers any goods it licenses to carry the "SUGAR BUSTERS!" name. Finally, we are unconvinced by plaintiff's argument that, by stating on the cover of its diet book that it may "[h]elp treat diabetes and other diseases" and then selling some of those books on the Internet, plaintiff provides a service substantially similar to a retail store that provides diabetic supplies. *See PepsiCo*, 416 F.2d at 286–89 (determining that pepper-flavored soft drink and cola-flavored soft drink are not substantially similar and therefore purported assignment was in gross and invalid). We therefore must conclude that plaintiff's purported service mark is invalid. Thus, its trademark infringement claim under 15 U.S.C. § 1114 cannot succeed on the merits and the district court improperly relied on this ground in granting plaintiff's request for a preliminary injunction.

{The court remanded the case for a determination of, among other things, whether the plaintiff's book title was protectable as an unregistered mark.}

Questions and Comments

1. *What about the similarity of the books' titles?* In a portion of the *Sugar Busters* opinion not excerpted here, the plaintiff argued that even if the assignment at issue was not valid, it nevertheless possessed trademark rights in the title of its book *Sugar Busters!*, and the defendant's title *Sugar Bust for Life!* would confuse consumers into mistakenly believing that the latter book was affiliated with the former. In analyzing this claim, the *Sugar Busters* court cited numerous cases in support of trademark law's longstanding rule that titles of single creative works are not registrable as trademarks, apparently because titles are merely descriptive. Titles are "the proper name of a specific thing, not the differential of a species." *Sugar Busters LLC v. Brennan*, 177 F.3d 258, 268–69 (5th Cir. 1999) (quoting *International Film Serv. Co. v. Associated Producers, Inc.*, 273 F. 585, 587 (S.D.N.Y.1921) (Hand, J.)). However, because titles of individual books may be protected under Lanham Act § 43(a) upon a showing of secondary meaning, the *Sugar Busters* court remanded the case back to the district court to determine if the title possessed the requisite secondary meaning. *See Sugar Busters*, 177 F.3d at 270. For more on the peculiar (and probably incoherent) treatment that trademark law affords to titles of individual creative works (including movies), see McCarthy § 10:4.

2. *Assignment and the importance of due diligence.* In 1998, Volkswagen AG purchased Rolls-Royce Motor Cars from Vickers PLC for £430 million ($712.7 million at the time, about $540 million currently), including the traditional manufacturing facility at Crewe, England. Inexplicably, what Volkswagen failed to appreciate was that the Rolls-Royce trademark for automobiles was owned not by Rolls-Royce Motor Cars but rather by Rolls-Royce PLC, the manufacturer of airplane engines. Rolls-Royce PLC had licensed the mark to Rolls-Royce Motor Cars under a license that terminated in the event that Rolls-Royce Motor Cars was sold. When the sale of Rolls-Royce Motor Cars triggered the termination of their license to use the Rolls-Royce trademark on automobiles, Rolls-Royce PLC licensed the mark instead to Volkswagen's rival BMW, which was Rolls-Royce PLC's manufacturing partner for various aircraft engines (and the entity that Rolls-Royce PLC had hoped would purchase the automaker). Thus, Volkswagen had purchased the means to manufacture Rolls-Royce automobiles in all but name. In an effort to avoid litigation, Rolls-Royce PLC, Volkswagen, and BMW eventually reached an agreement in which BMW paid Rolls-Royce PLC £40 million in exchange for the assignment to BMW of the Rolls-Royce trademark for automobiles. BMW agreed to lease the mark to Volkswagen

through 2002, after which Volkswagen would no longer be able to use the mark. On January 1, 2003, BMW-owned Rolls-Royce Motor Cars opened its new Goodwood manufacturing plant in England—thus freeing it of any need to rely on the Crewe, England plant. *See* Tom Buerkle, *BMW Wrests Rolls-Royce Name Away from VW*, N.Y. TIMES, July 29, 1998, http://www.nytimes.com/1998/07/29/news/bmw-wrests-rollsroyce-name-away-from-vw.html.

F.   The First Sale Doctrine

The first sale doctrine has been defined as follows:

> The resale of genuine trademarked goods generally does not constitute infringement. This is for the simple reason that consumers are not confused as to the origin of the goods: the origin has not changed as a result of the resale. Under what has sometimes been called the "first sale" or "exhaustion" doctrine, the trademark protections of the Lanham Act are exhausted after the trademark owner's first authorized sale of that product. Therefore, even though a subsequent sale is without a trademark owner's consent, the resale of a genuine good does not violate the [Lanham] Act.

> This doctrine does not hold true, however, when an alleged infringer sells trademarked goods that are materially different than those sold by the trademark owner . . . .

Davidoff & CIE, S.A. v. PLD Intern. Corp., 263 F.3d 1297, 1302 (11th Cir. 2001).

A crucial question under the first sale doctrine, then, is what constitutes a "material difference" such that the resale of the materially different good under the original trademark would violate the trademark owner's rights. The following three opinions address this issue. The first, *Champion Spark Plug Co. v. Sanders*, 331 U.S. 125 (1947), involving refurbished spark plugs, is one of the foundational first sale doctrine cases in U.S. trademark law. The second, *Davidoff & CIE, S.A. v. PLD Int'l Corp.*, 263 F.3d 1297 (11th Cir. 2001), is an oft-cited opinion considering whether the scratching off of batch codes on bottles constitutes a material difference. The third case, *Nitro Leisure Products, L.L.C. v. Acushnet Co.*, 341 F.3d 1356 (Fed. Cir. 2003), involves refurbished golf balls.

Note that the first sale doctrine is not strictly speaking a defense to trademark infringement in which the defendant bears the burden of persuasion. The plaintiff bears the overall burden of persuading the court that consumers would be confused as to the true nature of the goods sold by the defendant.

Champion Spark Plug Co. v. Sanders
331 U.S. 125 (1947)

Mr. Justice DOUGLAS delivered the opinion of the Court.

[1] Petitioner is a manufacturer of spark plugs which it sells under the trade mark 'Champion.' Respondents collect the used plugs, repair and recondition them, and resell them. Respondents retain the word 'Champion' on the repaired or reconditioned plugs. The outside box or carton in which the plugs are packed has stamped on it the word 'Champion,' together with the letter and figure denoting the particular style or type. They also have printed on them 'Perfect Process Spark Plugs Guaranteed Dependable' and 'Perfect Process Renewed Spark Plugs.' Each carton contains smaller boxes in which the plugs are individually packed. These inside boxes also carry legends indicating that the plug has been renewed.[1] But respondent company's business name or address is not printed on the cartons. It

---

[1] 'The process used in renewing this plug has been developed through 10 years continuous experience. This Spark Plug has been tested for firing under compression before packing.'

'This Spark Plug is guaranteed to be a selected used Spark Plug, thoroughly renewed and in perfect mechanical condition and is guaranteed to give satisfactory service for 10,000 miles.'

supplies customers with petitioner's charts containing recommendations for the use of Champion plugs. On each individual plug is stamped in small letters, blue on black, the word 'Renewed,' which at times is almost illegible.

[2] Petitioner brought this suit in the District Court, charging infringement of its trade mark and unfair competition. *See* Judicial Code s 24(1), (7), 28 U.S.C. s 41(1), (7), 28 U.S.C.A. s 41(1, 7). The District Court found that respondents had infringed the trade mark. It enjoined them from offering or selling any of petitioner's plugs which had been repaired or reconditioned unless (a) the trade mark and type and style marks were removed, (b) the plugs were repainted with a durable grey, brown, orange, or green paint, (c) the word 'Repaired' was stamped into the plug in letters of such size and depth as to retain enough white paint to display distinctly each letter of the word, (d) the cartons in which the plugs were packed carried a legend indicating that they contained used spark plugs originally made by petitioner and repaired and made fit for use up to 10,000 miles by respondent company.[2] The District Court denied an accounting. *See* 56 F.Supp. 782, 61 F.Supp. 247.

[3] The Circuit Court of Appeals held that respondents not only had infringed petitioner's trade mark but also were guilty of unfair competition. It likewise denied an accounting but modified the decree in the following respects: (a) it eliminated the provision requiring the trade mark and type and style marks to be removed from the repaired or reconditioned plugs; (b) it substituted for the requirement that the word 'Repaired' be stamped into the plug, etc., a provision that the word 'Repaired' or 'Used' be stamped and baked on the plug by an electrical hot press in a contrasting color so as to be clearly and distinctly visible, the plug having been completely covered by permanent aluminum paint or other paint or lacquer; and (c) it eliminated the provision specifying the precise legend to be printed on the cartons and substituted therefor a more general one.[3] The case is here on a petition for certiorari which we granted because of the apparent conflict between the decision below and *Champion Spark Plug Co. v. Reich*, 121 F.2d 769, decided by the Circuit Court of Appeals for the Eighth Circuit.

[4] There is no challenge here to the findings as to the misleading character of the merchandising methods employed by respondents, nor to the conclusion that they have not only infringed petitioner's trade mark but have also engaged in unfair competition. The controversy here relates to the adequacy of the relief granted, particularly the refusal of the Circuit Court of Appeals to require respondents to remove the word 'Champion' from the repaired or reconditioned plugs which they resell.

[5] We put to one side the case of a manufacturer or distributor who markets new or used spark plugs of one make under the trade mark of another. *See Bourjois & Co. v. Katzel*, 260 U.S. 689; *Old Dearborn Distributing Co. v. Seagram-Distillers Corp.*, 299 U.S. 183. Equity then steps in to prohibit defendant's use of the mark which symbolizes plaintiff's good will and 'stakes the reputation of the plaintiff upon the character of the goods.' *Bourjois & Co. v. Katzel, supra*, 260 U.S. at page 692

[6] We are dealing here with second-hand goods. The spark plugs, though used, are nevertheless Champion plugs and not those of another make. There is evidence to support what one would suspect,

---

[2] The prescribed legend read:

'Used spark plug(s) originally made by Champion Spark Plug Company repaired and made fit for use up to 10,000 miles by Perfect Recondition Spark Plug Co., 1133 Bedford Avenue, Brooklyn, N.Y.'

The decree also provided:

'the name and address of the defendants to be larger and more prominent than the legend itself, and the name of plaintiff may be in slightly larger type than the rest of the body of the legend.'

[3] 'The decree shall permit the defendants to state on cartons and containers, selling and advertising material, business records, correspondence and other papers, when published, the original make and type numbers provided it is made clear that any plug referred to therein is used and reconditioned by the defendants, and that such material contains the name and address of defendants."

that a used spark plug which has been repaired or reconditioned does not measure up to the specifications of a new one. But the same would be true of a second-hand Ford or Chevrolet car. And we would not suppose that one could be enjoined from selling a car whose valves had been reground and whose piston rings had been replaced unless he removed the name Ford or Chevrolet. *Prestonettes, Inc., v. Coty*, 264 U.S. 359, was a case where toilet powders had as one of their ingredients a powder covered by a trade mark and where perfumes which were trade marked were rebottled and sold in smaller bottles. The Court sustained a decree denying an injunction where the prescribed labels told the truth. Mr. Justice Holmes stated, 'A trade-mark only gives the right to prohibit the use of it so far as to protect the owner's good will against the sale of another's product as his. * * * When the mark is used in a way that does not deceive the public we see no such sanctity in the word as to prevent its being used to tell the truth. It is not taboo.' 264 U.S. at page 368.

[7] Cases may be imagined where the reconditioning or repair would be so extensive or so basic that it would be a misnomer to call the article by its original name, even though the words 'used' or 'repaired' were added. *Cf. Ingersoll v. Doyle*, D.C., 247 F. 620. But no such practice is involved here. The repair or reconditioning of the plugs does not give them a new design. It is no more than a restoration, so far as possible, of their original condition. The type marks attached by the manufacturer are determined by the use to which the plug is to be put. But the thread size and size of the cylinder hole into which the plug is fitted are not affected by the reconditioning. The heat range also has relevance to the type marks. And there is evidence that the reconditioned plugs are inferior so far as heat range and other qualities are concerned. But inferiority is expected in most second-hand articles. Indeed, they generally cost the customer less. That is the case here. Inferiority is immaterial so long as the article is clearly and distinctively sold as repaired or reconditioned rather than as new. The result is, of course, that the second-hand dealer gets some advantage from the trade mark. But under the rule of Prestonettes, Inc., v. Coty, supra, that is wholly permissible so long as the manufacturer is not identified with the inferior qualities of the product resulting from wear and tear or the reconditioning by the dealer. Full disclosure gives the manufacturer all the protection to which he is entitled.

[8] The decree as shaped by the Circuit Court of Appeals is fashioned to serve the requirements of full disclosure. We cannot say that of the alternatives available the ones it chose are inadequate for that purpose. We are mindful of the fact that this case, unlike *Prestonettes, Inc., v. Coty*, supra, involves unfair competition as well as trade mark infringement; and that where unfair competition is established, any doubts as to the adequacy of the relief are generally resolved against the transgressor. *Warner & Co. v. Lilly & Co.*, 256 U.S. 526, 532. But there was here no showing of fraud or palming off. Their absence, of course, does not undermine the finding of unfair competition. *Federal Trade Commission v. Winsted Hosiery Co.*, 258 U.S. 483, 493; *G. H. Mumm Champagne v. Eastern Wine Corp.*, 2 Cir., 142 F.2d 499, 501. But the character of the conduct giving rise to the unfair competition is relevant to the remedy which should be afforded. *See Jacob Siegel Co. v. Federal Trade Commission*, 327 U.S. 608. We cannot say that the conduct of respondents in this case, or the nature of the article involved and the characteristics of the merchandising methods used to sell it, called for more stringent controls than the Circuit Court of Appeals provided.

. . . .

[9] Affirmed.

Davidoff & CIE, S.A. v. PLD Int'l Corp.
263 F.3d 1297 (11th Cir. 2001)

ANDERSON, Chief Judge:

[1] This case appears to be the first time that this circuit has addressed the circumstances under which the resale of a genuine product with a registered trademark can be considered infringement. We recognize the general rule that a trademark owner's authorized initial sale of its product exhausts the trademark owner's right to maintain control over who thereafter resells the product; subsequent sales of the product by others do not constitute infringement even though such sales are not authorized by the trademark owner. However, we adopt from our sister circuits their exception to this general rule—i.e., the unauthorized resale of a materially different product constitutes infringement. Because we conclude that the resold products in the instant case are materially different, we affirm.

I. BACKGROUND

[2] Davidoff & Cie, S.A., a Swiss corporation, is the manufacturer of DAVIDOFF COOL WATER fragrance products and owns the U.S. trademark. Davidoff & Cie, S.A. exclusively licenses Lancaster Group US LLC (collectively "Davidoff") to distribute its products to retailers in the United States. Working outside of this arrangement, PLD International Corporation ("PLD") acquires DAVIDOFF fragrances that are intended for overseas sale or that are sold in duty-free sales. PLD then distributes them to discount retail stores in the United States.

[3] At the time that PLD acquires the product, the original codes on the bottom of the boxes are covered by white stickers, and batch codes on the bottles themselves have been obliterated with an etching tool. The etching leaves a mark on the bottle near its base on the side opposite the DAVIDOFF COOL WATER printing. The mark is approximately one and one-eighth inches in length and one-eighth of an inch wide. The batch codes are removed, according to PLD, to prevent Davidoff from discovering who sold the fragrances to PLD because Davidoff would stop selling to those vendors.

II. DISTRICT COURT PROCEEDINGS

[4] [T]he district court granted a preliminary injunction, prohibiting PLD from selling, repackaging or altering any product with the name "DAVIDOFF" and/or "COOL WATER" with an obliterated batch code. This appeal followed.

V. TRADEMARK INFRINGEMENT: LAW

. . . .

B. *Resale of a Genuine Trademarked Product and the Material Difference Exception*

[5] The resale of genuine trademarked goods generally does not constitute infringement. *See, e.g., Matrix Essentials, Inc. v. Emporium Drug Mart, Inc.,* 988 F.2d 587, 590 (5th Cir. 1993); *NEC Electronics v. CAL Circuit Abco,* 810 F.2d 1506, 1509 (9th Cir. 1987). This is for the simple reason that consumers are not confused as to the origin of the goods: the origin has not changed as a result of the resale. *See Enesco Corp. v. Price/Costco Inc.,* 146 F.3d 1083, 1085 (9th Cir. 1998) (quoting *NEC,* 810 F.2d at 1509). Under what has sometimes been called the "first sale" or "exhaustion" doctrine, the trademark protections of the Lanham Act are exhausted after the trademark owner's first authorized sale of that product. *See Iberia Foods,* 150 F.3d at 301 n. 4; *Enesco,* 146 F.3d at 1085; *Allison v. Vintage Sports Plaques,* 136 F.3d 1443, 1447-48 (11th Cir. 1998). Therefore, even though a subsequent sale is without a trademark owner's consent, the resale of a genuine good does not violate the Act.

[6] This doctrine does not hold true, however, when an alleged infringer sells trademarked goods that are materially different than those sold by the trademark owner. Our sister circuits have held that a materially different product is not genuine and therefore its unauthorized sale constitutes trademark infringement. *See Nestle,* 982 F.2d at 644 (1st Cir.); *Original Appalachian Artworks,* 816 F.2d at 73 (2d Cir.); *Iberia Foods,* 150 F.3d at 302-3 (3d Cir.); *Martin's Herend Imports, Inc. v. Diamond & Gem Trading USA, Co.,* 112 F.3d 1296, 1302 (5th Cir. 1997); *cf. Enesco,* 146 F.3d at 1087 (9th Cir.) (quoting *Warner-*

651

Lambert Co. v. Northside Dev. Corp., 86 F.3d 3, 6 (2d Cir. 1996)) (noting that a non-conforming product is not genuine and "its distribution constitutes trademark infringement"). We follow our sister circuits and hold that the resale of a trademarked product that is materially different can constitute a trademark infringement.[5] This rule is consistent with the purposes behind the Lanham Act, because materially different products that have the same trademark may confuse consumers and erode consumer goodwill toward the mark. *See Iberia Foods,* 150 F.3d at 303; *Nestle,* 982 F.2d at 638.

[7] Not just any difference will cause consumer confusion. A material difference is one that consumers consider relevant to a decision about whether to purchase a product. *See Martin's Herend Imports,* 112 F.3d at 1302; *Nestle,* 982 F.2d at 641. Because a myriad of considerations may influence consumer preferences, the threshold of materiality must be kept low to include even subtle differences between products. *See Iberia Foods,* 150 F.3d at 304; *Nestle,* 982 F.2d at 641.

[8] The caselaw supports the proposition that the resale of a trademarked product that has been altered, resulting in physical differences in the product, can create a likelihood of consumer confusion. Such alteration satisfies the material difference exception and gives rise to a trademark infringement claim. *Nestle,* 982 F.2d at 643-44 (applying the material difference exception, e.g., differences in the composition, presentation and shape of premium chocolates); *Original Appalachian Artworks,* 816 F.2d at 73 (applying the material difference exception where the infringing Cabbage Patch Kids dolls had Spanish language adoption papers and birth certificates, rather than English).

VI. APPLICATION OF THE EXCEPTION IN THIS CASE

[9] The district court found that etching the glass to remove the batch code degrades the appearance of the product and creates a likelihood of confusion. In addition, the court credited testimony of the marketing vice-president that the etching may make a consumer think that the product had been harmed or tampered with. We defer to the district court's finding that the etching degrades the appearance of the bottle. This finding is not clearly erroneous in light of the stylized nature of the fragrance bottle, which has an otherwise unblemished surface. Indeed, based on our own examination and comparison of the genuine fragrance bottle and the bottle sold by PLD, we agree with the district court that a consumer could very likely believe that the bottle had been tampered with. We agree with the district court that this alteration of the product could adversely affect Davidoff's goodwill, creates a likelihood of consumer confusion, satisfies the material difference exception to the first sale doctrine, and thus constitutes a trademark infringement. We believe that the material difference in this case is comparable to, or more pronounced than, the product differences in *Nestle* and *Original Appalachian Artworks* where the First and Second Circuits applied the material difference exception and found trademark infringement.

[10] PLD directs us to two cases, *Graham Webb International Ltd. Partnership v. Emporium Drug Mart, Inc.,* 916 F.Supp. 909 (E.D.Ark. 1995), and *John Paul Mitchell Systems v. Randalls Food Markets,*

---

[5] PLD argues that the material difference test only applies to so-called gray-market goods: foreign made goods bearing a trademark and intended for sale in a foreign country, but that are subsequently imported into the United States without the consent of the U.S. trademark owner. We reject this argument and join the Third Circuit in noting that infringement by materially different products "is not limited to gray goods cases . . . . The same theory has been used to enjoin the sale of domestic products in conditions materially different from those offered by the trademark owner." *Iberia Foods Corp. v. Romeo,* 150 F.3d 298, 302 (3d Cir. 1998). Indeed, several courts have held that the purchase and resale of goods solely within the United States may constitute infringement when differences exist in quality control or the products themselves. *See Enesco Corp. v. Price/Costco Inc.,* 146 F.3d 1083 (9th Cir. 1998); *Warner-Lambert Co. v. Northside Dev. Corp.,* 86 F.3d 3 (2d Cir. 1996); *Matrix Essentials, Inc. v. Emporium Drug Mart, Inc.,* 988 F.2d 587 (5th Cir. 1993); *Shell Oil Co. v. Commercial Petroleum Inc.,* 928 F.2d 104 (4th Cir. 1991).

Inc., 17 S.W.3d 721 (Tex.App. 2000), where courts have held that the removal of batch codes on hair care products does not constitute infringement. They are both distinguishable from the instant case. Neither court found that the removal affected the overall appearance of the product to the extent that it might be material to a consumer decision to purchase the product. In *Graham Webb,* the court noted that the removal of batch codes resulted in "almost imperceptible scratches" that were not likely to confuse consumers. 916 F.Supp. at 916. And in *Randalls Food Markets,* the court stated that "there was no evidence that removal of the batch codes defaced the bottles." 17 S.W.3d at 736. In the instant case, the etching on the fragrance bottle is more than almost imperceptible scratches. Indeed, the district court credited testimony that consumers may regard the bottles as harmed or tampered with. We agree with the district court that the physical difference created by the obliteration of the batch code on PLD's product constitutes a material difference. *See John Paul Mitchell Systems v. Pete-N-Larry's Inc.,* 862 F.Supp. 1020, 1027 (W.D.N.Y. 1994) (concluding that removal of batch codes from bottles of hair care products, leaving noticeable scars on the bottles and erasing some of the information printed, constitutes a material difference).

[11] PLD also attempts to cast the effect of the etching as minimal. PLD argues that the etching is on the back side of the bottle beneath several lines of printing that identifies the manufacturer and distributor, country of origin and volume, while the front side contains the trademarks in gold and black script letters. This may be true, but the etching is clearly noticeable to a consumer who examines the bottle. At oral argument, PLD argued that only the packaging but not the product itself—i.e., the liquid fragrance inside the bottle—had been altered by the etching. In marketing a fragrance, however, a vendor is not only selling the product inside the bottle, it is also selling the "commercial magnetism" of the trademark that is affixed to the bottle. *Mishawaka Rubber,* 316 U.S. at 205, 62 S.Ct. at 1024. The appearance of the product, which is associated with the trademark, is important to establishing this image. This makes the appearance of the bottle material to the consumer decision to purchase it. Because the etching degrades the appearance of the bottles, the DAVIDOFF fragrance that PLD distributes is materially different from that originally sold by Davidoff. Therefore, we agree with the district court that PLD's sale of this materially different product creates a likelihood of confusion, and satisfies Davidoff's burden of establishing a likelihood of success on the merits.

. . . .

Nitro Leisure Products, L.L.C. v. Acushnet Co.
341 F.3d 1356 (Fed. Cir. 2003)

LINN, Circuit Judge.

[1] Acushnet Company ("Acushnet") appeals from the denial of its motion for a preliminary injunction by the United States District Court for the Southern District of Florida. *In re Nitro Leisure Prods., L.L.C.,* No. 02–14008–CV–Middlebrooks (S.D.Fla. Aug. 9, 2002) ("*Order* "). Because the district court did not abuse its discretion in denying Acushnet's motion in view of Acushnet's failure to show a reasonable likelihood of success on the merits of its claims, we affirm.

BACKGROUND

[2] Acushnet manufactures and sells golfing equipment, and in particular, golf balls. Acushnet owns and has federally registered the trademarks TITLEIST, ACUSHNET, PINNACLE, and PRO V1. Of particular interest in this case, Acushnet manufactures and markets new golf balls under the TITLEIST name and trademark, including the TITLEIST PRO V1, asserted by Acushnet to be the best selling golf ball in the United States since February 2001. *Order* at 2–3.

[3] Nitro obtains and sells two categories of used golf balls at a discounted rate. The first category of balls are "recycled" balls. The recycled balls are those found in relatively good condition, needing

little more than washing, and are repackaged for resale. Recycled balls represent approximately 30% of Nitro's sales. The second category includes balls that are found with stains, scuffs or blemishes, requiring "refurbishing." Nitro's refurbishing process includes cosmetically treating the balls by removing the base coat of paint, the clear coat layer, and the trademark and model markings without damaging the covers of the balls, and then repainting the balls, adding a clear coat, and reaffixing the original manufacturer's trademark. Nitro also applies directly to each "refurbished" ball the legend "USED & REFURBISHED BY SECOND CHANCE" or "USED AND REFURBISHED BY GOLFBALLSDIRECT.COM." In these statements, the terms "Second Chance" and "Golfballsdirect.com" refer to businesses of Nitro. *Order* at 3. Some, but not all, of the refurbished balls also bear a Nitro trademark. Nitro's refurbished balls are packaged in containers displaying the following disclaimer:

> ATTENTION USED/REFURBISHED GOLF BALLS: The enclosed contents of used/refurbished golf balls are USED GOLF BALLS. Used/Refurbished golf balls are subject to performance variations from new ones. These used/refurbished balls were processed via one or more of the following steps: stripping, painting, stamping and/or clear coating in our factory. This product has NOT been endorsed or approved by the original manufacturer and the balls DO NOT fall under the original manufacturer's warranty.

According to Nitro, there is a large market for used golf balls. In 2001, Nitro saw annual sales of approximately $10 million, including $4.8 million for refurbished balls. *Id.*

[4] Nitro originally filed suit against Acushnet in the United States District Court for the Southern District of Florida, alleging, *inter alia,* unfair competition. Shortly thereafter, Acushnet filed suit in the United States District Court for the Central District of California, alleging that Nitro infringed a number of Acushnet's patents and violated federal and state trademark laws. Nitro amended its complaint in the Florida case to seek a declaratory judgment that it did not infringe Acushnet's patents. The California action was subsequently transferred to Florida, and the actions were consolidated.

[5] On April 23, 2002, Acushnet moved for a preliminary injunction on its trademark and patent claims. As to the trademark claims, Acushnet concedes that it has no trademark claim with respect to "recycled" balls and does not object to those sales. As to the "refurbished" balls, however, Acushnet asserts that "Nitro's refurbishing process produces a golf ball that bears no resemblance to a genuine Acushnet product in performance, quality or appearance" and that "Nitro's refurbishing process so alters the basic composition of Acushnet's golf balls that 'it would be a misnomer to call the article by its original name.'" Following oral argument, the district court on August 9, 2002, issued its *Order,* concluding that Acushnet had failed to show a likelihood of success on the merits and denying preliminary injunctive relief on both the trademark and the patent law claims.

[6] Before this court, Acushnet seeks review of the denial of its motion for preliminary injunction only as to its trademark infringement and dilution claims. We have jurisdiction pursuant to 28 U.S.C. §§ 1292(c)(1) and 1295(a)(1).

DISCUSSION

Standard of Review

[7] This court generally reviews procedural matters under the law of the regional circuit in which the district court sits. *See Payless Shoesource, Inc. v. Reebok Int'l Ltd.,* 998 F.2d 985, 987 (Fed.Cir. 1993). Additionally, we defer to the law of the regional circuit when addressing substantive legal issues over which we do not have exclusive subject matter jurisdiction. *See id.* In this case, we defer to the law of the Eleventh Circuit in reviewing the district court's denial of Acushnet's motion for preliminary injunctive relief from the alleged trademark infringement and dilution.

[8] The Eleventh Circuit reviews a district court's grant or denial of a preliminary injunction for abuse of discretion. *Davidoff & CIE, SA v. PLD Int'l Corp.,* 263 F.3d 1297, 1300 (11th Cir. 2001); *McDonald's Corp. v. Robertson,* 147 F.3d 1301, 1306 (11th Cir. 1998). Under the abuse of discretion

standard, a reviewing court "must affirm unless [it] at least determine[s] that the district court has made a 'clear error of judgment,' or has applied an incorrect legal standard." *CBS Broadcasting, Inc. v. EchoStar Commun. Corp.,* 265 F.3d 1193, 1200 (11th Cir. 2001) (citations omitted). A party seeking a preliminary injunction for trademark infringement must establish four elements: (1) that there is a substantial likelihood of success on the merits; (2) that it would be irreparably harmed if injunctive relief were denied; (3) that the threatened injury to the trademark owner outweighs whatever damage the injunction may cause to the alleged infringer; and (4) that the injunction, if issued, would not be adverse to the public interest. *Id.* It is well established in the Eleventh Circuit that "[a] preliminary injunction is an extraordinary and drastic remedy not to be granted unless the movant clearly established the 'burden of persuasion' as to all four elements." *Davidoff,* 263 F.3d at 1300 (quoting *Siegel v. LePore,* 234 F.3d 1163, 1176 (11th Cir. 2000) (en banc)).

[9] To succeed on the merits of a trademark infringement claim, a plaintiff must show that the defendant used the mark in commerce without its consent and "that the unauthorized use was likely to deceive, cause confusion, or result in mistake." *McDonald's Corp.,* 147 F.3d at 1307. The determination generally boils down to the existence of "likelihood of confusion." *AmBrit, Inc. v. Kraft, Inc.,* 812 F.2d 1531, 1538 (11th Cir. 1986).

ANALYSIS

I. Acushnet's Contentions

[10] Acushnet argues that the district court abused its discretion in denying its motion for preliminary injunction on the pleaded trademark infringement issues by applying an incorrect legal standard, by erroneously relying on a non-precedential consent judgment between Acushnet and an unrelated third party, and by making erroneous findings of fact and applications of law to fact, in concluding that Acushnet failed to show a likelihood of success on the merits of its trademark infringement and dilution claims. Acushnet requests that this court reverse the judgment of the district court, find that a likelihood of success on the merits has been shown, and remand with directions to enter the sought preliminary injunction or for further proceedings consistent with our opinion. We address each of Acushnet's arguments in turn.

II. Trademark Infringement

A. The Applicable Standard

[11] Acushnet first argues that the district court failed to apply the correct legal standard to the trademark infringement claim. Acushnet asserts that the district court misapplied *Champion Spark Plug Co. v. Sanders,* 331 U.S. 125 (1947), and Eleventh Circuit law by failing to extend the "material difference" test applied in the context of altered new goods in *Davidoff,* 263 F.3d at 1302, to the used and refurbished goods involved in the present case. Acushnet also contends that the district court's reliance on *Champion* was misplaced because the refurbished goods in this case differed from the original goods not by the ordinary wear and tear expected in used products but by the refurbishing actions taken by Nitro. Acushnet argues that the "undisputed evidence" presented, when analyzed under the correct legal standard, would have established the requisite likelihood of success on the merits to warrant a preliminary injunction, and that denial of the requested preliminary injunction was an abuse of discretion. We disagree and find no abuse of discretion.

[12] To succeed in its request for a preliminary injunction on its trademark infringement claim, Acushnet must show, *inter alia,* a likelihood of success on the merits. This means that it must show a likelihood of success on its claim that the sale by Nitro of its refurbished golf balls bearing re-applied Acushnet trademarks is likely to cause confusion. In considering this issue, the district court looked to *Champion*—clear precedent in the used goods context—and concluded, on the record presented at this preliminary stage, that the differences between Acushnet's new golf balls and Nitro's refurbished golf balls were not so great as to be a misnomer and that it was not an act of infringement, warranting

preliminary injunctive relief, for Nitro to re-apply Acushnet's trademarks to the Acushnet balls refurbished by Nitro and to re-sell those balls in packaging identifying them as used or refurbished.

[13] The Eleventh Circuit looks to the following factors in assessing a likelihood of confusion in trademark cases:

1. Type of mark

2. Similarity of mark

3. Similarity of the products the marks represent

4. Similarity of the parties' retail outlets (trade channels) and customers

5. Similarity of advertising media

6. Defendant's intent

7. Actual confusion

Frehling Enters., Inc. v. Int'l Select Group, Inc., 192 F.3d 1330, 1335 (11th Cir. 1999); *cf. Lipscher v. LRP Publ'ns, Inc.,* 266 F.3d 1305, 1313–14 (11th Cir. 2001) (noting that not all *Frehling* factors are relevant in each case). In the present case, the dispute centers around the differences between new and refurbished Acushnet golf balls, thus implicating the "similarity of the products" factor. Specifically, the question presented is the propriety of the re-application by Nitro of the Acushnet trademark, without Acushnet's consent, to genuine Acushnet golf balls that have been used, subjected to Nitro's refurbishing process, and then re-sold by Nitro as refurbished balls.

[14] The district court assessed that question by applying the standards applied to used and refurbished goods by the Supreme Court in the *Champion* case. The district court cited *Davidoff* but did not directly apply the "material differences" test articulated in that case. Acushnet urges us to conclude that the district court erred in not recognizing from *Davidoff* that the "material differences" standard used to assess likelihood of confusion in the sale by unrelated parties of new, genuine trademarked goods would also be used in the Eleventh Circuit as the standard for assessing trademark infringement in the sale of used, genuine trademarked goods. Acushnet argues from this that had the district court applied the *Davidoff* test, it would have found the refurbished golf balls sold by Nitro and bearing the Nitro re-applied Acushnet trademarks to be "materially different" from the original trademarked goods and thus an infringement of Acushnet's trademarks, warranting preliminary injunctive relief. Nitro argues that *Davidoff* is simply inapplicable, and attempts to distinguish this case from *Davidoff,* based on the fact that *Davidoff* considered new goods and because *Davidoff* did not include disclaimers. Nitro also attempts to distinguish the cases cited by Acushnet in support of adoption of the *Davidoff* "material differences" standard; namely, *Rolex Watch USA, Inc. v. Michel,* 179 F.3d 704 (9th Cir. 1999), *Rolex Watch USA, Inc. v. Meece,* 158 F.3d 816 (5th Cir. 1998), and *Intel Corp. v. Terabyte International, Inc.,* 6 F.3d 614 (9th Cir. 1993).

[15] Under 15 U.S.C. §§ 1114(1) and 1125(a)(1), any person who uses the trademark of another, without consent, in a manner that is likely to cause confusion, mistake, or to deceive may be liable in a civil action for trademark infringement. *McDonald's Corp.,* 147 F.3d at 1307. In the *Champion* case, a seminal opinion on the use of trademarks on used goods, the accused infringer collected genuine used Champion spark plugs, repaired and reconditioned the spark plugs, painted the spark plugs for aesthetic reasons, and resold the spark plugs, each labeled "Renewed." 331 U.S. at 126. The issue before the Supreme Court was simply whether the lower courts erred in not requiring the accused infringer to remove Champion's trademark name from the repaired and reconditioned spark plugs. *Id.* at 128. The Supreme Court acknowledged that, in some cases, used and repaired goods can be sold under the trademark of the original manufacturer, without "deceiv[ing] the public," so long as the accused infringer had attempted to restore "so far as possible" the original condition of the goods and full disclosure is made about the true nature of the goods, for example, as "used" or "repaired." *Id.* at 129–30. In *Champion,* the Supreme Court stated that "[w]hen the mark is used in a way that does not

656

deceive the public we see no such sanctity in the word as to prevent its being used to tell the truth." *Id.* at 129.

[16] The Supreme Court recognized that this standard results in the second-hand dealer getting some advantage from the trademark; however, this windfall is "wholly permissible so long as the manufacturer is not identified with the inferior qualities of the product." *Id.* at 130 (citing *Prestonettes, Inc. v. Coty*, 264 U.S. 359 (1924)). This advantage is not inconsistent with the stated purposes of the Lanham Act. In passing the Lanham Act, Congress noted that the purpose was "to protect legitimate business and consumers of the country." 92 Cong. Rec. 7524 (1946). To fulfill this purpose, the Act "protect[s] the public so it may be confident that, in purchasing a product bearing a particular trademark which it favorably knows, it will get the product which it asks for and wants to get." S.Rep. No. 79–1333 at 3 (1946), *reprinted in* 1946 U.S.S.C.A.N. 1274. Further, the owner of the trademark must have the energy and effort he expended in building goodwill in his trademark protected from misappropriation. *Id.* However, so long as the customer is getting a product with the expected characteristics, and so long as the goodwill built up by the trademark owner is not eroded by being identified with inferior quality, the Lanham Act does not prevent the truthful use of trademarks, even if such use results in the enrichment of others.

[17] The *Champion* court, while concluding that the facts of that case did not establish a likelihood of confusion, cautioned that there are limits on the use of a trademark by another on a used or repaired item. The Supreme Court explained that "[c]ases may be imagined where the reconditioning or repair would be so extensive or so basic that it would be a misnomer to call the article by its original name, even though the words 'used' or 'repaired' were added." 331 U.S. at 129. In *Champion*, the repair was such that it "[did] not give [the product] a new design," and the accused infringers had sought to restore the product "so far as possible, [to its] original condition," *id.* Thus, no infringement was found.

[18] Similar to the admonition expressed by the Supreme Court in connection with the sale of refurbished goods in *Champion*, the Eleventh Circuit in *Davidoff* cautioned that there are limits to the permissible uses of a trademark by re-sellers even on new, genuine trademarked goods. In *Davidoff*, the Eleventh Circuit found infringement in the use of a trademark by a party unrelated to the trademark owner for new, genuine trademarked goods sold in packaging that had been altered. In that case, accused infringer PLD purchased genuine bottles of Davidoff's perfumes and, prior to re-sale, etched and altered the bottles to remove batch code information from the bottoms of the bottles. Davidoff sought to end this practice, arguing that the etching of the bottles altered the product in a way that caused consumer confusion. The Eleventh Circuit agreed, holding that the removal of the batch code information was a material alteration that would affect a consumer's decision whether to purchase the product in question.

[19] The fundamental question examined in *Davidoff* was the same question considered in *Champion*—likelihood of confusion—but presented in the context of re-sales of new goods. The context is important because consumers of new goods have different expectations than consumers of used goods. For new goods, any variation of the product from a new condition—even as relatively modest as the obliteration of a name or batch number from the bottom of a container—may signal imitation, counterfeiting, falsity or some other irregularity affecting a customer's decision whether to purchase the product. *See, e.g., Societe Des Produits Nestle S.A. v. Casa Helvetia, Inc.*, 982 F.2d 633, 644 (1st Cir. 1992) (finding such differences as configuration, i.e., the number of different shapes of chocolates, and packaging, i.e., whether the packaging is shiny or matte and the colors of the packaging, to be material). For new goods, consumers are likely to be confused by the presence of such "material differences." *Davidoff*, 263 F.3d at 1302.

[20] For used or refurbished goods, customers have a different expectation. They do not expect the product to be in the same condition as a new product. *Champion*, 331 U.S. at 129. There is an understanding on the part of consumers of used or refurbished products that such products will be degraded or will show signs of wear and tear and will not measure up to or perform at the same level

657

as if new. *Id.* at 129–30. For used or refurbished products, consumers are not likely to be confused by—and indeed expect—differences in the goods compared to new, unused goods. *Id.* Thus, the tests applied to assess likelihood of confusion by courts will not necessarily be the same when determining trademark infringement in the resale of altered new goods and when considering trademark infringement in the resale of used and refurbished goods.

[21] Both *Champion* and *Davidoff* sought to define the boundaries of when the use of a trademark on genuine trademarked goods is no longer permitted. The tests applied in both cases focus on the similarities and differences between the accused infringing goods and the genuine trademarked goods and assess the likelihood of confusion resulting from contemporaneous sales of those goods.

[22] The *Davidoff* test looks to the effect on a consumer's decision to purchase of differences in an altered or modified new product from the original. It is a reasonable and workable test of the likelihood of confusion and the loss of goodwill represented by the trademark applied to the product, given consumer expectations as to the nature and quality of new products as offered for sale. The test has been adopted and applied to new, genuine trademarked goods in the First, Second, Third, Fifth, and Ninth Circuits. *See, e.g., Nestle,* 982 F.2d at 644 (1st Cir.) (finding material differences based on quality control, composition, configuration, packaging, and price); *Original Appalachian Artworks, Inc. v. Granada Elecs., Inc.,* 816 F.2d 68, 73 (2d Cir. 1987) (finding material differences where an imported doll comes with foreign language "adoption papers" and is not permitted to be "adopted" domestically); *Iberia Foods Corp. v. Romeo,* 150 F.3d 298, 302 (3d Cir. 1998) (finding material differences where quality control measures differ); *Martin's Herend Imports Inc. v. Diamond & Gem Trading USA, Co.,* 112 F.3d 1296, 1302 (5th Cir. 1997) (finding material differences when the trademark holder had chosen to sell only selected pieces in the United States and the accused infringer was selling other, genuine pieces in the United States); *Enesco Corp. v. Price/Costco Inc.,* 146 F.3d 1083, 1087 (9th Cir. 1998) (finding material differences where quality control measures differ).

[23] The *Champion* Court recognizes that consumers do not expect used or refurbished goods to be the same as new goods and that for such goods, "material differences" do not necessarily measure consumer confusion. According to *Champion,* what is more telling on the question of likelihood of confusion in the context of used goods is whether the used or refurbished goods are so different from the original that it would be a misnomer for them to be designated by the original trademark. We see no basis to conclude that the district court's reliance on *Champion* was improper.

[24] The district court in this case properly assessed likelihood of confusion in concluding: (1) that on the evidence before it, the differences in the goods were nothing more than what would be expected for used golf balls; (2) that it was therefore not a misnomer to apply the Acushnet mark to the used Acushnet balls; and (3) that Acushnet had not established a likelihood of success on the merits of its trademark "likelihood of confusion" case. This is all that was required, and there is no basis to conclude that the district court applied the wrong test or otherwise abused its discretion. This court need not predict whether the Eleventh Circuit would apply *Davidoff* to used goods. It would only be necessary to make such a prediction if application of the "material differences" test must be satisfied in all cases involving genuine trademarked goods. But *Davidoff* does not go that far and cannot be read to supplant the statutory "likelihood of confusion" test with a "material differences" test applicable to all cases involving the resale of genuine trademarked goods, both new and used.

[25] Alternatively, Acushnet argues that the district court's reliance on *Champion* is misplaced.[1] Acushnet attempts to distinguish *Champion,* arguing first that Nitro does not restore "so far as

---

[1] The dissent also attempts to distinguish *Champion* based on the notion of simply reselling versus reapplication of trademarks. *See* Dissent, *infra* at 1369 (stating that the *Champion* Court "ratified the resale of used spark plugs still bearing the Champion name"). However, this distinction overlooks the

possible" the used balls to their original condition, but rather masks the balls' condition, and second, that by masking rather than restoring, Nitro makes it more likely that customers will associate inferior performance with Acushnet. Acushnet argues that, although there was repainting of the spark plugs in *Champion*, such painting was merely cosmetic. Acushnet contends that the district court failed to recognize that Nitro's process of stripping and repainting was more than cosmetic and changed the fundamental attributes of the reprocessed balls. Moreover, Acushnet argues that it is Nitro's refurbishing process, not normal wear and tear, that degraded the quality of Nitro's used golf balls. Acushnet thus asserts that *Champion* is distinguishable on its facts and should not apply. We disagree with Acushnet's distinctions.

[26] First, while it is true that the spark plugs were repainted in *Champion*, the reconditioning also involved removing burned and pitted portions of the center electrodes, welding new metal to the side electrodes, wearing away the plug's porcelain insulators through sandblasting, and then cleaning and painting the spark plug. *Champion Spark Plug Co. v. Sanders*, 156 F.2d 488, 489 (2d Cir. 1946). The refurbishing process in *Champion*, then, was not merely cosmetic, and cannot be distinguished from the present case on that basis. Second, *Champion* also held that the source of any inferiority, whether the reconditioning or the refurbishing, is irrelevant, stating that inferiority is immaterial as long as the original manufacturer "is not identified with the inferior qualities of the product *resulting from wear and tear or the reconditioning*." *Champion*, 331 U.S. at 130 (emphasis added). In the *Champion* case, the district court noted that there was no proof whether the inferior qualities stemmed from either "wear and tear prior to the discarding of the plug by the original user, or to the process of repair as conducted by the defendants." *Champion Spark Plug Co. v. Sanders*, 61 F.Supp. 247, 248–49 (E.D.N.Y.1945). Acushnet's distinction on this point is similarly untenable.

[27] In this case, the district court carefully considered the extent of the alterations made by Nitro. *See Order* at 8–9 (citing *Rolex Watch USA, Inc. v. Michel*, 179 F.3d 704) ("[w]hether the modifications made to the product resulted in a new product"); *Intel*, 6 F.3d at 619. The district court also looked to a number of factors, outlined by the Ninth Circuit, to determine if the alterations resulted in a new product. *Order* at 9 ("These factors 'include the nature and extent of the alterations, the nature of the device and how it is designed ..., whether a market has developed for service or spare parts ... and, most importantly, whether end users of the product are likely to be misled as to the party responsible for the composition of the product.' *Karl Storz Endoscopy–America, Inc. v. Surgical Technologies, Inc.*, 285 F.3d 848, 856–57 (9th Cir. 2002)." (alterations in original)). The district court also considered: (a) evidence proffered by Nitro that the performance differences were not as extensive as claimed by Acushnet; (b) evidence of the use of disclaimers; and (c) evidence from customers of both Acushnet and Nitro on the question of confusion. *Order* at 9–12. On this record, the district court concluded that "Acushnet has not presented sufficient evidence to support its claim that the golf balls are so extensively repaired that they cannot be truly labeled with the Titleist marks." *Id.* at 9–10.

[28] Because the district court properly considered the *Frehling* factors; fully and carefully assessed the differences between Acushnet's new golf balls and Nitro's refurbished golf balls in determining likelihood of confusion; and correctly looked to *Champion* for the applicable legal standard, we find no abuse of discretion in the district court's denial of Acushnet's requested preliminary injunction based on its trademark infringement claim.

...

III. Dilution

---

fact that the refurbisher in Champion, at the very least, applied or reapplied Champion's trademark to its cartons and packaging. *Champion*, 331 U.S. at 126.

[The Court affirmed the district court's finding of no dilution].

CONCLUSION

[29] The district court did not abuse its discretion, commit an error of law, or seriously misjudge the evidence in concluding that Acushnet failed to show a reasonable likelihood of success on the merits of its trademark and dilution claims and in denying Acushnet's motion for a preliminary injunction based thereon. We therefore affirm.

AFFIRMED.

PAULINE NEWMAN, Circuit Judge, dissenting.

[1] I can think of nothing more destructive of the value of a famous trademark than for the law to permit unauthorized persons to re-affix the mark to a product that is so badly cut, scarred, dented, discolored, and bruised that its defects have to be concealed before it can be resold as "used"—and then, with the scars hidden and the surface repainted to look new, the product is resold with the benefit of the re-affixed trademark and its reputation for quality and performance. The court today holds that the trademark owner cannot object to this unauthorized, uncontrolled affixation of its famous Titleist7 mark, provided that the package is labeled "used/refurbished" and a disclaimer is presented.

[2] Neither trademark law nor any other law removes from the trademark owner control of the quality of the goods and use of the mark. To the contrary, the law requires the holder of the trademark to control both the use of the mark and the quality of the goods to which it is affixed, on pain of losing the mark as a trademark. The consequence of this law is that, whether on grounds of infringement, dilution, or tarnishment, Acushnet is likely to succeed on the merits of its case. From the denial of the requested preliminary injunction I must, respectfully, dissent.

DISCUSSION

[3] This case does not relate to the resale of used golf balls, washed and buffed and repackaged, bearing the original trademark. Acushnet is not objecting to that part of Nitro's activities. However, when the balls are so badly scarred or cut that they must be repainted and the damage concealed, the repainting also obscuring the original trademark, surely the trademark owner has the right to prevent re-application of its trademark (in identical script) to damaged goods covered with shiny new paint, goods of unsupervised quality but bearing the famous original trademark.

[4] Trademark law requires that the trademark owner police the quality of the goods to which the mark is applied, on pain of losing the mark entirely. Professor McCarthy explains:

> Sometimes a mark becomes abandoned to generic usage as a result of the trademark owner's failure to police the mark, so that widespread usage by competitors leads to a generic usage among the relevant public, who see many sellers using the same word or designation.

J. Thomas McCarthy et al., 2 *McCarthy on Trademarks and Unfair Competition* § 17:8, at 17–10 (4th ed., Rel.# 21, 3/2002). Yet here the trademark applier is unlicensed, the quality out of the control of the owner of the mark, and the flaws concealed from the consumer.

[5] These are fundamental principles of trademark law. The Federal Circuit, applying this law, has itself imposed loss of trademark rights based on inadequate control of use of a mark by others. *See BellSouth Corp. v. DataNational Corp.*, 60 F.3d 1565, 35 USPQ2d 1554 (Fed.Cir. 1995) (the "Walking Fingers" mark became generic because AT & T allowed others to use it). Although the law permits resale of used and refurbished products, it does not require the owner of the trademark to permit its use on inferior goods with concealed damage, simply by marking the goods as "used/refurbished." The presence of a famous trademark on such goods is not an indication of origin and quality, but a trap for the consumer.

660

[6] A trademark serves as an assurance of quality, consistency, and reliability, by indicating the source and control of the product bearing the mark:

> However, the quality function [of a trademark] does not replace the source function: it stands alongside it. In fact, one could accurately state that the quality theory is merely a facet of the older source theory. That is, the source theory has been broadened to include not only manufacturing source but also the source of standards of quality of goods bearing the mark: "[A] mark primarily functions to indicate a single quality control source of the goods or services." Under both the source and quality rationales, unity of source of manufacture or control appears essential.

1 *McCarthy, supra,* § 3:10, at 3–20. The law both permits and requires control by the trademark owner, even when the mark is licensed:

> Licensing a mark without adequate control over the quality of goods or services sold under the mark by the licensee may cause the mark to lose its significance as a symbol of equal quality-hence, abandonment.

Id., § 17:6, at 17–9.

[7] I repeat, the question is not whether Nitro can resell used golf balls, perhaps washed and buffed; the question is whether the owner of the Titleist7 and other famous trademarks can prevent reapplication of these trademarks to goods that have been materially changed. In explaining Nitro's operations, its President stated:

> The balls that are in sufficiently good condition to resell without refurbishing are then identified. Those golf balls are re-packaged and resold as used golf balls, i.e., "recycled" golf balls.

Acushnet does not object to Nitro's resale of these balls with the original trademarks. This case is about the next group, as Nitro's president further explained:

> The remaining balls, which suffer from one or more of the following detriments, e.g., scuff marks, cart path marks, tree marks, lack of clear coat, discoloration, etc., are sent to the final quality control sort.... The balls are refurbished by removing the base paint coat and the clear coat from the balls, which also has the effect of removing the marking from the balls....

Nitro then reapplies the base coat paint (on those balls that originally had a base coat). The balls are then re-stamped with the appropriate markings.... Nitro re-stamps the precise model type only for those models that its consumers have expressed a demand, e.g., Titleist Pro V1's.... Following the re-stamping process, Nitro re-applies the clear coat.

[8] The district court found Nitro's process not to be "intrusive," in that it "does not remove the dimples on the balls, nor does it take off the cover of the ball." The issue, however, is Nitro's right to re-apply the Titleist7 and Pro V–17 trademarks to the repainted balls.

[9] When goods have lost their identity and their quality, the trademark owner can not be forced to permit re-application of the original trademark to the doctored product. That is a reproach to the most fundamental principles of trademark law. *See Bulova Watch Co. v. Allerton Co.,* 328 F.2d 20, 24 (7th Cir. 1964) ("substitution of a different crown and case by defendants results in a different product," enjoining use of the trademark "Bulova" on the re-cased watches).

[10] There was evidence that these damaged balls did not have the characteristics of the original. Although Nitro argues that the difference is not great, that is not the issue. Trademarks are an indication of quality, on which the consumer can rely. The consumer is no less deceived if he does not know that the product is inferior, or if the extent of the inferiority is not great. The trademark owner is entitled, and required, to control the quality of the product:

One of the most valuable and important protections afforded by the Lanham Act is the right to control the quality of the goods manufactured and sold under the holder's trademark.... For this purpose the actual quality of the goods is irrelevant: it is the control of quality that a trademark holder is entitled to maintain.

El Greco Leather Products Co. v. Shoe World, Inc., 806 F.2d 392, 395 (2nd Cir. 1986).

[11] Even if the consumer has digested the notice on the Nitro package, the severity of the concealed defects are not known to the consumer, who will not know whether the refurbished ball has been stripped and painted, whether the balance is distorted, whether the all-important dimples are encumbered with fresh paint. The consumer will not know that the Titleist7 mark was re-applied to a ball that was so badly damaged that the original marking was lost.

[12] Although there was discussion at trial of the issues of section 1114 and section 1125 of the Trademark Act, there is prima facie infringement when a trademark is applied by unauthorized persons to an unlicensed product that has not met the quality standards of the trademark under the control of the owner of the mark. The law protects not only the trademark owner but also the consumer, for not only does an inferior product injure the Titleist7 and Pro V–1 7 reputation, but the consumer is deprived of the quality that the law demands of the trademark owner. Acushnet argues, with cogency, that inferior performance is more likely to be attributed to the Titleist7 source than to the refurbisher, for the degree of "refurbishment" is not specified, and the balls as repainted are clean and conceal their defects. This is not the same situation as in *Champion Spark Plug v. Sanders*, 331 U.S. 125 (1947), where the Court ratified the resale of used spark plugs still bearing the Champion name. The Court recognized that the trademark had been infringed, and that the issue was adequacy of the notice, considering "the equities of the case." In *Champion* there was no issue of concealed defects; the Court permitted retention of the identity of the original plugs "so long as the manufacturer is not identified with the inferior qualities of the product resulting from wear and tear or the reconditioning by the dealer." *Id.* at 130.

[13] My colleagues err in their ruling that the notice that the balls are used/refurbished "protects the public so it may be confident that, in purchasing a product bearing a particular trademark which it favorably knows, it will get the product which it asks for and wants to get." Maj. op. at 9. When the defects are concealed, that is not "full disclosure about the true nature" of the golf balls as the panel majority holds. Concealment is the antithesis of full disclosure. In purchasing a used golf ball that has been repainted, the consumer is not provided with knowledge of concealed damage as well as surface changes. When the consumer purchases a used golf ball bearing the Titleist7 mark, the purchaser does not know if this is an almost-new golf ball that went from tee to lake on the first stroke, or a ball so badly cut that it was discarded. This is not the "full disclosure" accommodated by *Champion*. The owner of the Titleist7 mark is surely entitled to prevent re-application of the mark to golf balls whose repainting covers the original mark.[1] The Court in *Champion* held that "the nature of the article involved and the characteristics of the merchandising methods used to sell it" are important considerations in devising an appropriate notice and disclaimer. 331 U.S. at 130–31. The nature of the refurbishment of a used spark plug is visible; the nature of the damage to a repainted golf ball is invisible, and any performance-deteriorating defects are permanently removed from view.

[14] In an ever more complex commercial economy, it is increasingly important to preserve standards of quality and confidence. Trademark law carries this burden. The record states that the Titleist7 balls are the premium balls in this market, and are recognized by the golfing public as of high and consistent quality and dependability. The producer of these products is entitled by law to protect

---

[1] There was also evidence that Nitro applied the Titleist7 mark to balls of other makers, when the original mark was obscured by repainting.

the reputation and the value of its marks. Consumer expectations of quality should not be thwarted by an inappropriate balance of interests.

[15] A trademark owner has the absolute right to prevent others from affixing the mark with neither license nor quality control by the trademark owner. This is not a case of likelihood of confusion or dilution through the use of similar marks; it is a case of unauthorized use of an original mark on goods that have been invisibly altered, such that the use approaches the counterfeit. The re-application of the obliterated trademark is not simply information about the original source of used golf balls; it is an unauthorized exploitation of the mark, identifying the original manufacturer with the disguised product. The role of the trademark is its assurance of quality, and its value depends on the consistent quality of the product that bears the mark. Again quoting Professor McCarthy:

> [T]he chief function of a trademark is a kind of 'warranty' to purchasers that they will receive, when they purchase goods bearing the mark, goods of the same character and source, anonymous as it may be, as other goods previously purchased bearing the mark that have already given the purchaser satisfaction.

1 *McCarthy, supra,* § 3:10, at 3–20, 3–21 (quotation marks and citations omitted).

[16] The trademark owner is required by law to police and preserve that quality; it cannot be deprived of that right and obligation. From the panel majority's contrary ruling and denial of the requested injunction I must, respectfully, dissent.

IV. False Advertising

A. False Advertising Under the Lanham Act

We turn now to federal false advertising law under Lanham Act § 43(a)(1)(B), 15 U.S.C. § 1125(a)(1)(B). Note from the very beginning that false advertising law covers much more than just § 43(a)(1)(B). Plaintiffs may seek redress from the Federal Trade Commission under the FTC Act, 15 U.S.C. §§ 41-58, from the "little" or "baby" FTC Acts of the states, from the common law, and from alternative forms of dispute resolution such as the National Advertising Division. However, we cover here only false advertising law under the Lanham Act. (For a comprehensive treatment of false advertising, see REBECCA TUSHNET & ERIC GOLDMAN, ADVERTISING & MARKETING LAW: CASES AND MATERIALS).

As originally drafted, § 43(a) covered only an advertiser's "false description or representation" about itself; it did not cover "commercial disparagement," i.e., the advertiser's false representations about someone else. The Trademark Law Revision Act of 1988 significantly expanded the scope of § 43(a) and made clear its application to a defendant's false representations about itself and others. Here is § 43(a)(1)(B) in its current form:

> (1) Any person who, on or in connection with any goods or services, or any container for goods, uses in commerce any word, term, name, symbol, or device, or any combination thereof, or any false designation of origin, false or misleading description of fact, or false or misleading representation of fact, which--
>
> . . . .
>
> (B) in commercial advertising or promotion, misrepresents the nature, characteristics, qualities, or geographic origin of his or her or another person's goods, services, or commercial activities,
>
> shall be liable in a civil action by any person who believes that he or she is or is likely to be damaged by such act.

15 U.S.C. § 1125(a)(1)(B).

In what follows, we will cover the various ways in which a statement may trigger liability under § 43(a)(1)(B):

- First (Part IV.A.1), a statement may be *literally false*, as in *S.C. Johnson & Son, Inc. v Clorox Co.*, 241 F.3d 232 (2d Cir. 2001), where the defendant's television commercial and print advertisements falsely depicted the rate of leakage of the plaintiff's resealable plastic bags.

- Second (Part IV.A.2), a statement may be *literally false by necessary implication*, as in *Time Warner Cable, Inc. v. DIRECTV, Inc.*, 497 F.3d 144 (2d Cir. 2007), where one of the defendant's television commercials made the false-by-necessary-implication claim that its transmitted picture quality was superior to the plaintiff's.

- Third (Part IV.A.3), a statement may be merely *misleading*, i.e., impliedly false, which is discussed in *Pizza Hut, Inc. v. Papa John's Intern., Inc.*, 227 F.3d 489 (5th Cir. 2000), in connection with the defendant's slogan "Better Ingredients. Better Pizza." Finally in Part IV.A.4, we will turn to the issue of substantiation, particularly in connection with advertisements that claim that "tests prove" or "studies show" some factual proposition.

The Basic Doctrine. Before we proceed, it may be helpful to set forth in somewhat mechanical fashion the basic blackletter doctrine that the following opinions will develop (and complicate).

Courts enumerate the elements of a false advertising cause of action under Lanham Act § 43(a)(1)(b), 15 U.S.C. § 1125(a)(1)(b), in a variety of ways, but the following is a good example of the five elements that the plaintiff must prove to prevail:

> A prima facie case of false advertising under section 43(a) requires the plaintiff to establish:

(1) A false or misleading statement of fact about a product;

(2) Such statement either deceived, or had the capacity to deceive a substantial segment of potential consumers;

(3) The deception is material, in that it is likely to influence the consumer's purchasing decision;

(4) The product is in interstate commerce; and

(5) The plaintiff has been or is likely to be injured as a result of the statement at issue.

Pizza Hut, Inc. v. Papa John's Int'l, 227 F.3d 489, 495 (5th Cir. 2000).

As the first element suggests, there are two modes of false advertising under Lanham Act § 43(a)(1)(b): (1) advertising that is literally false, and (2) advertising that is misleading. This dichotomy makes good sense in light of the statutory reference to any "*false or misleading* description of fact, or *false or misleading* representation of fact." Id. (emphasis added). This dichotomy is very important because if a court finds an advertisement to be literally false under the first element, the court need not have recourse to extrinsic evidence (e.g., survey evidence) to determine whether the advertisement deceives the public under the second element. The court may presume deception. *See Schering-Plough Healthcare Products, Inc. v. Schwarz Pharma, Inc.*, 586 F.3d 500, 512 (7th Cir. 2009) ("What the cases mean when they say that proof of literal falsity allows the plaintiff to dispense with evidence that anyone was misled or likely to be misled is that the seller who places an indisputably false statement in his advertising or labeling probably did so for a malign purpose, namely to sell his product by lies, and if the statement is false probably at least some people were misled, and since it was a lie why waste time on costly consumer surveys?"). By contrast, if a court finds an advertisement to be merely misleading, then it will require extrinsic evidence, typically in the form of survey evidence, to determine whether the advertisement deceives the public. Furthermore, if a court finds an advertisement to be literally false under the first element, the court will often also presume materiality under the third element and harm to the plaintiff under the fifth element.

In *Time Warner Cable, Inc. v. DIRECTV, Inc.* 497 F.3d 144 (2d Cir. 2007), excerpted below, the Second Circuit complicated the basic dichotomy between advertising that is literally false and advertising that is merely misleading by establishing that advertising that is "literally false by necessary implication" qualifies as literally false advertising—and thus triggers all the relevant presumptions under the other elements of a false advertising claim. What is the difference between advertising that is literally false by necessary implication and advertising that is merely misleading? As the *DIRECTTV* court seeks to explain, advertising that is literally false by necessary implication conveys one unambiguous false message, even if it does so implicitly. By contrast, advertising that is merely misleading may convey several messages, one of which may be false. *Id.* at 158 (paragraph 28 in the excerpted *DIRECTTV* opinion below). A court will require survey evidence to determine if consumers perceive that one false message. As you will see, the distinction between advertising that is literally false by necessary implication and advertising that is misleading, while relatively straightforward in theory, is far more subtle in practice. For more on this distinction, see 2 GILSON ON TRADEMARKS § 7.02 (2019).

Standing. Consumers do not have standing to bring suit under § 43(a)(1)(B). In *Lexmark International, Inc. v. Static Components, Inc.*, 134 S. Ct. 1377 (2014), the Supreme Court held that plaintiffs under § 43(a)(1)(B) have standing if (1) their interests fall within the "zone of interests" protected by § 43(a)(1)(B), which consists of "protecting persons engaged in commerce within the control of Congress", *id.* at 1389 (brackets removed), and (2) their injuries are proximately caused by violations of the statute. Because consumers are not engaged in commerce, they are unable to bring suit under § 43(a)(1)(B). *See* McCARTHY § 27.30.

1. Literal Falsity

S.C. Johnson & Son, Inc. v Clorox Co.
241 F.3d 232 (2d Cir. 2001)

HALL, District Judge:

[1] This case involves a Lanham Act challenge to the truthfulness of a television commercial and print advertisement depicting the plight of an animated goldfish in a Ziploc Slide–Loc bag that is being held upside down and is leaking water. Plaintiff-appellee S.C. Johnson & Son manufactures the Ziploc bags targeted by the advertisements. In an Order dated April 6, 2000, the United States District Court for the Southern District of New York (Griesa, J.) permanently enjoined the defendant-appellant, The Clorox Company, manufacturer of Ziploc's rival Glad–Lock resealable storage bags, from using these advertisements. *See S.C. Johnson & Son v. The Clorox Co.*, No. 99 Civ. 11079 (TPG), 2000 WL 423534, 2000 U.S. Dist. LEXIS 4977 (S.D.N.Y. Apr. 19, 2000) ("*S.C. Johnson II*"). We conclude that the district court did not abuse its discretion in entering this injunction and accordingly affirm.

BACKGROUND

[2] In August 1999, Clorox introduced a 15–second and a 30–second television commercial ("Goldfish I"), each depicting an S.C. Johnson Ziploc Slide–Loc resealable storage bag side-by-side with a Clorox Glad–Lock bag. The bags are identified in the commercials by brand name. Both commercials show an animated, talking goldfish in water inside each of the bags. In the commercials, the bags are turned upside-down, and the Slide–Loc bag leaks rapidly while the Glad–Lock bag does not leak at all. In both the 15– and 30–second Goldfish I commercials, the Slide–Loc goldfish says, in clear distress, "My Ziploc Slider is dripping. Wait a minute!," while the Slide Loc bag is shown leaking at a rate of approximately one drop per one to two seconds. In the 30–second Goldfish I commercial only, the

666

Slide–Loc bag is shown leaking while the Slide–Loc goldfish says, "Excuse me, a little help here," and then, "Oh, dripping, dripping." At the end of both commercials, the Slide Loc goldfish exclaims, "Can I borrow a cup of water!!!"

[3] On November 4, 1999, S.C. Johnson brought an action against Clorox under section 43(a) of the Lanham Act, 15 U.S.C. § 1125(a), for false advertising in the Goldfish I commercials. After S.C. Johnson moved for a preliminary injunction, the district court converted the evidentiary hearing on the motion to a trial on the merits under Fed.R.Civ.P. 65(a)(2).

[4] Dr. Phillip DeLassus, an outside expert retained by S.C. Johnson, conducted "torture testing," in which Slide–Loc bags were filled with water, rotated for 10 seconds, and held upside-down for an additional 20 seconds. He testified about the results of the tests he performed, emphasizing that 37 percent of all Slide–Loc bags tested did not leak at all. Of the remaining 63 percent that did leak, only a small percentage leaked at the rate depicted in the Goldfish I television commercials. The vast majority leaked at a rate between two and twenty times slower than that depicted in the Goldfish I commercials.

[5] On January 7, 2000, the district court entered findings of fact and conclusions of law on the record in support of an Order permanently enjoining Clorox from disseminating the Goldfish I television commercials. Specifically, the district court found that S.C. Johnson had shown by a preponderance of the evidence that the Goldfish I commercials are "literally false in respect to its depiction of the flow of water out of the Slide–Loc bag." *S.C. Johnson & Son, Inc. v. Clorox Co.*, No. 99 Civ. 11079 (TPG), 2000 WL 122209, at *1, 2000 U.S. Dist. LEXIS 3621, at *1–*2 (S.D.N.Y. Feb. 1, 2000) ("*S.C. Johnson I*").

[6] The court found that "the commercial impermissibly exaggerates the facts in respect to the flow of water or the leaking of water out of a Slide–Loc bag." *Id.,* at *1. The court further found that:

> [t]he commercial shows drops of water coming out of the bag at what appears to be a rapid rate. In fact, the rate is about one fairly large drop per second. Moreover, there is a depiction of the water level in the bag undergoing a substantial and rapid decline. Finally, there is an image of bubbles going through the water.

Id. at *1, 2000 U.S. Dist. LEXIS 3621, at *2–*3. The district court found that "the overall depiction in the commercial itself is of a rapid and substantial leakage and flow of water out of the Slide–Loc bag." *Id.* at *1, 2000 U.S. Dist. LEXIS 3621, at *3. The court noted that "[t]his is rendered even more graphic by the fact that there is a goldfish depicted in the bag which is shown to be in jeopardy because the water is running out at such a rate." *Id.*

[7] The district court found "that when these bags are subjected to the same kind of quality control test as used by Clorox for the Glad bags, there is some leakage in about two-thirds of the cases." *Id.* at *2, 2000 U.S. Dist. LEXIS 3621, at *4. However, the court found "that the great majority of those leaks are very small and at a very slow rate." *Id.* The court found that "[o]nly in about 10 percent of these bags is there leakage at the rate shown in the commercial, that is, one drop per second." *Id.* The district court further found that "[t]he problem with the commercial is that there is no depiction in the visual images to indicate anything else than the fact that the type of fairly rapid and substantial leakage shown in the commercial is simply characteristic of that kind of bag." *Id.*

[8] Accordingly, the court held that "the Clorox commercial in question misrepresents the Slide–Loc bag product," and that this "finding relates to the different sizes and types of the Slide–Loc bags because there is no attempt to limit the commercial to any particular category." *Id.* at *3, 2000 U.S. Dist. LEXIS 3621, at *7. The court entered an injunction, noting that S.C. Johnson had shown irreparable harm sufficient to support an injunction because, as the court found, the Goldfish I commercials are literally false. *Id.* The district court rejected S.C. Johnson's other theories of relief under section 43(a) of the Lanham Act, including a claim of implied falsity. *Id.* at *3, 2000 U.S. Dist. LEXIS 3621, at *6–*7. Clorox has not appealed this January 7 permanent injunction relating to the Goldfish I commercials.

[9] In February 2000, Clorox released a modified version of the Goldfish I television commercials as well as a related print advertisement ("Goldfish II"). In the 15 second Goldfish II television commercial, a Ziploc Slide–Loc bag and Glad–Lock bag are again shown side-by-side, filled with water and containing an animated, talking goldfish. The bags are then rotated, and a drop is shown forming and dropping in about a second from the Slide–Loc bag. During the approximately additional two seconds that it is shown, the Slide–Loc goldfish says, "My Ziploc slider is dripping. Wait a minute." The two bags are then off-screen for approximately eight seconds before the Slide–Loc bag is again shown, with a drop forming and falling in approximately one second. During this latter depiction of the Slide–Loc bag, the Slide–Loc goldfish says, "Hey, I'm gonna need a little help here." Both bags are identified by brand name, and the Glad–Lock bag does not leak at all. The second-to-last frame shows three puddles on an orange background that includes the phrase "Don't Get Mad."

[10] In the print advertisement, a large drop is shown forming and about to fall from an upside-down Slide–Loc bag in which a goldfish is partially out of the water. Bubbles are shown rising from the point of the leak in the Slide–Loc bag. Next to the Slide–Loc bag is a Glad–Lock bag that is not leaking and contains a goldfish that is completely submerged. Under the Slide–Loc bag appears: "Yikes! My Ziploc© Slide–Loc™ is dripping!" Under the Glad–Lock bag is printed: "My Glad is tight, tight, tight." On a third panel, three puddles and the words "Don't Get Mad" are depicted on a red background. In a fourth panel, the advertisement recites: "Only Glad has the Double–Lock™ green seal. That's why you'll be glad you got Glad. Especially if you're a goldfish."

[11] After these advertisements appeared, S.C. Johnson moved to enlarge the January 7 injunction to enjoin the airing and distribution of the Goldfish II advertisements. On April 6, 2000, after hearing oral argument, the district court entered another order on the record, setting forth further findings of fact and conclusions of law in support of an Order permanently enjoining the distribution of the Goldfish II television commercial and print advertisement. The district court explicitly noted that it was "in a position, in [its] view, to decide the case based on the existing evidence without further evidence." *S.C. Johnson II,* 2000 WL 423534, at *1, 2000 U.S. Dist. LEXIS 4977, at *1–*2.

[12] The court incorporated by reference its prior findings of fact from its January 7, 2000 Order, stating that it would "not attempt to repeat what was said in the earlier decision, although a great deal of it applies to the issue now presented to the court." *Id.* at *1, 2000 U.S. Dist. LEXIS 4977, at *2. The court then stated its finding that, "[f]ocusing now on the new television commercial, in my view it has the essential problems of the earlier 15 second commercial." *Id.* The court observed that the Goldfish II commercial "does not literally portray a rate of leakage which was portrayed in the earlier ad and which was the subject of certain of my findings in the earlier decision." *Id.* at *1, 2000 U.S. Dist. LEXIS 4977, at *3. Instead, the court noted,

> [t]here are two images shown of the slide-lock bag upside down with water coming out, two separate images. In each image a large drop immediately forms and the water drop falls. That is shown in the first image and then the commercial switches to some other subject and when the next image comes of the slide-lock bag there again is a large drop immediately forming and falling away.

Id. at *2, 2000 U.S. Dist. LEXIS 4977, at *4. The district court referenced its earlier finding that the Goldfish I commercials did not accurately depict either the rate or risk of leakage in Slide–Loc bags. *Id.* at *2, 2000 U.S. Dist. LEXIS 4977, at *4–*5. The court then found that:

> [E]ssentially the same problem that I commented upon in the earlier decision exists with this commercial, with the present commercial. There is nothing to indicate that anything goes on with the slide-lock bags except the leaking of large drops as shown in the only two depictions that are relevant. There is nothing indicated about slow rate or rapid rate. There is nothing shown except one image and that is an image of a big drop of water falling out of the bag.

There is nothing to indicate that this kind of leakage occurs in only some particular percentage of bags, and there is nothing to indicate the degree of risk of such leakage. There is only one image, and that is of a big drop falling out.

Id. at *2, 2000 U.S. Dist. LEXIS 4977, at *5.

[13] The court rejected Clorox's argument "that what is really shown [in the Goldfish II television commercial] is that the leakage occurs at a rather slow rate, perhaps about once every seven or eight seconds." *Id.* According to the court, Clorox "bases this argument on the fact that if you take the elapsed time between the leak or the drop in the first image and the drop in the second image, this amount of time elapses." *Id.* at *2, 2000 U.S. Dist. LEXIS 4977, at *5–*6. The district court found, however, that "[t]here is nothing visually or in words to indicate that what is being depicted is some kind of a continuum of the condition of the bag from one image to the other." *Id.* at *2, 2000 U.S. Dist. LEXIS 4977, at *6. Rather, "[a]ll that is depicted is two separate images, each of which shows the same thing." *Id.* The district court found that "[w]hat is shown is the images, and what is omitted is any indication about the actual rates and degree and amount of leakage that the detailed evidence at the trial showed." *Id.* The court further found that the Goldfish II commercial "portray[s] . . . a goldfish in danger of suffocating in air because of the outflow of water from the bag." *Id.*

[14] The court concluded that the Goldfish II television commercial "is decidedly contrary to what was portrayed in the actual evidence about the bags at the first trial, and all in all the television commercial in my view is literally false." *Id.* at *3, 2000 U.S. Dist. LEXIS 4977, at *6. The court then addressed the Goldfish II print advertisement, which, it found "is, if anything, worse," because "[i]t has a single image of a Slide–Loc bag with a large drop about to fall away and a goldfish in danger of suffocating because the water is as portrayed disappearing from the bag." *Id.* at *3, 2000 U.S. Dist. LEXIS 4977, at *7. The district court concluded that the Goldfish II print advertisement "is literally false." *Id.* The court also found that the inability of a Ziploc Slide–Loc bag to prevent leakage is portrayed as an inherent quality or characteristic of that product. Accordingly, the court found that the Goldfish II television commercial and print advertisement "portray[ ] the leakage as simply an ever-present characteristic of the Slide–Loc bags." *Id.* at *3, 2000 U.S. Dist. LEXIS 4977, at *8.

[15] The district court found, in the alternative, that the Goldfish II ads were false by necessary implication, a doctrine this court has not yet recognized, because consumers would necessarily believe that more viscous liquids such as soups and sauces would leak as rapidly as water. *Id.* at *3, 2000 U.S. Dist. LEXIS 4977, at *6–*7.

[16] Clorox now appeals from this April 6, 2000 Order permanently enjoining the use of the Goldfish II television commercial and print advertisement.

DISCUSSION

[17] "We review the District Court's entry of a permanent injunction for abuse of discretion, which may be found where the Court, in issuing the injunction, relied on clearly erroneous findings of fact or an error of law." *Knox v. Salinas*, 193 F.3d 123, 128–29 (2d Cir. 1999) (per curiam). "[T]he district judge's determination of the meaning of the advertisement [is] a finding of fact that 'shall not be set aside unless clearly erroneous.'" *Avis Rent A Car Sys., Inc. v. Hertz Corp.*, 782 F.2d 381, 384 (2d Cir. 1986) (quoting Fed.R.Civ.P. 52(a)).

[18] The district court found that the Goldfish II television commercial and print advertisement are literally false in violation of section 43(a). . . . "The Lanham Act does not prohibit false statements generally. It prohibits only false or misleading descriptions or false or misleading representations of fact made about one's own or another's goods or services." *Id.* at 1052.

[19] This court has recently restated the general requirements for a claim brought under section 43(a):

To establish a false advertising claim under Section 43(a), the plaintiff must demonstrate that the statement in the challenged advertisement is false. "Falsity may be established

669

by proving that (1) the advertising is literally false as a factual matter, or (2) although the advertisement is literally true, it is likely to deceive or confuse customers."

Nat'l Basketball Ass'n v. Motorola, Inc., 105 F.3d 841, 855 (2d Cir. 1997) (quoting *Lipton v. Nature Co.,* 71 F.3d 464, 474 (2d Cir. 1995)). It is also well-settled that, "in addition to proving falsity, the plaintiff must also show that the defendants misrepresented an 'inherent quality or characteristic' of the product. This requirement is essentially one of materiality, a term explicitly used in other circuits." *Id.* (citation and internal quotation marks omitted).

[20] In considering a false advertising claim, "[f]undamental to any task of interpretation is the principle that text must yield to context." *Avis,* 782 F.2d at 385.

> Thus, we have emphasized that in reviewing FTC actions prohibiting unfair advertising practices under the Federal Trade Commission Act a court must "consider the advertisement in its entirety and not ... engage in disputatious dissection. The entire mosaic should be viewed rather than each tile separately." Similar approaches have been taken in Lanham Act cases involving the claim that an advertisement was false on its face.

Id. (citations omitted). Moreover, we have explicitly looked to the visual images in a commercial to assess whether it is literally false. *See Coca–Cola Co. v. Tropicana Prods., Inc.,* 690 F.2d 312, 317–18 (2d Cir. 1982) (abrogated on other grounds by statute as noted in *Johnson & Johnson v. GAC Int'l, Inc.,* 862 F.2d 975, 979 (2d Cir. 1988)); *see also Avis,* 782 F.2d at 385.

[21] "Where the advertising claim is shown to be literally false, the court may enjoin the use of the claim 'without reference to the advertisement's impact on the buying public.' Additionally, a plaintiff must show that it will suffer irreparable harm absent the injunction." *McNeil–P.C.C., Inc. v. Bristol–Myers Squibb Co.,* 938 F.2d 1544, 1549 (2d Cir. 1991) (citations omitted). Under section 43(a), however, "[w]e will presume irreparable harm where plaintiff demonstrates a likelihood of success in showing literally false defendant's comparative advertisement which mentions plaintiff's product by name." *Castrol, Inc. v. Quaker State Corp.,* 977 F.2d 57, 62 (2d Cir. 1992).

I. The district court's findings of fact are not clearly erroneous.

[22] Clorox argues that the district court committed clear error in finding that its Goldfish II television commercial and print advertisement contain literal falsehoods. We find no clear error in the district court's findings of fact in support of its conclusion that the Goldfish II television commercial and print advertisement are literally false as a factual matter. We note that the court made its finding of literal falsity after a seven-day bench trial. The evidence presented at trial clearly indicates that, as the court found, only slightly more than one out of ten Slide–Loc bags tested dripped at a rate of one drop per second or faster, while more than one-third of the Slide–Loc bags tested leaked at a rate of less than one drop per five seconds. Over half of the Slide–Loc bags tested either did not leak at all or leaked at a rate no faster than one drop per 20 seconds. Moreover, less than two-thirds, or 63 percent, of Slide–Loc bags tested showed any leakage at all when subjected to the testing on which Clorox based its Goldfish I and II advertisements.

[23] The only Slide–Loc bag depicted in each of the two Goldfish II advertisements, on the other hand, is shown leaking and, when shown, is always leaking. Moreover, each time the Slide–Loc bag is on-screen, the Goldfish II television commercial shows a drop forming immediately and then falling from the Slide–Loc bag, all over a period of approximately two seconds. Accordingly, the commercial falsely depicts the risk of leakage for the vast majority of Slide–Loc bags tested.

[24] Clorox argues that, because approximately eight seconds pass between the images of the drops forming and falling in the Goldfish II television commercial, the commercial depicts an accurate rate of leakage. However, the commercial does not continuously show the condition of the Slide–Loc bag because the Slide–Loc bag is off-screen for eight seconds. Likewise, the print ad does not depict any rate of leakage at all, other than to indicate that the Slide–Loc bag is "dripping." Clorox's argument that its commercial shows a "continuum" also fails given that in each of the Goldfish II advertisements

is a background image containing three puddles of water, when only two drops form and fall in the television commercial and just one drop forms and nearly falls in the print advertisement.

[25] Given the highly deferential standard of review accorded to the district court's findings entered after a bench trial, we cannot say that, having viewed the record in its entirety, we are left with the definite and firm conviction that a mistake has been committed. *See Mobil Shipping and Transp. Co. v. Wonsild Liquid Carriers Ltd.,* 190 F.3d 64, 67–68 (2d Cir. 1999). We find no clear error in the district court's finding that the depiction of the risk of leakage from Slide–Loc bags in the Goldfish II television commercial and print advertisement is literally false as to an inherent quality or characteristic of Ziploc Slide–Loc storage bags.

II. The district court committed no error of law.

[26] Clorox alleges that the district court erred in finding literal falsity because "no facially false claim or depiction was present in the advertisements at issue in this case." As such, Clorox argues, the district court's finding of literal falsity "was based upon an interpretation of the ads that went beyond their facial or explicit claims." According to Clorox, the district court therefore must have based it injunction on the implied falsity of the ads. Clorox argues that the district court erred as a matter of law because "any alleged message beyond the literal claims in the advertisements [must] be proved by extrinsic evidence," upon which the district court undeniably did not rely in reaching its conclusions.

[27] We disagree. The district court properly concluded that the Goldfish II advertisements are literally false in violation of section 43(a) of the Lanham Act. The court looked at the Goldfish II television commercial and print advertisement in their entirety and determined that the risk of leakage from the Slide–Loc storage bag depicted in the ads is literally false based on the evidence presented at trial of the real risk and rate of leakage from Slide–Loc bags. The district court's conclusion that Clorox violated section 43(a) conforms to our earlier precedents applying the doctrine of literal falsity. In *Coca–Cola,* we reversed a district court's finding of no literal falsity in an orange juice commercial where:

> [t]he visual component of the ad makes an explicit representation that Premium Pack is produced by squeezing oranges and pouring the freshly-squeezed juice directly into the carton. This is not a true representation of how the product is prepared. Premium Pack juice is heated and sometimes frozen prior to packaging.

690 F.2d at 318. As in *Coca–Cola,* the Goldfish II advertisement depicts a literal falsity that requires no proof by extrinsic evidence: that Slide–Loc bags always leak when filled with water and held upside down.

[28] Furthermore, the district court did not erroneously enjoin Clorox's advertisements on the basis of implied falsity in the absence of extrinsic evidence. Contrary to Clorox's allegations on appeal, the district court's conclusion is not based on implied falsity or the district court's own subjective interpretation of the Goldfish II advertisements. Indeed, Clorox's purported "literal" reading of the Goldfish II ads requires the viewer to assume that the bag is not leaking while it is off-screen. It is therefore Clorox's interpretation that relies upon implication, not the district court's. The district court did not conclude that the Goldfish II advertisements are literally true but "nevertheless likely to mislead or confuse consumers." It correctly concluded that the advertisements are facially false. As such, our holding prohibiting a district judge from "determin[ing], based solely upon his or her own intuitive reaction, whether the advertisement is deceptive" under the doctrine of implied falsity is not implicated in this case. *Johnson & Johnson * Merck Consumer Pharms. Co. v. Smithkline Beecham Corp.,* 960 F.2d 294, 297 (2d Cir. 1992).

[29] Because we affirm the injunction on the basis of literal falsity, we need not reach the issue of whether the district court erred in concluding as an alternative ground that Clorox's Goldfish II television commercial and print advertisement are false "by necessary implication" because consumers

would necessarily believe that more viscous liquids than water would also leak rapidly from Ziploc Slide–Loc storage bags.

[30] Accordingly, we find no clearly erroneous findings of fact and no error of law. We therefore find that the district court did not abuse its discretion by permanently enjoining Clorox from disseminating the Goldfish II television commercial and print advertisement.

. . . .

We affirm the judgment of the district court.

Some further examples of literally false advertising may be instructive.

In *Coca-Cola Co. v. Tropicana Prods., Inc.*, 690 F.2d 312 (2d Cir. 1982), the defendant featured Olympic athlete Bruce Jenner in a television commercial for orange juice. In the commercial, Jenner was shown squeezing juice out of an orange into a glass bowl and then pouring that bowl into a Tropicana orange juice carton. Jenner did so while explaining: "It's pure pasteurized juice as it comes from the orange." (See the storyboard below). The Second Circuit determined that the commercial was literally false:

> We find, therefore, that the squeezing-pouring sequence in the Jenner commercial is false on its face. The visual component of the ad makes an explicit representation that Premium Pack is produced by squeezing oranges and pouring the freshly-squeezed juice directly into the carton. This is not a true representation of how the product is prepared. Premium Pack juice is heated and sometimes frozen prior to packaging. Additionally, the simultaneous audio component of the ad states that Premium Pack is "pasteurized juice as it comes from the orange." This statement is blatantly false—pasteurized juice does not come from oranges. Pasteurization entails heating the juice to approximately 200 degrees Fahrenheit to kill certain natural enzymes and microorganisms which cause spoilage. Moreover, even if the addition of the word "pasteurized" somehow made sense and effectively qualified the visual image, Tropicana's commercial nevertheless represented that the juice is only squeezed, heated and packaged when in fact it may actually also be frozen.

Id. at 318.

Tropicana 100% PURE ORANGE JUICE

"Only One Can Be The Best - Sprinters"

30 Seconds   BRTO 0733

BRUCE JENNER: Hi! I'm Bruce Jenner for Tropicana.

You're looking at five of the top hurdlers in America.

They're all good. But only one can be the best.

The same holds true for our All-American Drink. Orange Juice.

They're all good, but only one can be the best.

For me, it tastes freshest.

Tropicana Premium Pack.

It's pure pasteurized juice as it comes from the orange.

It's the only leading brand not made with concentrate and water.

Only one can be the best.

For me, it's Tropicana Premium Pack.

MCA ADVERTISING, INC.

In *Warner-Lambert Co. v. BreathAsure, Inc.*, 204 F.3d 87 (3d Cir. 2000), the court explained that "BreathAsure's breath freshening products are capsules that are swallowed . . . . BreathAsure[] heavily promoted its BreathAsure products as being effective against bad breath. The theme of much of the advertising was that the capsules worked effectively at the source of bad breath and were, therefore, superior to products that simply masked or covered bad breath such as gum, mints and mouthwash. One such ad contained a series of photographs depicting food, a couple appearing to share a tender moment, and a package of BreathAsure. The following captions appear beneath those images: 'if you eat and we all do,' 'and you want to get close,' 'you need BreathAsure the internal breath freshener,' 'BreathAsure for the confidence of clean fresh breath.'" *Id.* at 89. However, on the third day of the

673

district court bench trial, "BreathAsure stipulated that scientific evidence established that its 'BreathAsure' products were not effective against bad breath" and was subsequently permanently enjoined from advertising otherwise. *Id.* On appeal, the Third Circuit further determined that the name of the product, BreathAsure, was also literally false. "The name falsely tells the consumer that he or she has assurance of fresher breath when ingesting one of the defendant's capsules. That is not true." *Id.* at 97.

Finally, other cases are perhaps more ridiculous than instructive. *See, e.g., Hearst Bus. Pub. Inc. v. W.G. Nichols Inc.*, 76 F. Supp. 2d 459 (S.D.N.Y. 1999) (finding literal falsity where defendant stated that "Even our competition says Chilton's Professional Manuals are: '. . . the manuals which were established as the industry standard by decades of reliable accuracy . . . manuals that automotive repair professionals need or want,'" when competitor had in fact stated that defendant's manuals "are *not* the manuals which were established as the industry standard {and} are *not* the Chilton Profession{al} Repair Manuals that automative repair professionals need or want" (emphasis added)); *Telebrands Corp. v. Wilton Indus.*, 983 F. Supp. 471 (S.D.N.Y. 1997) (finding literal falsity where defendant stated that its product was "As Seen On T.V." when in fact the defendant ran no significant television advertising for its product while the plaintiff ran extensive television advertising for its very similar product); *Edmark Indus. Sdn. Bhd. v. South Asia Int'l (H.K.) Ltd.*, 89 F. Supp. 2d 840 (E.D. Tex. 2000) (finding literal falsity where defendant claimed that its food slicer "Features fine german [sic] surgical steel blades" when it fact the slicer used Japanese steel).

2.   Literal Falsity by Necessary Implication

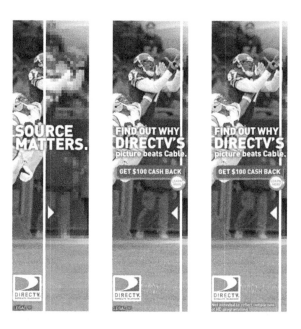

Time Warner Cable, Inc. v. DIRECTV, Inc.
497 F.3d 144 (2d Cir. 2007)

STRAUB, Circuit Judge:

[1] Defendant–Appellant DIRECTV, Inc. ("DIRECTV") appeals from the February 5, 2007 opinion and order of the United States District Court for the Southern District of New York (Laura Taylor Swain, Judge) preliminarily enjoining it from disseminating, in any market in which Plaintiff–Appellee Time Warner Cable, Inc. ("TWC") provides cable service, certain television commercials and Internet advertisements found likely to violate the Lanham Act on literal falsity grounds. *Time Warner Cable, Inc. v. DIRECTV, Inc.,* 475 F.Supp.2d 299 (S.D.N.Y.2007).

[2] This appeal requires us to clarify certain aspects of our false advertising doctrine. We make three clarifications in particular. First, we hold that an advertisement can be literally false even though

675

it does not explicitly make a false assertion, if the words or images, considered in context, necessarily and unambiguously imply a false message. Second, we decide that the category of non-actionable "puffery" encompasses visual depictions that, while factually inaccurate, are so grossly exaggerated that no reasonable consumer would rely on them in navigating the marketplace. Third, we conclude that the likelihood of irreparable harm may be presumed where the plaintiff demonstrates a likelihood of success in showing that the defendant's comparative advertisement is literally false and that given the nature of the market, it would be obvious to the viewing audience that the advertisement is targeted at the plaintiff, even though the plaintiff is not identified by name. Reviewing the District Court's decision under these principles, we affirm in part, vacate in part, and remand for further proceedings consistent with this opinion.

FACTUAL BACKGROUND[2]

A. The Parties

[3] TWC and DIRECTV are major players in the multichannel video service industry. TWC is the second-largest cable company in the United States, serving more than 13.4 million subscribers. Like all cable providers, TWC must operate through franchises let by local government entities; it is currently the franchisee in the greater part of New York City. DIRECTV is one of the country's largest satellite service providers, with more than 15.6 million customers nationwide. Because DIRECTV broadcasts directly via satellite, it is not subject to the same franchise limitations as cable companies. As a result, in the markets where TWC is the franchisee, DIRECTV and other satellite providers pose the greatest threat to its market share. The competition in these markets for new customers is extremely fierce, a fact to which the advertisements challenged in this case attest.

[4] TWC offers both analog and digital television services to its customers. DIRECTV, on the other hand, delivers 100% of its programming digitally. Both companies, however, offer high-definition ("HD") service on a limited number of their respective channels. Transmitted at a higher resolution than analog or traditional digital programming, HD provides the home viewer with theater-like picture quality on a wider screen. The picture quality of HD is governed by standards recommended by the Advanced Television Systems Committee ("ATSC"), an international non-profit organization that develops voluntary standards for digital television. To qualify as HD under ATSC standards, the screen resolution of a television picture must be at least 720p or 1080i.[3] TWC and DIRECTV do not set or alter the screen resolution for HD programming provided by the networks; instead, they make available sufficient bandwidth to permit the HD level of resolution to pass on to their customers. To view programming in HD format, customers of either provider must have an HD television set.

[5] There is no dispute, at least on the present record, that the HD programming provided by TWC and DIRECTV is equivalent in picture quality. In terms of non-HD programming, digital service generally yields better picture quality than analog service, because a digital signal is more resistant to interference. *See Consumer Elecs. Ass'n v. F.C.C.*, 347 F.3d 291, 293–94 (D.C.Cir. 2003). That said, TWC's analog cable service satisfies the technical specifications, *e.g.* signal level requirements and signal leakage limits, set by the Federal Communications Commission ("FCC"). *See* 47 C.F.R. § 76.1, *et seq.* According to a FCC fact sheet, analog service that meets these specifications produces a picture that is "high enough in quality to provide enjoyable viewing with barely perceptible impairments."

---

[2] This factual background is derived from the District Court's findings of fact, which are not in dispute. *See Time Warner Cable, Inc.*, 475 F.Supp.2d at 302–04.

[3] The "p" and "i" designations stand for "progressive" and "interlaced." In the progressive format, the full picture updates every sixtieth of a second, while in the interlaced format, half of the picture updates every sixtieth of a second. The higher the "p" or "i" number, the greater the resolution and the better the picture will appear to the viewer.

B. DIRECTV's "SOURCE MATTERS" Campaign

[6] In the fall of 2006, DIRECTV launched a multimedia advertising campaign based on the theme of "SOURCE MATTERS." The concept of the campaign was to educate consumers that to obtain HD-standard picture quality, it is not enough to buy an HD television set; consumers must also receive HD programming from the "source," *i.e.,* the television service provider.

1. Jessica Simpson Commercial

[7] As part of its new campaign, DIRECTV began running a television commercial in October 2006 featuring celebrity Jessica Simpson. In the commercial, Simpson, portraying her character of Daisy Duke from the movie *The Dukes of Hazzard,* says to some of her customers at the local diner:

> Simpson: Y'all ready to order?
>
> Hey, 253 straight days at the gym to get this body and you're not gonna watch me on DIRECTV HD?
>
> You're just not gonna get the best picture out of some fancy big screen TV without DIRECTV.
>
> It's broadcast in 1080i. I totally don't know what that means, but I want it.

The original version of the commercial concluded with a narrator saying, "For picture quality that beats cable, you've got to get DIRECTV."

[8] In response to objections by TWC, and pursuant to agreements entered into by the parties, DIRECTV pulled the original version of the commercial and replaced it with a revised one ("Revised Simpson Commercial"), which began airing in early December 2006. The Revised Simpson Commercial is identical to the original, except that it ends with a different tag line: "For an HD picture that can't be beat, get DIRECTV."

2. William Shatner Commercial

[9] DIRECTV debuted another commercial in October 2006, featuring actor William Shatner as Captain James T. Kirk, his character from the popular *Star Trek* television show and film series. The following conversation takes place on the Starship Enterprise:

> Mr. Chekov: Should we raise our shields, Captain?
>
> Captain Kirk: At ease, Mr. Chekov.
>
> Again with the shields. I wish he'd just relax and enjoy the amazing picture clarity of the DIRECTV HD we just hooked up.
>
> With what Starfleet just ponied up for this big screen TV, settling for cable would be illogical.
>
> Mr. Spock: [Clearing throat.]
>
> Captain Kirk: What, I can't use that line?

The original version ended with the announcer saying, "For picture quality that beats cable, you've got to get DIRECTV."

[10] DIRECTV agreed to stop running the Shatner commercial in November 2006. In January 2007, DIRECTV released a revised version of the commercial ("Revised Shatner Commercial") with the revamped tag line, "For an HD picture that can't be beat, get DIRECTV."

3. Internet Advertisements

[11] DIRECTV also waged its campaign in cyberspace, placing banner advertisements on various websites to promote the message that when it comes to picture quality, "source matters." The banner ads have the same basic structure. They open by showing an image that is so highly pixelated that it is impossible to discern what is being depicted. On top of this indistinct image is superimposed the slogan, "SOURCE MATTERS." After about a second, a vertical line splits the screen into two parts, one

677

labeled "OTHER TV" and the other "DIRECTV." On the OTHER TV side of the line, the picture is extremely pixelated and distorted, like the opening image. By contrast, the picture on the DIRECTV side is exceptionally sharp and clear. The DIRECTV screen reveals that what we have been looking at all along is an image of New York Giants quarterback Eli Manning; in another ad, it is a picture of two women snorkeling in tropical waters. The advertisements then invite browsers to "FIND OUT WHY DIRECTV'S picture beats cable" and to "LEARN MORE" about a special offer. In the original design, users who clicked on the "LEARN MORE" icon were automatically directed to the HDTV section of DIRECTV's website.

[12] In addition to the banner advertisements, DIRECTV created a demonstrative advertisement that it featured on its own website. Like the banner ads, the website demonstrative uses the split-screen technique to compare the picture quality of "DIRECTV" to that of "OTHER TV," which the ad later identifies as representing "basic cable," *i.e.,* analog cable. The DIRECTV side of the screen depicts, in high resolution, an image of football player Kevin Dyson making a touchdown at the Super Bowl. The portion of the image on the OTHER TV side is noticeably pixelated and blurry. This visual display is accompanied by the following text: "If you're hooking up your high-definition TV to basic cable, you're not getting the best picture on every channel. For unparalleled clarity, you need DIRECTV HD. You'll enjoy 100% digital picture and sound on every channel and also get the most sports in HD—including all your favorite football games in high definition with NFL SUNDAY TICKET."

PROCEDURAL HISTORY

A. Filing of Action and Stipulation

[13] On December 7, 2006, TWC filed this action charging DIRECTV with, *inter alia,* false advertising in violation of § 43(a) of the Lanham Act. 15 U.S.C. § 1114, *et seq.* Initial negotiations led to the execution of a stipulation, in which DIRECTV agreed that pending final resolution of the action, it would stop running the original versions of the Simpson and Shatner commercials and also disable the link on the banner advertisements that routed customers to the HDTV page of its website. DIRECTV further stipulated that it would not claim in any advertisement, either directly or by implication, that "the picture quality presently offered by DIRECTV's HDTV service is superior to the picture offered presently by Time Warner Cable's HDTV service, or the present HDTV services of cable television providers in general." Finally, DIRECTV agreed that any breach of the stipulation would result in irreparable harm to TWC. The stipulation contained the caveat, however, that nothing in it "shall be construed to be a finding on the merits of this action." The District Court entered an order on the stipulation on December 12, 2006.

B. Preliminary Injunction Motion

[14] The following week, on December 18, TWC filed a motion for a preliminary injunction against the Revised Simpson Commercial, as well as the banner advertisements and website demonstrative (collectively, "Internet Advertisements"), none of which were specifically covered by the stipulation. TWC claimed that each of these advertisements was literally false, obviating the need for extrinsic evidence of consumer confusion. TWC further argued that as DIRECTV's direct competitor, it was entitled to a presumption of irreparable injury. On January 4, 2007, after discovering that DIRECTV had started running the Revised Shatner Commercial, TWC filed supplemental papers requesting that this commercial also be preliminarily enjoined on literal falsity grounds.

[15] DIRECTV vigorously opposed the motion. It asserted that the Revised Simpson and Shatner Commercials were not literally false because no single statement in the commercials explicitly claimed that DIRECTV HD is superior to cable HD in terms of picture quality. DIRECTV did not deny that the Internet Advertisements' depictions of cable were facially false. Rather, it argued that the Internet Advertisements did not violate the Lanham Act because the images constituted non-actionable puffery.

Finally, DIRECTV argued that irreparable harm could not be presumed because none of the contested advertisements identified TWC by name.

C. The District Court's February 5, 2007 Opinion and Order

[16] On February 5, 2007, the District Court issued a decision granting TWC's motion. The District Court determined that TWC had met its burden of showing that each of the challenged advertisements was likely to be proven literally false. Addressing the television commercials, the District Court held that the meaning of particular statements had to be determined in light of the overall context, and not in a vacuum as urged by DIRECTV. Given the commercials' obvious focus on HD picture quality, the District Court found that the Simpson's assertion that a viewer cannot "get the best picture out of some big fancy big screen TV without DIRECTV" and Shatner's quip that "settling for cable would be illogical" could only be understood as making the literally false claim that DIRECTV HD is superior to cable HD in picture quality. *See Time Warner Cable, Inc.,* 475 F.Supp.2d at 305–06. As for the Internet Advertisements, the District Court found that the facially false depictions of cable's picture quality could not be discounted as mere puffery because it was possible that consumers unfamiliar with HD technology would actually rely on the images in deciding whether to hook up their HD television sets to DIRECTV or analog cable. *See id.* at 306–08.

[17] In assessing irreparable harm *vel non*, the District Court observed that under Second Circuit case law, irreparable harm could be presumed where the movant "demonstrates a likelihood of success in showing literally false defendant's comparative advertisement which mentions plaintiff's product by name." *Id.* at 308 (quoting *Castrol, Inc. v. Quaker State Corp.,* 977 F.2d 57, 62 (2d Cir. 1992) (internal quotation marks omitted)). The District Court acknowledged that the Revised Shatner Commercial and the Internet Advertisements did not specifically name TWC, but concluded that a presumption of irreparable harm was nevertheless appropriate because the advertisements made explicit references to "cable," and in the markets where TWC is the franchisee, "cable" is functionally synonymous with "Time Warner Cable." *See id.* As for the Revised Simpson Commercial, the District Court reasoned that although the advertisement did not explicitly reference "cable," irreparable harm should be presumed because "TWC is DIRECTV's main competitor in markets served by TWC." *Id.* The District Court further noted that DIRECTV had breached the stipulation by continuing to run the contested commercials and that this breach also supported a finding of irreparable harm. *See id.* at n. 5.

[18] In accordance with its opinion, the District Court entered a preliminary injunction barring DIRECTV from disseminating, "in any market in which [TWC] provides cable service,"

> (1) the Revised Simpson Commercial and Revised Shatner Commercial, "and any other advertisement disparaging the visual or audio quality of TWC or cable high-definition ("HDTV") programming as compared to that of DIRECTV or satellite HDTV programming"; and

> (2) the Internet Advertisements "and any other advertisement making representations that the service provided by Time Warner Cable, or cable service in general, is unwatchable due to blurriness, distortion, pixellation or the like, or inaudible due to static or other interference."

DISCUSSION

[19] A party seeking preliminary injunctive relief must establish: (1) either (a) a likelihood of success on the merits of its case or (b) sufficiently serious questions going to the merits to make them a fair ground for litigation and a balance of hardships tipping decidedly in its favor, *and* (2) a likelihood of irreparable harm if the requested relief is denied. *See Coca–Cola Co. v. Tropicana Prods., Inc.,* 690 F.3d 312, 314–15 (2d Cir. 1982), *abrogated on other grounds by* Fed.R.Civ.P. 52(a). We review the entry of a preliminary injunction for excess of discretion, which may be found where the district court, in issuing the injunction, relied upon clearly erroneous findings of fact or errors of law. *S.C. Johnson & Son, Inc. v. Clorox Co.,* 241 F.3d 232, 237 (2d Cir. 2001). "[T]he district judge's determination of the meaning

of the advertisement [is] a finding of fact that shall not be set aside unless clearly erroneous." *Id.* (alterations in original; internal quotation marks omitted); *see also Johnson & Johnson v. GAC Int'l, Inc.,* 862 F.2d 975, 979 (2d Cir. 1988) (*"GAC Int'l, Inc."*).

A. Likelihood of Success on the Merits

    1. Television Commercials

      . . . .

[20] Two different theories of recovery are available to a plaintiff who brings a false advertising action under § 43(a) of the Lanham Act. First, the plaintiff can demonstrate that the challenged advertisement is literally false, *i.e.,* false on its face. *See GAC Int'l, Inc.,* 862 F.2d at 977. When an advertisement is shown to be literally or facially false, consumer deception is presumed, and "the court may grant relief without reference to the advertisement's [actual] impact on the buying public." *Coca-Cola Co.,* 690 F.2d at 317. "This is because plaintiffs alleging a literal falsehood are claiming that a statement, on its face, conflicts with reality, a claim that is best supported by comparing the statement itself with the reality it purports to describe." *Schering Corp. v. Pfizer Inc.,* 189 F.3d 218, 229 (2d Cir. 1999).

[21] Alternatively, a plaintiff can show that the advertisement, while not literally false, is nevertheless likely to mislead or confuse consumers. *See Coca–Cola Co.,* 690 F.2d at 317. "[P]laintiffs alleging an implied falsehood are claiming that a statement, whatever its literal truth, has left an impression on the listener [or viewer] that conflicts with reality"—a claim that "invites a comparison of the impression, rather than the statement, with the truth." *Schering Corp.,* 189 F.3d at 229. Therefore, whereas "plaintiffs seeking to establish a literal falsehood must generally show the substance of what is conveyed, . . . a district court *must* rely on extrinsic evidence [of consumer deception or confusion] to support a finding of an implicitly false message." *Id.* (internal quotation marks omitted).[4]

[22] Here, TWC chose to pursue only the first path of literal falsity, and the District Court granted the preliminary injunction against the television commercials on that basis. In this appeal, DIRECTV does not dispute that it would be a misrepresentation to claim that the picture quality of DIRECTV HD is superior to that of cable HD. Rather, it argues that neither commercial explicitly makes such a claim and therefore cannot be literally false.

    a. Revised Simpson Commercial

[23] DIRECTV's argument is easily dismissed with respect to the Revised Simpson Commercial. In the critical lines, Simpson tells audiences, "You're just not gonna get the best picture out of some fancy big screen TV without DIRECTV. It's broadcast in 1080i." These statements make the explicit assertion that it is impossible to obtain "the best picture"—*i.e.,* a "1080i"-resolution picture—from any source other than DIRECTV. This claim is flatly untrue; the uncontroverted factual record establishes that viewers can, in fact, get the same "best picture" by ordering HD programming from their cable service provider. We therefore affirm the District Court's determination that the Revised Simpson Commercial's contention "that a viewer cannot 'get the best picture' without DIRECTV is . . . likely to be proven literally false." *Time Warner Cable, Inc.,* 475 F.Supp.2d at 306.

---

[4] Under either theory, the plaintiff must also demonstrate that the false or misleading representation involved an inherent or material quality of the product. *See S.C. Johnson & Son, Inc.,* 241 F.3d at 238; *Nat'l Basketball Ass'n v. Motorola, Inc.,* 105 F.3d 841, 855 (2d Cir. 1997). TWC has met this requirement, as it is undisputed that picture quality is an inherent and material characteristic of multichannel video service.

b. Revised Shatner Commercial

[24] The issue of whether the Revised Shatner Commercial is likely to be proven literally false requires more analysis. When interpreting the controversial statement, "With what Starfleet just ponied up for this big screen TV, settling for cable would be illogical," the District Court looked not only at that particular text, but also at the surrounding context. In light of Shatner's opening comment extolling the "amazing picture quality of [ ] DIRECTV HD" and the announcer's closing remark highlighting the unbeatable "HD picture" provided by DIRECTV, the District Court found that the line in the middle—"settling for cable would be illogical"—clearly referred to cable's HD picture quality. Since it would only be "illogical" to "settle" for cable's HD picture if it was materially inferior to DIRECTV's HD picture, the District Court concluded that TWC was likely to establish that the statement was literally false.

[25] DIRECTV argues that the District Court's ruling was clearly erroneous because the actual statement at issue, "settling for cable would be illogical," does not explicitly compare the picture quality of DIRECTV *HD* with that of cable *HD,* and indeed, does not mention *HD* at all. In DIRECTV's view, the District Court based its determination of literal falsity not on the words actually used, but on what it subjectively perceived to be the general message conveyed by the commercial as a whole. DIRECTV contends that this was plainly improper under this Court's decision in *American Home Products Corp. v. Johnson & Johnson,* 577 F.2d 160 (2d Cir. 1978).

[26] TWC, on the other hand, maintains that the District Court properly took context into account in interpreting the commercial, as directed by this Court in *Avis Rent A Car System, Inc. v. Hertz Corp.,* 782 F.2d 381 (2d Cir. 1986). TWC argues that under *Avis Rent A Car,* an advertisement can be literally false even though no "combination of words between two punctuation signals" is untrue, if the clear meaning of the statement, considered in context, is false. Given the commercial's repeated references to "HD picture," TWC contends that the District Court correctly found that "settling for cable would be illogical" literally made the false claim that cable's HD picture quality is inferior to DIRECTV's.

. . . .

[27] These two cases {*American Home Products Corp. v. Johnson & Johnson,* 577 F.2d 160 (2d Cir. 1978) and *Avis Rent A Car System, Inc. v. Hertz Corp.,* 782 F.2d 381 (2d Cir. 1986)}, read together, compel us to now formally adopt what is known in other circuits as the "false by necessary implication" doctrine. *See, e.g., Scotts Co. v. United Indus. Corp.,* 315 F.3d 264, 274 (4th Cir. 2002); *Clorox Co. Puerto Rico v. Proctor & Gamble Commercial Co.,* 228 F.3d 24, 34–35 (1st Cir. 2000); *Southland Sod Farms v. Stover Seed Co.,* 108 F.3d 1134, 1139 (9th Cir. 1997); *Castrol Inc. v. Pennzoil Co.,* 987 F.2d 939, 946–47 (3d Cir. 1993) ("*Pennzoil Co.*").[5] Under this doctrine, a district court evaluating whether an advertisement is literally false "must analyze the message conveyed in full context," *Pennzoil Co.,* 987 F.2d at 946, *i.e.,* it "must consider the advertisement in its entirety and not . . . engage in disputatious dissection," *Avis Rent A Car,* 782 F.2d at 385 (internal quotation marks omitted). If the words or images, considered in context, necessarily imply a false message, the advertisement is literally false and no extrinsic evidence of consumer confusion is required. *See Novartis Consumer Health, Inc. v. Johnson & Johnson–Merck Pharm. Co.,* 290 F.3d 578, 586–87 (3d Cir. 2002) ("A 'literally false' message may be either explicit or 'conveyed by necessary implication when, considering the advertisement in its entirety, the audience would recognize the claim as readily as if it had been explicitly stated.'" (quoting *Clorox Co. Puerto Rico,* 228 F.3d at 35)). However, "only an *unambiguous* message can be literally false." *Id.* at 587. Therefore, if the language or graphic is susceptible to more than one

---

[5] Several district courts in this Circuit have already embraced the doctrine. *See, e.g., Johnson & Johnson–Merck Consumer Pharm. Co. v. Procter & Gamble Co.,* 285 F.Supp.2d 389, 391 (S.D.N.Y.2003), *aff'd,* 90 Fed.Appx. 8 (2d Cir.2003); *Tambrands, Inc. v. Warner–Lambert Co.,* 673 F.Supp. 1190, 1193–94 (S.D.N.Y.1987).

reasonable interpretation, the advertisement cannot be literally false. *See Scotts Co.,* 315 F.3d at 275 (stating that a literal falsity argument fails if the statement or image "can reasonably be understood as conveying different messages"); *Clorox Co. Puerto Rico,* 228 F.3d at 35 ("[A] factfinder might conclude that the message conveyed by a particular advertisement remains so balanced between several plausible meanings that the claim made by the advertisement is too uncertain to serve as the basis of a literal falsity claim . . . ."). There may still be a "basis for a claim that the advertisement is misleading," *Clorox Co. Puerto Rico,* 228 F.3d at 35, but to resolve such a claim, the district court must look to consumer data to determine what "the person to whom the advertisement is addressed find[s] to be the message," *Am. Home Prods.,* 577 F.2d at 166 (citation omitted). In short, where the advertisement does not unambiguously make a claim, "the court's reaction is at best not determinative and at worst irrelevant." *Id.*

[28] Here, the District Court found that Shatner's assertion that "settling for cable would be illogical," considered in light of the advertisement as a whole, unambiguously made the false claim that cable's HD picture quality is inferior to that of DIRECTV's. We cannot say that this finding was clearly erroneous, especially given that in the immediately preceding line, Shatner praises the "amazing picture clarity of DIRECTV HD." We accordingly affirm the District Court's conclusion that TWC established a likelihood of success on its claim that the Revised Shatner Commercial is literally false.

2. Internet Advertisements

[29] We have made clear that a district court must examine not only the words, but also the "visual images . . . to assess whether [the advertisement] is literally false." *S.C. Johnson & Son, Inc.,* 241 F.3d at 238. It is uncontroverted that the images used in the Internet Advertisements to represent cable are inaccurate depictions of the picture quality provided by cable's digital or analog service. The Internet Advertisements are therefore explicitly and literally false. *See Coca–Cola Co.,* 690 F.2d at 318 (reversing the district court's finding of no literal falsity in an orange juice commercial where "[t]he visual component of the ad makes an explicit representation that Premium Pack is produced by squeezing oranges and pouring the freshly-squeezed juice directly into the carton. This is not a true representation of how the product is prepared. Premium Pack juice is heated and sometimes frozen prior to packaging.").

[30] DIRECTV does not contest this point. Rather, it asserts that the images are so grossly distorted and exaggerated that no reasonable buyer would take them to be accurate depictions "of how a consumer's television picture would look when connected to cable." Consequently, DIRECTV argues, the images are obviously just puffery, which cannot form the basis of a Lanham Act violation. Notably, TWC agrees that no Lanham Act action would lie against an advertisement that was so exaggerated that no reasonable consumer would rely on it in making his or her purchasing decisions. TWC contends, however, that DIRECTV's own evidence—which indicates that consumers are highly confused about HD technology—shows that the Internet Advertisements pose a real danger of consumer reliance.

[31] This Court has had little occasion to explore the concept of puffery in the false advertising context. In *Lipton v. Nature Co.,* 71 F.3d 464 (2d Cir. 1995), the one case where we discussed the subject in some depth, we characterized puffery as "[s]ubjective claims about products, which cannot be proven either true or false." *Id.* at 474 (internal quotation marks omitted). We also cited to the Third Circuit's description of puffery in *Pennzoil Co.:* "Puffery is an exaggeration or overstatement expressed in broad, vague, and commendatory language. 'Such sales talk, or puffing, as it is commonly called, is considered to be offered and understood as an expression of the seller's opinion only, which is to be discounted as such by the buyer . . . . The 'puffing' rule amounts to a seller's privilege to lie his head off, so long as he says nothing specific.'" *Pennzoil Co.,* 987 F.2d at 945 (quoting W. Page Keeton et al., *Prosser and Keeton on the Law of Torts* § 109, at 756–57 (5th ed.1984)). Applying this definition, we concluded that the defendant's contention that he had conducted "thorough" research was just puffery, which was not actionable under the Lanham Act. *See Lipton,* 71 F.3d at 474.

[32] *Lipton*'s and *Pennzoil Co.*'s definition of puffery does not translate well into the world of images. Unlike words, images cannot be vague or broad. *Cf. Pennzoil Co.,* 987 F.2d at 945. To the contrary, visual depictions of a product are generally "specific and measurable," *id.* at 946, and can therefore "be proven either true or false," *Lipton,* 71 F.3d at 474 (internal quotation marks omitted), as this case demonstrates. Yet, if a visual representation is so grossly exaggerated that no reasonable buyer would take it at face value, there is no danger of consumer deception and hence, no basis for a false advertising claim. *Cf. Johnson & Johnson Merck Consumer Pharm. Co. v. Smithkline Beecham Corp.,* 960 F.2d 294, 298 (2d Cir. 1992) ("[T]he injuries redressed in false advertising cases are the result of public deception. Thus, where the plaintiff cannot demonstrate that a statistically significant part of the commercial audience holds the false belief allegedly communicated by the challenged advertisement, the plaintiff cannot establish that it suffered any injury as a result of the advertisement's message. Without injury there can be no claim, regardless of commercial context, prior advertising history, or audience sophistication."); *see also U.S. Healthcare, Inc. v. Blue Cross of Greater Philadelphia,* 898 F.2d 914, 922 (3d Cir. 1990) ("Mere puffery, advertising that is not deceptive for no one would rely on its exaggerated claims, is not actionable under § 43(a)." (internal quotation marks omitted)).

[33] Other circuits have recognized that puffery can come in at least two different forms. *See, e.g., Pizza Hut, Inc. v. Papa John's Int'l, Inc.,* 227 F.3d 489, 497 (5th Cir. 2000). The first form we identified in *Lipton*—"a general claim of superiority over comparable products that is so vague that it can be understood as nothing more than a mere expression of opinion." *Id.; see Lipton,* 71 F.3d at 474. The second form of puffery, which we did not address in *Lipton,* is "an exaggerated, blustering, and boasting statement upon which no reasonable buyer would be justified in relying." *Pizza Hut, Inc.,* 227 F.3d at 497; *accord United Indus. Corp. v. Clorox Co.,* 140 F.3d 1175, 1180 (8th Cir. 1998) ("Puffery is exaggerated advertising, blustering, and boasting upon which no reasonable buyer would rely and is not actionable under § 43(a)." (internal quotation marks omitted)). We believe that this second conception of puffery is a better fit where, as here, the "statement" at issue is expressed not in words, but through images.

[34] The District Court determined that the Internet Advertisements did not satisfy this alternative definition of puffery because DIRECTV's own evidence showed that "many HDTV equipment purchasers are confused as to what image quality to expect when viewing non-HD broadcasts, as their prior experience with the equipment is often limited to viewing HD broadcasts or other digital images on floor model televisions at large retail chains." *Time Warner Cable, Inc.,* 475 F.Supp.2d at 307. Given this confusion, the District Court reasoned that "consumers unfamiliar with HD equipment could be led to believe that using an HD television set with an analog cable feed might result in the sort of distorted images showcased in DIRECTV's Internet Advertisements, especially since those advertisements make reference to 'basic cable.'" *Id.*

[35] Our review of the record persuades us that the District Court clearly erred in rejecting DIRECTV's puffery defense. The "OTHER TV" images in the Internet Advertisements are—to borrow the words of Ronald Boyer, TWC's Senior Network Engineer—"unwatchably blurry, distorted, and pixelated, and . . . nothing like the images a customer would ordinarily see using Time Warner Cable's cable service." Boyer further explained that

> the types of gross distortions shown in DIRECTV's Website Demonstrative and Banner Ads are not the type of disruptions that could naturally happen to an analog or non-HD digital cable picture. These advertisements depict the picture quality of cable television as a series of large colored square blocks, laid out in a grid like graph paper, which nearly entirely obscure the image. This is not the type of wavy or "snowy" picture that might occur from degradation of an unconverted analog cable picture, or the type of macro-blocking or "pixelization" that might occur from degradation of a digital cable picture. Rather, the patchwork of colored blocks that DIRECTV depicts in its advertisement appears to be the type of distortion that would result if someone took a low-resolution

photograph and enlarged it too much or zoomed in too close. If DIRECTV intended the advertisement to depict a pixelization problem, this is a gross exaggeration of one.

[36] As Boyer's declaration establishes, the Internet Advertisements' depictions of cable are not just inaccurate; they are not even remotely realistic. It is difficult to imagine that any consumer, whatever the level of sophistication, would actually be fooled by the Internet Advertisements into thinking that cable's picture quality is so poor that the image is "nearly entirely obscure [d]." As DIRECTV states in its brief, "even a person not acquainted with cable would realize TWC could not realistically supply an unwatchably blurry image and survive in the marketplace."

[37] In reaching the contrary conclusion, the District Court relied heavily on the declaration of Jon Gieselman, DIRECTV's Senior Vice–President of Advertising and Public Relations. However, Gieselman merely stated that the common misconception amongst first-time purchasers of HD televisions is that "they will automatically get exceptional clarity on every channel" just by plugging their new television sets into the wall. Nothing in Gieselman's declaration indicates that consumers mistakenly believe that hooking up their HD televisions to an analog cable feed will produce an unwatchably distorted picture. More importantly, the Internet Advertisements do not claim that the "OTHER TV" is an HD television set, or that the corresponding images represent what happens when an HD television is connected to basic cable. The Internet Advertisements simply purport to compare the picture quality of DIRECTV's programming to that of basic cable programming, and as discussed above, the comparison is so obviously hyperbolic that "no reasonable buyer would be justified in relying" on it in navigating the marketplace. *Pizza Hut, Inc.*, 227 F.3d at 497.

[38] For these reasons, we conclude that the District Court exceeded its permissible discretion in preliminarily enjoining DIRECTV from disseminating the Internet Advertisements.

. . . .

3. Literally True But Misleading Advertising

The following opinion, which emerged out of litigation between two companies that both claim to make pizza, is lengthy and detailed. It is included here because it covers a variety of important issues in false advertising law, such as what qualifies as a representation of fact (rather than as opinion or puffery) and what kind of evidence is necessary to prove that a misleading statement is material to consumers' decision to purchase.

V7.0/2020-07-14

Pizza Hut, Inc. v. Papa John's Intern., Inc.
227 F.3d 489 (5th Cir. 2000)

E. GRADY JOLLY, Circuit Judge:

[1] This appeal presents a false advertising claim under section 43(a) of the Lanham Act, resulting in a jury verdict for the plaintiff, Pizza Hut. At the center of this appeal is Papa John's four word slogan "Better Ingredients. Better Pizza."

[2] The appellant, Papa John's International Inc. ("Papa John's"), argues that the slogan "cannot and does not violate the Lanham Act" because it is "not a misrepresentation of fact." The appellee, Pizza Hut, Inc., argues that the slogan, when viewed in the context of Papa John's overall advertising campaign, conveys a false statement of fact actionable under section 43(a) of the Lanham Act. The district court, after evaluating the jury's responses to a series of special interrogatories and denying Papa John's motion for judgment as a matter of law, entered judgment for Pizza Hut stating:

> When the "Better Ingredients. Better Pizza." slogan is considered in light of the entirety of Papa John's post-May 1997 advertising which violated provisions of the Lanham Act and in the context in which it was juxtaposed with the false and misleading statements contained in Papa John's print and broadcast media advertising, the slogan itself became tainted to the extent that its continued use should be enjoined.

We conclude that (1) the slogan, standing alone, is not an objectifiable statement of fact upon which consumers would be justified in relying, and thus not actionable under section 43(a); and (2) while the slogan, when utilized in connection with some of the post-May 1997 comparative advertising—specifically, the sauce and dough campaigns—conveyed objectifiable and misleading facts, Pizza Hut has failed to adduce any evidence demonstrating that the facts conveyed by the slogan were material to the purchasing decisions of the consumers to which the slogan was directed. Thus, the district court erred in denying Papa John's motion for judgment as a matter of law. We therefore reverse the judgment of the district court denying Papa John's motion for judgment as a matter of law, vacate its final judgment, and remand the case to the district court for entry of judgment for Papa John's.

I

A

[3] Pizza Hut is a wholly owned subsidiary of Tricon Global Restaurants. With over 7000 restaurants (both company and franchisee-owned), Pizza Hut is the largest pizza chain in the United States. In 1984, John Schnatter founded Papa John's Pizza in the back of his father's tavern. Papa John's has grown to over 2050 locations, making it the third largest pizza chain in the United States.

[4] In May 1995, Papa John's adopted a new slogan: "Better Ingredients. Better Pizza." In 1996, Papa John's filed for a federal trademark registration for this slogan with the United States Patent &

685

Trademark Office ("PTO"). Its application for registration was ultimately granted by the PTO. Since 1995, Papa John's has invested over $300 million building customer goodwill in its trademark "Better Ingredients. Better Pizza." The slogan has appeared on millions of signs, shirts, menus, pizza boxes, napkins and other items, and has regularly appeared as the "tag line" at the end of Papa John's radio and television ads, or with the company logo in printed advertising.

[5] On May 1, 1997, Pizza Hut launched its "Totally New Pizza" campaign. This campaign was the culmination of "Operation Lightning Bolt," a nine-month, $50 million project in which Pizza Hut declared "war" on poor quality pizza. From the deck of a World War II aircraft carrier, Pizza Hut's president, David Novak, declared "war" on "skimpy, low quality pizza." National ads aired during this campaign touted the "better taste" of Pizza Hut's pizza, and "dared" anyone to find a "better pizza."

[6] In early May 1997, Papa John's launched its first national ad campaign. The campaign was directed towards Pizza Hut, and its "Totally New Pizza" campaign. In a pair of TV ads featuring Pizza Hut's co-founder Frank Carney, Carney touted the superiority of Papa John's pizza over Pizza Hut's pizza. Although Carney had left the pizza business in the 1980's, he returned as a franchisee of Papa John's because he liked the taste of Papa John's pizza better than any other pizza on the market. The ad campaign was remarkably successful. During May 1997, Papa John's sales increased 11.7 percent over May 1996 sales, while Pizza Hut's sales were down 8 percent.

[7] On the heels of the success of the Carney ads, in February 1998, Papa John's launched a second series of ads touting the results of a taste test in which consumers were asked to compare Papa John's and Pizza Hut's pizzas. In the ads, Papa John's boasted that it "won big time" in taste tests. The ads were a response to Pizza Hut's "dare" to find a "better pizza." The taste test showed that consumers preferred Papa John's traditional crust pizzas over Pizza Hut's comparable pizzas by a 16–point margin (58% to 42%). Additionally, consumers preferred Papa John's thin crust pizzas by a fourteen-point margin (57% to 43%).

[8] Following the taste test ads, Papa John's ran a series of ads comparing specific ingredients used in its pizzas with those used by its "competitors." During the course of these ads, Papa John's touted the superiority of its sauce and its dough. During the sauce campaign, Papa John's asserted that its sauce was made from "fresh, vine-ripened tomatoes," which were canned through a process called "fresh pack," while its competitors—including Pizza Hut—make their sauce from remanufactured tomato paste. During the dough campaign, Papa John's stated that it used "clear filtered water" to make its pizza dough, while the "biggest chain" uses "whatever comes out of the tap." Additionally, Papa John's asserted that it gives its yeast "several days to work its magic," while "some folks" use "frozen dough or dough made the same day." At or near the close of each of these ads, Papa John's punctuated its ingredient comparisons with the slogan "Better Ingredients. Better Pizza."

[9] Pizza Hut does not appear to contest the truthfulness of the underlying factual assertions made by Papa John's in the course of these ads. Pizza Hut argues, however, that its own independent taste tests and other "scientific evidence" establishes that filtered water makes no difference in pizza dough, that there is no "taste" difference between Papa John's "fresh-pack" sauce and Pizza Hut's "remanufactured" sauce, and that fresh dough is not superior to frozen dough. In response to Pizza Hut's "scientific evidence," Papa John's asserts that "each of these 'claims' involves a matter of common sense choice (fresh versus frozen, canned vegetables and fruit versus remanufactured paste, and filtered versus unfiltered water) about which individual consumers can and do form preferences every day without 'scientific' or 'expert' assistance."

[10] In November 1997, Pizza Hut filed a complaint regarding Papa John's "Better Ingredients. Better Pizza." advertising campaign with the National Advertising Division of the Better Business Bureau, an industry self-regulatory body. This complaint, however, did not produce satisfactory results for Pizza Hut.

B

[11] On August 12, 1998, Pizza Hut filed a civil action in the United States District Court for the Northern District of Texas charging Papa John's with false advertising in violation of Section 43(a)(1)(B) of the Lanham Act. The suit sought relief based on the above-described TV ad campaigns, as well as on some 249 print ads. On March 10, 1999, Pizza Hut filed an amended complaint. Papa John's answered the complaints by denying that its advertising and slogan violated the Lanham Act. Additionally, Papa John's asserted a counterclaim, charging Pizza Hut with engaging in false advertising. The parties consented to a jury trial before a United States magistrate judge. The parties further agreed that the liability issues were to be decided by the jury, while the equitable injunction claim and damages award were within the province of the court.

[12] The trial began on October 26, 1999, and continued for over three weeks. At the close of Pizza Hut's case, and at the close of all evidence, Papa John's moved for a judgment as a matter of law. The motions were denied each time. The district court, without objection, submitted the liability issue to the jury through special interrogatories.[6] The special issues submitted to the jury related to (1) the slogan and (2) over Papa John's objection, certain classes of groups of advertisements referred to as "sauce claims," "dough claims," "taste test claims," and "ingredients claims."

[13] On November 17, 1999, the jury returned its responses to the special issues finding that Papa John's slogan, and its "sauce claims" and "dough claims" were false or misleading and deceptive or likely to deceive consumers.[7] The jury also determined that Papa John's "taste test" ads were not deceptive or likely to deceive consumers, and that Papa John's "ingredients claims" were not false or misleading.[8] As to Papa John's counterclaims against Pizza Hut, the jury found that two of the three

---

[6] Although Papa John's did not object to the submission of the issue of Lanham Act liability to the jury via special interrogatories, it did object to the district court's refusal to submit special interrogatories on the essential elements of materiality and injury. Specifically, Papa John's submitted the following proposed jury interrogatories: (1) "Do you find that any false or misleading description or representation of fact in Papa John's Slogan 'Better Ingredients. Better Pizza.' *are material in that they are likely to influence the purchasing decisions of prospective purchasers of pizza?* " (emphasis added); and (2) "Do you find that any facts or misleading descriptions or representations of fact in Papa John's Slogan 'Better Ingredients. Better Pizza.' are likely to cause injury or damage to Pizza Hut in terms of declining sales or loss of good will?" The district court, without issuing written reasons, denied Papa John's request for special jury interrogatories on these two elements of Pizza Hut's prima facie case.

[7] Specifically, the jury answered "Yes" to each of the following interrogatories: (1) Did you find that Papa John's "Better Ingredients. Better Pizza" slogan is false or misleading, and was a false or misleading description or representation of fact which deceived or was likely to deceive a substantial number of the consumers to whom the slogan was directed; (2) Did you find that Papa John's "sauce" claims are false or misleading, and was a false or misleading description or representation of fact which deceived or was likely to deceive a substantial number of the consumers to whom the slogan was directed; and (3) Did you find that Papa John's "dough" claims are false or misleading, and was a false or misleading description or representation of fact which deceived or was likely to deceive a substantial number of the consumers to whom the slogan was directed? Although the jury was specifically asked whether the advertisements were likely to deceive consumers, the interrogatories failed to ask whether the deception created by these advertisements was material to the consumers to which the ads were directed—that is, whether consumers actually relied on the misrepresentations in making purchasing decisions.

[8] Specifically, the jury answered "No" to the following interrogatories: (1) Did you find that Papa John's "taste test" commercials are a false or misleading description or representation of fact which deceived or was likely to deceive a substantial number of the consumers to whom the slogan was directed; and (2) Did you find that Papa John's "ingredients" claims are false or misleading? The "ingredients" ads found not to be false or misleading did not include any of the "sauce" or "dough" ads.

Pizza Hut television ads at issue were false or misleading and deceptive or likely to deceive consumers.[9]

[14] On January 3, 2000, the trial court, based upon the jury's verdict and the evidence presented by the parties in support of injunctive relief and on the issue of damages, entered a Final Judgment and issued a Memorandum Opinion and Order. The court concluded that the "Better Ingredients. Better Pizza." slogan was "consistent with the legal definition of non-actionable puffery" from its introduction in 1995 until May 1997. However, the slogan "became tainted . . . in light of the entirety of Papa John's post-May 1997 advertising." Based on this conclusion, the magistrate judge permanently enjoined Papa John's from "using any slogan in the future that constitutes a recognizable variation of the phrase 'Better Ingredients. Better Pizza.' or which uses the adjective 'Better' to modify the terms 'ingredients' and/or 'pizza'." Additionally, the court enjoined Papa John's from identifying Frank Carney as a co-founder of Pizza Hut, "unless such advertising includes a voice-over, printed statement or a superimposed message which states that Frank Carney has not been affiliated with Pizza Hut since 1980," and enjoined the dissemination of any advertising that was produced or disseminated prior to the date of this judgment and that explicitly or implicitly states or suggested that "Papa John's component is superior to the same component of Pizza Hut's pizzas." Finally, the court enjoined Papa John's from "explicitly or implicitly claim[ing] that a component of Papa John's pizza is superior to the same component of Pizza Hut's unless the superiority claim is supported by either (1) scientifically demonstrated attributes of superiority or (2) taste test surveys." Additionally, the injunction required that if the claim is supported by taste test surveys, the advertising shall include a printed statement, voice-over or "super," whichever is appropriate, stating the localities where the tests were conducted, the inclusive dates on which the surveys were performed, and the specific pizza products that were tested. The court also awarded Pizza Hut $467,619.75 in damages for having to run corrective ads.

[15] On January 20, 2000, Papa John's filed a notice of appeal with our court. On January 26, we granted Papa John's motion to stay the district court's injunction pending appeal.

II

[16] We review the district court's denial of a motion for judgment as a matter of law de novo applying the same standards as the district court. . . . Thus, for purposes of this appeal, we will review the evidence, in the most favorable light to Pizza Hut, to determine if, as a matter of law, it is sufficient to support a claim of false advertising under section 43(a) of the Lanham Act.

III

. . . .

B

[17] The law governing false advertising claims under section 43(a) of the Lanham Act is well settled. In order to obtain monetary damages or equitable relief in the form of an injunction, "a plaintiff must demonstrate that the commercial advertisement or promotion is either literally false, or that [if the advertisement is not literally false,] it is likely to mislead and confuse consumers." *Seven–Up*, 86 F.3d at 1390 (citing *McNeil–P.C.C., Inc. v. Bristol–Myers Squibb Co.*, 938 F.2d 1544, 1548–49 (2d Cir. 1991)); *see also Johnson & Johnson v. Smithkline Beecham Corp.*, 960 F.2d 294, 298 (2d Cir. 1992).[10] If

---

[9] Pizza Hut has not sought to appeal the jury's verdict regarding its advertising.

[10] When construing the allegedly false or misleading statement to determine if it is actionable under section 43(a), the statement must be viewed in the light of the overall context in which it appears. *See Avis*, 782 F.2d at 385; *Southland*, 108 F.3d at 1139. "Fundamental to any task of interpretation is the principle that text must yield to context." *Avis*, 782 F.2d at 385. Context will often help to determine whether the statement at issue is so overblown and exaggerated that no reasonable

688

the statement is shown to be misleading, the plaintiff must also introduce evidence of the statement's impact on consumers, referred to as materiality. *American Council of Certified Podiatric Physicians and Surgeons v. American Bd. of Podiatric Surgery, Inc.,* 185 F.3d 606, 614 (6th Cir. 1999).

(1)

(a)

[18] Essential to any claim under section 43(a) of the Lanham Act is a determination of whether the challenged statement is one of fact—actionable under section 43(a)—or one of general opinion—not actionable under section 43(a). Bald assertions of superiority or general statements of opinion cannot form the basis of Lanham Act liability . . . . Rather the statements at issue must be a "specific and measurable claim, capable of being proved false or of being reasonably interpreted as a statement of objective fact." *Coastal Abstract Serv., Inc. v. First Am. Title Ins. Co.,* 173 F.3d 725, 731 (9th Cir. 1999); *see also American Council,* 185 F.3d at 614 (stating that "a Lanham Act claim must be based upon a statement of fact, not of opinion"). As noted by our court in *Presidio:* "[A] statement of fact is one that (1) admits of being adjudged true or false in a way that (2) admits of empirical verification." *Presidio,* 784 F.2d at 679; *see also Southland Sod Farms v. Stover Seed Co.,* 108 F.3d 1134, 1145 (9th Cir. 1997) (stating that in order to constitute a statement of fact, a statement must make "a specific and measurable advertisement claim of product superiority").

(b)

[19] One form of non-actionable statements of general opinion under section 43(a) of the Lanham Act has been referred to as "puffery." Puffery has been discussed at some length by other circuits. The Third Circuit has described "puffing" as "advertising that is not deceptive for no one would rely on its exaggerated claims." *U.S. Healthcare, Inc. v. Blue Cross of Greater Philadelphia,* 898 F.2d 914 (3d Cir. 1990) . . . .[11]

[20] These definitions of puffery are consistent with the definitions provided by the leading commentaries in trademark law. A leading authority on unfair competition has defined "puffery" as an "exaggerated advertising, blustering, and boasting upon which no reasonable buyer would rely," or "a general claim of superiority over a comparative product that is so vague, it would be understood as a mere expression of opinion." 4 J. Thomas McCarthy, McCarthy on Trademark and Unfair Competition § 27.38 (4th ed.1996).[12] Similarly, Prosser and Keeton on Torts defines "puffing" as "a seller's privilege

---

consumer would likely rely upon it. As the court in *Federal Express Corporation v. United States Postal Service,* 40 F.Supp.2d 943 (W.D.Tenn.1999), noted:

> On its face, [the statement at issue] does not seem to be the type of vague, general exaggeration which no reasonable person would rely upon in making a purchasing decision. Nevertheless, the determination of whether an advertising statement should be deemed puffery is driven by the context in which the statement is made. Where the context of an advertising statement may lend greater specificity to an otherwise vague representation, the court should not succumb to the temptation to hastily rule a phrase to be unactionable under the Lanham Act.

Id. at 956.

[11] In the same vein, the Second Circuit has observed that "statements of opinion are generally not the basis for Lanham Act liability." *Groden v. Random House,* 61 F.3d 1045, 1051 (2d Cir. 1995). When a statement is "obviously a statement of opinion," it cannot "reasonably be seen as stating or implying provable facts." *Id.* "The Lanham Act does not prohibit false statements generally. It prohibits only false or misleading description or false or misleading representations of fact made about one's own or another's goods or services." *Id.* at 1052.

[12] McCarthy on Trademarks goes on to state: "[V]ague advertising claims that one's product is 'better' than that of competitors' can be dismissed as mere puffing that is not actionable as false

to lie his head off, so long as he says nothing specific, on the theory that no reasonable man would believe him, or that no reasonable man would be influenced by such talk." W. Page Keeton, et al., Prosser and Keeton on the Law of Torts § 109, at 757 (5th ed.1984).

[21] Drawing guidance from the writings of our sister circuits and the leading commentators, we think that non-actionable "puffery" comes in at least two possible forms: (1) an exaggerated, blustering, and boasting statement upon which no reasonable buyer would be justified in relying; or (2) a general claim of superiority over comparable products that is so vague that it can be understood as nothing more than a mere expression of opinion.

(2)

(a)

[22] With respect to materiality, when the statements of fact at issue are shown to be literally false, the plaintiff need not introduce evidence on the issue of the impact the statements had on consumers. *See Castrol, Inc. v. Quaker State Corp.*, 977 F.2d 57, 62 (2d Cir. 1992); *Avila v. Rubin*, 84 F.3d 222, 227 (7th Cir. 1996). In such a circumstance, the court will assume that the statements actually misled consumers. *See American Council*, 185 F.3d at 614; *Johnson & Johnson, Inc. v. GAC Int'l, Inc.*, 862 F.2d 975, 977 (2d Cir. 1988); *U–Haul Inter'l, Inc. v. Jartran, Inc.*, 793 F.2d 1034, 1040 (9th Cir. 1986). On the other hand, if the statements at issue are either ambiguous or true but misleading, the plaintiff must present evidence of actual deception. *See American Council*, 185 F.3d at 616; *Smithkline*, 960 F.2d at 297 (stating that when a "plaintiff's theory of recovery is premised upon a claim of implied falsehood, a plaintiff must demonstrate, by extrinsic evidence, that the challenged commercials tend to mislead or confuse"); *Avila*, 84 F.3d at 227. The plaintiff may not rely on the judge or the jury to determine, "based solely upon his or her own intuitive reaction, whether the advertisement is deceptive." *Smithkline*, 960 F.2d at 297. Instead, proof of actual deception requires proof that "consumers were actually deceived by the defendant's ambiguous or true-but-misleading statements." *American Council*, 185 F.3d at 616 . . . .

(b)

[23] The type of evidence needed to prove materiality also varies depending on what type of recovery the plaintiff seeks. Plaintiffs looking to recover monetary damages for false or misleading advertising that is not literally false must prove actual deception . . . . Plaintiffs attempting to prove actual deception have to produce evidence of actual consumer reaction to the challenged advertising or surveys showing that a substantial number of consumers were actually misled by the advertisements. *See, e.g., PPX Enters., Inc. v. Audiofidelity Enters., Inc.*, 818 F.2d 266, 271 (2d Cir. 1987) ("Actual consumer confusion often is demonstrated through the use of direct evidence, e.g., testimony from members of the buying public, as well as through circumstantial evidence, e.g., consumer surveys or consumer reaction tests.").

[24] Plaintiffs seeking injunctive relief must prove that defendant's representations "have a tendency to deceive consumers." *Balance Dynamics*, 204 F.3d 683 at 690 . . . . Although this standard requires less proof than actual deception, plaintiffs must still produce evidence that the advertisement tends to deceive consumers . . . . To prove a tendency to deceive, plaintiffs need to show that at least some consumers were confused by the advertisements. *See, e.g., American Council*, 185 F.3d at 618 ("Although plaintiff need not present consumer surveys or testimony demonstrating actual deception, it must present evidence of some sort demonstrating that consumers were misled.")

IV

---

advertising." 4 J. Thomas McCarthy, McCarthy on Trademarks and Unfair Competition § 27:38 (4th ed.1997).

[25] We turn now to consider the case before us. Reduced to its essence, the question is whether the evidence, viewed in the most favorable light to Pizza Hut, established that Papa John's slogan "Better Ingredients. Better Pizza." is misleading and violative of section 43(a) of the Lanham Act. In making this determination, we will first consider the slogan "Better Ingredients. Better Pizza." standing alone to determine if it is a statement of fact capable of deceiving a substantial segment of the consuming public to which it was directed. Second, we will determine whether the evidence supports the district court's conclusion that after May 1997, the slogan was tainted, and therefore actionable, as a result of its use in a series of ads comparing specific ingredients used by Papa John's with the ingredients used by its "competitors."

A

[26] The jury concluded that the slogan itself was a "false or misleading" statement of fact, and the district court enjoined its further use. Papa John's argues, however, that this statement "quite simply is not a statement of fact, [but] rather, a statement of belief or opinion, and an argumentative one at that." Papa John's asserts that because "a statement of fact is either true or false, it is susceptible to being proved or disproved. A statement of opinion or belief, on the other hand, conveys the speaker's state of mind, and even though it may be used to attempt to persuade the listener, it is a subjective communication that may be accepted or rejected, but not proven true or false." Papa John's contends that its slogan "Better Ingredients. Better Pizza." falls into the latter category, and because the phrases "better ingredients" and "better pizza" are not subject to quantifiable measures, the slogan is non-actionable puffery.

[27] We will therefore consider whether the slogan standing alone constitutes a statement of fact under the Lanham Act. Bisecting the slogan "Better Ingredients. Better Pizza.," it is clear that the assertion by Papa John's that it makes a "Better Pizza." is a general statement of opinion regarding the superiority of its product over all others. This simple statement, "Better Pizza.," epitomizes the exaggerated advertising, blustering, and boasting by a manufacturer upon which no consumer would reasonably rely. *See, e.g., In re Boston Beer Co.,* 198 F.3d 1370, 1372 (Fed.Cir. 1999) (stating that the phrase "The Best Beer in America" was "trade puffery" and that such a general claim of superiority "should be freely available to all competitors in any given field to refer to their products or services"); *Atari Corp. v. 3D0 Co.,* 1994 WL 723601, *2 (N.D.Cal. 1994) (stating that a manufacturer's slogan that its product was "the most advanced home gaming system in the universe" was non-actionable puffery); *Nikkal Indus., Ltd. v. Salton, Inc.,* 735 F.Supp. 1227, 1234 n. 3 (S.D.N.Y. 1990) (stating that a manufacturers claim that its ice cream maker was "better" than competition ice cream makers is non-actionable puffery). Consequently, it appears indisputable that Papa John's assertion "Better Pizza." is non-actionable puffery.[13]

[28] Moving next to consider separately the phrase "Better Ingredients.," the same conclusion holds true. Like "Better Pizza.," it is typical puffery. The word "better," when used in this context is unquantifiable. What makes one food ingredient "better" than another comparable ingredient, without further description, is wholly a matter of individual taste or preference not subject to scientific quantification. Indeed, it is difficult to think of any product, or any component of any product, to which the term "better," without more, is quantifiable. As our court stated in *Presidio:*

> The law recognizes that a vendor is allowed some latitude in claiming merits of his wares
> by way of an opinion rather than an absolute guarantee, so long as he hews to the line of

---

[13] It should be noted that Pizza Hut uses the slogan "The Best Pizza Under One Roof." Similarly, other nationwide pizza chains employ slogans touting their pizza as the "best": (1) Domino's Pizza uses the slogan "Nobody Delivers Better."; (2) Danato's uses the slogan "Best Pizza on the Block."; (3) Mr. Gatti's uses the slogan "Best Pizza in Town: Honest!"; and (4) Pizza Inn uses the slogans "Best Pizza Ever." and "The Best Tasting Pizza."

rectitude in matters of fact. Opinions are not only the lifestyle of democracy, they are the brag in advertising that has made for the wide dissemination of products that otherwise would never have reached the households of our citizens. If we were to accept the thesis set forth by the appellees, [that all statements by advertisers were statements of fact actionable under the Lanham Act,] the advertising industry would have to be liquidated in short order.

Presidio, 784 F.2d at 685. Thus, it is equally clear that Papa John's assertion that it uses "Better Ingredients." is one of opinion not actionable under the Lanham Act.

[29] Finally, turning to the combination of the two non-actionable phrases as the slogan "Better Ingredients. Better Pizza.," we fail to see how the mere joining of these two statements of opinion could create an actionable statement of fact. Each half of the slogan amounts to little more than an exaggerated opinion of superiority that no consumer would be justified in relying upon. It has not been explained convincingly to us how the combination of the two phrases, without more, changes the essential nature of each phrase so as to make it actionable. We assume that "Better Ingredients." modifies "Better Pizza." and consequently gives some expanded meaning to the phrase "Better Pizza," i.e., our pizza is better because our ingredients are better. Nevertheless, the phrase fails to give "Better Pizza." any more quantifiable meaning. Stated differently, the adjective that continues to describe "pizza" is "better," a term that remains unquantifiable, especially when applied to the sense of taste. Consequently, the slogan as a whole is a statement of non-actionable opinion. Thus, there is no legally sufficient basis to support the jury's finding that the slogan standing alone is a "false or misleading" statement of fact.

B

[30] We next will consider whether the use of the slogan "Better Ingredients. Better Pizza." in connection with a series of comparative ads found by the jury to be misleading—specifically, ads comparing Papa John's sauce and dough with the sauce and dough of its competitors—"tainted" the statement of opinion and made it misleading under section 43(a) of the Lanham Act. Before reaching the ultimate question of whether the slogan is actionable under the Lanham Act, we will first examine the sufficiency of the evidence supporting the jury's conclusion that the comparison ads were misleading.

(1)

[31] After the jury returned its verdict, Papa John's filed a post-verdict motion under Federal Rule of Civil Procedure 50 for a judgment as a matter of law. In denying Papa John's motion, the district court, while apparently recognizing that the slogan "Better Ingredients. Better Pizza." standing alone is non-actionable puffery under the Lanham Act, concluded that after May 1997, the slogan was transformed as a result of its use in connection with a series of ads that the jury found misleading. These ads had compared specific ingredients used by Papa John's with the ingredients used by its competitors.[14] In essence, the district court held that the comparison ads in which the slogan appeared

---

[14] In its memorandum opinion addressing Papa John's post-verdict Rule 50 motion, the court stated:

> Although Papa John's started in May 1995 with a slogan which was essentially ambiguous and self-laudatory, consistent with the legal definition of non-actionable puffery, Papa John's deliberately and intentionally exploited its slogan as a centerpiece of its subsequent advertising campaign after May 1997 which falsely portrayed Papa Johns's tomato sauce and pizza dough as being superior to the sauce and dough components used in Pizza Hut's pizza products. When the "Better Ingredients. Better Pizza." slogan is considered in light of the entirety of Papa John's post-May 1997 advertising which violated the provisions of the Lanham Act and in the context in which it was juxtaposed

as the tag line gave objective, quantifiable, and fact-specific meaning to the slogan. Consequently, the court concluded that the slogan was misleading and actionable under section 43(a) of the Lanham Act and enjoined its further use.

(2)

[32] We are obligated to accept the findings of the jury unless the facts point so overwhelmingly in favor of one party that no reasonable person could arrive at a different conclusion. *See Scottish Heritable Trust v. Peat Marwick Main & Co.,* 81 F.3d 606, 610 (5th Cir. 1996). In examining the record evidence, we must view it the way that is most favorable to upholding the verdict. *See Hiltgen v. Sumrall,* 47 F.3d 695, 700 (5th Cir. 1995). Viewed in this light, it is clear that there is sufficient evidence to support the jury's conclusion that the sauce and dough ads were misleading statements of fact actionable under the Lanham Act.

[33] Turning first to the sauce ads, the evidence establishes that despite the differences in the methods used to produce their competing sauces: (1) the primary ingredient in both Pizza Hut and Papa John's sauce is vine-ripened tomatoes; (2) at the point that the competing sauces are placed on the pizza, just prior to putting the pies into the oven for cooking, the consistency and water content of the sauces are essentially identical; and (3) as noted by the district court, at no time "prior to the close of the liability phase of trial was any credible evidence presented [by Papa John's] to demonstrate the existence of demonstrable differences" in the competing sauces. Consequently, the district court was correct in concluding that: "Without any scientific support or properly conducted taste preference test, by the written and/or oral negative connotations conveyed that pizza made from tomato paste concentrate is inferior to the 'fresh pack' method used by Papa John's, its sauce advertisements conveyed an impression which is misleading . . . ." Turning our focus to the dough ads, while the evidence clearly established that Papa John's and Pizza Hut employ different methods in making their pizza dough, again, the evidence established that there is no quantifiable difference between pizza dough produced through the "cold or slow-fermentation method" (used by Papa John's), or the "frozen dough method" (used by Pizza Hut).[15] Further, although there is some evidence indicating that the texture of the dough used by Papa John's and Pizza Hut is slightly different, this difference is not related to the manufacturing process used to produce the dough. Instead, it is due to a difference in the wheat used to make the dough. Finally, with respect to the differences in the pizza dough resulting from the use of filtered water as opposed to tap water, the evidence was sufficient for the jury to conclude that there is no quantifiable difference between dough produced with tap water, as opposed to dough produced with filtered water.

[34] We should note again that Pizza Hut does not contest the truthfulness of the underlying factual assertions made by Papa John's in the course of the sauce and dough ads. Pizza Hut concedes that it uses "remanufactured" tomato sauce to make its pizza sauce, while Papa John's uses "fresh-pack." Further, in regard to the dough, Pizza Hut concedes the truth of the assertion that it uses tap water in making its pizza dough, which is often frozen, while Papa John's uses filtered water to make its dough, which is fresh—never frozen. Consequently, because Pizza Hut does not contest the factual basis of Papa John's factual assertions, such assertions cannot be found to be factually false, but only impliedly false or misleading.

---

with the false and misleading statements contained in Papa John's print and broadcast media advertising, the slogan itself became tainted to the extent that its continued use should be enjoined.

[15] The testimony of Pizza Hut's expert, Dr. Faubion, established that although consumers stated a preference for fresh dough rather than frozen dough, when taste tests were conducted, respondents were unable to distinguish between pizza made on fresh as opposed to frozen dough.

693

[35] Thus, we conclude by saying that although the ads were true about the ingredients Papa John's used, it is clear that there was sufficient evidence in the record to support the jury's conclusion that Papa John's sauce and dough ads were misleading—but not false—in their suggestion that Papa John's ingredients were superior.

(3)

[36] Thus, having concluded that the record supports a finding that the sauce and dough ads are misleading statements of fact, we must now determine whether the district court was correct in concluding that the use of the slogan "Better Ingredients. Better Pizza." in conjunction with these misleading ads gave quantifiable meaning to the slogan making a general statement of opinion misleading within the meaning of the Lanham Act.

[37] In support of the district court's conclusion that the slogan was transformed, Pizza Hut argues that "in construing any advertising statement, the statement must be considered in the overall context in which it appears." Building on the foundation of this basic legal principle, *see Avis,* 782 F.2d at 385, Pizza Hut argues that "[t]he context in which Papa John's slogan must be viewed is the 2 1/2 year campaign during which its advertising served as 'chapters' to demonstrate the truth of the 'Better Ingredients. Better Pizza.' book." Pizza Hut argues, that because Papa John's gave consumers specific facts supporting its assertion that its sauce and dough are "better"—specific facts that the evidence, when viewed in the light most favorable to the verdict, are irrelevant in making a better pizza—Papa John's statement of opinion that it made a "Better Pizza" became misleading. In essence, Pizza Hut argues, that by using the slogan "Better Ingredients. Better Pizza." in combination with the ads comparing Papa John's sauce and dough with the sauce and dough of its competitions, Papa John's gave quantifiable meaning to the word "Better" rendering it actionable under section 43(a) of the Lanham Act.

[38] We agree that the message communicated by the slogan "Better Ingredients. Better Pizza." is expanded and given additional meaning when it is used as the tag line in the misleading sauce and dough ads. The slogan, when used in combination with the comparison ads, gives consumers two fact-specific reasons why Papa John's ingredients are "better." Consequently, a reasonable consumer would understand the slogan, *when considered in the context of the comparison ads,* as conveying the following message: Papa John's uses "better ingredients," which produces a "better pizza" because Papa John's uses "fresh-pack" tomatoes, fresh dough, and filtered water. In short, Papa John's has given definition to the word "better." Thus, when the slogan is used in this context, it is no longer mere opinion, but rather takes on the characteristics of a statement of fact. When used in the context of the sauce and dough ads, the slogan is misleading for the same reasons we have earlier discussed in connection with the sauce and dough ads.[16]

---

[16] The judgment of the district court enjoining the future use by Papa John's of the slogan "Better Ingredients. Better Pizza." did not simply bar Papa John's use of the slogan in future ads comparing its sauce and dough with that of its competitors. Rather, the injunction permanently enjoined any future use of the slogan "in association with the sale, promotion and/or identification of pizza products sold under the Papa John's name." Further, the injunction precluded Papa John's from using the "adjective 'better' to modify the terms 'ingredients' and/or 'pizza.' " While it is clear that the jury did not make any finding to support such a broad injunction, and Pizza Hut offered no survey evidence indicating how potential consumers viewed the slogan, the district court concluded that the evidence established that

> Papa John's deliberately and intentionally exploited its slogan as a centerpiece of its
> subsequent advertising campaign after May 1997 which falsely portrayed Papa John's
> tomato sauce and pizza dough as being superior to the sauce and dough components

694

(4)

[39] Concluding that when the slogan was used as the tag line in the sauce and dough ads it became misleading, we must now determine whether reasonable consumers would have a tendency to rely on this misleading statement of fact in making their purchasing decisions. We conclude that Pizza Hut has failed to adduce evidence establishing that the misleading statement of fact conveyed by the ads and the slogan was material to the consumers to which the slogan was directed. Consequently, because such evidence of materiality is necessary to establish liability under the Lanham Act, the district court erred in denying Papa John's motion for judgment as a matter of law.

[40] As previously discussed, none of the underlying facts supporting Papa John's claims of ingredient superiority made in connection with the slogan were literally false. Consequently, in order to satisfy its prima facie case, Pizza Hut was required to submit evidence establishing that the impliedly false or misleading statements were material to, that is, they had a tendency to influence the purchasing decisions of, the consumers to which they were directed.[17] *See American Council,* 185 F.3d at 614 (stating that "a plaintiff relying upon statements that are literally true yet misleading cannot obtain relief by arguing how consumers could react; it must show how consumers actually do react"); . . . *see also* 4 J. Thomas McCarthy, McCarthy on Trademarks and Unfair Competition, § 27:35 (4th ed.1997)(stating that the "[p]laintiff must make some showing that the defendant's misrepresentation was 'material' in the sense that it would have some effect on consumers' purchasing decision").[18] We conclude that the evidence proffered by Pizza Hut fails to make an adequate showing.

---

used in Pizza Hut's products . . . . [Thus,] the slogan itself became tainted to the extent that its continued use should be enjoined.

Our review of the record convinces us that there is simply no evidence to support the district court's conclusion that the slogan was irreparably tainted as a result of its use in the misleading comparison sauce and dough ads. At issue in this case were some 249 print ads and 29 television commercials. After a thorough review of the record, we liberally construe eight print ads to be sauce ads, six print ads to be dough ads, and six print ads to be both sauce and dough ads. Further, we liberally construe nine television commercials to be sauce ads and two television commercials to be dough ads. Consequently, out of a total of 278 print and television ads, the slogan appeared in only 31 ads that could be liberally construed to be misleading sauce or dough ads.

We find simply no evidence, survey or otherwise, to support the district court's conclusion that the advertisements that the jury found misleading—ads that constituted only a small fraction of Papa John's use of the slogan—somehow had become encoded in the minds of consumers such that the mention of the slogan reflectively brought to mind the misleading statements conveyed by the sauce and dough ads. Thus, based on the record before us, Pizza Hut has failed to offer sufficient evidence to support the district court's conclusion that the slogan had become forever "tainted" by its use as the tag line in the handful of misleading comparison ads.

[17] Since Pizza Hut sought only equitable relief and no monetary damages, it was required to offer evidence sufficient to establish that the claims made by Papa John's had the *"tendency to deceive consumers,"* rather than evidence indicating that the claims made by Papa John's *actually deceived consumers. American Council,* 185 F.3d at 606; *see also Balance Dynamics,* 204 F.3d at 690 (emphasis added).

[18] In *Johnson & Johnson v. Smithkline Beecham Corp.,* 960 F.2d 294 (2d Cir. 1992), the Second Circuit discussed this requirement in some detail:

Where, as here, a plaintiff's theory of recovery is premised upon a claim of implied falsehood, a plaintiff must demonstrate, by extrinsic evidence, that the challenged commercials tend to mislead or confuse consumers. It is not for the judge to determine, based solely upon his or her own intuitive reaction whether the advertisement is deceptive. Rather, as we have reiterated in the past, "the question in such cases is—what

695

[41] In its appellate brief and during the course of oral argument, Pizza Hut directs our attention to three items of evidence in the record that it asserts establishes materiality to consumers. First, Pizza Hut points to the results of a survey conducted by an "independent expert" (Dr. Dupont) regarding the use of the slogan "Better Ingredients. Better Pizza." as written on Papa John's pizza box (the box survey). The results of the box survey, however, were excluded by the district court.[19] Consequently, these survey results provide no basis for the jury's finding.

[42] Second, Pizza Hut points to two additional surveys conducted by Dr. Dupont that attempted to measure consumer perception of Papa John's "taste test" ads. This survey evidence, however, fails to address Pizza Hut's claim of materiality with respect to the slogan. Moreover, the jury rejected Pizza Hut's claims of deception with regard to Papa John's "taste test" ads—the very ads at issue in these surveys.

[43] Finally, Pizza Hut attempts to rely on Papa John's own tracking studies and on the alleged subjective intent of Papa John's executives "to create a perception that Papa John's in fact uses better ingredients" to demonstrate materiality. Although Papa John's 1998 Awareness, Usage & Attitude Tracking Study showed that 48% of the respondents believe that "Papa John's has better ingredients than other national pizza chains," the study failed to indicate whether the conclusions resulted from the advertisements at issue, or from personal eating experiences, or from a combination of both. Consequently, the results of this study are not reliable or probative to test whether the slogan was material. Further, Pizza Hut provides no precedent, and we are aware of none, that stands for the proposition that the subjective intent of the defendant's corporate executives to convey a particular message is evidence of the fact that consumers in fact relied on the message to make their purchases. Thus, this evidence does not address the ultimate issue of materiality.

[44] In short, Pizza Hut has failed to offer probative evidence on whether the misleading facts conveyed by Papa John's through its slogan were material to consumers: that is to say, there is no evidence demonstrating that the slogan had the tendency to deceive consumers so as to affect their purchasing decisions. *See American Council,* 185 F.3d at 614; *Blue Dane,* 178 F.3d at 1042–43; *Sandoz Pharm. Corp. v. Richardson–Vicks, Inc.,* 902 F.2d 222, 228–29 (3d Cir. 1990). Thus, the district court erred in denying Papa John's motion for judgment as a matter of law.

[45] Additionally, we note that the district court erred in requiring Papa John's to modify the Carney ads and the taste test ads. The Carney ads were removed from the jury's consideration by Pizza Hut, and the jury expressly concluded that the taste test ads were not actionable under section 43(a) of the Lanham Act. Thus, the district court, lacking the necessary factual predicate, abused its discretion in ordering Papa John's to modify these ads.

V

[46] In sum, we hold that the slogan "Better Ingredients. Better Pizza." standing alone is not an objectifiable statement of fact upon which consumers would be justified in relying. Thus, it does not constitute a false or misleading statement of fact actionable under section 43(a) of the Lanham Act.

---

does the person to whom the advertisement is addressed find to be the message?" That is, what does the public perceive the message to be.

The answer to this question is pivotal because, where the advertisement is literally true, it is often the only measure by which a court can determine whether a commercial's net communicative effect is misleading. Thus, the success of a plaintiff's implied falsity claim usually turns on the persuasiveness of a consumer survey.

Id. at 287–98.

[19] Pizza Hut has not sought review on appeal of the district court's ruling that the results of the box survey were inadmissible.

[47] Additionally, while the slogan, when appearing in the context of some of the post-May 1997 comparative advertising—specifically, the sauce and dough campaigns—was given objectifiable meaning and thus became misleading and actionable, Pizza Hut has failed to adduce sufficient evidence establishing that the misleading facts conveyed by the slogan were material to the consumers to which it was directed. Thus, Pizza Hut failed to produce evidence of a Lanham Act violation, and the district court erred in denying Papa John's motion for judgment as a matter of law.

[48] Therefore, the judgment of the district court denying Papa John's motion for judgment as a matter of law is REVERSED; the final judgment of the district court is VACATED; and the case is REMANDED for entry of judgment for Papa John's.

REVERSED, VACATED, and REMANDED with instructions.

Questions and Comments

1. *Consumer Deception as Distinct from Materiality.* As stated in the introductory paragraphs of Part IV.A, among the five elements that a plaintiff must show to prevail on a false advertising claim are: (2) the advertising statement "either deceived or had the capacity to deceive a substantial segment of potential consumers" and (3) "[t]he deception is material, in that it is likely to influence the consumer's purchasing decision." *Pizza Hut, Inc. v. Papa John's Int'l*, 227 F.3d 489, 495 (5th Cir. 2000). In its discussion of materiality, and specifically in paragraphs 22 and 44 of the opinion as excerpted, the *Pizza Hut* court may appear to merge these two elements together. *See Johnson & Johnson Vision Care, Inc. v. 1-800 Contacts, Inc.*, 299 F.3d 1242, 1250 (11th Cir. 2002) ("[I]t appears that the Fifth Circuit blurred the boundary between the two elements in its recent *Pizza Hut* decision."). It is worth keeping in mind that courts typically treat these two elements separately. As to the consumer deception element, literally false advertising (including advertising that is false by necessary implication) typically triggers a presumption of consumer deception, while true but misleading advertising typically requires extrinsic evidence (often in the form of survey evidence) to show that consumers are deceived. *See* DAVID H. BERNSTEIN & BRUCE P. KELLER, THE LAW OF ADVERTISING, MARKETING AND PROMOTIONS § 2.07 (2019). As to the materiality element, if an advertising statement is literally false, this typically triggers a presumption of materiality, while true but misleading advertising requires evidence that the statement is material to consumers' decision to purchase. *See* MCCARTHY § 27:35. Importantly, however, in certain circuits, even literally false advertising will not trigger a presumption of materiality, which must instead be independently shown in all cases. *See, e.g., Johnson & Johnson Vision Care, Inc. v. 1-800 Contacts, Inc.*, 299 F.3d 1242, 1250–51 (11th Cir. 2002) ("To the extent that the Fifth Circuit {*Pizza Hut*} decision marks a circuit split, we stand with the First and Second Circuits, concluding that the plaintiff must establish materiality even when a defendant's advertisement has been found literally false.").

4. Substantiation

a. "Tests Prove" Claims

When the defendant represents that "tests prove," "studies show," or "surveys show" some asserted fact, special doctrinal rules apply under Lanham Act § 43(a)(1)(B), 15 U.S.C. § 1125(a)(1)(B). David Bernstein and Bruce Keller explain:

> Under the Lanham Act, the plaintiff always has the burden of proving the defendant's claim false. If an advertisement asserts a fact, then it is not enough for a Lanham Act plaintiff to show that the claim was unsubstantiated. When, however, the defendant makes what is known as an "establishment claim," the plaintiff's burden to prove the claim false is reduced. An establishment claim conveys an express or implied message that "tests prove" a particular fact, or that "studies show" a particular claim, or any similar message indicating to the consumer that scientific or experimental evidence supports an advertising claim. In order to prove that an establishment claim is literally

697

false, the plaintiff need only prove that the tests cited by the advertiser do not establish the proposition for which they are cited . . . .

Generally, a plaintiff may prove that the cited tests do not support the proposition for which they are cited in one of two ways. First, the plaintiff may show that the tests, even if valid, do not establish the claims actually made by an advertisement. Second, an alternative method of proof is to show that the advertiser's cited tests are invalid and objectively unreliable.

DAVID H. BERNSTEIN & BRUCE P. KELLER, THE LAW OF ADVERTISING, MARKETING AND PROMOTIONS § 2.07 (2019) (footnotes omitted).

Establishment claims may be express or implied. Even when an advertisement does not use the phrase "tests prove" or its equivalents, the advertisement may be held to convey the same meaning through non-verbal indicia, such as when it depicts graphs or diagrams or scientists at work in a laboratory setting. *See, e.g., L & F Prod., a Div. of Sterling Winthrop, Inc. v. Procter & Gamble Co.*, 845 F. Supp. 984, 1000 (S.D.N.Y. 1994), aff'd, 45 F.3d 709 (2d Cir. 1995) ("The commercials make no explicit reference to tests or studies. Nonetheless, a commercial may imply that tests or studies support a superiority claim. For example, a product comparison performed by actors dressed as scientists on a set appearing to be a laboratory may imply that tests or studies were conducted. Plaintiffs bear the burden of demonstrating that commercials convey such implied messages.").

The following case, *Castrol Inc. v. Quaker State Corp.*, 977 F.2d 57 (2d Cir. 1992), remains one of the most important foundational cases setting forth establishment claim doctrine under Lanham Act § 43(a)(1)(B).

Castrol Inc. v. Quaker State Corp.
977 F.2d 57 (2d Cir. 1992)

WALKER, Circuit Judge:

[1] A Quaker State television commercial asserts that "tests prove" its 10W–30 motor oil provides better protection against engine wear at start-up. In a thoughtful opinion reported at 1992 WL 47981 (S.D.N.Y. March 2, 1992), the United States District Court for the Southern District of New York (Charles S. Haight, *Judge*) held that plaintiff-appellee Castrol, Inc. ("Castrol") had proven this advertised claim literally false pursuant to § 43(a) of the Lanham Act, 15 U.S.C. § 1125(a) (1988). The district court issued a March 20, 1992 Order preliminarily enjoining defendants-appellants Quaker State Corporation, Quaker State Oil Refining Corporation, and Grey Advertising Inc., ("Quaker State"), from airing the commercial. We agree that Castrol has shown a likelihood of success in proving the commercial literally false. We accordingly affirm.

BACKGROUND

[2] Judge Haight's March 2, 1992 opinion thoroughly recites the facts of this case. We describe only those facts essential to the disposition of this appeal.

The voiceover to Quaker State's 10W–30 motor oil commercial states:

Warning: Up to half of all engine wear can happen when you start your car.

At this critical time, tests prove Quaker State 10W–30 protects better than any other leading 10W–30 motor oil.

In an overwhelming majority of engine tests, Quaker State 10W–30 flowed faster to all vital parts. In all size engines tested, Quaker State protected faster, so it protected better.

Get the best protection against start up wear. Today's Quaker State! It's one tough motor oil.

[3] Visually, the commercial begins with a man entering a car and then shows a bottle of Quaker State 10W–30 motor oil. Large, block letters, superimposed over the bottle, "crawl" across the screen with the words:

AT START UP QUAKER STATE 10W–30 PROTECTS BETTER THAN ANY OTHER LEADING 10W–30 MOTOR OIL.

Originally, this "crawl" used the words "tests prove" instead of "at start up," but shortly after the filing of the current lawsuit Quaker State revised the message. The commercial then shows an engine, superimposed over which are bottles of Quaker State and four competing motor oils (including Castrol GTX 10W–30) and a bar graph depicting the speed with which each oil flowed to components of a Chrysler engine. The Quaker State bar is higher than all four competitors indicating that it flowed faster. The commercial closes with the words: "ONE TOUGH MOTOR OIL."

[4] Polymethacrylate or "PMA," an additive intended to quicken oil flow to engine parts, is the source of Quaker State's superiority claim. The competitors listed in its commercial use olefin copolymer or "OCP," another additive. Two laboratory tests, the first run in 1987 and the second in 1991, have compared Quaker State's PMA–based oil with competing OCP–based oils. Rohm and Haas, the Pennsylvania corporation which manufactures PMA, conducted both tests.

[5] Rohm and Haas' 1987 tests measured two performance indicators: "oiling time," or the time it takes for oil to reach distant parts in a just-started engine, and engine wear, measured through the amount of metal debris observed in the oil after the engine had run. Rohm and Haas technicians filled engines, in all other respects similar, with either Quaker State's PMA–based 10W–30 oil, or with a generic OCP–based oil known as "Texstar." During numerous engine starts, Quaker State's oil demonstrated a substantially faster oiling time, reaching distant engine parts as much as 100 seconds earlier than the Texstar competitor. Contrary to expectations, however, this did not translate into reduced engine wear. A Rohm and Haas report stated that "[a]fter 64 starts … the Quaker State oil gave marginally better results, but there was no significant difference in wear metals accumulation between the two oils."

[6] Rohm and Haas initially attributed the poor engine wear results to the presence of "residual oil" remaining from the prior engine starts. They theorized that this oil might be lubricating the engine in the period between ignition and arrival of the new oil, and so might be preventing the faster flowing Quaker State oil from demonstrating better protection that is statistically significant. To address this, they conducted additional engine starts with a warm-up between each run so as to burn off the residual oil. The Rohm and Haas report, however, concluded that "[w]ear metals analysis for this test cycle also failed to differentiate significantly between the two oils …." Thus, while the 1987 Rohm and Haas tests demonstrated faster oil flow, they could not prove better protection against engine wear that is statistically significant.

[7] The 1991 Rohm and Haas tests compared Quaker State's oiling time with that of four leading OCP–based competitors, including Castrol GTX 10W–30. Again, Quaker State's PMA–based oil flowed significantly faster to engine parts. Using a 1991 2.2 liter Chrysler engine with a sump temperature of minus 20 degrees Fahrenheit, for example, the Quaker State oiling time was 345 seconds, as compared to the competing oils' times of 430, 430, 505 and 510 seconds. In the 1991 tests, as opposed to the 1987 studies, Rohm and Haas made no attempt to measure whether this faster oiling time resulted in reduced engine wear.

[8] Quaker State broadcast their commercial in November, 1991. On December 19, 1991, Castrol initiated the present action. Castrol asserted that no studies supported the commercial's claim that "tests prove" Quaker State's oil provides better protection, and that this claim of test-proven superiority constituted false advertising. It sought preliminary and permanent injunctive relief and damages pursuant to § 43(a) of the Lanham Act, 15 U.S.C. § 1125(a), New York General Business Law §§ 349, 350, and common law unfair competition.

[9] At the hearing on the motion for a preliminary injunction, Quaker State relied on the Rohm and Haas tests. It argued that the Rohm and Haas oiling time findings support the advertised claim of better protection because oil which flows faster to engine parts necessarily protects them better. Dr. Elmer Klaus, Quaker State's sole expert witness, explained this "faster means better" theory as follows: Prior to start-up "the metal parts [of an engine] are not separated by a film of oil. The solid members are sitting on each other," a condition referred to as "boundary lubrication." Upon ignition, engine wear begins to occur. Soon, however, the movement of the parts generates a film of lubrication from the "residual oil" remaining from a prior running of the engine and engine wear ceases. But the heat of the running engine thins the residual oil which can no longer keep the parts sufficiently apart. The engine returns to a condition of boundary lubrication and wear again occurs until the arrival of the new oil. Dr. Klaus concluded that the faster the new oil flows to the engine parts, the better job it does of minimizing this second period of boundary lubrication. Faster oil flow, therefore, means better protection.

[10] Castrol's three experts focused on the role of residual oil. They testified that the small amount of residual oil left from a prior running of an engine provides more than adequate lubrication at the next start-up. Moreover, they asserted that this residual oil remains functional for a significant period of time so that both PMA–based and OCP–based 10W–30 motor oils reach the engine parts *before* this residual oil burns off. Thus, they maintained, there is no second boundary lubrication period and Quaker State's faster oiling time is irrelevant to engine wear.

[11] Castrol's experts supported their residual oil theory with a Rohm and Haas videotape, produced in the course of its tests, which shows the residual oil present on the cam lobe interface of a Chrysler 2.2 liter engine. Dr. Hoult, who narrated the tape for the court, explained that "as the film goes on the lubricant there will never go away[,] which means it's lubricated throughout the starting process and that's the basic reason that the time for the replenishment oil to reach these parts is not related to wear[,] because the parts have already lubricated okay."

[12] The experts also cited the near absence of catastrophic engine failure since the imposition of mandatory "pumpability" standards, known as "J300" standards, in the early 1980's. Pumpability refers to the ease with which the pump can spread oil throughout the engine. As pumpability increases, oiling times decrease. Prior to the J300 standards, certain oils became unpumpable in cold weather. This, the experts testified, caused engines to suffer catastrophic failure within a "fraction" of a second after the residual oil had burned off. The J300 standards, however, required increased pumpability and have virtually eradicated reported cases of engine failure. The experts inferred that all 10W–30 oils, which are required to meet the J300 standards, must therefore be reaching the engine before the residual oil burns off. At best, there is only a "fraction" of a second between residual oil burn-off and catastrophic failure during which a faster flowing oil could conceivably reduce engine wear.

[13] The district court assessed the parties' conflicting testimony in its March 2, 1991 opinion. Judge Haight found Dr. Klaus' testimony lacking in credibility because

> [Dr. Klaus'] current research programs at Pennsylvania State University are funded in significant part by Quaker State or an industry association to which Quaker State belongs. Klaus arrived at his opinions not on the basis of independent research but by digesting technical papers furnished to him by Quaker State and Rohm and Haas in preparation for his testimony; and he acknowledged that he reached his conclusion concerning Quaker State's better protection before even being made aware of the contrary 1987 Rohm and Haas tests.

Judge Haight credited the testimony of Castrol's three experts. In addition, he found their testimony corroborated by three key facts: (1) the failure of the 1987 Rohm and Haas tests to demonstrate reduced engine wear; (2) the Rohm and Haas technician's 1987 hypothesis that the presence of residual oil might be the reason for the failure to show better engine wear protection that is statistically significant; and (3) the virtual disappearance of catastrophic engine failure following the imposition of the J300 standards. Judge Haight accordingly "accept[ed]" the residual oil theory put forth by these experts. The court explained that an engine is like "a fort besieged by an encircling and encroaching enemy." The enemy is engine wear; the fort's supplies are residual oil; and a relief column on its way to reinforce the fort is the new oil. "If that relief column does not reach the bearing surfaces before the residual oil is burned away, the engine will suffer not only wear but catastrophic failure . . . . [T]he Quaker State commercial is false because the evidence shows that during the time differentials demonstrated by the [Rohm and Haas] oiling tests, residual oil holds the fort."

[14] Judge Haight concluded that because residual oil "holds the fort," Rohm and Haas' faster oiling time findings did not necessarily prove better protection. He consequently held that "Castrol has established the likelihood of proving at trial the falsity of Quaker State's claim that tests prove its oil protects better against start-up engine wear." On March 20, 1992, 1992 WL 73569 the district court entered an Order granting preliminary injunctive relief. Quaker State appeals.

DISCUSSION

. . . .

To succeed under § 43(a), a plaintiff must demonstrate that "an advertisement is either literally false or that the advertisement, though literally true, is likely to mislead and confuse consumers . . . . Where the advertising claim is shown to be literally false, the court may enjoin the use of the claim 'without reference to the advertisement's impact on the buying public.'" *McNeil–P.C.C., Inc. v. Bristol–Myers Squibb Co.*, 938 F.2d 1544, 1549 (2d Cir. 1991) (quoting *Coca–Cola*, 690 F.2d at 317) (citations omitted). Here, Castrol contends that the challenged advertisement is literally false. It bears the burden of proving this to a "likelihood of success" standard.

[15] As we have on two occasions explained, plaintiff bears a different burden in proving literally false the advertised claim that tests prove defendant's product superior, than it does in proving the falsity of a superiority claim which makes no mention of tests. In *Procter & Gamble Co. v. Chesebrough–Pond's, Inc.*, 747 F.2d 114 (2d Cir. 1984), for example, Chesebrough alleged the literal falsity of Procter's advertised claim that "clinical tests" proved its product superior. *Id.* at 116. Procter, in return, challenged as literally false a Chesebrough commercial which, making no mention of tests, asserted that its lotion was equal in effectiveness to any leading brand. *Id.* We explained that in order to prove literally false Procter's claim of "test-proven superiority," Chesebrough bore the burden of "showing that the tests referred to by P & G were not sufficiently reliable to permit one to conclude with reasonable certainty that they established the proposition for which they were cited." *Id.* at 119. We held that Procter could prove false Chesebrough's advertisement, however, "only upon adducing evidence" that affirmatively showed Chesebrough's claim of parity to be false. *Id.*

[16] We drew this same distinction in *McNeil–P.C.C., Inc. v. Bristol–Myers Squibb Co.*, 938 F.2d 1544 (2d Cir. 1991). Bristol–Myers initially advertised to trade professionals that "clinical studies" had shown its analgesic provided better relief than McNeil's. *Id.* at 1546. Bristol–Myers' later televised commercial made the product superiority claim but "did not refer to clinical studies." *Id.* We held that, with respect to the initial trade advertising, "McNeil could . . . meet its burden of proof by demonstrating that these studies did not establish that AF Excedrin provided superior pain relief." *Id.* at 1549. With respect to the televised commercial, however, McNeil bore the burden of generating "scientific proof that the challenged advertisement was false." *Id.*

[17] A plaintiff's burden in proving literal falsity thus varies depending on the nature of the challenged advertisement. Where the defendant's advertisement claims that its product is superior, plaintiff must affirmatively prove defendant's product equal or inferior. Where, as in the current case, defendant's ad explicitly or implicitly represents that tests or studies prove its product superior, plaintiff satisfies its burden by showing that the tests did not establish the proposition for which they were cited. *McNeil*, 938 F.2d at 1549. We have held that a plaintiff can meet this burden by

701

demonstrating that the tests were not sufficiently reliable to permit a conclusion that the product is superior. *Procter,* 747 F.2d at 119.... The *Procter* "sufficiently reliable" standard of course assumes that the tests in question, if reliable, would prove the proposition for which they are cited. If the plaintiff can show that the tests, even if reliable, do not establish the proposition asserted by the defendant, the plaintiff has obviously met its burden. In such a case, tests which may or may not be "sufficiently reliable," are simply irrelevant.

[18] The district court held that Castrol had met this latter burden, stating that "Castrol has established the likelihood of proving at trial the falsity of Quaker State's claim that tests prove its oil protects better...." In this Lanham Act case, we will reverse the district court's order of preliminary injunctive relief "only upon a showing that it abused its discretion, which may occur when a court bases its decision on clearly erroneous findings of fact or on errors as to applicable law." *Procter,* 747 F.2d at 118.

I. The district court committed no errors of law.

[19] Quaker State contends that the district court improperly shifted the burden of proof to the defendant when it stated that "the claim that tests demonstrate ... superiority is false because no test does so and [Dr.] Klaus' analysis fails to fill the gap." It argues that plaintiff bears the burden in a false advertising action and there should be no "gap" for defendant to fill.

[20] Where a plaintiff challenges a test-proven superiority advertisement, the defendant must identify the cited tests. Plaintiff must then prove that these tests did not establish the proposition for which they were cited. *McNeil,* 938 F.2d at 1549. At the hearing, Quaker State cited the 1987 and 1991 Rohm and Haas oiling time tests in conjunction with Dr. Klaus' theory of engine wear at the second boundary lubrication period. Castrol's burden was to prove that neither the Rohm and Haas tests alone, nor the tests in conjunction with Dr. Klaus' theory, permitted the conclusion to a reasonable certainty that Quaker State's oil protected better at start-up. The district court's statement that "no test [demonstrates superiority] and Klaus' analysis fails to fill the gap" is a finding that Castrol, through its residual oil theory, met its burden. It is, in substance, a finding that the Quaker State tests, which proved faster oiling time, are irrelevant to their claim that Quaker State's oil protects better at start-up. Therefore, we need not consider the tests' reliability. The district court's statement does not shift the burden to defendant.

[21] Quaker State also contends that the district court should have subjected the 1987 Rohm and Haas engine wear results to *Procter's* "sufficiently reliable" test before relying on them. It argues, in other words, that the *Procter* standard applies not only to the studies offered to support defendant's claim of test-proven superiority, but also to plaintiff's evidence offered to rebut this claim.

[22] Quaker State misreads *Procter.* In that case, we established that a plaintiff proves false a test-proven superiority claim when it shows that "the tests referred to by [defendant were] not sufficiently reliable...." *Id.* at 119. This phrase merely establishes plaintiff's burden of proof with respect to defendant's tests. It in no way limits the evidence which plaintiff may use in meeting this burden. Such evidence is governed by the usual standards of admissibility. It was not error for the district court to consider the 1987 tests in this regard.

II. The district court's findings as to the role of residual oil were not clearly erroneous.

[23] Quaker State asserts that the district court's factual findings as to the role of residual oil are clearly erroneous. *See* Fed.R.Civ.P. 52(a). We disagree.

. . . .

III. Is the district court's injunction overly broad?

[24] In a March 20, 1992 memorandum opinion accompanying its simultaneously-issued Order of Preliminary Injunction, the district court explained its intent "to enjoin preliminarily Quaker State

from claiming 'that tests prove its oil protects better against start-up engine wear.'" The injunction, however, goes beyond this limited intent. Paragraph 2 of the injunction states that

> Defendants ... are preliminarily enjoined from broadcasting, publishing or disseminating, in any manner or in any medium, any advertisement, commercial, or promotional matter ... that claims, directly or by clear implication, that:
>
> (a) Quaker State 10W–30 motor oil provides superior protection against engine wear at start-up;
>
> (b) Quaker State 10W–30 motor oil provides better protection against engine wear at start-up than other leading 10W–30 motor oils, including Castrol GTX 10W–30; or
>
> (c) Castrol GTX 10W–30 motor oil provides inferior protection against engine wear at start-up.

This paragraph enjoins Quaker State from distributing *any* advertisement claiming that its oil provides superior protection against engine wear at start-up, whether or not the ad claims test-proven superiority. As explained above, Castrol bears a different burden of proof with respect to this broader injunction than it does in seeking to enjoin only commercials which make the test-proven superiority claim.

[25] The district court expressly found that Castrol had met its burden with respect to any test-proven superiority advertisement. It stated that "Castrol has established the likelihood of proving at trial the falsity of Quaker State's claim that tests prove its oil protects better ...." Its injunction would be too broad, however, absent the additional finding that Castrol had met its burden with respect to superiority advertisements that omit the "tests prove" language. As we have noted above, Castrol meets this burden by adducing proof that Quaker State's oil is not, in fact, superior.

[26] Judge Haight made this additional finding. Castrol submitted the report from the 1987 Rohm and Haas tests as proof that Quaker State's oil did not protect better. This submission was proper under our holding that "[plaintiff can] rel[y] on and analy[se] data generated by [defendant] as scientific proof that the challenged advertisement was false." *McNeil–P.C.C.,* 938 F.2d at 1549. The district court, referring to this document, stated that "the record makes it crystal clear that to the extent tests were performed to demonstrate better wear protection (as opposed to faster flowing), *the tests contradict, rather than support* the claim. I refer to the 1987 Rohm and Haas tests ...." (emphasis added). The court went on to find that "Quaker State presents no convincing argument to counter the unequivocal conclusion of Roland [author of the 1987 report], a Rohm and Haas scientist, that the 1987 tests failed to demonstrate a superiority in protection against engine wear ...." These statements amount to a finding that Castrol has met the additional burden. The injunction is not overly broad.

[27] Quaker State also asks us to limit the injunction to advertisements based on the 1987 and 1991 Rohm and Haas tests. It contends that it should not be barred from advertising a superiority claim if later tests should support it.

[28] Any time a court issues a preliminary injunction there is some chance that, after the issuance of the order but prior to a full adjudication on the merits, changes in the operative facts will undercut the court's rationale. We will not, however, require the district court to draft a technical and narrow injunction to address the possibility of additional tests which are, at this time, purely hypothetical. If tests supporting its claim do come to light, Quaker State may move to modify or dissolve the injunction. *See Flavor Corp. of Am. v. Kemin Indus., Inc.,* 503 F.2d 729, 732 (8th Cir. 1974); 11 C. Wright & A. Miller, *Federal Practice and Procedure,* § 2961 at 604 (1973). We will likely have jurisdiction to review the district court's disposition of such a motion, and can consider the issue at that point if necessary. *See* 28 U.S.C. § 1292(a)(1) (1988); *United States v. City of Chicago,* 534 F.2d 708, 711 (7th Cir. 1976) (denial of motion to dissolve preliminary injunction is appealable pursuant to 28 U.S.C. § 1292(a)(1)); *Int'l Brotherhood of Teamsters v. Western Penn. Motor Carriers Ass'n,* 660 F.2d 76, 80 (3d Cir. 1981) (denial of motion to amend injunction is appealable).

CONCLUSION

[29] We affirm the district court's March 20, 1992 Order granting the preliminary injunction.

b.   Comparative Claims

Firms often make comparative statements of fact (rather than mere subjective opinion or exaggerated puffery) about the merits of their products, and they often do so without reference to studies or any other kind of scientific basis for their claims. Such statements are not "establishment claims" but they are nevertheless subject to particular doctrinal rules. Bernstein and Keller explain:

> Comparative claims are generally of two sorts: superiority and parity claims. Statements that consumers "prefer" a product or that it is "more effective" than its competitor's product are comparative superiority claims. Proving these claims false requires evidence that the competitor's product is superior or equivalent to the advertiser's product as to the claim at issue. A claim that consumers think that a product is "as good as" a competitor's, or that "nothing is more effective," by contrast, is a parity (or equivalence) claim that can be proved false by showing that the competitor's product is superior.

BERNSTEIN & KELLER § 2.08 (2019).

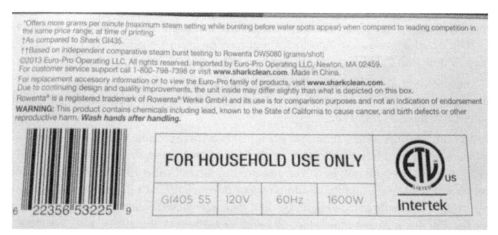

Groupe SEB USA, Inc. v. Euro-Pro Operating LLC
774 F.3d 192 (3d Cir. 2014)

FISHER, Circuit Judge.

[1] In this false advertising case, Euro–Pro Operating, LLC ("Euro–Pro") appeals the District Court's order granting a motion for a preliminary injunction brought by Groupe SEB USA, Inc. ("SEB"). The District Court found that two advertising claims on Euro–Pro's steam irons likely violated section 43(a) of the Lanham Act, 15 U.S.C. § 1125(a), and enjoined Euro–Pro from using those claims. Euro–Pro raises several issues on appeal, but we principally consider how courts should interpret an advertising claim when the packaging or label unambiguously defines a claim term. The District Court decided that the packaging's definition of a claim term applies to the claim's explicit message. Based on this decision, the District Court disregarded consumer survey evidence offering alternative meanings for the claim term. We agree with the District Court and find its approach firmly based in false advertising law and logic. And because we conclude that the District Court did not otherwise abuse its discretion in granting the preliminary injunction, we will affirm.

I.

A.

[2] SEB distributes and sells various household consumer products under several brand names throughout the country. This case involves SEB's electric steam irons sold under the Rowenta brand name, namely the Rowenta Focus, Model No. DW5080 ("Rowenta DW5080"), and the Rowenta Steamium, Model No. DW9080 ("Rowenta DW9080"). Euro–Pro manufactures, markets, and distributes kitchen and household appliances. It sells these products under the Shark brand name. The dispute here arises from advertising claims on the packaging of two Shark steam irons, the Shark Professional, Model No. GI405–55 ("Shark 405"), and the Shark Ultimate Professional, Model No. GI505–55 ("Shark 505").

[3] The Shark 405 packaging includes two advertising claims. First, text on the bottom right of the front packaging asserts that the Shark 405 offers "MORE POWERFUL STEAM vs. Rowenta®†† at half the price." J.A. at A3, A805. The "††" characters refer to a fine-print footnote on the bottom of the packaging, which states that the claim is "††[b]ased on independent comparative steam burst testing to Rowenta DW5080 (grams/shot)." *Id.* Text on the top right of the front packaging also asserts that the Shark 405 delivers "# 1 MOST POWERFUL STEAM*." *Id.* Again, there is a fine-print reference to this

705

claim on the bottom of the packaging that states the Shark 405 " *[o]ffers more grams per minute (maximum steam setting while bursting before water spots appear) when compared to leading competition in the same price range, at time of printing." *Id.* The Shark 505 packaging makes substantially the same claims.

[4] Additionally, both the Shark 405 and the Shark 505 include hang tags on the steam irons for store displays. The hang tags claim that the Shark steam irons deliver "MORE POWERFUL STEAM vs. Rowenta ... at half the price." J.A. at A4. The hang tags also include a reference stating that the claim is "[b]ased on independent comparative steam burst testing" to the respective Rowenta steam irons in "(grams/shot)." *Id.*

[5] SEB first learned of the comparative advertising claims on the Shark steam irons in October 2013. Soon thereafter, SEB directed its internal laboratory to conduct testing to determine whether the claims were true. The lab ran tests comparing the Shark 505 and the Rowenta DW9080. The tests measured (1) the variable steam rate in grams per minute according to International Electrical Corporation ("IEC") 60311 protocol and (2) the mass of a shot of steam in grams per shot according to IEC 60311 protocol.[2] The test results showed that the Rowenta DW9080 performed the same as the Shark 505 in terms of variable steam rate in grams per minute, with both measuring 37 grams per minute. In the test measuring grams per shot of steam, the Rowenta DW9080 outperformed the Shark 505, with measurements of 1.34 grams per shot and 1.00 grams per shot, respectively.

[6] Because SEB's internal test results were inconsistent with the Shark advertising claims, SEB commissioned SLG Prüfund Zertifizierungs GmbH ("SLG"), an independent laboratory based in Germany, to conduct independent tests based on the Shark claims. SLG tested three steam irons of each model in accordance with IEC 60311 protocol, and it delivered its findings to SEB in a comprehensive thirty-eight page report ("SLG Test Report"). The SLG Test Report showed that the Rowenta DW5080 and the Rowenta DW9080 outperformed the Shark 405 and the Shark 505, respectively, in terms of grams per minute. For the test measuring steam power in grams per shot, the SLG Test Report showed that two of the three Shark 405 steam irons performed worse than all three Rowenta DW5080 steam irons, but one Shark 405 steam iron outperformed all three Rowenta DW5080 steam irons. The Rowenta DW5080's average performance was higher than the Shark 405's average performance.[3] The SLG Test Report also showed that two of the three Rowenta DW9080 steam irons performed better in grams per shot than all three Shark 505 steam irons, and one Rowenta DW9080 performed worse than all three Shark 505 steam irons. The Rowenta DW9080's average performance was higher than the Shark 505's average performance.

B.

[7] On January 29, 2014, SEB filed a complaint in the United States District Court for the Western District of Pennsylvania, asserting claims for false advertising under the Lanham Act, 15 U.S.C. § 1125(a), and for unfair competition under Pennsylvania common law. The following day, SEB moved for a preliminary injunction to enjoin Euro–Pro from making the claims on the Shark 405 and the Shark 505.

[8] The District Court held an evidentiary hearing on March 19, 2014, to address SEB's motion for a preliminary injunction. At the hearing, SEB introduced the aforementioned internal test results and the independent SLG Test Report to show that the claims on the Shark steam irons are false. Euro–Pro introduced testimony and a study from its scientific expert, Dr. Abid Kemal (collectively referred to as

---

[2] As the District Court found, the IEC is the leading "international standards organization that prepares and publishes international standards for all electrical, electronic[,] and related technologies, collectively known as 'electrotechnology.' " J.A. at A5. The IEC standards for steam irons are laid out in IEC 60311.

the "Kemal Report"). According to the Kemal Report, steam power is the kinetic energy of a steam burst divided by the duration of the burst. Using this measurement for steam power, the Kemal Report showed that the Shark 405 and the Shark 505 deliver more powerful steam than the Rowenta DW5080 and the Rowenta DW9080, respectively. The Kemal Report also showed that "the mass of a shot of steam expelled from [the Shark steam irons] is comparable to the mass of a shot of steam (grams/shot) expelled from [the respective Rowenta steam irons]." Additionally, Euro–Pro introduced a consumer survey report prepared by Dr. Gary Ford ("the Ford Survey") showing that consumers do not have a uniform understanding of the meaning of the phrase "more powerful steam."

. . . .

III.

. . . .

A.

. . . .

[9] A plaintiff can prevail in a false advertising action if it proves that the advertisement "is either (1) literally false or (2) literally true or ambiguous, but has the tendency to deceive consumers." *Novartis Consumer Health, Inc. v. Johnson & Johnson–Merck Consumer Pharm. Co.,* 290 F.3d 578, 586 (3d Cir.2002). Proof of literal falsity relieves the plaintiff of its burden to prove actual consumer deception. *Id.* Here, the only dispute is whether the Shark claims are literally false.

[10] "A determination of literal falsity rests on an analysis of the message in context." *Johnson & Johnson–Merck Consumer Pharm. Co. v. Rhone–Poulenc Rorer Pharm., Inc.,* 19 F.3d 125, 129 (3d Cir.1994). In deciding whether an advertising claim is literally false, a court must decide first whether the claim conveys an unambiguous message and second whether that unambiguous message is false. *Novartis,* 290 F.3d at 586. "A 'literally false' message may be either explicit or 'conveyed by necessary implication when, considering the advertisement in its entirety, the audience would recognize the claim as readily as if it had been explicitly stated.' " *Id.* at 586–87 (quoting *Clorox Co. P.R. v. Proctor & Gamble Commercial Co.,* 228 F.3d 24, 35 (1st Cir.2000)). Unless the claim is unambiguous, however, it cannot be literally false. *Id.* at 587. " 'The greater the degree to which a message relies upon the viewer or consumer to integrate its components and draw the apparent conclusion ... the less likely it is that a finding of literal falsity will be supported.' " *Id.* (quoting *United Indus. Corp. v. Clorox Co.,* 140 F.3d 1175, 1181 (8th Cir.1998)). We review a district court's findings that an advertising claim is unambiguous and literally false for clear error. *See id.* at 589.

[11] The District Court analyzed the two advertising claims at issue separately. It first determined that Euro–Pro's claim that the Shark steam irons offer "MORE POWERFUL STEAM vs. Rowenta" is unambiguous. The District Court found that the footnote reference to this claim governs the claim's meaning, as the packaging explicitly claims that the Shark steam irons offer more powerful steam measured in grams per shot than the respective Rowenta steam irons. The District Court also determined that the "# 1 MOST POWERFUL STEAM" claim is unambiguous but for different reasons. Recognizing that the reference to this claim explicitly restricts the claim to comparisons to steam irons in the same price range and that Rowenta steam irons are in a higher price range, the District Court still found an unambiguous message of superiority over Rowenta steam irons conveyed by necessary implication due to the claim's close proximity to the "MORE POWERFUL STEAM vs. Rowenta" claim.

[12] With respect to the question of falsity, the District Court found that both claims are false because all the scientific evidence that measured steam power in grams per shot and grams per minute—the measurements for steam power provided on the Shark packaging—disproved Euro–Pro's claims of superiority over Rowenta. The District Court rejected Euro–Pro's scientific evidence, the Kemal Report, as irrelevant because it did not measure steam power in grams per shot or grams per minute. The District Court also observed that Euro–Pro failed to come forward with any other evidence that actually supported its claims.

707

1.

[13] We agree with the District Court that the "MORE POWERFUL STEAM vs. Rowenta" claim is unambiguous. When a product's packaging includes an advertising claim and unambiguously defines a claim term, the packaging's definition of the claim term applies to the claim's explicit message. As explained below, we think this rule is consistent with false advertising law and common sense.

[14] In certain cases, determining the message conveyed by a claim is a simple exercise because the claim is explicit and unambiguous. *See Novartis,* 290 F.3d at 586. And so it is here. To make something explicit is to state it clearly and precisely. Therefore, when Euro–Pro took the affirmative step to include a reference on the Shark packaging that clearly defined the key term in its claim—that steam power is measured in grams per shot—it made an explicit claim. The claim is also unambiguous because grams per shot is a unit of measurement provided by the IEC, the leading independent publisher of standards for electrotechnology, including steam irons. Thus, there is no " 'apparent conclusion' " to be drawn about this claim's meaning, *id.* at 587 (quoting *United Indus.,* 140 F.3d at 1181), nor is its meaning "balanced between several plausible meanings," *Clorox Co. P.R.,* 228 F.3d at 35. There is only one available conclusion and only one plausible meaning—the claim means exactly what the reference on the packaging says it does.

[15] Moreover, as we previously discussed, courts deciding whether a claim is literally false must view the claim in the context of the entire advertisement. *See Rhone–Poulenc,* 19 F.3d at 129. Here, the reference that defines the meaning of steam power is on the Shark packaging, and the claim expressly links to the reference using a symbol—"††" on the Shark 405 and "†" on the Shark 505. Thus, ignoring the reference in our analysis would be not only to read the claim out of context, but also to ignore part of the claim itself denoted by the symbol.

[16] Our holding is also consistent with other areas of the law where courts interpreting a term's meaning apply a specific definition if one is provided by the author. *See, e.g., Meese v. Keene,* 481 U.S. 465, 484, 107 S.Ct. 1862, 95 L.Ed.2d 415 (1987) ("It is axiomatic that the statutory definition of the term excludes unstated meanings of that term."); *Phillips v. AWH Corp.,* 415 F.3d 1303, 1316 (Fed.Cir.2005) (en banc) ("[O]ur cases recognize that the specification may reveal a special definition given to a claim term by the patentee that differs from the meaning it would otherwise possess. In such cases, the inventor's lexicography governs."); *J.C. Penney Life Ins. Co. v. Pilosi,* 393 F.3d 356, 363 (3d Cir.2004) (applying Pennsylvania law to interpret an insurance contract, and explaining that words expressly defined in a policy will be given that definition by courts interpreting the policy); 12 Richard A. Lord, *Williston on Contracts,* § 34:11, at 123 (4th ed. 2012) ("Another method for excluding usage is to have the contract define terms in a manner that is different from the industry or trade definitions for those terms. Then the contract definitions govern and usage is inapplicable...."). We see no reason to depart from this principle here.

[17] We therefore agree entirely with the District Court that the reference's definition of steam power governs the term's meaning in the "MORE POWERFUL STEAM vs. Rowenta" claim. Accordingly, the claim's explicit and unambiguous message is that the Shark steam irons offer more powerful steam measured in grams per shot than the respective Rowenta steam irons.

[18] The fact that the references are in fine-print footnotes and presumably less likely to be read by consumers does not alter our analysis, as Euro–Pro urges it should. We understand that other courts have held that footnote disclaimers purporting to make a false or misleading claim literally true cannot cure the claim's false or misleading message. *See, e.g., Am. Home Prods. Corp. v. Johnson & Johnson,* 654 F.Supp. 568, 590 (S.D.N.Y.1987). We have not addressed this issue, *see Pernod,* 653 F.3d at 252 n. 13 (declining to address the situation when an allegedly misleading claim is corrected by a true statement contained in fine print), and we do not decide it today. Our rather unremarkable holding here is analytically distinct. It is that what a product's packaging says a claim term means is in fact part

708

of the claim's explicit message. If that explicit message is both unambiguous and false, the claim is literally false.

[19] Nor does the presence of consumer survey evidence showing alternative meanings for a defined term affect our holding. Euro–Pro would have us ignore the packaging's definition of steam power and instead credit consumer survey evidence demonstrating that the meaning of steam power is ambiguous. According to Euro–Pro, the District Court's decision to ignore the Ford Survey is inconsistent with our decision in *Pernod Ricard USA, LLC v. Bacardi U.S.A., Inc.,* 653 F.3d 241 (3d Cir.2011). The crux of Euro–Pro's argument is that consumer surveys must be considered by courts in determining whether a claim's message is ambiguous. As explained below, Euro–Pro's argument does not hold up.

[20] In *Pernod,* we addressed whether courts must always consider survey evidence showing that consumers are misled by an advertising claim. There, the appellant asserted that the name of a brand of rum, "Havana Club," misled consumers about the brand's geographic origin. *Id.* at 247. Beneath the "Havana Club" name, the label prominently stated that it was "Puerto Rican Rum," an accurate statement of where the rum was distilled. *Id.* at 245–46. The District Court found that the label made no false or misleading statement, so it disregarded consumer survey evidence showing that eighteen percent of consumers were confused about the brand's geographic origin. *See id.* at 247–48.

[21] We held that the district court properly disregarded the consumer survey evidence. Our conclusion rested on the principle "that there is and must be a point at which language is used plainly enough that the question ceases to be 'what does this mean' and becomes instead 'now that it is clear what this means, what is the legal consequence.' " *Id.* at 251. Applying this principle, we observed that the label contained a "factually accurate, unambiguous statement of geographic origin," prominently stating that it was "Puerto Rican Rum." *Id.* at 252. As a consequence, we concluded that no reasonable consumer could be misled by the "Havana Club" name when it was considered in the context of this prominent truthful statement on the label. *Id.* at 252–53. Consumer survey evidence was therefore immaterial because the Lanham Act does not prohibit a claim that "reasonable people would have to acknowledge is not false or misleading." *Id.* at 253. But we cautioned that judges should not "lightly disregard" consumer surveys because they may reveal "potential ambiguities in an advertisement" that show reasonable consumers may in fact be misled by the advertisement. *Id.* at 254–55. Finally, we noted that "a district court's decision to disregard survey evidence is reviewable de novo, since it is founded on a legal conclusion based on underlying facts, that is that no reasonable consumer would be misled by an advertisement." *Id.* at 255 n. 18.

[22] As our discussion of *Pernod* demonstrates, it is readily distinguishable from the issue before us here. Unlike *Pernod,* the case before us involves claims of literal falsity, so evidence of actual consumer deception is not required. *See Novartis,* 290 F.3d at 586. By disregarding the consumer survey evidence in this case, the District Court did not make the same legal conclusion we recognized in *Pernod:* that no consumers could be misled by the advertisement. The District Court instead made a factual finding about what the claim means and that its message is clear and unambiguous.

[23] *Pernod* does not license courts to use consumer survey evidence to define the meaning of words in an advertising claim. In fact, our analysis in *Pernod* recognized that words may be used plainly enough and carry baseline meanings such that consumer survey evidence is irrelevant. *See* 653 F.3d at 251 (discussing *Mead Johnson & Co. v. Abbott Labs.,* 201 F.3d 883, 886 (7th Cir.2000), *opinion amended on denial of reh'g,* 209 F.3d 1032 (7th Cir.2000) (explaining that "never before has survey research been used to determine the meaning of words, or to set the standard to which objectively verifiable claims must be held")). In this case, Euro–Pro plainly explained on the packaging what it meant by its claim, so we are puzzled by Euro–Pro's characterization of the District Court's approach as a court inserting its "own perception" ahead of consumer perception. Far from using its own perception of the claim's meaning, the District Court used the definition provided by Euro–Pro in the reference, and, concluding that Euro–Pro's message was explicit and unambiguous, it reasonably

709

declined to substitute the uninformed first impressions of consumers about the claim's meaning. *See Mead Johnson,* 201 F.3d at 886. Euro–Pro chose a definition for steam power and now must live with it. It cannot use a consumer survey to create an ambiguity out of whole cloth. Accordingly, we conclude that the District Court did not err in failing to consider the Ford Survey in its analysis.

[24] Turning to the "# 1 MOST POWERFUL STEAM" claim, we again agree with the District Court that this claim unambiguously conveys that Shark steam irons deliver more powerful steam than Rowenta steam irons. Unlike the "MORE POWERFUL STEAM vs. Rowenta" claim, however, the relevant message here is not explicit. The corresponding reference to the "# 1 MOST POWERFUL STEAM" claim states that the Shark steam irons "[o]ffer[ ] more grams per minute ... when compared to leading competition in the same price range," and the parties agree that Rowenta steam irons are in a different price range. But, as we discussed earlier, a literally false claim may also be conveyed by necessary implication when considering the advertisement in its entirety. *See Novartis,* 290 F.3d at 586–87. The question here is whether, "based on a facial analysis of the product name or advertising, ... the consumer will unavoidably receive a false message." *Id.* at 587. Here, the answer is yes. The "# 1 MOST POWERFUL STEAM" claim appears directly above the "MORE POWERFUL STEAM vs. Rowenta" claim, and the proximity of the two claims necessarily and unavoidably conveys a message that Shark steam irons offer the most powerful steam, even when compared to Rowenta steam irons. We therefore cannot say the District Court's finding is clearly erroneous.

2.

[25] Having decided that the claims convey unambiguous messages, the next question is whether those messages are false. We find no clear error in the District Court's determination that the messages are false. The District Court reasonably relied on SEB's internal test results and the SLG Test Report. Both tests measured steam power in grams per shot and grams per minute—the measurements for steam power provided on the Shark packaging—in accordance with independent, objective standards promulgated by the IEC. Both tests also showed that the Rowenta steam irons either outperformed or performed as well as the Shark steam irons. Moreover, the Kemal Report acknowledged that there is no difference in grams per shot of steam between the Shark steam irons and the respective Rowenta steam irons. Put simply, all the relevant evidence before the District Court refuted Euro–Pro's claims of superiority.

. . . .

C.

[26] Euro–Pro's final challenge is to the constitutionality and scope of the District Court's injunction. "District Courts are afforded considerable discretion in framing injunctions." *Meyer v. CUNA Mut. Ins. Soc.,* 648 F.3d 154, 169 (3d Cir.2011). At the same time, an injunction "should be 'no more burdensome to the defendant than necessary to provide complete relief to plaintiffs.' " *Novartis,* 290 F.3d at 598 (quoting *Califano v. Yamasaki,* 442 U.S. 682, 702, 99 S.Ct. 2545, 61 L.Ed.2d 176 (1979)). "Moreover, because commercial speech is entitled to appropriate protection under the First Amendment, an injunction restraining allegedly false or misleading speech must be narrowly tailored to cover only the speech most likely to deceive consumers and harm [the plaintiff]." *Id.* (alteration in original) (internal quotation marks omitted).

[27] Here, the District Court's order granting the preliminary injunction requires Euro–Pro to place stickers over the "MORE POWERFUL STEAM vs. Rowenta" and the "# 1 MOST POWERFUL STEAM" claims on both the Shark 405 and the Shark 505. Also, the order directs Euro–Pro to remove the hang tags from the steam irons.

[28] Commercial speech conveying a literally false message is not protected by the First Amendment. *See id.* ("We conclude that the injunction does not violate the First Amendment ... because each of these messages is false."). As we have explained, we agree with the District Court's conclusion

710

that SEB will likely prevail on its false advertising claims. Therefore, we see no First Amendment violation.

[29] Euro–Pro contends that the District Court's injunction is overbroad because it requires Euro–Pro to cover the advertising claims themselves rather than only the references to the claims. Euro–Pro correctly points out that the references are critical to the literal falsity analysis. Without the definitions from the references, the claims about relative steam power may be considered ambiguous, and as such, could not be literally false. *See id.* at 587. Thus, Euro–Pro argues that the injunction should have targeted only the references.

[30] We disagree with Euro–Pro's narrow characterization of its advertising claims. Although the references provide the definition for steam power that the District Court appropriately adopted in this case, the references and the advertising claims together compose the literally false messages. Therefore, the injunction is not overbroad because it is limited to reaching claims that are literally false. *See Castrol Inc. v. Pennzoil Co.,* 987 F.2d 939, 949 (3d Cir.1993). Moreover, the logic underlying Euro–Pro's argument would create an unworkable framework. Under Euro–Pro's suggested approach, district courts could not just enjoin the dissemination of literally false advertising claims, but they also would need to parse each part of those literally false claims to see if the removal of a word or a portion here and there would render the remainder true. We cannot say that the District Court abused its discretion when it required Euro–Pro to place stickers over the entirety of the false advertising claims rather than only part of them.

c.   False Demonstrations

Schick Mfg., Inc. v. Gillette Co.
372 F.Supp.2d 273 (D. Conn. 2005)

HALL, District Judge.

[1] The plaintiff, Schick Manufacturing Company ("Schick"), seeks a preliminary injunction enjoining the defendant, The Gillette Company ("Gillette"), from making certain claims about its M3 Power razor system ("M3 Power"). Schick contends that Gillette has made various false claims in violation of section 43(a) of the Lanham Act, 15 U.S.C. § 1125(a) and the Connecticut Unfair Trade Practices Act ("CUTPA"), Conn. Gen.Stat. § 42–110a, *et seq.*

. . . .

[2] In order to succeed on its false advertising claim, Schick must prove five elements of this claim. *Omega Engineering, Inc. v. Eastman Kodak Co.,* 30 F.Supp.2d 226, 255 (D.Conn.1998) (citing various treatises and cases). These are the following:

(1) The defendant has made a false or misleading statement of fact. The statement must be (a) literally false as a factual matter or (b) likely to deceive or confuse. *S.C. Johnson & Son, Inc. v. Clorox Company,* 241 F.3d 232, 238 (2d Cir. 2001).

(2) The statement must result in actual deception or capacity for deception "Where the advertising claim is shown to be literally false, the court may enjoin the use of the claim without reference to the advertisement's impact on the buying public." *Id.* (internal quotations omitted).

(3) The deception must be material. "[I]n addition to proving falsity, the plaintiff must also show that the defendants misrepresented an inherent quality or characteristic of the product." *Id.* (internal quotations omitted).

712

(4) Schick must demonstrate that it has been injured because of potential decline in sales. Where parties are head-to-head competitors, the fact that the defendant's advertising is misleading presumptively injures the plaintiff. *Coca–Cola Co. v. Tropicana Products, Inc.*, 690 F.2d 312, 317 (2d Cir. 1982) (abrogated on other grounds by statute as noted in *Johnson & Johnson v. GAC Int'l, Inc.*, 862 F.2d 975, 979 (2d Cir. 1988)).

(5) The advertised goods must travel in interstate commerce.

FACTS

[3] The court held a scheduling conference on the preliminary injunction motion on March 2, 2005. The court allowed the parties to conduct limited discovery prior to conducting a hearing on Schick's motion for a preliminary injunction. The hearing on the motion was conducted over four days: April 12, 13, 22, and May 2, 2005. During the hearing, Schick called five witnesses: Adel Mekhail, Schick's Director of Marketing; Peter M. Clay, Gillette's Vice–President for Premium Systems; Dr. David J. Leffell, Professor of Dermatology; Christopher Kohler, Schick Research Technician; and John Thornton, statistical consultant. Gillette also called five witnesses during the hearing: Dr. Kevin L. Powell, Gillette's Director of the Advanced Technology Centre; Dr. Michael A. Salinger, Professor of Economics; Peter M. Clay, Gillette's Vice–President for Premium Systems; Dr. Ian Saker, Gillette Group Leader at the Advanced Technology Centre and Dr. Michael P. Philpott, Professor of Cutaneous Biology.

[4] The men's systems razor and blade market is worth about $1.1 billion per year in the United States. Gillette holds about 90% of the dollar share of that market, while Schick holds about 10%. The parties are engaged in head-to-head competition and the court credits testimony that growth in the razor systems market results not from volume increases but "with the introduction of high price, new premium items." Hr'g Tr. 39:20–21.

[5] Schick launched its Quattro razor system in September of 2003 and expended many millions of dollars in marketing the product. Although Schick had projected $100 million in annual sales for the Quattro, its actual sales fell short by approximately $20 million. From May 2004 to December 2004, Quattro's market share fell from 21% of dollar sales to 13.9% of dollar sales.

[6] Gillette launched the M3 Power in the United States on May 24, 2004. In preparation for that launch, it began advertising that product on May 17, 2004. The M3 Power is sold throughout the United States. The M3 Power includes a number of components including a handle, a cartridge, guard bar, a lubricating strip, three blades, and a battery-powered feature which causes the razor to oscillate. The market share of the M3 Power, launched in May 2004, was 42% of total dollar sales in December 2004.

[7] Gillette's original advertising for the M3 Power centered on the claim that "micropulses raise hair up and away from skin," thus allowing a consumer to achieve a closer shave. This "hair-raising" or hair extension claim was advertised in various media, including the internet, television, print media, point of sale materials, and product packaging. For example, Gillette's website asserted that, in order to combat the problem of "[f]acial hair grow[ing] in different directions," the M3 Power's "[m]icro-pulses raise hair up and away from skin ..." PX 2, Hr'g Tr. 33:25–34:22. Of Gillette's expenditures on advertising, 85% is spent on television advertising. At the time of the launch, the television advertising stated, "turn on the first micro-power shaving system from Gillette and turn on the amazing new power-glide blades. Micro-pulses raise the hair, so you shave closer in one power stroke." PX 14.2(C). The advertisement also included a 1.8 second-long animated dramatization of hairs growing. In the animated cartoon, the oscillation produced by the M3 Power is shown as green waves moving over hairs. In response, the hairs shown extended in length in the direction of growth and changed angle towards a more vertical position.

[8] The court notes that eight months passed between the launch of the M3 Power and the date Schick initiated the instant suit. Schick maintains that there are two factors that excuse this delay. First, Schick invested time in developing a stroke machine and test protocol that would allow it to test the

713

M3 Power with some degree of confidence and effectiveness.[20] Specifically, the development of a machine that would deliver a stroke of consistent pressure to a test subject's face took time. Second, after completing its first tests of Gillette's claims that the M3 Power raises hair in October, Schick chose to pursue its claims in Germany. In November of 2004, Schick sued Gillette in Germany to enjoin it from making claims that the M3 Power raised hairs. In late December of 2004, the Hamburg Regional Court affirmed the lower court's order enjoining Gillette from making such claims in Germany.

[9] While the court finds that it may have been possible to develop testing protocols in a quicker fashion, the court finds the M3 Power was a new product with a feature (the use of battery power) that had never before been present in wet shavers. The court finds the time Schick took to develop testing of and to test the M3 Power is excusable. The court has been presented with no evidence of bad faith or strategic maneuvering behind the timing of the instant lawsuit.

[10] In late January of 2005, Gillette revised its television commercials for the M3 Power in the United States. It chose to do so based on both the German litigation as well as conversations between the parties about Schick's discomfort with certain claims made in the advertising. The animated product demonstration in the television commercials was revised so that the hairs in the demonstration no longer changed angle, and some of the hairs are shown to remain static. The voice-over was changed to say, "Turn it on and micropulses raise the hair so the blades can shave closer." PX 14.10C. The product demonstration in the revised advertisements depicts the oscillations to lengthen many hairs significantly. The depiction in the revised advertisements of how much the hair lengthens—the magnitude of the extension—is not consistent with Gillette's own studies regarding the effect of micropulses on hair. The animated product demonstration depicts many hairs extending, in many instances, multiple times the original length. Gillette began broadcasting the revised television commercials on or about January 31, 2005. Schick provided credible evidence, however, that the prior version of the advertisement is still featured on the Internet and on product packaging.

[11] Television advertisements aim to provide consumers a "reason to believe," that is, the reason consumers should buy the advertised product. Because of the expense of television advertising, companies have a very short period of time in which to create a "reason to believe" and are generally forced to pitch only the key qualities and characteristics of the product advertised.

[12] Gillette conceded during the hearing that the M3 Power's oscillations do not cause hair to change angle on the face. Its original advertisements depicting such an angle change are both unsubstantiated and inaccurate. Gillette also concedes that the animated portion of its television advertisement is not physiologically exact insofar as the hairs and skin do not appear as they would at such a level of magnification and the hair extension effect is "somewhat exaggerated." Gillette Co.'s Prop. Findings of Fact [Dkt. No. 114] ¶ 33. The court finds that the hair "extension" in the commercial is greatly exaggerated. Gillette does contend, however, that the M3 Power's oscillations cause beard hairs to be raised out of the skin. Gillette contends that the animated product demonstration showing hair extension in its revised commercials is predicated on its testing showing that oscillations cause "trapped" facial hairs to lengthen from the follicle so that more of these hairs' length is exposed. Gillette propounds two alternative physiological bases for its "hair extension" theory. First, Gillette hypothesizes that a facial hair becomes "bound" within the follicle due to an accumulation of sebum and corneocytes (dead skin cells). Gillette contends that the oscillations could free such a "bound" hair. Second, Gillette hypothesizes that hairs may deviate from their normal paths in the follicle and become "trapped" outside the path until vibrations from the M3 Power restore them to their proper path.

---

[20] The court also notes that time spent by Schick testing Gillette's "angle-change" claim, which claim Gillette abandoned in January of 2005.

[13] Schick's expert witness, Dr. David Leffell, Professor of Dermatology and Chief of Dermatologic Surgery at the Yale School of Medicine, testified that, based on his clinical and dermatological expertise, he is aware of no scientific basis for the claim that the oscillations of the M3 Power would result in hair extension, as Gillette contends. Dr. Leffell stated that Gillette's "hair extension" theory is inconsistent with his 20 years of experience in dermatology. He testified that he has never seen a hair trapped in a sub-clinical manner, as hypothesized by Gillette. Dr. Leffell testified that, in certain circumstances, trapped hairs will result in clinical symptoms, such as infection or inflammation. With respect to Gillette's hypothesis that the interaction between sebum and corneocytes trap hairs, however, Dr. Leffell stated, and the court credits, that in non-clinical circumstances, sebum and comeocytes do not accumulate sufficiently to inhibit hair growth. Moreover, everyday activities such as washing or shaving remove accumulations of sebum and corneocytes.

[14] Gillette's expert hair biologist, Dr. Michael Philpott, has studied hair biology for almost twenty years. He testified that, prior to his retention as an expert by Gillette, he had never seen a hair trapped in the manner posited by Gillette. Only after being retained by Gillette did Dr. Philpott first claim to have encountered this hair extension theory. Dr. Philpott acknowledged that neither of Gillette's two hypothesis of hair extension have any support in medical or scientific literature. With regard to Gillette's theory that hair could become bound in the follicle by sebum and corneocytes, Dr. Philpott admitted that no evidence supports that theory. Dr. Leffell testified that erector pili muscles, which cause hairs to stand up in response to various stimuli, as is commonly seen in the case of goosebumps, may also provide a biologicial mechanism for hair extension. Neither Dr. Leffell nor Dr. Philpott, however, testified on the relationship between the application of mechanical energy and the erector pili muscles, and neither party has contended that these muscles play a role in Gillette's hair extension theory.

[15] In addition to positing biological mechanisms that might support the claim that the M3 Power's oscillations raise hairs, Gillette introduced evidence of experiments and testing to support those claims. Gillette provided summaries of said testing which were not prepared contemporaneously with the testing, conducted in the early 1990's, they purport to memorialize. Instead, they were prepared in anticipation of litigation in late 2004.

[16] Gillette performed experiments using oscillating razors in 1990, 1991 and 2003. In 1990 and 1991, Gillette performed studies using prototype oscillating razor handles fitted with razor systems other than the M3 Power, the Atra Plus and Sensor razor cartridge, two other Gillette products. In each of these initial experiments, a circle was drawn on a test subject's face. Twenty beard hairs within the circled region were measured with an imaging stereomicroscope manufactured by the Leica Company. That instrument measures hairs three-dimensionally to a resolution of three to four microns. The test subject then stroked the area using an oscillating razor with blunted blades. Then, twenty beard hairs within the circled region were again measured with a stereomicroscope. The same protocol was followed using a non-oscillating razor with blunted blades, and the changes in hair measurement were compared.

[17] The Atra Plus study was performed in 1990 and included 10 test subjects. The study results show that the panelists' average hair length increased by 83.3 microns after five strokes with the oscillating razor versus 6.3 microns with the non-oscillating razor. The Sensor study was performed from 1990 to 1991 and also involved 10 test subjects. The subjects' mean hair length increased by 27.9 microns versus 12.9 microns with the non-oscillating razor. While both tests provided some evidence of a hair extension effect and the magnitude of that effect, neither test indicated what percentage of hairs were lengthened.

[18] Notably, while Gillette found that use of both the oscillating Atra Plus and Sensor razors resulted in an increase in beard hair length, there was significant difference between the average increase caused by the Atra Plus and that caused by the Sensor. Furthermore, no evidence was presented to the court regarding similarities or differences between the M3 Power razor and the Atra

715

Plus or Sensor. The sample size, ten test subjects per study, was small. The twenty beard hairs measured prior to stroking were not necessarily the same hairs measured after stroking. The test included no efforts to keep constant the variables of pressure on the razor or speed of the shaving stroke. In addition, Gillette's chief scientist, Kevin Powell, testified that the pressure or load applied by consumers co-varies to a statistically significant degree with whether a razor oscillates. All these deficiencies cause this court not to credit the studies' finding that oscillations cause hair lengthening.[21]

[19] In 2003, Gillette performed a study using a prototype of the M3 Power. In the fall of 2003, Gillette tested a Mach 3 cartridge fitted with an oscillating handle. That prototype was called the "Swan." The Swan prototype's motor, handle, and cartridge differ from those features of the actually-marketed M3 Power. Four test subjects were used.[22] The test protocol was identical to that used in 1990 and 1991 except that, instead of using blunted blades, Gillette removed the blades from the razor. The study results suggest that the oscillating-Swan-prototype produced an average increase in hair length of between 32 and 40 microns while the non-oscillating prototype yielded no average increase. That 32 to 40 micron increase represented an average of eight to ten percent increase in hair length. The test does not indicate what percentage of hairs experience any lengthening as a result of oscillations. The court does not credit Dr. Powell's opinion that the differences between the model used in the test and the marketed product has no impact on the testing. Failure to use the marketed product is critical. The court cites the varied results Gillette reports between the Atra Plus, Sensor, and "Swan" tests as only one reason to conclude that failure to use the market product undercuts the 2003 testing. Further, the test protocol and sample size cause the court to question the validity of these study findings.

[20] In addition to testing oscillating battery-powered razors, Gillette conducted what has been called the Microwatcher study. The Microwatcher is a commercially available product consisting of a miniature camera with an illumination system that channels light into an orifice at the tip of a transparent hemispherical dome. The device allows the user to impart mechanical energy into the top and underlying layers of the skin, which, according to Gillette, replicates the mechanical energy imparted by the oscillating razor.[23] The recorded video images introduced into evidence show individual hairs releasing from just below the skin surface. Gillette did not introduce evidence to describe what the various elements of the photo were. When asked by the court to identify the various elements appearing in the video were, Dr. Philpott could not identify or explain important skin features. For example, the court pointed to an area surrounding the individual hair, of darker hue than the rest of the skin, on the video, but Dr. Philpott could not explain what that area was or what might explain its coloration. The court further finds that Gillette provides no evidence to suggest the relationship between the amount of mechanical energy imparted by the Microwatcher and that imparted by the M3 Power.

[21] Schick performed its own study which it contends proves the falsity of Gillette's advertising with respect to claims regarding hair extension.[24] Schick's study took place over three days and included 37 test subjects. With respect to each test subject, twenty hairs were measured before and

---

[21] In Gillette's testing, no effort was made to control for variables, such as pressure on, or speed of, the razor. Failure to control for variable makes Gillette's "results" unscientific and not supportive of any conclusion.

[22] The sample size of four was chosen because the 2003 study, according to Gillette, was merely "confirmatory." Because the court finds the earlier tests deficient, the 2003 study cannot be "confirmatory."

[23]

[24] Schick first performed tests to determine whether the M3 Power changes the angle of beard hairs.

after strokes with an M3 Power razor with blunted blades in both the power-on and power-off modes. The strokes were taken using an automated shaving device developed specially by Schick for the purposes of testing the M3 Power razor and Gillette's claims with respect to it. Images of the hairs were taken before and after the razor strokes using a camera with a plate that flattened hair onto the face. The images were then downloaded to a computer and hair lengths were assessed using ImagePro software. An independent statistician evaluated the data for all three days. Schick argues that its data indicates that there was no statistically significant difference between the change in hair length with power off and the change in hair length with power on.

[22] Again, however, the court finds the test protocol lacking and results questionable. Schick's testing shows that some hairs shrunk even in the absence of the use of water, which Gillette's testing has found to result in hair shrinkage. Schick's expert testified that this may have been the result of measurement error, and the court agrees.[25] Furthermore, Gillette provided expert testimony that the glass plate used to flatten hairs so that they could be measured would likely result in distortion, making it difficult to accurately measure hair lengths. Such flaws in Schick's testing cause the court to be skeptical of Schick's test results and the suggestion that these results demonstrate that the M3 Power does not cause hairs to extend.

[23] The flaws in testing conducted by both parties prevent the court from concluding whether, as a matter of fact, the M3 Power raises beard hairs.

II. ANALYSIS

. . . .

B. False Advertising

[24] **1. Literal Falsity.** "Falsity may be established by proving that (1) the advertising is literally false as a factual matter, or (2) although the advertising is literally true, it is likely to deceive or confuse customers." *Nat'l Basketball Ass'n v. Motorola, Inc.*, 105 F.3d 841, 855 (2d Cir. 1997). "A plaintiff's burden in proving literal falsity thus varies depending on the nature of the challenged advertisement." *Castrol, Inc.*, 977 F.2d at 63. The Second Circuit has found that where an advertisement alleges that tests have established a product's superiority, a plaintiff must demonstrate that the tests or studies did not prove such superiority. "[A] plaintiff can meet this burden by demonstrating that the tests were not sufficiently reliable to permit a conclusion that the product is superior." *Id.* In addition, "[i]f the plaintiff can show that the tests, even if reliable, do not establish the proposition asserted by the defendant, the plaintiff has obviously met its burden." *Id.*

[25] Where, however, as here, the accused advertising does not allege that tests or clinical studies have proven a particular fact, the plaintiff's burden to come forward with affirmative evidence of falsity is qualitatively different. "To prove that an advertising claim is literally false, a plaintiff must do more than show that the tests supporting the challenged claim are unpersuasive." *Mc–Neil–P.C.C., Inc. v. Bristol–Myers Squibb Co.*, 938 F.2d 1544, 1549 (2d Cir. 1991). The plaintiff must prove falsity by a preponderance of the evidence, either using its own scientific testing or that of the defendant. If a plaintiff is to prevail by relying on the defendant's own studies, it cannot do so simply by criticizing the defendant's studies. It must prove either that "such tests 'are not sufficiently reliable to permit one to conclude with reasonable certainty that they established' the claim made" or that the defendant's studies establish that the defendant's claims are false. *Id.* at 1549–50.

[26] The challenged advertising consists of two basic components: an animated representation of the effect of the M3 Power razor on hair and skin and a voice-over that describes that effect. The animation, which lasts approximately 1.8 seconds, shows many hairs growing at a significant rate,

---

[25] It may also result from the application of a glass plate meant to flatten the hairs so that they could be measured in two dimensions.

many by as much as four times the original length. During the animation, the voice-over states the following: "Turn it on and micropulses raise the hair so the blades can shave closer." Schick asserts that this M3 Power advertising is false in three ways: first, it asserts the razor changes the angle of beard hairs; second, it portrays a false amount of extension; and third, it asserts that the razor raises or extends the beard hair.

[27] With regard to the first claim of falsity, if the voiceover means that the razor changes the angle of hairs on the face, the claim is false. Although Gillette removed the "angle changing" claim from its television advertisements, it is unclear whether it has completely removed all material asserting this angle-change claim. The court concludes that the current advertising claim of "raising" hair does not unambiguously mean to changes angles.[26] *See Novartis Consumer Health, Inc. v. Johnson & Johnson–Merck Consumer Pharmaceuticals Co.,* 290 F.3d 578, 587 (3d Cir. 2002) ("only an unambiguous message can be literally false"). Thus, the revised advertising is not literally false on this basis.

[28] With regard to the second asserted basis of falsity, the animation, Gillette concedes that the animation exaggerates the effect that the razor's vibration has on hair. Its own tests show hairs extending approximately 10% on average, when the animation shows a significantly greater extension. The animation is not even a "reasonable approximation," which Gillette claims is the legal standard for non-falsity. *See* Gillette's Prop. Conclusions of Law at ¶ 32, 37–38 [Dkt. No. 114]. Here, Schick can point to Gillette's own studies to prove that the animation is false. *See Mc–Neil–P.C.C., Inc.,* 938 F.2d at 1549.

[29] Gillette argues that such exaggeration does not constitute falsity. However, case law in this circuit indicates that a defendant cannot argue that a television advertisement is "approximately" correct or, alternatively, simply a representation in order to excuse a television ad or segment thereof that is literally false. *S.C. Johnson & Son, Inc.,* 241 F.3d at 239–40 (finding that depiction of leaking plastic bag was false where rate at which bag leaked in advertisement was faster than rate tests indicated); *Coca–Cola Co.,* 690 F.2d at 318 (finding that advertisement that displaced fresh-squeezed orange juice being poured into a Tropicana carton was false). Indeed, "[the Court of Appeals has] explicitly looked to the visual images in a commercial to assess whether it is literally false." *S.C. Johnson,* 241 F.3d at 238.[27]

[30] Gillette's argument that the animated portion of its advertisement need not be exact is wrong as a matter of law. Clearly, a cartoon will not exactly depict a real-life situation, here, *e.g.,* the actual uneven surface of a hair or the details of a hair plug. However, a party may not distort an inherent quality of its product in either graphics or animation. Gillette acknowledges that the magnitude of beard hair extension in the animation is false. The court finds, therefore, that any claims with respect to changes in angle and the animated portion of Gillette's current advertisement are literally false.

[31] The court does not make such a finding with respect to Schick's third falsity ground, Gillette's hair extension theory generally. Gillette claims that the razor's vibrations raise some hairs trapped under the skin to come out of the skin. While its own studies are insufficient to establish the truth of this claim, the burden is on Schick to prove falsity. Neither Schick's nor Gillette's testing can support a finding of falsity.

[32] While there can be no finding of literal falsity with respect to Gillette's hair extension claim at this stage in the instant litigation, the court expresses doubt about that claim. As described earlier, Gillette's own testing is suspect. Furthermore, Schick introduced expert testimony and elicited

---

[26] It is the words "up and away" when combined with "raises" that suggest both extension and angle change.

[27] At least one other circuit has held that picture depictions can constitute false advertising. *Scotts Co. v. United Indus. Corp.,* 315 F.3d 264 (4th Cir.2002) (finding that while ambiguous graphic on packaging did not constitute literally false advertising, an unambiguous graphic could do so).

evidence from Gillette's expert regarding the lack of scientific foundation for any biological mechanism that would explain the effect described by Gillette in its advertising. Gillette's own expert, Dr. Philpott, testified that no scientific foundation exists to support Gillette's hypothesis that beard hairs might be trapped under the skin by sebum and comeocytes and that the application of mechanical energy might release such hairs. While Dr. Philpott put forward another hypothesis—that a hair's curliness might cause it to be trapped-he also conceded that, prior to his engagement as an expert on Gillette's behalf, in twenty years of studying hair, he had never come across such a phenomenon. The court credits the testimony of Schick's expert, Dr. Leffell, that while certain clinical conditions are characterized by hairs trapped under the surface of the skin, there is no such non-clinical phenomenon.

[33] Nevertheless, putting forth credible evidence that there is no known biological mechanism to support Gillette's contention that the M3Power raises hairs is insufficient to meet Schick's burden. Such evidence is not affirmative evidence of falsity. Further, while Schick successfully attacked Gillette's testing, that attack did not result in evidence of falsity. Unlike in *McNeil*, here Gillette's own tests do not prove hair extension does not occur. Schick merely proved that Gillette's testing is inadequate to prove it does occur.

[34] **2. Actual Deception.** Schick need not prove actual deception if Gilette's advertising is determined to be literally false. *Mc–Neil–P.C.C., Inc.*, 938 F.2d at 1549 ("Where the advertising claim is shown to be literally false, the court may enjoin the use of the claim without reference to the advertisement's impact on the buying public." (internal quotation marks and citations omitted)). Because the court finds that claims regarding angle change and the magnitude and frequency of hair extension portrayed in the animated portion of Gillette's television advertisement are both literally false, it presumes that these claims result in actual deception.

[35] **3. Materiality.** "It is also well-settled that, in addition to proving falsity, the plaintiff must also show that the defendants misrepresented an inherent quality or characteristic of the product. This requirement is essentially one of materiality, a term explicitly used in other circuits." *S.C. Johnson & Son, Inc.*, 241 F.3d at 238 (internal quotation marks and citations omitted). In determining that certain allegedly false statements were not material, the Second Circuit considered the relevance of the statements and the fact that "[t]he inaccuracy in the statements would not influence customers." *Nat'l Basketball Ass'n v. Motorola, Inc.*, 105 F.3d 841, 855 (2d Cir. 1997).

[36] It is clear that whether the M3 Power raises hairs is material. Gillette's employees testified that television advertising time is too valuable to include things that are "unimportant". Furthermore, in this case, hair extension is the "reason to believe" that the M3 Power is a worthwhile product. The magnitude and frequency of that effect are also, therefore, material. Whether a material element of a product's performance happens very often and how often that element happens are, in themselves, material.

[37] **4. Injury.** The court finds that, in light of the advertisement's literal falsity, the fact that the parties are head-to-head competitors, and recent declines in the sale of Schick's premiere wet shave system injury will be presumed. *Coca–Cola Co.*, 690 F.2d at 316–317. While Schick has not submitted consumer surveys or market research, the fact that the parties are head-to-head competitors supports an inference of causation.

[38] **5. Interstate Commerce.** The parties do not dispute that this element of the claim has been established.

[39] Accordingly, the court finds that Schick has established a likelihood of success on the merits of its claims insofar as Gillette's claims regarding changes in hair angle and its animation depicting an exaggerated amount of hair extension are literally false. The court finds that Schick has failed to establish a likelihood of success, or even serious questions going to the merits, on the claim of hair "extension."

BOND

719

[40] Gillette has requested a bond of $49,579,248. It contends that this amount represents estimated lost profits on future M3 Power sales, over a twelve-month period, if later found to have been wrongfully enjoined. Schick submits that a bond of $50,000 to $100,000 is appropriate.

[41] Gillette's calculations assume a precipitous drop in sales as a result of a mandate to correct two admitted falsities in its advertisement.[28] The court is skeptical that this calculation represents an appropriate bond amount.[29] Instead, the court imposes a bond of $200,000 on Schick. Absent a record created by Gillette, the court concludes this amount, generally in the range for false advertising cases, is sufficient to protect Gillette. Gillette may move to increase the bond amount upon a showing of likely injury.

CONCLUSION

[42] For the reasons stated above the Motion for Preliminary Injunction [Dkt. No. 7] is GRANTED in part and DENIED in part. The injunction is entered as stated in the accompanying order. Schick's Motion for Leave to Amend [Dkt. No. 103] is GRANTED.

---

[28] While Gillette contends that the animated portion of its advertisement is not literally false as a matter of law, it has conceded that, as a factual matter, the animation represents an exaggerated hair-extension effect.

[29] Does it claim that it cannot sell one M3 Power razor without making false claims regarding angle change or the magnitude of hair extension? When it ceased television and print advertising with the "angle change," did its sales drop precipitously?

B. Endorsements, Testimonials, and Reviews

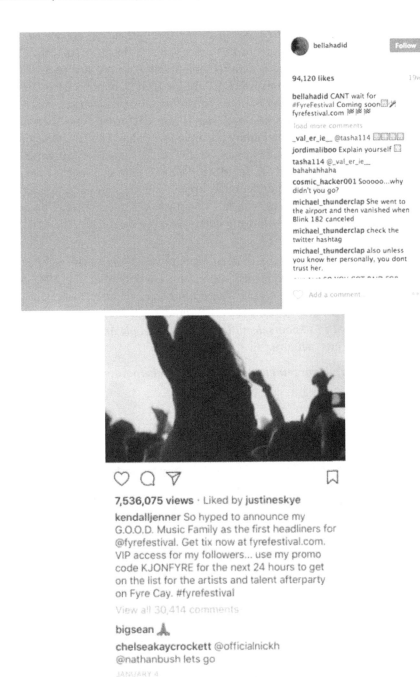

The mission of the Federal Trade Commission (FTC) is to prevent "unfair methods of competition in or affecting commerce and unfair or deceptive acts or practices in or affecting commerce." FTC Act § 5(a)(2), 15 U.S.C. § 45(a)(2). As its name suggests, the FTC's Bureau of Competition focuses on "unfair methods of competition" and shares with the Antitrust Division of the Department of Justice authority to enforce American antitrust laws. The FTC's Bureau of Consumer Protection focuses on the protection of consumers from "unfair or deceptive acts or practices," including abusive lending and telemarketing practices, violation of data privacy laws, and false advertising. Due to the increasing prominence of endorsements and reviews in social media and on online marketplaces such as Amazon,

721

this subpart briefly surveys FTC policies prohibiting deceptive endorsements and reviews, particularly in the online context.

The FTC Act empowers the FTC to investigate matters either *sua sponte* or in response to complaints submitted to the agency. Pursuant to FTC Act § 20, 15 U.S.C. § 57b-1, the FTC may issue a Civil Investigative Demand ("CID"), which is akin to a subpoena but may also require the recipient to "file written reports or answers to questions." 15 U.S.C. § 57b-1(c)(1). If the FTC has "reason to believe" that a violation of law has occurred, it may issue a complaint stating its charges. FTC Act § 5(a)(2), 15 U.S.C. § 45(a)(2). The respondent may settle and sign a consent order (which is subject to public comment) or contest the charges before an administrative law judge. The FTC typically seeks a cease and desist order, though it may also pursue injunctive relief such as an order for corrective advertising or consumer refunds. FTC Act § 5(l), 15 U.S.C. Sec. 45(l). The FTC may also seek civil penalties. FTC Act § 5(m), 15 U.S.C. Sec. 45(m). A losing respondent may appeal the ALJ's decision to the full Commission typically consisting of five Commissioners. The full Commission's decision may be appealed to any Court of Appeals that has personal jurisdiction and venue over the defendant. The FTC Act provides for no private right of action.

The FTC also engages in formal and informal rulemaking. Its informal rulemaking often takes the form of *FTC Guides* or *FTC Policy Statements* addressing conduct that the FTC considers to be permissible and impermissible. The *FTC Guides Concerning Use of Endorsements and Testimonials in Advertising* offers a comprehensive review of FTC guidelines with respect to endorsements, testimonials, and reviews. *The FTC's Endorsement Guides: What People Are Asking* focuses on conduct in social media, blogs, and other internet fora.

FTC Guides Concerning Use of Endorsements and Testimonials in Advertising
16 C.F.R. § 255

§255.0 Purpose and definitions.

(a) The Guides in this part represent administrative interpretations of laws enforced by the Federal Trade Commission for the guidance of the public in conducting its affairs in conformity with legal requirements. Specifically, the Guides address the application of Section 5 of the FTC Act (15 U.S.C. 45) to the use of endorsements and testimonials in advertising. The Guides provide the basis for voluntary compliance with the law by advertisers and endorsers. Practices inconsistent with these Guides may result in corrective action by the Commission under Section 5 if, after investigation, the Commission has reason to believe that the practices fall within the scope of conduct declared unlawful by the statute. The Guides set forth the general principles that the Commission will use in evaluating endorsements and testimonials, together with examples illustrating the application of those principles. The Guides do not purport to cover every possible use of endorsements in advertising. Whether a particular endorsement or testimonial is deceptive will depend on the specific factual circumstances of the advertisement at issue.

(b) For purposes of this part, an endorsement means any advertising message (including verbal statements, demonstrations, or depictions of the name, signature, likeness or other identifying personal characteristics of an individual or the name or seal of an organization) that consumers are likely to believe reflects the opinions, beliefs, findings, or experiences of a party other than the sponsoring advertiser, even if the views expressed by that party are identical to those of the sponsoring advertiser. The party whose opinions, beliefs, findings, or experience the message appears to reflect will be called the endorser and may be an individual, group, or institution.

(c) The Commission intends to treat endorsements and testimonials identically in the context of its enforcement of the Federal Trade Commission Act and for purposes of this part. The term endorsements is therefore generally used hereinafter to cover both terms and situations.

(d) For purposes of this part, the term product includes any product, service, company or industry.

(e) For purposes of this part, an expert is an individual, group, or institution possessing, as a result of experience, study, or training, knowledge of a particular subject, which knowledge is superior to what ordinary individuals generally acquire.

Example 1: A film critic's review of a movie is excerpted in an advertisement. When so used, the review meets the definition of an endorsement because it is viewed by readers as a statement of the critic's own opinions and not those of the film producer, distributor, or exhibitor. Any alteration in or quotation from the text of the review that does not fairly reflect its substance would be a violation of the standards set by this part because it would distort the endorser's opinion. [*See* §255.1(b).]

Example 2: A TV commercial depicts two women in a supermarket buying a laundry detergent. The women are not identified outside the context of the advertisement. One comments to the other how clean her brand makes her family's clothes, and the other then comments that she will try it because she has not been fully satisfied with her own brand. This obvious fictional dramatization of a real life situation would not be an endorsement.

Example 3: In an advertisement for a pain remedy, an announcer who is not familiar to consumers except as a spokesman for the advertising drug company praises the drug's ability to deliver fast and lasting pain relief. He purports to speak, not on the basis of his own opinions, but rather in the place of and on behalf of the drug company. The announcer's statements would not be considered an endorsement.

Example 4: A manufacturer of automobile tires hires a well-known professional automobile racing driver to deliver its advertising message in television commercials. In these commercials, the driver speaks of the smooth ride, strength, and long life of the tires. Even though the message is not expressly declared to be the personal opinion of the driver, it may nevertheless constitute an endorsement of the tires. Many consumers will recognize this individual as being primarily a racing driver and not merely a spokesperson or announcer for the advertiser. Accordingly, they may well believe the driver would not speak for an automotive product unless he actually believed in what he was saying and had personal knowledge sufficient to form that belief. Hence, they would think that the advertising message reflects the driver's personal views. This attribution of the underlying views to the driver brings the advertisement within the definition of an endorsement for purposes of this part.

Example 5: A television advertisement for a particular brand of golf balls shows a prominent and well-recognized professional golfer practicing numerous drives off the tee. This would be an endorsement by the golfer even though she makes no verbal statement in the advertisement.

Example 6: An infomercial for a home fitness system is hosted by a well-known entertainer. During the infomercial, the entertainer demonstrates the machine and states that it is the most effective and easy-to-use home exercise machine that she has ever tried. Even if she is reading from a script, this statement would be an endorsement, because consumers are likely to believe it reflects the entertainer's views.

Example 7: A television advertisement for a housewares store features a well-known female comedian and a well-known male baseball player engaging in light-hearted banter about products each one intends to purchase for the other. The comedian says that she will buy him a Brand X, portable, high-definition television so he can finally see the strike zone. He says that he will get her a Brand Y juicer so she can make juice with all the fruit and vegetables thrown at her during her performances. The comedian and baseball player are not likely to be deemed endorsers because consumers will likely realize that the individuals are not expressing their own views.

Example 8: A consumer who regularly purchases a particular brand of dog food decides one day to purchase a new, more expensive brand made by the same manufacturer. She writes in her personal blog that the change in diet has made her dog's fur noticeably softer and shinier, and that in her opinion, the new food definitely is worth the extra money. This posting would not be deemed an endorsement under the Guides.

723

Assume that rather than purchase the dog food with her own money, the consumer gets it for free because the store routinely tracks her purchases and its computer has generated a coupon for a free trial bag of this new brand. Again, her posting would not be deemed an endorsement under the Guides.

Assume now that the consumer joins a network marketing program under which she periodically receives various products about which she can write reviews if she wants to do so. If she receives a free bag of the new dog food through this program, her positive review would be considered an endorsement under the Guides.

§255.1 General considerations.

(a) Endorsements must reflect the honest opinions, findings, beliefs, or experience of the endorser. Furthermore, an endorsement may not convey any express or implied representation that would be deceptive if made directly by the advertiser. [*See* §255.2(a) and (b) regarding substantiation of representations conveyed by consumer endorsements.]

(b) The endorsement message need not be phrased in the exact words of the endorser, unless the advertisement affirmatively so represents. However, the endorsement may not be presented out of context or reworded so as to distort in any way the endorser's opinion or experience with the product. An advertiser may use an endorsement of an expert or celebrity only so long as it has good reason to believe that the endorser continues to subscribe to the views presented. An advertiser may satisfy this obligation by securing the endorser's views at reasonable intervals where reasonableness will be determined by such factors as new information on the performance or effectiveness of the product, a material alteration in the product, changes in the performance of competitors' products, and the advertiser's contract commitments.

(c) When the advertisement represents that the endorser uses the endorsed product, the endorser must have been a bona fide user of it at the time the endorsement was given. Additionally, the advertiser may continue to run the advertisement only so long as it has good reason to believe that the endorser remains a bona fide user of the product. [*See* §255.1(b) regarding the "good reason to believe" requirement.]

(d) Advertisers are subject to liability for false or unsubstantiated statements made through endorsements, or for failing to disclose material connections between themselves and their endorsers [*see* §255.5]. Endorsers also may be liable for statements made in the course of their endorsements.

Example 1: A building contractor states in an advertisement that he uses the advertiser's exterior house paint because of its remarkable quick drying properties and durability. This endorsement must comply with the pertinent requirements of §255.3 (Expert Endorsements). Subsequently, the advertiser reformulates its paint to enable it to cover exterior surfaces with only one coat. Prior to continued use of the contractor's endorsement, the advertiser must contact the contractor in order to determine whether the contractor would continue to specify the paint and to subscribe to the views presented previously.

Example 2: A television advertisement portrays a woman seated at a desk on which rest five unmarked computer keyboards. An announcer says, "We asked X, an administrative assistant for over ten years, to try these five unmarked keyboards and tell us which one she liked best." The advertisement portrays X typing on each keyboard and then picking the advertiser's brand. The announcer asks her why, and X gives her reasons. This endorsement would probably not represent that X actually uses the advertiser's keyboard at work. In addition, the endorsement also may be required to meet the standards of §255.3 (expert endorsements).

Example 3: An ad for an acne treatment features a dermatologist who claims that the product is "clinically proven" to work. Before giving the endorsement, she received a write-up of the clinical study in question, which indicates flaws in the design and conduct of the study that are so serious that they preclude any conclusions about the efficacy of the product. The dermatologist is subject to liability for the false statements she made in the advertisement. The advertiser is also liable for misrepresentations made through the endorsement. [*See* §255.3 regarding the product evaluation that an expert endorser must conduct].

Example 4: A well-known celebrity appears in an infomercial for an oven roasting bag that purportedly cooks every chicken perfectly in thirty minutes. During the shooting of the infomercial, the celebrity watches five attempts to cook chickens using the bag. In each attempt, the chicken is undercooked after thirty minutes and requires sixty minutes of cooking time. In the commercial, the celebrity places an uncooked chicken in the oven roasting bag and places the bag in one oven. He then takes a chicken roasting bag from a second oven, removes from the bag what appears to be a perfectly cooked chicken, tastes the chicken, and says that if you want perfect chicken every time, in just thirty minutes, this is the product you need. A significant percentage of consumers are likely to believe the celebrity's statements represent his own views even though he is reading from a script. The celebrity is subject to liability for his statement about the product. The advertiser is also liable for misrepresentations made through the endorsement.

Example 5: A skin care products advertiser participates in a blog advertising service. The service matches up advertisers with bloggers who will promote the advertiser's products on their personal blogs. The advertiser requests that a blogger try a new body lotion and write a review of the product on her blog. Although the advertiser does not make any specific claims about the lotion's ability to cure skin conditions and the blogger does not ask the advertiser whether there is substantiation for the claim, in her review the blogger writes that the lotion cures eczema and recommends the product to her blog readers who suffer from this condition. The advertiser is subject to liability for misleading or unsubstantiated representations made through the blogger's endorsement. The blogger also is subject to liability for misleading or unsubstantiated representations made in the course of her endorsement. The blogger is also liable if she fails to disclose clearly and conspicuously that she is being paid for her services. [*See* §255.5.]

In order to limit its potential liability, the advertiser should ensure that the advertising service provides guidance and training to its bloggers concerning the need to ensure that statements they make are truthful and substantiated. The advertiser should also monitor bloggers who are being paid to promote its products and take steps necessary to halt the continued publication of deceptive representations when they are discovered.

§255.2 Consumer endorsements.

(a) An advertisement employing endorsements by one or more consumers about the performance of an advertised product or service will be interpreted as representing that the product or service is effective for the purpose depicted in the advertisement. Therefore, the advertiser must possess and rely upon adequate substantiation, including, when appropriate, competent and reliable scientific evidence, to support such claims made through endorsements in the same manner the advertiser would be required to do if it had made the representation directly, *i.e.*, without using endorsements. Consumer endorsements themselves are not competent and reliable scientific evidence.

(b) An advertisement containing an endorsement relating the experience of one or more consumers on a central or key attribute of the product or service also will likely be interpreted as representing that the endorser's experience is representative of what consumers will generally achieve with the advertised product or service in actual, albeit variable, conditions of use. Therefore, an advertiser should possess and rely upon adequate substantiation for this representation. If the advertiser does not have substantiation that the endorser's experience is representative of what consumers will generally achieve, the advertisement should clearly and conspicuously disclose the generally expected performance in the depicted circumstances, and the advertiser must possess and rely on adequate substantiation for that representation.[1]

(c) Advertisements presenting endorsements by what are represented, directly or by implication, to be "actual consumers" should utilize actual consumers in both the audio and video, or clearly and conspicuously disclose that the persons in such advertisements are not actual consumers of the advertised product.

Example 1: A brochure for a baldness treatment consists entirely of testimonials from satisfied customers who say that after using the product, they had amazing hair growth and their hair is as thick and strong as it was when they were teenagers. The advertiser must have competent and reliable scientific evidence that its product is effective in producing new hair growth.

The ad will also likely communicate that the endorsers' experiences are representative of what new users of the product can generally expect. Therefore, even if the advertiser includes a disclaimer such as, "Notice: These testimonials do not prove our product works. You should not expect to have similar results," the ad is likely to be deceptive unless the advertiser has adequate substantiation that new users typically will experience results similar to those experienced by the testimonialists.

Example 2: An advertisement disseminated by a company that sells heat pumps presents endorsements from three individuals who state that after installing the company's heat pump in their homes, their monthly utility bills went down by $100, $125, and $150, respectively. The ad will likely be interpreted as conveying that such savings are representative of what consumers who buy the company's heat pump can generally expect. The advertiser does not have substantiation for that representation because, in fact, less than 20% of purchasers will save $100 or more. A disclosure such as, "Results not typical" or, "These testimonials are based on the experiences of a few people and you are not likely to have similar results" is insufficient to prevent this ad from being deceptive because consumers will still interpret the ad as conveying that the specified savings are representative of what consumers can generally expect. The ad is less likely to be deceptive if it clearly and conspicuously discloses the generally expected savings and the advertiser has adequate substantiation that homeowners can achieve those results. There are multiple ways that such a disclosure could be phrased, *e.g.*, "the average homeowner saves $35 per month," "the typical family saves $50 per month during cold months and $20 per month in warm months," or "most families save 10% on their utility bills."

Example 3: An advertisement for a cholesterol-lowering product features an individual who claims that his serum cholesterol went down by 120 points and does not mention having made any lifestyle changes. A well-conducted clinical study shows that the product reduces the cholesterol levels of individuals with elevated cholesterol by an average of 15% and the advertisement clearly and conspicuously discloses this fact. Despite the presence of this disclosure, the advertisement would be

---

[1] The Commission tested the communication of advertisements containing testimonials that clearly and prominently disclosed either "Results not typical" or the stronger "These testimonials are based on the experiences of a few people and you are not likely to have similar results." Neither disclosure adequately reduced the communication that the experiences depicted are generally representative. Based upon this research, the Commission believes that similar disclaimers regarding the limited applicability of an endorser's experience to what consumers may generally expect to achieve are unlikely to be effective.

Nonetheless, the Commission cannot rule out the possibility that a strong disclaimer of typicality could be effective in the context of a particular advertisement. Although the Commission would have the burden of proof in a law enforcement action, the Commission notes that an advertiser possessing reliable empirical testing demonstrating that the net impression of its advertisement with such a disclaimer is non-deceptive will avoid the risk of the initiation of such an action in the first instance.

deceptive if the advertiser does not have adequate substantiation that the product can produce the specific results claimed by the endorser (*i.e.,* a 120-point drop in serum cholesterol without any lifestyle changes).

Example 4: An advertisement for a weight-loss product features a formerly obese woman. She says in the ad, "Every day, I drank 2 WeightAway shakes, ate only raw vegetables, and exercised vigorously for six hours at the gym. By the end of six months, I had gone from 250 pounds to 140 pounds." The advertisement accurately describes the woman's experience, and such a result is within the range that would be generally experienced by an extremely overweight individual who consumed WeightAway shakes, only ate raw vegetables, and exercised as the endorser did. Because the endorser clearly describes the limited and truly exceptional circumstances under which she achieved her results, the ad is not likely to convey that consumers who weigh substantially less or use WeightAway under less extreme circumstances will lose 110 pounds in six months. (If the advertisement simply says that the endorser lost 110 pounds in six months using WeightAway together with diet and exercise, however, this description would not adequately alert consumers to the truly remarkable circumstances leading to her weight loss.)The advertiser must have substantiation, however, for any performance claims conveyed by the endorsement (e.g., that WeightAway is an effective weight loss product).

If, in the alternative, the advertisement simply features "before" and "after" pictures of a woman who says "I lost 50 pounds in 6 months with WeightAway," the ad is likely to convey that her experience is representative of what consumers will generally achieve. Therefore, if consumers cannot generally expect to achieve such results, the ad should clearly and conspicuously disclose what they can expect to lose in the depicted circumstances (*e.g.,* "most women who use WeightAway for six months lose at least 15 pounds").

If the ad features the same pictures but the testimonialist simply says, "I lost 50 pounds with WeightAway," and WeightAway users generally do not lose 50 pounds, the ad should disclose what results they do generally achieve (*e.g.,* "most women who use WeightAway lose 15 pounds").

Example 5: An advertisement presents the results of a poll of consumers who have used the advertiser's cake mixes as well as their own recipes. The results purport to show that the majority believed that their families could not tell the difference between the advertised mix and their own cakes baked from scratch. Many of the consumers are actually pictured in the advertisement along with relevant, quoted portions of their statements endorsing the product. This use of the results of a poll or survey of consumers represents that this is the typical result that ordinary consumers can expect from the advertiser's cake mix.

Example 6: An advertisement purports to portray a "hidden camera" situation in a crowded cafeteria at breakfast time. A spokesperson for the advertiser asks a series of actual patrons of the cafeteria for their spontaneous, honest opinions of the advertiser's recently introduced breakfast cereal. Even though the words "hidden camera" are not displayed on the screen, and even though none of the actual patrons is specifically identified during the advertisement, the net impression conveyed to consumers may well be that these are actual customers, and not actors. If actors have been employed, this fact should be clearly and conspicuously disclosed.

Example 7: An advertisement for a recently released motion picture shows three individuals coming out of a theater, each of whom gives a positive statement about the movie. These individuals are actual consumers expressing their personal views about the movie. The advertiser does not need to have substantiation that their views are representative of the opinions that most consumers will have about the movie. Because the consumers' statements would be understood to be the subjective opinions of only three people, this advertisement is not likely to convey a typicality message.

If the motion picture studio had approached these individuals outside the theater and offered them free tickets if they would talk about the movie on camera afterwards, that arrangement should be clearly and conspicuously disclosed. [*See* §255.5.]

§255.3 Expert endorsements.

(a) Whenever an advertisement represents, directly or by implication, that the endorser is an expert with respect to the endorsement message, then the endorser's qualifications must in fact give the endorser the expertise that he or she is represented as possessing with respect to the endorsement.

(b) Although the expert may, in endorsing a product, take into account factors not within his or her expertise (*e.g.*, matters of taste or price), the endorsement must be supported by an actual exercise of that expertise in evaluating product features or characteristics with respect to which he or she is expert and which are relevant to an ordinary consumer's use of or experience with the product and are available to the ordinary consumer. This evaluation must have included an examination or testing of the product at least as extensive as someone with the same degree of expertise would normally need to conduct in order to support the conclusions presented in the endorsement. To the extent that the advertisement implies that the endorsement was based upon a comparison, such comparison must have been included in the expert's evaluation; and as a result of such comparison, the expert must have concluded that, with respect to those features on which he or she is expert and which are relevant and available to an ordinary consumer, the endorsed product is at least equal overall to the competitors' products. Moreover, where the net impression created by the endorsement is that the advertised product is superior to other products with respect to any such feature or features, then the expert must in fact have found such superiority. [*See* §255.1(d) regarding the liability of endorsers.]

Example 1: An endorsement of a particular automobile by one described as an "engineer" implies that the endorser's professional training and experience are such that he is well acquainted with the design and performance of automobiles. If the endorser's field is, for example, chemical engineering, the endorsement would be deceptive.

Example 2: An endorser of a hearing aid is simply referred to as "Doctor" during the course of an advertisement. The ad likely implies that the endorser is a medical doctor with substantial experience in the area of hearing. If the endorser is not a medical doctor with substantial experience in audiology, the endorsement would likely be deceptive. A non-medical "doctor" (e.g., an individual with a Ph.D. in exercise physiology) or a physician without substantial experience in the area of hearing can endorse the product, but if the endorser is referred to as "doctor," the advertisement must make clear the nature and limits of the endorser's expertise.

Example 3: A manufacturer of automobile parts advertises that its products are approved by the "American Institute of Science." From its name, consumers would infer that the "American Institute of Science" is a bona fide independent testing organization with expertise in judging automobile parts and that, as such, it would not approve any automobile part without first testing its efficacy by means of valid scientific methods. If the American Institute of Science is not such a bona fide independent testing organization (*e.g.*, if it was established and operated by an automotive parts manufacturer), the endorsement would be deceptive. Even if the American Institute of Science is an independent bona fide expert testing organization, the endorsement may nevertheless be deceptive unless the Institute has conducted valid scientific tests of the advertised products and the test results support the endorsement message.

Example 4: A manufacturer of a non-prescription drug product represents that its product has been selected over competing products by a large metropolitan hospital. The hospital has selected the product because the manufacturer, unlike its competitors, has packaged each dose of the product separately. This package form is not generally available to the public. Under the circumstances, the endorsement would be deceptive because the basis for the hospital's choice—convenience of

728

packaging—is neither relevant nor available to consumers, and the basis for the hospital's decision is not disclosed to consumers.

Example 5: A woman who is identified as the president of a commercial "home cleaning service" states in a television advertisement that the service uses a particular brand of cleanser, instead of leading competitors it has tried, because of this brand's performance. Because cleaning services extensively use cleansers in the course of their business, the ad likely conveys that the president has knowledge superior to that of ordinary consumers. Accordingly, the president's statement will be deemed to be an expert endorsement. The service must, of course, actually use the endorsed cleanser. In addition, because the advertisement implies that the cleaning service has experience with a reasonable number of leading competitors to the advertised cleanser, the service must, in fact, have such experience, and, on the basis of its expertise, it must have determined that the cleaning ability of the endorsed cleanser is at least equal (or superior, if such is the net impression conveyed by the advertisement) to that of leading competitors' products with which the service has had experience and which remain reasonably available to it. Because in this example the cleaning service's president makes no mention that the endorsed cleanser was "chosen," "selected," or otherwise evaluated in side-by-side comparisons against its competitors, it is sufficient if the service has relied solely upon its accumulated experience in evaluating cleansers without having performed side-by-side or scientific comparisons.

Example 6: A medical doctor states in an advertisement for a drug that the product will safely allow consumers to lower their cholesterol by 50 points. If the materials the doctor reviewed were merely letters from satisfied consumers or the results of a rodent study, the endorsement would likely be deceptive because those materials are not what others with the same degree of expertise would consider adequate to support this conclusion about the product's safety and efficacy.

§255.4 Endorsements by organizations.

Endorsements by organizations, especially expert ones, are viewed as representing the judgment of a group whose collective experience exceeds that of any individual member, and whose judgments are generally free of the sort of subjective factors that vary from individual to individual. Therefore, an organization's endorsement must be reached by a process sufficient to ensure that the endorsement fairly reflects the collective judgment of the organization. Moreover, if an organization is represented as being expert, then, in conjunction with a proper exercise of its expertise in evaluating the product under §255.3 (expert endorsements), it must utilize an expert or experts recognized as such by the organization or standards previously adopted by the organization and suitable for judging the relevant merits of such products. [*See* §255.1(d) regarding the liability of endorsers.]

Example: A mattress seller advertises that its product is endorsed by a chiropractic association. Because the association would be regarded as expert with respect to judging mattresses, its endorsement must be supported by an evaluation by an expert or experts recognized as such by the organization, or by compliance with standards previously adopted by the organization and aimed at measuring the performance of mattresses in general and not designed with the unique features of the advertised mattress in mind.

§255.5 Disclosure of material connections.

When there exists a connection between the endorser and the seller of the advertised product that might materially affect the weight or credibility of the endorsement (*i.e.,* the connection is not reasonably expected by the audience), such connection must be fully disclosed. For example, when an endorser who appears in a television commercial is neither represented in the advertisement as an expert nor is known to a significant portion of the viewing public, then the advertiser should clearly and conspicuously disclose either the payment or promise of compensation prior to and in exchange for the endorsement or the fact that the endorser knew or had reason to know or to believe that if the endorsement favored the advertised product some benefit, such as an appearance on television, would be extended to the endorser. Additional guidance, including guidance concerning endorsements made through other media, is provided by the examples below.

Example 1: A drug company commissions research on its product by an outside organization. The drug company determines the overall subject of the research (*e.g.*, to test the efficacy of a newly developed product) and pays a substantial share of the expenses of the research project, but the research organization determines the protocol for the study and is responsible for conducting it. A subsequent advertisement by the drug company mentions the research results as the "findings" of that research organization. Although the design and conduct of the research project are controlled by the outside research organization, the weight consumers place on the reported results could be materially affected by knowing that the advertiser had funded the project. Therefore, the advertiser's payment of expenses to the research organization should be disclosed in this advertisement.

Example 2: A film star endorses a particular food product. The endorsement regards only points of taste and individual preference. This endorsement must, of course, comply with §255.1; but regardless of whether the star's compensation for the commercial is a $1 million cash payment or a royalty for each product sold by the advertiser during the next year, no disclosure is required because such payments likely are ordinarily expected by viewers.

Example 3: During an appearance by a well-known professional tennis player on a television talk show, the host comments that the past few months have been the best of her career and during this time she has risen to her highest level ever in the rankings. She responds by attributing the improvement in her game to the fact that she is seeing the ball better than she used to, ever since having laser vision correction surgery at a clinic that she identifies by name. She continues talking about the ease of the procedure, the kindness of the clinic's doctors, her speedy recovery, and how she can now engage in a variety of activities without glasses, including driving at night. The athlete does not disclose that, even though she does not appear in commercials for the clinic, she has a contractual relationship with it, and her contract pays her for speaking publicly about her surgery when she can do so. Consumers might not realize that a celebrity discussing a medical procedure in a television interview has been paid for doing so, and knowledge of such payments would likely affect the weight or credibility consumers give to the celebrity's endorsement. Without a clear and conspicuous disclosure that the athlete has been engaged as a spokesperson for the clinic, this endorsement is likely to be deceptive. Furthermore, if consumers are likely to take away from her story that her experience was typical of those who undergo the same procedure at the clinic, the advertiser must have substantiation for that claim.

Assume that instead of speaking about the clinic in a television interview, the tennis player touts the results of her surgery—mentioning the clinic by name—on a social networking site that allows her fans to read in real time what is happening in her life. Given the nature of the medium in which her endorsement is disseminated, consumers might not realize that she is a paid endorser. Because that information might affect the weight consumers give to her endorsement, her relationship with the clinic should be disclosed.

Assume that during that same television interview, the tennis player is wearing clothes bearing the insignia of an athletic wear company with whom she also has an endorsement contract. Although this contract requires that she wear the company's clothes not only on the court but also in public appearances, when possible, she does not mention them or the company during her appearance on the show. No disclosure is required because no representation is being made about the clothes in this context.

Example 4: An ad for an anti-snoring product features a physician who says that he has seen dozens of products come on the market over the years and, in his opinion, this is the best ever. Consumers would expect the physician to be reasonably compensated for his appearance in the ad. Consumers are unlikely, however, to expect that the physician receives a percentage of gross product

730

sales or that he owns part of the company, and either of these facts would likely materially affect the credibility that consumers attach to the endorsement. Accordingly, the advertisement should clearly and conspicuously disclose such a connection between the company and the physician.

Example 5: An actual patron of a restaurant, who is neither known to the public nor presented as an expert, is shown seated at the counter. He is asked for his "spontaneous" opinion of a new food product served in the restaurant. Assume, first, that the advertiser had posted a sign on the door of the restaurant informing all who entered that day that patrons would be interviewed by the advertiser as part of its TV promotion of its new soy protein "steak." This notification would materially affect the weight or credibility of the patron's endorsement, and, therefore, viewers of the advertisement should be clearly and conspicuously informed of the circumstances under which the endorsement was obtained.

Assume, in the alternative, that the advertiser had not posted a sign on the door of the restaurant, but had informed all interviewed customers of the "hidden camera" only after interviews were completed and the customers had no reason to know or believe that their response was being recorded for use in an advertisement. Even if patrons were also told that they would be paid for allowing the use of their opinions in advertising, these facts need not be disclosed.

Example 6: An infomercial producer wants to include consumer endorsements for an automotive additive product featured in her commercial, but because the product has not yet been sold, there are no consumer users. The producer's staff reviews the profiles of individuals interested in working as "extras" in commercials and identifies several who are interested in automobiles. The extras are asked to use the product for several weeks and then report back to the producer. They are told that if they are selected to endorse the product in the producer's infomercial, they will receive a small payment. Viewers would not expect that these "consumer endorsers" are actors who were asked to use the product so that they could appear in the commercial or that they were compensated. Because the advertisement fails to disclose these facts, it is deceptive.

Example 7: A college student who has earned a reputation as a video game expert maintains a personal weblog or "blog" where he posts entries about his gaming experiences. Readers of his blog frequently seek his opinions about video game hardware and software. As it has done in the past, the manufacturer of a newly released video game system sends the student a free copy of the system and asks him to write about it on his blog. He tests the new gaming system and writes a favorable review. Because his review is disseminated via a form of consumer-generated media in which his relationship to the advertiser is not inherently obvious, readers are unlikely to know that he has received the video game system free of charge in exchange for his review of the product, and given the value of the video game system, this fact likely would materially affect the credibility they attach to his endorsement. Accordingly, the blogger should clearly and conspicuously disclose that he received the gaming system free of charge. The manufacturer should advise him at the time it provides the gaming system that this connection should be disclosed, and it should have procedures in place to try to monitor his postings for compliance.

Example 8: An online message board designated for discussions of new music download technology is frequented by MP3 player enthusiasts. They exchange information about new products, utilities, and the functionality of numerous playback devices. Unbeknownst to the message board community, an employee of a leading playback device manufacturer has been posting messages on the discussion board promoting the manufacturer's product. Knowledge of this poster's employment likely would affect the weight or credibility of her endorsement. Therefore, the poster should clearly and conspicuously disclose her relationship to the manufacturer to members and readers of the message board.

Example 9: A young man signs up to be part of a "street team" program in which points are awarded each time a team member talks to his or her friends about a particular advertiser's products.

Team members can then exchange their points for prizes, such as concert tickets or electronics. These incentives would materially affect the weight or credibility of the team member's endorsements. They should be clearly and conspicuously disclosed, and the advertiser should take steps to ensure that these disclosures are being provided.

The FTC's Endorsement Guides: What People Are Asking (September 2017)

Introduction

Suppose you meet someone who tells you about a great new product. She tells you it performs wonderfully and offers fantastic new features that nobody else has. Would that recommendation factor into your decision to buy the product? Probably.

Now suppose the person works for the company that sells the product – or has been paid by the company to tout the product. Would you want to know that when you're evaluating the endorser's glowing recommendation? You bet. That common-sense premise is at the heart of the Federal Trade Commission's (FTC) Endorsement Guides.

The Guides, at their core, reflect the basic truth-in-advertising principle that endorsements must be honest and not misleading. An endorsement must reflect the honest opinion of the endorser and can't be used to make a claim that the product's marketer couldn't legally make.

In addition, the Guides say, if there's a connection between an endorser and the marketer that consumers would not expect and it would affect how consumers evaluate the endorsement, that connection should be disclosed. For example, if an ad features an endorser who's a relative or employee of the marketer, the ad is misleading unless the connection is made clear. The same is usually true if the endorser has been paid or given something of value to tout the product. The reason is obvious: Knowing about the connection is important information for anyone evaluating the endorsement.

Say you're planning a vacation. You do some research and find a glowing review on someone's blog that a particular resort is the most luxurious place he has ever stayed. If you knew the hotel had paid the blogger hundreds of dollars to say great things about it or that the blogger had stayed there for several days for free, it could affect how much weight you'd give the blogger's endorsement. The blogger should, therefore, let his readers know about that relationship.

Another principle in the Guides applies to ads that feature endorsements from people who achieved exceptional, or even above average, results. An example is an endorser who says she lost 20 pounds in two months using the advertised product. If the advertiser doesn't have proof that the endorser's experience represents what people will generally achieve using the product as described in the ad (for example, by just taking a pill daily for two months), then an ad featuring that endorser must make clear to the audience what the generally expected results are.

Here are answers to some of our most frequently asked questions from advertisers, ad agencies, bloggers, and others.

About the Endorsement Guides

Do the Endorsement Guides apply to social media?

Yes. Truth in advertising is important in all media, whether they have been around for decades (like television and magazines) or are relatively new (like blogs and social media).

Isn't it common knowledge that bloggers are paid to tout products or that if you click a link on a blogger's site to buy a product, the blogger will get a commission?

No. Some bloggers who mention products in their posts have no connection to the marketers of those products – they don't receive anything for their reviews or get a commission. They simply recommend those products to their readers because they believe in them.

Moreover, the financial arrangements between some bloggers and advertisers may be apparent to industry insiders, but not to everyone else who reads a particular blog. Under the law, an act or practice is deceptive if it misleads "a significant minority" of consumers. Even if some readers are aware of these deals, many readers aren't. That's why disclosure is important.

Are you monitoring bloggers?

Generally not, but if concerns about possible violations of the FTC Act come to our attention, we evaluate them case by case. If law enforcement becomes necessary, our focus usually will be on advertisers or their ad agencies and public relations firms. Action against an individual endorser, however, might be appropriate in certain circumstances, such as if the endorser has continued to fail to make required disclosures despite warnings.

Does the FTC hold bloggers to a higher standard than reviewers for traditional media outlets?

No. The FTC Act applies across the board. The issue is – and always has been – whether the audience understands the reviewer's relationship to the company whose products are being recommended. If the audience understands the relationship, a disclosure isn't needed.

If you're employed by a newspaper or TV station to give reviews – whether online or offline – your audience probably understands that your job is to provide your personal opinion on behalf of the newspaper or television station. In that situation, it's clear that you did not buy the product yourself – whether it's a book or a car or a movie ticket. On a personal blog, a social networking page, or in similar media, the reader might not realize that the reviewer has a relationship with the company whose products are being recommended. Disclosure of that relationship helps readers decide how much weight to give the review.

What is the legal basis for the Guides?

The FTC conducts investigations and brings cases involving endorsements made on behalf of an advertiser under Section 5 of the FTC Act, which generally prohibits deceptive advertising.

The Guides are intended to give insight into what the FTC thinks about various marketing activities involving endorsements and how Section 5 might apply to those activities. The Guides themselves don't have the force of law. However, practices inconsistent with the Guides may result in law enforcement actions alleging violations of the FTC Act. Law enforcement actions can result in orders requiring the defendants in the case to give up money they received from their violations and to abide by various requirements in the future. Despite inaccurate news reports, there are no "fines" for violations of the FTC Act.

When Does the FTC Act Apply to Endorsements?

I'm a blogger. I heard that every time I mention a product on my blog, I have to say whether I got it for free or paid for it myself. Is that true?

No. If you mention a product you paid for yourself, there isn't an issue. Nor is it an issue if you get the product for free because a store is giving out free samples to its customers.

The FTC is only concerned about endorsements that are made on behalf of a sponsoring advertiser. For example, an endorsement would be covered by the FTC Act if an advertiser – or someone working for an advertiser – pays you or gives you something of value to mention a product. If you receive free products or other perks with the expectation that you'll promote or discuss the advertiser's products in your blog, you're covered. Bloggers who are part of network marketing programs, where they sign up to receive free product samples in exchange for writing about them, also are covered.

What if all I get from a company is a $1-off coupon, an entry in a sweepstakes or a contest, or a product that is only worth a few dollars? Does that still have to be disclosed?

The question you need to ask is whether knowing about that gift or incentive would affect the weight or credibility your readers give to your recommendation. If it could, then it should be disclosed. For example, being entered into a sweepstakes or a contest for a chance to win a thousand dollars in exchange for an endorsement could very well affect how people view that endorsement. Determining whether a small gift would affect the weight or credibility of an endorsement could be difficult. It's always safer to disclose that information.

Also, even if getting one free item that's not very valuable doesn't affect your credibility, continually getting free stuff from an advertiser or multiple advertisers could suggest you expect future benefits from positive reviews. If a blogger or other endorser has a relationship with a marketer or a network that sends freebies in the hope of positive reviews, it's best to let readers know about the free stuff.

Even an incentive with no financial value might affect the credibility of an endorsement and would need to be disclosed. The Guides give the example of a restaurant patron being offered the opportunity to appear in television advertising before giving his opinion about a product. Because the chance to appear in a TV ad could sway what someone says, that incentive should be disclosed.

My company makes a donation to charity anytime someone reviews our product. Do we need to make a disclosure?

Some people might be inclined to leave a positive review in an effort to earn more money for charity. The overarching principle remains: If readers of the reviews would evaluate them differently knowing that they were motivated in part by charitable donations, there should be a disclosure. Therefore, it might be better to err on the side of caution and disclose that donations are made to charity in exchange for reviews.

What if I upload a video to YouTube that shows me reviewing several products? Should I disclose that I got them from an advertiser?

Yes. The guidance for videos is the same as for websites or blogs.

What if I return the product after I review it? Should I still make a disclosure?

That might depend on the product and how long you are allowed to use it. For example, if you get free use of a car for a month, we recommend a disclosure even though you have to return it. But even for less valuable products, it's best to be open and transparent with your readers.

I have a website that reviews local restaurants. It's clear when a restaurant pays for an ad on my website, but do I have to disclose which restaurants give me free meals?

If you get free meals, you should let your readers know so they can factor that in when they read your reviews.

I'm opening a new restaurant. To get feedback on the food and service, I'm inviting my family and friends to eat for free. If they talk about their experience on social media, is that something that should be disclosed?

You've raised two issues here. First, it may be relevant to readers that people endorsing your restaurant on social media are related to you. Therefore, they should disclose that personal relationship. Second, if you are giving free meals to anyone and seeking their endorsement, then their reviews in social media would be viewed as advertising subject to FTC jurisdiction. But even if you don't specifically ask for their endorsement, there may be an expectation that attendees will spread the word about the restaurant. Therefore, if someone who eats for free at your invitation posts about your restaurant, readers of the post would probably want to know that the meal was on the house.

I have a YouTube channel that focuses on hunting, camping, and the outdoors. Sometimes I'll do a product review. Knife manufacturers know how much I love knives, so they send me knives as free gifts, hoping that I will review them. I'm under no obligation to talk about any knife and getting

the knives as gifts really doesn't affect my judgment. Do I need to disclose when I'm talking about a knife I got for free?

Even if you don't think it affects your evaluation of the product, what matters is whether knowing that you got the knife for free might affect how *your audience* views what you say about the knife. It doesn't matter that you aren't required to review every knife you receive. Your viewers may assess your review differently if they knew you got the knife for free, so we advise disclosing that fact.

Several months ago a manufacturer sent me a free product and asked me to write about it in my blog. I tried the product, liked it, and wrote a favorable review. When I posted the review, I disclosed that I got the product for free from the manufacturer. I still use the product. Do I have to disclose that I got the product for free every time I mention it in my blog?

It might depend on what you say about it, but each new endorsement made without a disclosure could be deceptive because readers might not see the original blog post where you said you got the product free from the manufacturer.

A trade association hired me to be its "ambassador" and promote its upcoming conference in social media, primarily on Facebook, Twitter, and in my blog. The association is only hiring me for five hours a week. I disclose my relationship with the association in my blogs and in the tweets and posts I make about the event during the hours I'm working. But sometimes I get questions about the conference in my off time. If I respond via Twitter when I'm not officially working, do I need to make a disclosure? Can that be solved by placing a badge for the conference in my Twitter profile?

You have a financial connection to the company that hired you and that relationship exists whether or not you are being paid for a particular tweet. If you are endorsing the conference in your tweets, your audience has a right to know about your relationship. That said, some of your tweets responding to questions about the event might not be endorsements, because they aren't communicating your opinions about the conference (for example, if someone just asks you for a link to the conference agenda).

Also, if you respond to someone's questions about the event via email or text, that person probably already knows your affiliation or they wouldn't be asking you. You probably wouldn't need a disclosure in that context. But when you respond via social media, all your followers see your posts and some of them might not have seen your earlier disclosures.

With respect to posting the conference's badge on your Twitter profile page, a disclosure on a profile page isn't sufficient because many people in your audience probably won't see it. Also, depending upon what it says, the badge may not adequately inform consumers of your connection to the trade association. If it's simply a logo or hashtag for the event, it won't tell consumers of your relationship to the association.

I'm a blogger and a company wants me to attend the launch of its new product. They will fly me to the launch and put me up in a hotel for a couple of nights. They aren't paying me or giving me anything else. If I write a blog sharing my thoughts about the product, should I disclose anything?

Yes. Knowing that you received free travel and accommodations could affect how much weight your readers give to your thoughts about the product, so you should disclose that you have a financial relationship with the company.

I share in my social media posts about products I use. Do I actually have to say something positive about a product for my posts to be endorsements covered by the FTC Act?

Simply posting a picture of a product in social media, such as on Pinterest, or a video of you using it could convey that you like and approve of the product. If it does, it's an endorsement.

You don't necessarily have to use words to convey a positive message. If your audience thinks that what you say or otherwise communicate about a product reflects your opinions or beliefs about the product, and you have a relationship with the company marketing the product, it's an endorsement subject to the FTC Act.

Of course, if you don't have any relationship with the advertiser, then your posts simply are not subject to the FTC Act, no matter what you show or say about the product. The FTC Act covers only endorsements made on behalf of a sponsoring advertiser.

If I post a picture of myself to Instagram and tag the brand of dress I'm wearing, but don't say anything about the brand in my description of the picture, is that an endorsement? And, even if it is an endorsement, wouldn't my followers understand that I only tag the brands of my sponsors?

Tagging a brand you are wearing is an endorsement of the brand and, just like any other endorsement, could require a disclosure if you have a relationship with that brand. Some influencers only tag the brands of their sponsors, some tag brands with which they don't have relationships, and some do a bit of both. Followers might not know why you are tagging a dress and some might think you're doing it just because you like the dress and want them to know.

Say a car company pays a blogger to write that he wants to buy a certain new sports car and he includes a link to the company's site. But the blogger doesn't say he's going to actually buy the car – or even that he's driven it. Is that still an endorsement subject to the FTC's Endorsement Guides?

Yes, an endorsement can be aspirational. It's an endorsement if the blogger is explicitly or implicitly expressing his or her views about the sports car (*e.g.*, "I want this car"). If the blogger was paid, it should be disclosed.

I'm a book author and I belong to a group where we agree to post reviews in social media for each other. I'll review someone else's book on a book review site or a bookstore site if he or she reviews my book. No money changes hands. Do I need to make a disclosure?

It sounds like you have a connection that might materially affect the weight or credibility of your endorsements (that is, your reviews), since bad reviews of each others' books could jeopardize the arrangement. There doesn't have to be a monetary payment. The connection could be friendship, family relationships, or strangers who make a deal.

My Facebook page identifies my employer. Should I include an additional disclosure when I post on Facebook about how useful one of our products is?

It's a good idea. People reading your posts in their news feed – or on your profile page – might not know where you work or what products your employer makes. Many businesses are so diversified that readers might not realize that the products you're talking about are sold by your company.

A famous athlete has thousands of followers on Twitter and is well-known as a spokesperson for a particular product. Does he have to disclose that he's being paid every time he tweets about the product?

It depends on whether his followers understand that he's being paid to endorse that product. If they know he's a paid endorser, no disclosure is needed. But if a significant portion of his followers don't know that, the relationship should be disclosed. Determining whether followers are aware of a relationship could be tricky in many cases, so we recommend disclosure.

A famous celebrity has millions of followers on Twitter. Many people know that she regularly charges advertisers to mention their products in her tweets. Does she have to disclose when she's being paid to tweet about products?

It depends on whether her followers understand that her tweets about products are paid endorsements. If a significant portion of her followers don't know that, disclosures are needed. Again, determining that could be tricky, so we recommend disclosure.

I'm a video blogger who lives in London. I create sponsored beauty videos on YouTube. The products that I promote are also sold in the U.S. Am I under any obligation to tell my viewers that I have been paid to endorse products, considering that I'm not living in the U.S.?

To the extent it is reasonably foreseeable that your YouTube videos will be seen by and affect U.S. consumers, U.S. law would apply and a disclosure would be required. Also, the U.K. and many other countries have similar laws and policies, so you'll want to check those, too.

Product Placements

What does the FTC have to say about product placements on television shows?

Federal Communications Commission law (FCC, not FTC) requires TV stations to include disclosures of product placement in TV shows.

The FTC has expressed the opinion that under the FTC Act, product placement (that is, merely showing products or brands in third-party entertainment content – as distinguished from sponsored content or disguised commercials) doesn't require a disclosure that the advertiser paid for the placement.

What if the host of a television talk show expresses her opinions about a product – let's say a videogame – and she was paid for the promotion? The segment is entertainment, it's humorous, and it's not like the host is an expert. Is that different from a product placement and does the payment have to be disclosed?

If the host endorses the product – even if she is just playing the game and saying something like "wow, this is awesome" – it's more than a product placement. If the payment for the endorsement isn't expected by the audience and it would affect the weight the audience gives the endorsement, it should be disclosed. It doesn't matter that the host isn't an expert or the segment is humorous as long as the endorsement has credibility that would be affected by knowing about the payment. However, if what the host says is obviously an advertisement – think of an old-time television show where the host goes to a different set, holds up a cup of coffee, says "Wake up with ABC Coffee. It's how I start my day!" and takes a sip – a disclosure probably isn't necessary.

Endorsements by Individuals on Social Networking Sites

Many social networking sites allow you to share your interests with friends and followers by clicking a button or sharing a link to show that you're a fan of a particular business, product, website or service. Is that an "endorsement" that needs a disclosure?

Many people enjoy sharing their fondness for a particular product or service with their social networks.

If you write about how much you like something you bought on your own and you're not being rewarded, you don't have to worry. However, if you're doing it as part of a sponsored campaign or you're being compensated – for example, getting a discount on a future purchase or being entered into a sweepstakes for a significant prize – then a disclosure is appropriate.

I am an avid social media user who often gets rewards for participating in online campaigns on behalf of brands. Is it OK for me to click a "like" button, pin a picture, or share a link to show that I'm a fan of a particular business, product, website or service as part of a paid campaign?

Using these features to endorse a company's products or services as part of a sponsored brand campaign probably requires a disclosure.

We realize that some platforms – like Facebook's "like" buttons – don't allow you to make a disclosure. Advertisers shouldn't encourage endorsements using features that don't allow for clear and conspicuous disclosures. Whether the Commission may take action would depend on the overall impression, including whether consumers take "likes" to be material in their decision to patronize a business or buy a product.

However, an advertiser buying fake "likes" is very different from an advertiser offering incentives for "likes" from actual consumers. If "likes" are from non-existent people or people who have no experience using the product or service, they are clearly deceptive, and both the purchaser and the seller of the fake "likes" could face enforcement action.

I posted a review of a service on a website. Now the marketer has taken my review and changed it in a way that I think is misleading. Am I liable for that? What can I do?

737

No, you aren't liable for the changes the marketer made to your review. You could, and probably should, complain to the marketer and ask them to stop using your altered review. You also could file complaints with the FTC, your local consumer protection organization, and the Better Business Bureau.

How Should I Disclose That I Was Given Something for My Endorsement?

Is there special wording I have to use to make the disclosure?

No. The point is to give readers the essential information. A simple disclosure like "Company X gave me this product to try . . . ." will usually be effective.

Do I have to hire a lawyer to help me write a disclosure?

No. What matters is effective communication. A disclosure like "Company X gave me [name of product], and I think it's great" gives your readers the information they need. Or, at the start of a short video, you might say, "The products I'm going to use in this video were given to me by their manufacturers." That gives the necessary heads-up to your viewers.

Do I need to list the details of everything I get from a company for reviewing a product?

No. What matters is whether the information would have an effect on the weight readers would give your review. So whether you got $100 or $1,000 you could simply say you were "paid." (That wouldn't be good enough, however, if you're an employee or co-owner.) And if it is something so small that it would not affect the weight readers would give your review, you may not need to disclose anything.

When should I say more than that I got a product for free?

It depends on whether you got something else from the company. Saying that you got a product for free suggests that you didn't get anything else.

For example, if an app developer gave you their 99-cent app for free for you to review it, that information might not have much effect on the weight that readers give to your review. But if the app developer also gave you $100, knowledge of that payment would have a much greater effect on the credibility of your review. So a disclosure that simply said you got the app for free wouldn't be good enough, but as discussed above, you don't have to disclose exactly how much you were paid.

Similarly, if a company gave you a $50 gift card to give away to one of your readers and a second $50 gift card to keep for yourself, it wouldn't be good enough only to say that the company gave you a gift card to give away.

I'm doing a review of a videogame that hasn't been released yet. The manufacturer is paying me to try the game and review it. I was planning on disclosing that the manufacturer gave me a "sneak peek" of the game. Isn't that enough to put people on notice of my relationship to the manufacturer?

No, it's not. Getting early access doesn't mean that you got paid. Getting a "sneak peek" of the game doesn't even mean that you get to keep the game. If you get early access, you can say that, but if you get to keep the game or are paid, you should say so.

Would a single disclosure on my home page that "many of the products I discuss on this site are provided to me free by their manufacturers" be enough?

A single disclosure on your home page doesn't really do it because people visiting your site might read individual reviews or watch individual videos without seeing the disclosure on your home page.

If I upload a video to YouTube and that video requires a disclosure, can I just put the disclosure in the description that I upload together with the video?

No, because consumers can easily miss disclosures in the video description. Many people might watch the video without even seeing the description page, and those who do might not read the disclosure. The disclosure has the most chance of being clear and prominent if it's included in the video itself. That's not to say that you couldn't have disclosures in both the video and the description.

What about a disclosure in the description of an Instagram post?

When people view Instagram streams on most smartphones, longer descriptions (currently more than two lines) are truncated, with only the beginning lines displayed. To see the rest, you have to click "more." If an Instagram post makes an endorsement through the picture or the beginning lines of the description, any required disclosure should be presented without having to click "more."

Would a button that says DISCLOSURE, LEGAL, or something like that which links to a full disclosure be sufficient?

No. A hyperlink like that isn't likely to be sufficient. It does not convey the importance, nature, and relevance of the information to which it leads and it is likely that many consumers will not click on it and therefore will miss necessary disclosures. The disclosures we are talking about are brief and there is no space-related reason to use a hyperlink to provide access to them.

The social media platform I use has a built-in feature that allows me to disclose paid endorsements. Is it sufficient for me to rely on that tool?

Not necessarily. Just because a platform offers a feature like that is no guarantee it's an effective way for influencers to disclose their material connection to a brand. It still depends on an evaluation of whether the tool clearly and conspicuously discloses the relevant connection. One factor the FTC will look to is placement. The disclosure should catch users' attention and be placed where they aren't likely to miss it. A key consideration is how users view the screen when using a particular platform. For example, on a photo platform, users paging through their streams will likely look at the eye-catching images. Therefore, a disclosure placed above a photo may not attract their attention. Similarly, a disclosure in the lower corner of a video could be too easy for users to overlook. Second, the disclosure should use a simple-to-read font with a contrasting background that makes it stand out. Third, the disclosure should be a worded in a way that's understandable to the ordinary reader. Ambiguous phrases are likely to be confusing. For example, simply flagging that a post contains paid content might not be sufficient if the post mentions multiple brands and not all of the mentions were paid. The big-picture point is that the ultimate responsibility for clearly disclosing a material connection rests with the influencer and the brand – not the platform.

How can I make a disclosure on Snapchat or in Instagram Stories?

You can superimpose a disclosure on Snapchat or Instagram Stories just as you can superimpose any other words over the images on those platforms. The disclosure should be easy to notice and read in the time that your followers have to look at the image. In determining whether your disclosure passes muster, factors you should consider include how much time you give your followers to look at the image, how much competing text there is to read, how large the disclosure is, and how well it contrasts against the image. (You might want to have a solid background behind the disclosure.) Keep in mind that if your post includes video and you include an audio disclosure, many users of those platforms watch videos without sound. So they won't hear an audio-only disclosure. Obviously, other general disclosure guidance would also apply.

What about a platform like Twitter? How can I make a disclosure when my message is limited to 140 characters?

The FTC isn't mandating the specific wording of disclosures. However, the same general principle – that people get the information they need to evaluate sponsored statements – applies across the board, regardless of the advertising medium. The words "Sponsored" and "Promotion" use only 9 characters. "Paid ad" only uses 7 characters. Starting a tweet with "Ad:" or "#ad" – which takes only 3 characters – would likely be effective.

You just talked about putting "#ad" at the beginning of a social media post. What about "#ad" at or near the end of a post?

We're not necessarily saying that "#ad" has to be at the beginning of a post. The FTC does not dictate where you have to place the "#ad." What the FTC will look at is whether it is easily noticed and understood. So, although we aren't saying it has to be at the beginning, it's less likely to be effective in the middle or at the end. Indeed, if #ad is mixed in with links or other hashtags at the end, some readers may just skip over all of that stuff.

What if we combine our company name, "Cool Stylle" with "ad" as in "#coolstyllead"?

There is a good chance that consumers won't notice and understand the significance of the word "ad" at the end of a hashtag, especially one made up of several words combined like "#coolstyllead." Disclosures need to be easily noticed and understood.

Is it good enough if an endorser says "thank you" to the sponsoring company?

No. A "thank you" to a company or a brand doesn't necessarily communicate that the endorser got something for free or that they were given something in exchange for an endorsement. The person posting in social media could just be thanking a company or brand for providing a great product or service. But "Thanks XYZ for the free product" or "Thanks XYZ for the gift of ABC product" would be good enough – if that's all you got from XYZ. If that's too long, there's "Sponsored" or "Ad."

What about saying, "XYZ Company asked me to try their product"?

Depending on the context of the endorsement, it might be clear that the endorser got the product for free and kept it after trying it. If that isn't clear, then that disclosure wouldn't be good enough. Also, that disclosure might not be sufficient if, in addition to receiving a free product, the endorser was paid.

I provide marketing consulting and advice to my clients. I'm also a blogger and I sometimes promote my client's products. Are "#client" "#advisor" and "#consultant" all acceptable disclosures?

Probably not. Such one-word hashtags are ambiguous and likely confusing. In blogs, there isn't an issue with a limited number of characters available. So it would be much clearer if you say something like, "I'm a paid consultant to the marketers of XYZ" or "I work with XYZ brand"(where XYZ is a brand name).

Of course, it's possible that that some shorter message might be effective. For example, something like "XYZ_Consultant" or "XYZ_Advisor" might work. But even if a disclosure like that is clearer, no disclosure is effective if consumers don't see it and read it.

Would "#ambassador" or "#[BRAND]_Ambassador" work in a tweet?

The use of "#ambassador" is ambiguous and confusing. Many consumers are unlikely to know what it means. By contrast, "#XYZ_Ambassador" will likely be more understandable (where XYZ is a brand name). However, even if the language is understandable, a disclosure also must be prominent so it will be noticed and read.

I'm a blogger, and XYZ Resort Company is flying me to one of its destinations and putting me up for a few nights. If I write an article sharing my thoughts about the resort destination, how should I disclose the free travel?

Your disclosure could be just, "XYZ Resort paid for my trip" or "Thanks to XYZ Resort for the free trip." It would also be accurate to describe your blog as "sponsored by XYZ Resort."

The Guides say that disclosures have to be clear and conspicuous. What does that mean?

To make a disclosure "clear and conspicuous," advertisers should use plain and unambiguous language and make the disclosure stand out. Consumers should be able to notice the disclosure easily. They should not have to look for it. In general, disclosures should be:

- close to the claims to which they relate;
- in a font that is easy to read;
- in a shade that stands out against the background;
- for video ads, on the screen long enough to be noticed, read, and understood;
- for audio disclosures, read at a cadence that is easy for consumers to follow and in words consumers will understand.

740

A disclosure that is made in both audio and video is more likely to be noticed by consumers. Disclosures should <u>not</u> be hidden or buried in footnotes, in blocks of text people are not likely to read, or in hyperlinks. If disclosures are hard to find, tough to understand, fleeting, or buried in unrelated details, or if other elements in the ad or message obscure or distract from the disclosures, they don't meet the "clear and conspicuous" standard. With respect to online disclosures, FTC staff has issued a guidance document, ".com Disclosures: How to Make Effective Disclosures in Digital Advertising," which is available on ftc.gov.

Where in my blog should I disclose that my review is sponsored by a marketer? I've seen some say it at the top and others at the bottom. Does it matter?

Yes, it matters. A disclosure should be placed where it easily catches consumers' attention and is difficult to miss. Consumers may miss a disclosure at the bottom of a blog or the bottom of a page. A disclosure at the very top of the page, outside of the blog, might also be overlooked by consumers. A disclosure is more likely to be seen if it's very close to, or part of, the endorsement to which it relates.

I've been paid to endorse a product in social media. My posts, videos, and tweets will be in Spanish. In what language should I disclose that I've been paid for the promotion?

The connection between an endorser and a marketer should be disclosed in whatever language or languages the endorsement is made, so your disclosures should be in Spanish.

I guess I need to make a disclosure that I've gotten paid for a video review that I'm uploading to YouTube. When in the review should I make the disclosure? Is it ok if it's at the end?

It's more likely that a disclosure at the end of the video will be missed, especially if someone doesn't watch the whole thing. Having it at the beginning of the review would be better. Having multiple disclosures during the video would be even better. Of course, no one should promote a link to your review that bypasses the beginning of the video and skips over the disclosure. If YouTube has been enabled to run ads during your video, a disclosure that is obscured by ads is not clear and conspicuous.

I'm getting paid to do a videogame playthrough and give commentary while I'm playing. The playthrough – which will last several hours – will be live streamed. Would a disclosure at the beginning of the stream be ok?

Since viewers can tune in any time, they could easily miss a disclosure at the beginning of the stream or at any other single point in the stream. If there are multiple, periodic disclosures throughout the stream people are likely to see them no matter when they tune in. To be cautious, you could have a continuous, clear and conspicuous disclosure throughout the entire stream.

Other Things for Endorsers to Know

Besides disclosing my relationship with the company whose product I'm endorsing, what are the essential things I need to know about endorsements?

The most important principle is that an endorsement has to represent the accurate experience and opinion of the endorser:

- You can't talk about your experience with a product if you haven't tried it.
- If you were paid to try a product and you thought it was terrible, you can't say it's terrific.

You can't make claims about a product that would require proof the advertiser doesn't have. The Guides give the example of a blogger commissioned by an advertiser to review a new body lotion. Although the advertiser does not make any claims about the lotion's ability to cure skin conditions and the blogger does not ask the advertiser whether there is substantiation for the claim, she writes that the lotion cures eczema. The blogger is subject to liability for making claims without having a reasonable basis for those claims.

Social Media Contests

741

My company runs contests and sweepstakes in social media. To enter, participants have to send a Tweet or make a pin with the hashtag, #XYZ_Rocks. ("XYZ" is the name of my product.) Isn't that enough to notify readers that the posts were incentivized?

No, it is likely that many readers would not understand such a hashtag to mean that those posts were made as part of a contest or that the people doing the posting had received something of value (in this case, a chance to win the contest prize). Making the word "contest" or "sweepstakes" part of the hashtag should be enough. However, the word "sweeps" probably isn't, because it is likely that many people would not understand what that means.

Online Review Programs

My company runs a retail website that includes customer reviews of the products we sell. We believe honest reviews help our customers and we give out free products to a select group of our customers for them to review. We tell them to be honest, whether it's positive or negative. What we care about is how helpful the reviews are. Do we still need to disclose which reviews were of free products?

Yes. Knowing that reviewers got the product they reviewed for free would probably affect the weight your customers give to the reviews, even if you didn't intend for that to happen. And even assuming the reviewers in your program are unbiased, your customers have the right to know which reviewers were given products for free. It's also possible that the reviewers may wonder whether your company would stop sending them products if they wrote several negative reviews – despite your assurances that you only want their honest opinions – and that could affect their reviews. Also, reviewers given free products might give the products higher ratings on a scale like the number of stars than reviewers who bought the products. If that's the case, consumers may be misled if they just look at inflated average ratings rather than reading individual reviews with disclosures. Therefore, if you give free products to reviewers you should disclose next to any average or other summary rating that it includes reviewers who were given free products.

My company, XYZ, operates one of the most popular multi-channel networks on YouTube. We just entered into a contract with a videogame marketer to pay some of our network members to produce and upload video reviews of the marketer's games. We're going to have these reviewers announce at the beginning of each video (before the action starts) that it's "sponsored by XYZ" and also have a prominent simultaneous disclosure on the screen saying the same thing. Is that good enough?

Many consumers could think that XYZ is a neutral third party and won't realize from your disclosures that the review was really sponsored (and paid for) by the videogame marketer, which has a strong interest in positive reviews. If the disclosure said, "Sponsored by [name of the game company]," that would be good enough.

Soliciting Endorsements

My company wants to contact customers and interview them about their experiences with our service. If we like what they say about our service, can we ask them to allow us to quote them in our ads? Can we pay them for letting us use their endorsements?

Yes, you can ask your customers about their experiences with your product and feature their comments in your ads. If they have no reason to expect compensation or any other benefit before they give their comments, there's no need to disclose your payments to them.

However, if you've given these customers a reason to expect a benefit from providing their thoughts about your product, you should disclose that fact in your ads. For example, if customers are told in advance that their comments might be used in advertising, they might expect to receive a payment for a positive review, and that could influence what they say, even if you tell them that you want their honest opinion. In fact, even if you tell your customers that you aren't going to pay them but that they might be featured in your advertising, that opportunity might be seen as having a value, so the fact that they knew this when they gave the review should be disclosed (e.g., "Customers were told in advance they might be featured in an ad.").

I'm starting a new Internet business. I don't have any money for advertising, so I need publicity. Can I tell people that if they say good things about my business on Yelp or Etsy, I'll give them a discount on items they buy through my website?

It's not a good idea. Endorsements must reflect the honest opinions or experiences of the endorser, and your plan could cause people to make up positive reviews even if they've never done business with you. However, it's okay to invite people to post reviews of your business after they've actually used your products or services. If you're offering them something of value in return for these reviews, tell them in advance that they should disclose what they received from you. You should also inform potential reviewers that the discount will be conditioned upon their making the disclosure. That way, other consumers can decide how much stock to put in those reviews.

A company is giving me a free product to review on one particular website or social media platform. They say that if I voluntarily review it on another site or on a different social media platform, I don't need to make any disclosures. Is that true?

No. If you received a free or discounted product to provide a review somewhere, your connection to the company should be disclosed everywhere you endorse the product.

Does it matter how I got the free product to review?

No, it doesn't. Whether they give you a code, ship it directly to you, or give you money to buy it yourself, it's all the same for the purpose of having to disclose that you got the product for free. The key question is always the same: If consumers knew the company gave it to you for free (or at a substantial discount), might that information affect how much weight they give your review?

My company wants to get positive reviews. We are thinking about distributing product discounts through various services that encourage reviews. Some services require individuals who want discount codes to provide information allowing sellers to read their other reviews before deciding which reviewers to provide with discount codes. Other services send out offers of a limited number of discount codes and then follow up by email to see whether the recipients have reviewed their products. Still others send offers of discount codes to those who previously posted reviews in exchange for discounted products. All of these services say that reviews are not required. Does it matter which service I choose? I would prefer that recipients of my discount codes not have to disclose that they received discounts.

Whichever service you choose, the recipients of your discount codes need to disclose that they received a discount from you to encourage their reviews. Even though the services might say that a review is not "required," it's at least implied that a review is expected.

What Are an Advertiser's Responsibilities for What Others Say in Social Media?

Our company uses a network of bloggers and other social media influencers to promote our products. We understand we're responsible for monitoring our network. What kind of monitoring program do we need? Will we be liable if someone in our network says something false about our product or fails to make a disclosure?

Advertisers need to have reasonable programs in place to train and monitor members of their network. The scope of the program depends on the risk that deceptive practices by network participants could cause consumer harm – either physical injury or financial loss. For example, a network devoted to the sale of health products may require more supervision than a network promoting, say, a new fashion line. Here are some elements every program should include:

1. Given an advertiser's responsibility for substantiating objective product claims, explain to members of your network what they can (and can't) say about the products – for example, a list of the health claims they can make for your products, along with instructions not to go beyond those claims;

2. Instruct members of the network on their responsibilities for disclosing their connections to you;

3. Periodically search for what your people are saying; and

4. Follow up if you find questionable practices.

It's unrealistic to expect you to be aware of every single statement made by a member of your network. But it's up to you to make a reasonable effort to know what participants in your network are saying. That said, it's unlikely that the activity of a rogue blogger would be the basis of a law enforcement action if your company has a reasonable training, monitoring, and compliance program in place.

Our company's social media program is run by our public relations firm. We tell them to make sure that what they and anyone they pay on our behalf do complies with the FTC's Guides. Is that good enough?

Your company is ultimately responsible for what others do on your behalf. You should make sure your public relations firm has an appropriate program in place to train and monitor members of its social media network. Ask for regular reports confirming that the program is operating properly and monitor the network periodically. Delegating part of your promotional program to an outside entity doesn't relieve you of responsibility under the FTC Act.

What About Intermediaries?

I have a small network marketing business. Advertisers pay me to distribute their products to members of my network who then try the product for free. How do the principles in the Guides affect me?

You should tell the participants in your network that if they endorse products they have received through your program, they should make it clear they got them for free. Advise your clients – the advertisers – that if they provide free samples directly to your members, they should remind them of the importance of disclosing the relationship when they talk about those products. Put a program in place to check periodically whether your members are making those disclosures, and to deal with anyone who isn't complying.

My company recruits "influencers" for marketers who want them to endorse their products. We pay and direct the influencers. What are our responsibilities?

Like an advertiser, your company needs to have reasonable programs in place to train and monitor the influencers you pay and direct.

What About Affiliate or Network Marketing?

I'm an affiliate marketer with links to an online retailer on my website. When people read what I've written about a particular product and then click on those links and buy something from the retailer, I earn a commission from the retailer. What do I have to disclose? Where should the disclosure be?

If you disclose your relationship to the retailer clearly and conspicuously on your site, readers can decide how much weight to give your endorsement.

In some instances – like when the affiliate link is embedded in your product review – a single disclosure may be adequate. When the review has a clear and conspicuous disclosure of your relationship and the reader can see both the review containing that disclosure and the link at the same time, readers have the information they need. You could say something like, "I get commissions for purchases made through links in this post." But if the product review containing the disclosure and the link are separated, readers may not make the connection.

As for where to place a disclosure, the guiding principle is that it has to be clear and conspicuous. The closer it is to your recommendation, the better. Putting disclosures in obscure places – for example, buried on an ABOUT US or GENERAL INFO page, behind a poorly labeled hyperlink or in a "terms of service" agreement – isn't good enough. Neither is placing it below your review or below the link to the online retailer so readers would have to keep scrolling after they finish reading. Consumers should be able to notice the disclosure easily. They shouldn't have to hunt for it.

Is "affiliate link" by itself an adequate disclosure? What about a "buy now" button?

Consumers might not understand that "affiliate link" means that the person placing the link is getting paid for purchases through the link. Similarly, a "buy now" button would not be adequate.

What if I'm including links to product marketers or to retailers as a convenience to my readers, but I'm not getting paid for them?

Then there isn't anything to disclose.

Does this guidance about affiliate links apply to links in my product reviews on someone else's website, to my user comments, and to my tweets?

Yes, the same guidance applies anytime you endorse a product and get paid through affiliate links.

It's clear that what's on my website is a paid advertisement, not my own endorsement or review of the product. Do I still have to disclose that I get a commission if people click through my website to buy the product?

If it's clear that what's on your site is a paid advertisement, you don't have to make additional disclosures. Just remember that what's clear to you may not be clear to everyone visiting your site, and the FTC evaluates ads from the perspective of reasonable consumers.

Expert Endorsers Making Claims Outside of Traditional Advertisements

One of our company's paid spokespersons is an expert who appears on news and talk shows promoting our product, sometimes along with other products she recommends based on her expertise. Your Guides give an example of a celebrity spokesperson appearing on a talk show and recommend that the celebrity disclose her connection to the company she is promoting. Does that principle also apply to expert endorsers?

Yes, it does. Your spokesperson should disclose her connection when promoting your products outside of traditional advertising media (in other words, on programming that consumers won't recognize as paid advertising). The same guidance also would apply to comments by the expert in her blog or on her website.

Employee Endorsements

I work for a terrific company. Can I mention our products to people in my social networks? How about on a review site? My friends won't be misled since it's clear in my online profiles where I work.

If your company allows employees to use social media to talk about its products, you should make sure that your relationship is disclosed to people who read your online postings about your company or its products. Put yourself in the reader's shoes. Isn't the employment relationship something you would want to know before relying on someone else's endorsement? Listing your employer on your profile page isn't enough. After all, people who just read what you post on a review site won't get that information.

People reading your posting on a review site probably won't know who you are. You definitely should disclose your employment relationship when making an endorsement.

On her own initiative and without us asking, one of our employees used her personal social network simply to "like" or "share" one of our company's posts. Does she need to disclose that she works for our company?

Whether there should be any disclosure depends upon whether the "like" or "share" could be viewed as an advertisement for your company. If the post is an ad, then employees endorsing the post should disclose their relationship to the company. With a share, that's fairly easy to do, "Check out my company's great new product ...." Regarding "likes," see what we said above about "likes."

Our company's policy says that employees shouldn't post positive reviews online about our products without clearly disclosing their relationship to the company. All of our employees agree to abide by this policy when they are hired. But we have several thousand people working here and we can't monitor what they all do on their own computers and other devices when they aren't

745

at work. Are we liable if an employee posts a review of one of our products, either on our company website or on a social media site and doesn't disclose that relationship?

It wouldn't be reasonable to expect you to monitor every social media posting by all of your employees. However, you should establish a formal program to remind employees periodically of your policy, especially if the company encourages employees to share their opinions about your products. Also, if you learn that an employee has posted a review on the company's website or a social media site without adequately disclosing his or her relationship to the company, you should remind them of your company policy and ask them to remove that review or adequately disclose that they're an employee.

What about employees of an ad agency or public relations firm? Can my agency ask our employees to spread the buzz about our clients' products?

First, an ad agency (or any company for that matter) shouldn't ask employees to say anything that isn't true. No one should endorse a product they haven't used or say things they don't believe about a product, and an employer certainly shouldn't encourage employees to engage in such conduct.

Moreover, employees of an ad agency or public relations firm have a connection to the advertiser, which should be disclosed in all social media posts. Agencies asking their employees to spread the word must instruct those employees about their responsibilities to disclose their relationship to the product they are endorsing, e.g., "My employer is paid to promote [name of product]," or simply "Advertisement," or when space is an issue, "Ad" or "#ad."

My company XYX wants to tell our employees what to disclose in social media. Is "#employee" good enough?

Consumers may be confused by "#employee." Consumers would be more likely to understand "#XYZ_Employee." Then again, if consumers don't associate your company's name with the product or brand being endorsed, that disclosure might not work. It would be much clearer to use the words "my company" or "employer's" in the body of the message. It's a lot easier to understand and harder to miss.

Using Testimonials That Don't Reflect the Typical Consumer Experience

We want to run ads featuring endorsements from consumers who achieved the best results with our company's product. Can we do that?

Testimonials claiming specific results usually will be interpreted to mean that the endorser's experience reflects what others can also expect. Statements like "Results not typical" or "Individual results may vary" won't change that interpretation. That leaves advertisers with two choices:

1. Have adequate proof to back up the claim that the results shown in the ad are typical, or

2. Clearly and conspicuously disclose the generally expected performance in the circumstances shown in the ad.

How would this principle about testimonialists who achieved exceptional results apply in a real ad?

The Guides include several examples with practical advice on this topic. One example is about an ad in which a woman says, "I lost 50 pounds in 6 months with WeightAway." If consumers can't generally expect to get those results, the ad should say how much weight consumers can expect to lose in similar circumstances – for example, "Most women who use WeightAway for six months lose at least 15 pounds."

Our company website includes testimonials from some of our more successful customers who used our product during the past few years and mentions the results they got. We can't figure out now what the "generally expected results" were back then. What should we do? Do we have to remove those testimonials?

There are two issues here. First, according to the Guides, if your website says or implies that the endorser currently uses the product in question, you can use that endorsement only as long as you have good reason to believe the endorser does still use the product. If you're using endorsements that are a few years old, it's your obligation to make sure the claims still are accurate. If your product has changed, it's best to get new endorsements.

Second, if your product is the same as it was when the endorsements were given and the claims are still accurate, you probably can use the old endorsements if the disclosures are consistent with what the generally expected results are now.

The following is an example of a complaint issued by the FTC, this one in connection with a social media "product bomb" campaign launched by the department store Lord & Taylor. Excerpts from the exhibits referenced in the complaint appear after the text of the complaint. At the conclusion of the matter, Lord & Taylor agreed in a consent order in essence to follow the FTC's rules in the future. It received no other penalties. The FTC did not apparently contact the influencers cited in the complaint.

In the Matter of Lord & Taylor, LLC
FTC Matter/File No. 153-3181 | C4576 (2016)

COMPLAINT

The Federal Trade Commission, having reason to believe that Lord & Taylor, LLC, a limited liability company ("Respondent"), has violated the provisions of the Federal Trade Commission Act, and it appearing to the Commission that this proceeding is in the public interest, alleges:

1. Respondent Lord & Taylor is a New York limited liability company with its principal office or place of business at 424 5th Avenue, New York, NY, 10018.

2. Respondent has manufactured, advertised, labeled, offered for sale, sold, and distributed women's, men's, and children's apparel, accessories, cosmetics, and other retail merchandise to consumers.

3. The acts and practices of Respondent alleged in this complaint have been in or affecting commerce, as "commerce" is defined in Section 4 of the Federal Trade Commission Act.

Lord & Taylor's Design Lab Instagram Campaign

4. In the Fall of 2014, Respondent Lord & Taylor developed plans to promote its new Design Lab collection, a private label clothing line aimed at women ages 18-35. Respondent's Design Lab marketing plan included a comprehensive social media campaign ("product bomb") launched at the end of March 2015. The campaign was comprised of Lord & Taylor-branded blog posts, photos, video uploads, native advertising editorials in online fashion magazines, and use of a team of fashion influencers recruited for their fashion style and extensive base of followers on social media platforms, all focused on a single article of clothing, the Design Lab Paisley Asymmetrical Dress.

5. Lord & Taylor gifted the Paisley Asymmetrical Dress to 50 select fashion influencers who were paid, in amounts ranging from $1,000 to $4,000, to post on the social media platform Instagram one photo of themselves wearing the Design Lab dress during a specified timeframe during the weekend of March 27-28, 2015. While the influencers were given the freedom to style the dress in any way they saw fit, Lord & Taylor contractually obligated them to exclusively mention the company using the "@lordandtaylor" Instagram user designation and the campaign hashtag "#DesignLab" in the photo caption. The influencers also were required to tag their photos of the dress using the "@lordandtaylor" Instagram designation.

6. Although Lord & Taylor's Design Lab influencer contracts detailed the manner in which Respondent was to be mentioned in each Instagram posting, the contracts did not require the

influencers to disclose in their postings that Respondent had compensated them, nor did Respondent otherwise obligate the influencers to disclose that they had been compensated.

7. In advance of the March 27-28, 2015 Design Lab debut, Respondent's representatives preapproved each of the influencers' Instagram posts to ensure that the required campaign hashtag and the @lordandtaylor Instagram user designation were included in the photo captions. Respondent also made certain other stylistic edits to the influencers' proposed text. None of the Instagram posts presented to Respondent for pre-approval included a disclosure that the influencer had received the dress for free, that she had been compensated for the post, or that the post was a part of a Lord & Taylor advertising campaign. Respondent Lord & Taylor did not edit any of the 50 posts to add such disclosures. *See* Exhibit A (representative Design Lab Instagram posts from the weekend of March 27-28, 2015).

8. The Design Lab Instagram campaign reached 11.4 million individual Instagram users, resulted in 328,000 brand engagements with Lord & Taylor's own Instagram user handle (such as likes, comments, or re-postings), and the dress subsequently sold out.

9. Respondent's Design Lab debut also included strategic placement of Lord & Taylor-edited Instagram posts and an article in online fashion magazines. One such magazine was Nylon, a pop culture and fashion publication owned by Nylon Media, LLC, the company that represented the majority of the fashion influencers involved in Respondent's Design Lab Instagram campaign. Nylon posted a photo of the Paisley Asymmetrical Dress, along with a Lord & Taylor-edited caption, on its Instagram account during the product bomb weekend. *See* Exhibit B (Nylon.com Design Lab Instagram Post). Although paid for, reviewed, and pre-approved by Lord & Taylor, Nylon's Instagram post failed to disclose that Lord & Taylor had paid for the posting.

10. Nylon Magazine also ran an article about the Design Lab collection in its online magazine on March 31, 2015. Under the terms of its contract with Nylon Magazine, Lord & Taylor reviewed and pre-approved the paid-for Nylon Design Lab article, yet the article did not disclose or otherwise make clear this commercial arrangement. *See* Exhibit C (Nylon.com Design Lab magazine article).

COUNT I
Misrepresentations About the Design Lab Instagram Postings

11. Through the means described in Paragraphs 4 through 7, Respondent represented, directly or indirectly, expressly or by implication, that the 50 Instagram images and captions reflected the independent statements of impartial fashion influencers.

12. In fact, the 50 Instagram images and captions did not reflect the independent statements of impartial fashion influencers. Respondent's influencers specifically created the postings as part of an advertising campaign to promote sales of Respondent's Design Lab collection. Therefore, the representation set forth in Paragraph 11 is false or misleading.

COUNT II
Failure to Disclose Influencers' Material Connection to Lord & Taylor

13. Through the means described in Paragraphs 4 through 7, Respondent represented, directly or indirectly, expressly or by implication, that the 50 Instagram images and captions posted on March 27 and 28, 2015 about the Paisley Asymmetrical Dress reflected the opinions of individuals with expertise in new trends in fashion. In numerous instances, Respondent failed to disclose or disclose adequately that these individuals were paid endorsers for Respondent. These facts would be material to consumers in their decision to purchase the Paisley Asymmetrical Dress. The failure to disclose these facts, in light of the representation made, was and is, a deceptive practice.

COUNT III
Misrepresentations About the Nylon Instagram Post and the March 31, 2015 Nylon Magazine Article

14. Through the means described in Paragraphs 9 and 10, Respondent represented, directly or indirectly, expressly or by implication, that the article that appeared on the March 31, 2015 Nylon Magazine website and the Design Lab posting on Nylon's Instagram account, were independent statements and opinions regarding the launch of Respondent's Design Lab collection.

15. In fact, neither the Nylon Magazine article nor the Nylon Instagram post were independent statements or opinions regarding Respondent's Design Lab collection; they were paid commercial advertising. Therefore, the representation set forth in Paragraph 14 is false or misleading.

16. The acts and practices of Respondent as alleged in this complaint constitute unfair or deceptive acts or practices in or affecting commerce in violation of Section 5(a) of the FTC Act, 15 U.S.C. § 45(a).

THEREFORE, the Federal Trade Commission this twentieth day of May, 2016, has issued this Complaint against Respondent.

By the Commission.

Donald S. Clark

Secretary

Exhibit A

Exhibit B

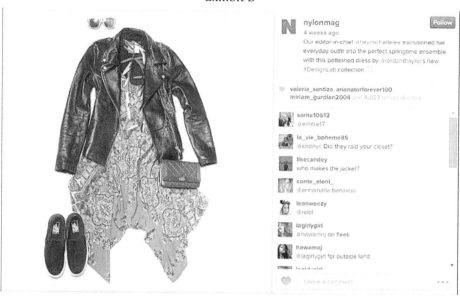

Exhibit C

V.   Right of Publicity

The right of publicity protects a person's identity against unauthorized commercial exploitation. *See* J. THOMAS MCCARTHY, THE RIGHTS OF PUBLICITY AND PRIVACY § 1:3 (2d ed. Apr. 2014) (defining the right of publicity as "the inherent right of every human being to control the commercial use of his or her identity"). There is no federal right of publicity, though as we will see below, Lanham Act § 43(a), 15 U.S.C. § 1125(a), may form the basis for a cause of action akin to one that protects publicity rights. Right of publicity claims are typically pursued under state common law or state statutory law. Thirty-three of the fifty states provide some form of right of publicity protection,[2] either through common law protection, state statutory protection, or both.

Right of Publicity Law by State (as of May 2020)

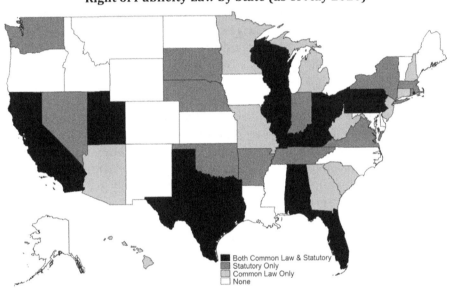

Because of their importance to the entertainment and media industries, and because their differences are typical of the differences among the laws of the many states, California and New York's schemes of publicity rights protection are detailed below.

But before delving into the specifics of the right of publicity, it may be worthwhile to ask: why should we protect a person's identity from unauthorized commercial exploitation? This question is important because the answer we give may guide how we apply the doctrine and what exceptions we allow to publicity rights. Borrowing from trademark law, should we do so simply to prevent false endorsements that may mislead consumers as to who is actually endorsing a product? *See generally* Stacey L. Dogan & Mark A. Lemley, *What the Right of Publicity Can Learn from Trademark Law*, 58 STAN. L. REV. 1161 (2006). Or are there further, independent justifications? Some commentators have proposed moral or ethical rationales for the right of publicity, based on an individual's human right to privacy or on an individual's right to autonomous self-definition—so that a sportsman opposed to alcohol should not have to see his identity used to promote alcoholic beverages. *See e.g.*, Mark McKenna, *The Right of Publicity and Autonomous Self-Definition*, 67 U. PITT. L. REV. 225 (2005); *but see*

---

[2] *See* J. THOMAS MCCARTHY, THE RIGHTS OF PUBLICITY AND PRIVACY § 6:2 (April 2019). *See also* Jennifer Rothman's http://www.rightofpublicityroadmap.com/.

O'Brien v. Pabst Sales Co., 124 F.2d 167 (5th Cir. 1941) (denying football player Davy O'Brien's privacy-based right of publicity claim against a beer producer). Others have proposed a Lockean justification for the right of publicity, in that the unauthorized exploitation of someone's identity constitutes a misappropriation of the fruits of the labor of whoever created that identity. *See* Michael Madow, *Private Ownership of Public Image*, 81 CAL. L. REV. 127 (1993) (discussing but not endorsing this view). Commentators have also proposed economic justifications for the right of publicity, based on the proposition that the right of publicity provides an economic incentive to celebrities to do more and better of whatever it is that makes them celebrities, or that the right of publicity prevents "congestion externalities," i.e., the dilution of the distinctiveness of a celebrity's identity that might occur if that identity is associated with too many products or services. *See* WILLIAM M. LANDES & RICHARD A. POSNER, THE ECONOMIC STRUCTURE OF INTELLECTUAL PROPERTY LAW 222-228 (2003). (In what sense is antidilution law essentially a right of publicity scheme of protection for brand names?).

Which of these rationales for the right of publicity strikes you as the most or least persuasive?

One other initial question: must a person be a celebrity to qualify for the right of publicity? The answer is that it depends on state law. Most states that recognize a right of publicity do not require that the plaintiff be a celebrity or have a commercially-valuable identity. *See, e.g,. Onassis v. Christian Dior-New York, Inc.*, 472 N.Y.S.2d 254, 260 (Sup 1984) ("The principle to be distilled from a study of the statute and of the cases construing it is that all persons, of whatever station in life, from the relatively unknown to the world famous, are to be secured against rapacious commercial exploitation."); *Fraley v. Facebook*, 830 F.Supp. 2d 785, 807-08 (N.D. Cal. 2011) (declining to endorse a heightened pleading standard for non-celebrities asserting a misappropriation cause of action under California Civil Code § 3344); *id.* at 807 ("California courts have clearly held that 'the statutory right of publicity exists for celebrity and non-celebrity plaintiffs alike.'" (*citing KNB Enterprises v. Matthews*, 78 Cal. App. 4th 362, 373 n. 12 (2000)). For an example of a state statute that probably requires a showing that the plaintiff's identity have some preexisting commercial value, see Utah Code § 45-3-1 et seq. *See also Cox v. Hatch*, 761 P.2d 556, 564 (Utah 1988) ("[T]he complaint fails because it must allege that the plaintiffs' names or likenesses have some 'intrinsic value' that was used or appropriated for the defendants' benefit." (citations omitted)); *id.* at 566 (reasoning that "[f]or all practical purposes, the plaintiffs' pictures were wholly fungible with those of any other persons" in plaintiffs' position).

New York and California law offer typical examples of the elements that the plaintiff must prove to prevail on a right of publicity cause of action. Under New York statutory law, "[t]he elements of a cause of action for violation of the statutory right to privacy are: (1) the use of a person's name, portrait, picture or voice (2) within the State of New York (3) for advertising purposes or the purposes of trade, (4) without written consent." *Nussenzweig v. diCorcia*, 38 A.D.3d 339, 346 n. 4 (2007). In California,

> [t]o state a common law cause of action for misappropriation, a plaintiff must plead sufficient facts to establish (1) the defendant's use of the plaintiff's identity; (2) the appropriation of plaintiff's name or likeness to defendant's advantage, commercially or otherwise; (3) lack of consent; and (4) resulting injury. To state a statutory cause of action under § 3344, a plaintiff must plead all the elements of the common law action and must also prove (5) a knowing use by the defendant, and (6) a direct connection between the alleged use and the commercial purpose.

Fraley v. Facebook, Inc., 830 F. Supp. 2d 785, 803 (N.D. Cal. 2011) (quotations and citations omitted).

A. State Right of Publicity Statutory Provisions

New York's right of publicity statute, excerpted below, is generally understood to be based on the individual's right to privacy. Accordingly, New York law does not provide for the descendibilty of the right of publicity, which ceases in New York with the death of the individual. By contrast, California's statute, also excerpted below, is generally understood to conceive of the right of publicity as a property

752

right, which is descendible for 70 years after the death of the individual. CAL. CIV. CODE. § 3344.1(g). Commentators routinely declare California's right of publicity to be freely assignable, while the New York case law has not clearly established the assignability of the right in New York, but scholarship has suggested that the alienability of the right of publicity is considerably more complicated across the states. *See* Jennifer E. Rothman, *The Inalienable Right of Publicity*, 101 GEO. L.J. 185 (2012).

Note that N.Y. Civil Rights Law § 51 below appears as a single paragraph in the statute. Parts of its have been rendered in indents to make it human-readable.

N.Y. Civil Rights Law § 51. Action for injunction and for damages

Any person whose name, portrait, picture or voice is used within this state for advertising purposes or for the purposes of trade without the written consent first obtained as above provided may maintain an equitable action in the supreme court of this state against the person, firm or corporation so using his name, portrait, picture or voice, to prevent and restrain the use thereof; and may also sue and recover damages for any injuries sustained by reason of such use and if the defendant shall have knowingly used such person's name, portrait, picture or voice in such manner as is forbidden or declared to be unlawful by section fifty of this article, the jury, in its discretion, may award exemplary damages.

- But nothing contained in this article shall be so construed as to prevent any person, firm or corporation from selling or otherwise transferring any material containing such name, portrait, picture or voice in whatever medium to any user of such name, portrait, picture or voice, or to any third party for sale or transfer directly or indirectly to such a user, for use in a manner lawful under this article;

- nothing contained in this article shall be so construed as to prevent any person, firm or corporation, practicing the profession of photography, from exhibiting in or about his or its establishment specimens of the work of such establishment, unless the same is continued by such person, firm or corporation after written notice objecting thereto has been given by the person portrayed;

- and nothing contained in this article shall be so construed as to prevent any person, firm or corporation from using the name, portrait, picture or voice of any manufacturer or dealer in connection with the goods, wares and merchandise manufactured, produced or dealt in by him which he has sold or disposed of with such name, portrait, picture or voice used in connection therewith; or from using the name, portrait, picture or voice of any author, composer or artist in connection with his literary, musical or artistic productions which he has sold or disposed of with such name, portrait, picture or voice used in connection therewith.

- Nothing contained in this section shall be construed to prohibit the copyright owner of a sound recording from disposing of, dealing in, licensing or selling that sound recording to any party, if the right to dispose of, deal in, license or sell such sound recording has been conferred by contract or other written document by such living person or the holder of such right. Nothing contained in the foregoing sentence shall be deemed to abrogate or otherwise limit any rights or remedies otherwise conferred by federal law or state law.

California Civil Code §§ 3344 & 3344.1.

§ 3344. Use of another's name, voice, signature, photograph, or likeness for advertising or selling or soliciting purposes

(a) Any person who knowingly uses another's name, voice, signature, photograph, or likeness, in any manner, on or in products, merchandise, or goods, or for purposes of advertising or selling, or soliciting purchases of, products, merchandise, goods or services, without such person's prior consent, or, in the case of a minor, the prior consent of his parent or legal guardian, shall be liable for any damages sustained by the person or persons injured as a result thereof. In addition, in any action brought under this section, the person who violated the section shall be liable to the injured party or parties in an amount equal to the greater of seven hundred fifty dollars ($750) or the actual damages suffered by him or her as a result of the unauthorized use, and any profits from the unauthorized use that are attributable to the use and are not taken into account in computing the actual damages. In establishing such profits, the injured party or parties are required to present proof only of the gross revenue attributable to such use, and the person who violated this section is required to prove his or her deductible expenses. Punitive damages may also be awarded to the injured party or parties. The prevailing party in any action under this section shall also be entitled to attorney's fees and costs.

(b) As used in this section, "photograph" means any photograph or photographic reproduction, still or moving, or any videotape or live television transmission, of any person, such that the person is readily identifiable.

(1) A person shall be deemed to be readily identifiable from a photograph when one who views the photograph with the naked eye can reasonably determine that the person depicted in the photograph is the same person who is complaining of its unauthorized use.

(2) If the photograph includes more than one person so identifiable, then the person or persons complaining of the use shall be represented as individuals rather than solely as members of a definable group represented in the photograph. A definable group includes, but is not limited to, the following examples: a crowd at any sporting event, a crowd in any street or public building, the audience at any theatrical or stage production, a glee club, or a baseball team.

(3) A person or persons shall be considered to be represented as members of a definable group if they are represented in the photograph solely as a result of being present at the time the photograph was taken and have not been singled out as individuals in any manner.

(c) Where a photograph or likeness of an employee of the person using the photograph or likeness appearing in the advertisement or other publication prepared by or in behalf of the user is only incidental, and not essential, to the purpose of the publication in which it appears, there shall arise a rebuttable presumption affecting the burden of producing evidence that the failure to obtain the consent of the employee was not a knowing use of the employee's photograph or likeness.

(d) For purposes of this section, a use of a name, voice, signature, photograph, or likeness in connection with any news, public affairs, or sports broadcast or account, or any political campaign, shall not constitute a use for which consent is required under subdivision (a).

(e) The use of a name, voice, signature, photograph, or likeness in a commercial medium shall not constitute a use for which consent is required under subdivision (a) solely because the material containing such use is commercially sponsored or contains paid advertising. Rather it shall be a question of fact whether or not the use of the person's name, voice, signature, photograph, or likeness was so directly connected with the commercial sponsorship or with the paid advertising as to constitute a use for which consent is required under subdivision (a).

(f) Nothing in this section shall apply to the owners or employees of any medium used for advertising, including, but not limited to, newspapers, magazines, radio and television networks and stations, cable television systems, billboards, and transit ads, by whom any advertisement or solicitation in violation of this section is published or disseminated, unless it is established that such owners or employees had knowledge of the unauthorized use of the person's name, voice, signature, photograph, or likeness as prohibited by this section.

(g) The remedies provided for in this section are cumulative and shall be in addition to any others provided for by law.

§ 3344.1. Deceased personality's name, voice, signature, photograph, or likeness; unauthorized use; damages and profits from use; protected uses; persons entitled to exercise rights; successors in interest or licensees; registration of claim

. . . .

(a)(2) For purposes of this subdivision, a play, book, magazine, newspaper, musical composition, audiovisual work, radio or television program, single and original work of art, work of political or newsworthy value, or an advertisement or commercial announcement for any of these works, shall not be considered a product, article of merchandise, good, or service if it is fictional or nonfictional entertainment, or a dramatic, literary, or musical work.

. . . .

(j) For purposes of this section, the use of a name, voice, signature, photograph, or likeness in connection with any news, public affairs, or sports broadcast or account, or any political campaign, shall not constitute a use for which consent is required under subdivision (a).

B. Right of Publicity Case Law

Provided below are opinions from two significant right of publicity cases. The first, older case is *White v. Samsung Electronics America, Inc.*, 971 F.2d 1395 (9th Cir. 1992), which addressed television hostess Vanna White's claims that a series of Samsung advertisements featuring a robot likeness of her violated her intellectual property rights. Excerpted below is the Ninth Circuit's majority opinion in the case and Judge Kozinski's dissent from a denial of *en banc* review of that majority opinion. The second case, *In re NCAA Student–Athlete Name & Likeness Licensing Litigation*, 724 F.3d 1268 (9th Cir. 2013), is of much more recent vintage and was issued on the same day as *Brown v. Electronic Arts*, 724 F.3d 1235 (9th Cir. 2013), which rejected retired football player Jim Brown's Lanham Act § 43(a) claim against a video game producer who used his likeness in a video game. By contrast, *In re NCAA Student-Athlete Name & Likeness Licensing* (sometimes known as the "Keller case"), the court addressed a California Civil Code § 3344 claim against the video game producer brought by a one-time college football player. As you will see, the California right of publicity claim was more successful than Jim Brown's Lanham Act § 43(a) claim.

As you read through the *White v. Samsung* opinions, consider the following questions:

- If you are persuaded by the simple false endorsement justification for right of publicity protection, then does *White v. Samsung* support that justification? Does Samsung's homage to Vanna White constitute false endorsement? How might a court properly determine the answer to this latter question?

- In *Midler v. Ford Motor Co.*, 849 F.2d 460 (9th Cir. 1988) and *Waits v. Frito-Lay, Inc.,* 978 F.2d 1093 (9th Cir. 1992), the defendants employed impersonators to mimic the singing styles of Bette Midler and Tom Waits, respectively, both of whom adamantly refuse to allow their art to be used to sell goods and services. Defendants were found liable under Lanham Act § 43(a) in both cases. If you are persuaded by Judge Kozinski's dissent, then how would you rule in *Midler* and *Waits*?

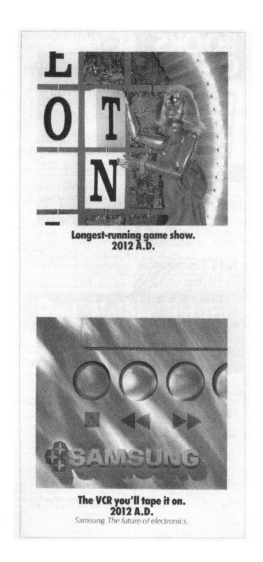

Longest-running game show.
2012 A.D.

The VCR you'll tape it on.
2012 A.D.
Samsung. The future of electronics.

White v. Samsung Electronics America, Inc.
971 F.2d 1395 (9th Cir. 1992)

GOODWIN, Senior Circuit Judge:

[1] This case involves a promotional "fame and fortune" dispute. In running a particular advertisement without Vanna White's permission, defendants Samsung Electronics America, Inc. (Samsung) and David Deutsch Associates, Inc. (Deutsch) attempted to capitalize on White's fame to enhance their fortune. White sued, alleging infringement of various intellectual property rights, but the district court granted summary judgment in favor of the defendants. We affirm in part, reverse in part, and remand.

[2] Plaintiff Vanna White is the hostess of "Wheel of Fortune," one of the most popular game shows in television history. An estimated forty million people watch the program daily. Capitalizing on the fame which her participation in the show has bestowed on her, White markets her identity to various advertisers.

[3] The dispute in this case arose out of a series of advertisements prepared for Samsung by Deutsch. The series ran in at least half a dozen publications with widespread, and in some cases national, circulation. Each of the advertisements in the series followed the same theme. Each depicted a current item from popular culture and a Samsung electronic product. Each was set in the twenty-first

756

century and conveyed the message that the Samsung product would still be in use by that time. By hypothesizing outrageous future outcomes for the cultural items, the ads created humorous effects. For example, one lampooned current popular notions of an unhealthy diet by depicting a raw steak with the caption: "Revealed to be health food. 2010 A.D." Another depicted irreverent "news"-show host Morton Downey Jr. in front of an American flag with the caption: "Presidential candidate. 2008 A.D."

[4] The advertisement which prompted the current dispute was for Samsung video-cassette recorders (VCRs). The ad depicted a robot, dressed in a wig, gown, and jewelry which Deutsch consciously selected to resemble White's hair and dress. The robot was posed next to a game board which is instantly recognizable as the Wheel of Fortune game show set, in a stance for which White is famous. The caption of the ad read: "Longest-running game show. 2012 A.D." Defendants referred to the ad as the "Vanna White" ad. Unlike the other celebrities used in the campaign, White neither consented to the ads nor was she paid.

[5] Following the circulation of the robot ad, White sued Samsung and Deutsch in federal district court under: (1) California Civil Code § 3344; (2) the California common law right of publicity; and (3) § 43(a) of the Lanham Act, 15 U.S.C. § 1125(a). The district court granted summary judgment against White on each of her claims. White now appeals.

I. Section 3344

[6] White first argues that the district court erred in rejecting her claim under section 3344. Section 3344(a) provides, in pertinent part, that "[a]ny person who knowingly uses another's name, voice, signature, photograph, or likeness, in any manner, ... for purposes of advertising or selling, ... without such person's prior consent ... shall be liable for any damages sustained by the person or persons injured as a result thereof."

[7] White argues that the Samsung advertisement used her "likeness" in contravention of section 3344. In *Midler v. Ford Motor Co.*, 849 F.2d 460 (9th Cir. 1988), this court rejected Bette Midler's section 3344 claim concerning a Ford television commercial in which a Midler "sound-alike" sang a song which Midler had made famous. In rejecting Midler's claim, this court noted that "[t]he defendants did not use Midler's name or anything else whose use is prohibited by the statute. The voice they used was [another person's], not hers. The term 'likeness' refers to a visual image not a vocal imitation." *Id.* at 463.

[8] In this case, Samsung and Deutsch used a robot with mechanical features, and not, for example, a manikin molded to White's precise features. Without deciding for all purposes when a caricature or impressionistic resemblance might become a "likeness," we agree with the district court that the robot at issue here was not White's "likeness" within the meaning of section 3344. Accordingly, we affirm the court's dismissal of White's section 3344 claim.

II. Right of Publicity

[9] White next argues that the district court erred in granting summary judgment to defendants on White's common law right of publicity claim. In *Eastwood v. Superior Court,* 149 Cal.App.3d 409, 198 Cal.Rptr. 342 (1983), the California court of appeal stated that the common law right of publicity cause of action "may be pleaded by alleging (1) the defendant's use of the plaintiff's identity; (2) the appropriation of plaintiff's name or likeness to defendant's advantage, commercially or otherwise; (3) lack of consent; and (4) resulting injury." *Id.* at 417, 198 Cal.Rptr. 342 (citing Prosser, Law of Torts (4th ed. 1971) § 117, pp. 804–807). The district court dismissed White's claim for failure to satisfy *Eastwood's* second prong, reasoning that defendants had not appropriated White's "name or likeness" with their robot ad. We agree that the robot ad did not make use of White's name or likeness. However, the common law right of publicity is not so confined.

[10] The *Eastwood* court did not hold that the right of publicity cause of action could be pleaded only by alleging an appropriation of name or likeness. *Eastwood* involved an unauthorized use of photographs of Clint Eastwood and of his name. Accordingly, the *Eastwood* court had no occasion to consider the extent beyond the use of name or likeness to which the right of publicity reaches. That court held only that the right of publicity cause of action "may be" pleaded by alleging, *inter alia,* appropriation of name or likeness, not that the action may be pleaded *only* in those terms.

[11] The "name or likeness" formulation referred to in *Eastwood* originated not as an element of the right of publicity cause of action, but as a description of the types of cases in which the cause of action had been recognized. The source of this formulation is Prosser, *Privacy*, 48 Cal.L.Rev. 383, 401–07 (1960), one of the earliest and most enduring articulations of the common law right of publicity cause of action. In looking at the case law to that point, Prosser recognized that right of publicity cases involved one of two basic factual scenarios: name appropriation, and picture or other likeness appropriation. *Id.* at 401–02, nn. 156–57.

[12] Even though Prosser focused on appropriations of name or likeness in discussing the right of publicity, he noted that "[i]t is not impossible that there might be appropriation of the plaintiff's identity, as by impersonation, without the use of either his name or his likeness, and that this would be an invasion of his right of privacy." *Id.* at 401, n. 155.[1] At the time Prosser wrote, he noted however, that "[n]o such case appears to have arisen." *Id.*

[13] Since Prosser's early formulation, the case law has borne out his insight that the right of publicity is not limited to the appropriation of name or likeness. In *Motschenbacher v. R.J. Reynolds Tobacco Co.*, 498 F.2d 821 (9th Cir. 1974), the defendant had used a photograph of the plaintiff's race car in a television commercial. Although the plaintiff appeared driving the car in the photograph, his features were not visible. Even though the defendant had not appropriated the plaintiff's name or likeness, this court held that plaintiff's California right of publicity claim should reach the jury.

[14] In *Midler,* this court held that, even though the defendants had not used Midler's name or likeness, Midler had stated a claim for violation of her California common law right of publicity because "the defendants . . . for their own profit in selling their product did appropriate part of her identity" by using a Midler sound-alike. *Id.* at 463–64.

[15] In *Carson v. Here's Johnny Portable Toilets, Inc.,* 698 F.2d 831 (6th Cir. 1983), the defendant had marketed portable toilets under the brand name "Here's Johnny"—Johnny Carson's signature "Tonight Show" introduction—without Carson's permission. The district court had dismissed Carson's Michigan common law right of publicity claim because the defendants had not used Carson's "name or likeness." *Id.* at 835. In reversing the district court, the sixth circuit found "the district court's conception of the right of publicity . . . too narrow" and held that the right was implicated because the defendant had appropriated Carson's identity by using, *inter alia,* the phrase "Here's Johnny." *Id.* at 835–37.

[16] These cases teach not only that the common law right of publicity reaches means of appropriation other than name or likeness, but that the specific means of appropriation are relevant only for determining whether the defendant has in fact appropriated the plaintiff's identity. The right of publicity does not require that appropriations of identity be accomplished through particular means to be actionable. It is noteworthy that the *Midler* and *Carson* defendants not only avoided using the plaintiff's name or likeness, but they also avoided appropriating the celebrity's voice, signature, and photograph. The photograph in *Motschenbacher* did include the plaintiff, but because the plaintiff was

---

[1] Under Professor Prosser's scheme, the right of publicity is the last of the four categories of the right to privacy. Prosser, 48 Cal.L.Rev. at 389.

not visible the driver could have been an actor or dummy and the analysis in the case would have been the same.

[17] Although the defendants in these cases avoided the most obvious means of appropriating the plaintiffs' identities, each of their actions directly implicated the commercial interests which the right of publicity is designed to protect. As the *Carson* court explained:

> [t]he right of publicity has developed to protect the commercial interest of celebrities in their identities. The theory of the right is that a celebrity's identity can be valuable in the promotion of products, and the celebrity has an interest that may be protected from the unauthorized commercial exploitation of that identity.... If the celebrity's identity is commercially exploited, there has been an invasion of his right whether or not his "name or likeness" is used.

Carson, 698 F.2d at 835. It is not important *how* the defendant has appropriated the plaintiff's identity, but *whether* the defendant has done so. *Motschenbacher, Midler,* and *Carson* teach the impossibility of treating the right of publicity as guarding only against a laundry list of specific means of appropriating identity. A rule which says that the right of publicity can be infringed only through the use of nine different methods of appropriating identity merely challenges the clever advertising strategist to come up with the tenth.

[18] Indeed, if we treated the means of appropriation as dispositive in our analysis of the right of publicity, we would not only weaken the right but effectively eviscerate it. The right would fail to protect those plaintiffs most in need of its protection. Advertisers use celebrities to promote their products. The more popular the celebrity, the greater the number of people who recognize her, and the greater the visibility for the product. The identities of the most popular celebrities are not only the most attractive for advertisers, but also the easiest to evoke without resorting to obvious means such as name, likeness, or voice.

[19] Consider a hypothetical advertisement which depicts a mechanical robot with male features, an African–American complexion, and a bald head. The robot is wearing black hightop Air Jordan basketball sneakers, and a red basketball uniform with black trim, baggy shorts, and the number 23 (though not revealing "Bulls" or "Jordan" lettering). The ad depicts the robot dunking a basketball one-handed, stiff-armed, legs extended like open scissors, and tongue hanging out. Now envision that this ad is run on television during professional basketball games. Considered individually, the robot's physical attributes, its dress, and its stance tell us little. Taken together, they lead to the only conclusion that any sports viewer who has registered a discernible pulse in the past five years would reach: the ad is about Michael Jordan.

[20] Viewed separately, the individual aspects of the advertisement in the present case say little. Viewed together, they leave little doubt about the celebrity the ad is meant to depict. The female-shaped robot is wearing a long gown, blond wig, and large jewelry. Vanna White dresses exactly like this at times, but so do many other women. The robot is in the process of turning a block letter on a game-board. Vanna White dresses like this while turning letters on a game-board but perhaps similarly attired Scrabble-playing women do this as well. The robot is standing on what looks to be the Wheel of Fortune game show set. Vanna White dresses like this, turns letters, and does this on the Wheel of Fortune game show. She is the only one. Indeed, defendants themselves referred to their ad as the "Vanna White" ad. We are not surprised.

[21] Television and other media create marketable celebrity identity value. Considerable energy and ingenuity are expended by those who have achieved celebrity value to exploit it for profit. The law protects the celebrity's sole right to exploit this value whether the celebrity has achieved her fame out of rare ability, dumb luck, or a combination thereof. We decline Samsung and Deutch's invitation to permit the evisceration of the common law right of publicity through means as facile as those in this case. Because White has alleged facts showing that Samsung and Deutsch had appropriated her

759

identity, the district court erred by rejecting, on summary judgment, White's common law right of publicity claim.

III. The Lanham Act

[22] White's final argument is that the district court erred in denying her claim under § 43(a) of the Lanham Act, 15 U.S.C. § 1125(a). The version of section 43(a) applicable to this case[2] provides, in pertinent part, that "[a]ny person who shall ... use, in connection with any goods or services ... any false description or representation ... shall be liable to a civil action ... by any person who believes that he is or is likely to be damaged by the use of any such false description or designation." 15 U.S.C. § 1125(a).

[23] To prevail on her Lanham Act claim, White is required to show that in running the robot ad, Samsung and Deutsch created a likelihood of confusion, *Academy of Motion Picture Arts v. Creative House*, 944 F.2d 1446, 1454 (9th Cir. 1991); *Toho Co. Ltd. v. Sears Roebuck & Co.*, 645 F.2d 788, 790 (9th Cir. 1981) *New West Corp. v. NYM Co. of California*, 595 F.2d 1194, 1201 (9th Cir. 1979), over whether White was endorsing Samsung's VCRs. *HMH Publishing Co. v. Brincat*, 504 F.2d 713 (9th Cir. 1974); *Allen v. National Video, Inc.*, 610 F.Supp. 612 (D.C.N.Y.1985).

[24] This circuit recognizes several different multi-factor tests for determining whether a likelihood of confusion exists. *See Academy*, 944 F.2d at 1454, n. 3. None of these tests is correct to the exclusion of the others. *Eclipse Associates Ltd. v. Data General Corp.*, 894 F.2d 1114, 1118 (9th Cir. 1990). Normally, in reviewing the district court's decision, this court will look to the particular test that the district court used. *Academy*, 944 F.2d at 1454, n. 3; *Eclipse*, 894 F.2d at 1117–1118. However, because the district court in this case apparently did not use any of the multi-factor tests in making its likelihood of confusion determination, and because this case involves an appeal from summary judgment and we review de novo the district court's determination, we will look for guidance to the 8–factor test enunciated in *AMF, Inc. v. Sleekcraft Boats*, 599 F.2d 341 (9th Cir. 1979). According to *AMF*, factors relevant to a likelihood of confusion include:

(1) strength of the plaintiff's mark;

(2) relatedness of the goods;

(3) similarity of the marks;

(4) evidence of actual confusion;

(5) marketing channels used;

(6) likely degree of purchaser care;

(7) defendant's intent in selecting the mark;

(8) likelihood of expansion of the product lines.

599 F.2d at 348–49. We turn now to consider White's claim in light of each factor.

[25] In cases involving confusion over endorsement by a celebrity plaintiff, "mark" means the celebrity's persona. *See Allen*, 610 F.Supp. at 627. The "strength" of the mark refers to the level of recognition the celebrity enjoys among members of society. *See Academy*, 944 F.2d at 1455. If Vanna White is unknown to the segment of the public at whom Samsung's robot ad was directed, then that segment could not be confused as to whether she was endorsing Samsung VCRs. Conversely, if White is well-known, this would allow the possibility of a likelihood of confusion. For the purposes of the *Sleekcraft* test, White's "mark," or celebrity identity, is strong.

---

[2] The statute was amended after White filed her complaint. The amendments would not have altered the analysis in this case however.

[26] In cases concerning confusion over celebrity endorsement, the plaintiff's "goods" concern the reasons for or source of the plaintiff's fame. Because White's fame is based on her televised performances, her "goods" are closely related to Samsung's VCRs. Indeed, the ad itself reinforced the relationship by informing its readers that they would be taping the "longest-running game show" on Samsung's VCRs well into the future.

[27] The third factor, "similarity of the marks," both supports and contradicts a finding of likelihood of confusion. On the one hand, all of the aspects of the robot ad identify White; on the other, the figure is quite clearly a robot, not a human. This ambiguity means that we must look to the other factors for resolution.

[28] The fourth factor does not favor White's claim because she has presented no evidence of actual confusion.

[29] Fifth, however, White has appeared in the same stance as the robot from the ad in numerous magazines, including the covers of some. Magazines were used as the marketing channels for the robot ad. This factor cuts toward a likelihood of confusion.

[30] Sixth, consumers are not likely to be particularly careful in determining who endorses VCRs, making confusion as to their endorsement more likely.

[31] Concerning the seventh factor, "defendant's intent," the district court found that, in running the robot ad, the defendants had intended a spoof of the "Wheel of Fortune." The relevant question is whether the defendants "intended to profit by confusing consumers" concerning the endorsement of Samsung VCRs. *Toho*, 645 F.2d 788. We do not disagree that defendants intended to spoof Vanna White and "Wheel of Fortune." That does not preclude, however, the possibility that defendants also intended to confuse consumers regarding endorsement. The robot ad was one of a series of ads run by defendants which followed the same theme. Another ad in the series depicted Morton Downey Jr. as a presidential candidate in the year 2008. Doubtless, defendants intended to spoof presidential elections and Mr. Downey through this ad. Consumers, however, would likely believe, and would be correct in so believing, that Mr. Downey was paid for his permission and was endorsing Samsung products. Looking at the series of advertisements as a whole, a jury could reasonably conclude that beneath the surface humor of the series lay an intent to persuade consumers that celebrity Vanna White, like celebrity Downey, was endorsing Samsung products.

[32] Finally, the eighth factor, "likelihood of expansion of the product lines," does not appear apposite to a celebrity endorsement case such as this.

[33] Application of the *Sleekcraft* factors to this case indicates that the district court erred in rejecting White's Lanham Act claim at the summary judgment stage. In so concluding, we emphasize two facts, however. First, construing the motion papers in White's favor, as we must, we hold only that White has raised a genuine issue of material fact concerning a likelihood of confusion as to her endorsement. *Cohen v. Paramount Pictures Corp.*, 845 F.2d 851, 852–53 (9th Cir. 1988). Whether White's Lanham Act claim should succeed is a matter for the jury. Second, we stress that we reach this conclusion in light of the peculiar facts of this case. In particular, we note that the robot ad identifies White and was part of a series of ads in which other celebrities participated and were paid for their endorsement of Samsung's products.

IV. The Parody Defense

[34] In defense, defendants cite a number of cases for the proposition that their robot ad constituted protected speech. The only cases they cite which are even remotely relevant to this case are *Hustler Magazine v. Falwell*, 485 U.S. 46, 108 S.Ct. 876, 99 L.Ed.2d 41 (1988) and *L.L. Bean, Inc. v. Drake Publishers, Inc.*, 811 F.2d 26 (1st Cir. 1987). Those cases involved parodies of advertisements run for the purpose of poking fun at Jerry Falwell and L.L. Bean, respectively. This case involves a true advertisement run for the purpose of selling Samsung VCRs. The ad's spoof of Vanna White and Wheel

761

of Fortune is subservient and only tangentially related to the ad's primary message: "buy Samsung VCRs." Defendants' parody arguments are better addressed to non-commercial parodies.[3] The difference between a "parody" and a "knock-off" is the difference between fun and profit.

V. Conclusion

[35] In remanding this case, we hold only that White has pleaded claims which can go to the jury for its decision.

AFFIRMED IN PART, REVERSED IN PART, and REMANDED.

{Judge Alarcon's dissent is not included.}

---

[3] In warning of a first amendment chill to expressive conduct, the dissent reads this decision too broadly. *See Dissent* at 1407. This case concerns only the market which exists in our society for the exploitation of celebrity to sell products, and an attempt to take a free ride on a celebrity's celebrity value. Commercial advertising which relies on celebrity fame is different from other forms of expressive activity in two crucial ways.

First, for celebrity exploitation advertising to be effective, the advertisement must evoke the celebrity's identity. The more effective the evocation, the better the advertisement. If, as Samsung claims, its ad was based on a "generic" game-show hostess and not on Vanna White, the ad would not have violated anyone's right of publicity, but it would also not have been as humorous or as effective.

Second, even if some forms of expressive activity, such as parody, do rely on identity evocation, the first amendment hurdle will bar most right of publicity actions against those activities. *Cf. Falwell,* 485 U.S. at 46. In the case of commercial advertising, however, the first amendment hurdle is not so high. *Central Hudson Gas & Electric Corp. v. Public Service Comm'n of New York,* 447 U.S. 557, 566 (1980). Realizing this, Samsung attempts to elevate its ad above the status of garden-variety commercial speech by pointing to the ad's parody of Vanna White. Samsung's argument is unavailing. *See Board of Trustees, State Univ. of N.Y. v. Fox,* 492 U.S. 469, 474–75 (1988); *Bolger v. Youngs Drug Products Corp.,* 463 U.S. 60, 67–68, (1983). Unless the first amendment bars all right of publicity actions—and it does not, *see Zachini v. Scripps–Howard Broadcasting Co.,* 433 U.S. 562 (1977)—then it does not bar this case.

Vanna White   Ms. C3PO?

White v. Samsung Electronics America, Inc.
989 F.2d 1512 (9th Cir. 1993)

Before GOODWIN, PREGERSON and ALARCON, Circuit Judges.

[1] The panel has voted unanimously to deny the petition for rehearing. Circuit Judge Pregerson has voted to reject the suggestion for rehearing en banc, and Circuit Judge Goodwin so recommends. Circuit Judge Alarcon has voted to accept the suggestion for rehearing en banc.

[2] The full court has been advised of the suggestion for rehearing en banc. An active judge requested a vote on whether to rehear the matter en banc. The matter failed to receive a majority of the votes of the nonrecused active judges in favor of en banc consideration. Fed.R.App.P. 35.

[3] The petition for rehearing is DENIED and the suggestion for rehearing en banc is REJECTED.

KOZINSKI, Circuit Judge, with whom Circuit Judges O'SCANNLAIN and KLEINFELD join, dissenting from the order rejecting the suggestion for rehearing en banc.

I

Saddam Hussein wants to keep advertisers from using his picture in unflattering contexts.[1] Clint Eastwood doesn't want tabloids to write about him.[2] Rudolf Valentino's heirs want to control his film biography.[3] The Girl Scouts don't want their image soiled by association with certain activities.[4] George

---

[1] *See* Eben Shapiro, *Rising Caution on Using Celebrity Images,* N.Y. Times, Nov. 4, 1992, at D20 (Iraqi diplomat objects on right of publicity grounds to ad containing Hussein's picture and caption "History has shown what happens when one source controls all the information").

[2] *Eastwood v. Superior Court,* 149 Cal.App.3d 409, 198 Cal.Rptr. 342 (1983).

[3] *Guglielmi v. Spelling-Goldberg Prods.,* 25 Cal.3d 860, 160 Cal.Rptr. 352, 603 P.2d 454 (1979) (Rudolph Valentino); *see also Maheu v. CBS, Inc.,* 201 Cal.App.3d 662, 668, 247 Cal.Rptr. 304 (1988) (aide to Howard Hughes). *Cf.* Frank Gannon, *Vanna Karenina,* in *Vanna Karenina and Other Reflections* (1988) (A humorous short story with a tragic ending. "She thought of the first day she had met

Lucas wants to keep Strategic Defense Initiative fans from calling it "Star Wars."[5] Pepsico doesn't want singers to use the word "Pepsi" in their songs.[6] Guy Lombardo wants an exclusive property right to ads that show big bands playing on New Year's Eve.[7] Uri Geller thinks he should be paid for ads showing psychics bending metal through telekinesis.[8] Paul Prudhomme, that household name, thinks the same about ads featuring corpulent bearded chefs.[9] And scads of copyright holders see purple when their creations are made fun of.[10]

VR_SKY. How foolish she had been. How could she love a man who wouldn't even tell her all the letters in his name?").

[4] *Girl Scouts v. Personality Posters Mfg.,* 304 F.Supp. 1228 (S.D.N.Y.1969) (poster of a pregnant girl in a Girl Scout uniform with the caption "Be Prepared").

[5] *Lucasfilm Ltd. v. High Frontier,* 622 F.Supp. 931 (D.D.C.1985).

[6] Pepsico Inc. claimed the lyrics and packaging of grunge rocker Tad Doyle's "Jack Pepsi" song were "offensive to [it] and [. . .] likely to offend [its] customers," in part because they "associate [Pepsico] and its Pepsi marks with intoxication and drunk driving." Deborah Russell, *Doyle Leaves Pepsi Thirsty for Compensation,* Billboard, June 15, 1991, at 43. Conversely, the Hell's Angels recently sued Marvel Comics to keep it from publishing a comic book called "Hell's Angel," starring a character of the same name. Marvel settled by paying $35,000 to charity and promising never to use the name "Hell's Angel" again in connection with any of its publications. *Marvel, Hell's Angels Settle Trademark Suit,* L.A. Daily J., Feb. 2, 1993, § II, at 1.

Trademarks are often reflected in the mirror of our popular culture. *See* Truman Capote, *Breakfast at Tiffany's* (1958); Kurt Vonnegut, Jr., *Breakfast of Champions* (1973); Tom Wolfe, *The Electric Kool-Aid Acid Test* (1968) (which, incidentally, includes a chapter on the Hell's Angels); Larry Niven, *Man of Steel, Woman of Kleenex,* in *All the Myriad Ways* (1971); *Looking for Mr. Goodbar* (1977); *The Coca-Cola Kid* (1985) (using Coca-Cola as a metaphor for American commercialism); *The Kentucky Fried Movie* (1977); *Harley Davidson and the Marlboro Man* (1991); *The Wonder Years* (ABC 1988-present) ("Wonder Years" was a slogan of Wonder Bread); Tim Rice & Andrew Lloyd Webber, *Joseph and the Amazing Technicolor Dream Coat* (musical).

Hear Janis Joplin, *Mercedes Benz,* on *Pearl* (CBS 1971); Paul Simon, *Kodachrome,* on *There Goes Rhymin' Simon* (Warner 1973); Leonard Cohen, *Chelsea Hotel,* on *The Best of Leonard Cohen* (CBS 1975); Bruce Springsteen, *Cadillac Ranch,* on *The River* (CBS 1980); Prince, *Little Red Corvette, on 1999* (Warner 1982); dada, *Dizz Knee Land,* on *Puzzle* (IRS 1992) ("I just robbed a grocery store—I'm going to Disneyland / I just flipped off President George—I'm going to Disneyland"); Monty Python, *Spam,* on *The Final Rip Off* (Virgin 1988); Roy Clark, *Thank God and Greyhound [You're Gone],* on *Roy Clark's Greatest Hits Volume I* (MCA 1979); Mel Tillis, *Coca-Cola Cowboy,* on *The Very Best of* (MCA 1981) ("You're just a Coca-Cola cowboy / You've got an Eastwood smile and Robert Redford hair . . .").

Dance to Talking Heads, *Popular Favorites 1976-92: Sand in the Vaseline* (Sire 1992); Talking Heads, *Popsicle,* on *id. Admire* Andy Warhol, *Campbell's Soup Can. Cf.* REO Speedwagon, 38 Special, and Jello Biafra of the Dead Kennedys.

The creators of some of these works might have gotten permission from the trademark owners, though it's unlikely Kool-Aid relished being connected with LSD, Hershey with homicidal maniacs, Disney with armed robbers, or Coca-Cola with cultural imperialism. Certainly no free society can *demand* that artists get such permission.

[7] *Lombardo v. Doyle, Dane & Bernbach, Inc.,* 58 A.D.2d 620, 396 N.Y.S.2d 661 (1977).

[8] *Geller v. Fallon McElligott,* No. 90-Civ-2839 (S.D.N.Y. July 22, 1991) (involving a Timex ad).

[9] Prudhomme v. Procter & Gamble Co., 800 F.Supp. 390 (E.D.La.1992).

[10] E.g., Acuff-Rose Music, Inc. v. Campbell, 972 F.2d 1429 (6th Cir. 1992); Cliffs Notes v. Bantam Doubleday Dell Publishing Group, Inc., 886 F.2d 490 (2d Cir. 1989); Fisher v. Dees, 794 F.2d 432 (9th Cir. 1986); MCA, Inc. v. Wilson, 677 F.2d 180 (2d Cir. 1981); Elsmere Music, Inc. v. NBC, 623 F.2d 252 (2d Cir. 1980); Walt Disney Prods. v. The Air Pirates, 581 F.2d 751 (9th Cir. 1978); Berlin v. E.C. Publications, Inc., 329 F.2d 541 (2d Cir. 1964); Lowenfels v. Nathan, 2 F.Supp. 73 (S.D.N.Y.1932).

[4] Something very dangerous is going on here. Private property, including intellectual property, is essential to our way of life. It provides an incentive for investment and innovation; it stimulates the flourishing of our culture; it protects the moral entitlements of people to the fruits of their labors. But reducing too much to private property can be bad medicine. Private land, for instance, is far more useful if separated from other private land by public streets, roads and highways. Public parks, utility rights-of-way and sewers reduce the amount of land in private hands, but vastly enhance the value of the property that remains.

[5] So too it is with intellectual property. Overprotecting intellectual property is as harmful as underprotecting it. Creativity is impossible without a rich public domain. Nothing today, likely nothing since we tamed fire, is genuinely new: Culture, like science and technology, grows by accretion, each new creator building on the works of those who came before. Overprotection stifles the very creative forces it's supposed to nurture.[11]

[6] The panel's opinion is a classic case of overprotection. Concerned about what it sees as a wrong done to Vanna White, the panel majority erects a property right of remarkable and dangerous breadth: Under the majority's opinion, it's now a tort for advertisers to *remind* the public of a celebrity. Not to use a celebrity's name, voice, signature or likeness; not to imply the celebrity endorses a product; but simply to evoke the celebrity's image in the public's mind. This Orwellian notion withdraws far more from the public domain than prudence and common sense allow. It conflicts with the Copyright Act and the Copyright Clause. It raises serious First Amendment problems. It's bad law, and it deserves a long, hard second look.

II

[7] Samsung ran an ad campaign promoting its consumer electronics. Each ad depicted a Samsung product and a humorous prediction: One showed a raw steak with the caption "Revealed to be health food. 2010 A.D." Another showed Morton Downey, Jr. in front of an American flag with the caption "Presidential candidate. 2008 A.D."[12] The ads were meant to convey—humorously—that Samsung products would still be in use twenty years from now.

[8] The ad that spawned this litigation starred a robot dressed in a wig, gown and jewelry reminiscent of Vanna White's hair and dress; the robot was posed next to a Wheel-of-Fortune-like game board. *See* Appendix. The caption read "Longest-running game show. 2012 A.D." The gag here, I take it, was that Samsung would still be around when White had been replaced by a robot.

[9] Perhaps failing to see the humor, White sued, alleging Samsung infringed her right of publicity by "appropriating" her "identity." Under California law, White has the exclusive right to use her name, likeness, signature and voice for commercial purposes. Cal.Civ.Code § 3344(a); *Eastwood v. Superior Court,* 149 Cal.App.3d 409, 417, 198 Cal.Rptr. 342, 347 (1983). But Samsung didn't use her name, voice or signature, and it certainly didn't use her likeness. The ad just wouldn't have been funny had it depicted White or someone who resembled her—the whole joke was that the game show host(ess) was a robot, not a real person. No one seeing the ad could have thought this was supposed to be White in 2012.

[10] The district judge quite reasonably held that, because Samsung didn't use White's name, likeness, voice or signature, it didn't violate her right of publicity. 971 F.2d at 1396-97. Not so, says the panel majority: The California right of publicity can't possibly be limited to name and likeness. If it were, the majority reasons, a "clever advertising strategist" could avoid using White's name or likeness

---

[11] See Wendy J. Gordon, A Property Right in Self Expression: Equality and Individualism in the Natural Law of Intellectual Property, 102 Yale L.J. 1533, 1556-57 (1993).

[12] I had never heard of Morton Downey, Jr., but I'm told he's sort of like Rush Limbaugh, but not as shy.

but nevertheless remind people of her with impunity, "effectively eviscerat[ing]" her rights. To prevent this "evisceration," the panel majority holds that the right of publicity must extend beyond name and likeness, to any "appropriation" of White's "identity"—anything that "evoke[s]" her personality. *Id.* at 1398-99.

III

[11] But what does "evisceration" mean in intellectual property law? Intellectual property rights aren't like some constitutional rights, absolute guarantees protected against all kinds of interference, subtle as well as blatant.[13] They cast no penumbras, emit no emanations: The very point of intellectual property laws is that they protect only against certain specific kinds of appropriation. I can't publish unauthorized copies of, say, *Presumed Innocent;* I can't make a movie out of it. But I'm perfectly free to write a book about an idealistic young prosecutor on trial for a crime he didn't commit.[14] So what if I got the idea from *Presumed Innocent?* So what if it reminds readers of the original? Have I "eviscerated" Scott Turow's intellectual property rights? Certainly not. All creators draw in part on the work of those who came before, referring to it, building on it, poking fun at it; we call this creativity, not piracy.[15]

[12] The majority isn't, in fact, preventing the "evisceration" of Vanna White's existing rights; it's creating a new and much broader property right, a right unknown in California law.[16] It's replacing the existing balance between the interests of the celebrity and those of the public by a different balance, one substantially more favorable to the celebrity. Instead of having an exclusive right in her name, likeness, signature or voice, every famous person now has an exclusive right to *anything that reminds the viewer of her.* After all, that's all Samsung did: It used an inanimate object to remind people of White, to "evoke [her identity]." 971 F.2d at 1399.[17]

---

[13] *Cf., e.g., Guinn v. United States,* 238 U.S. 347, 364-65, 35 S.Ct. 926, 931, 59 L.Ed. 1340 (1915) (striking down grandfather clause that was a clear attempt to evade the Fifteenth Amendment).

[14] It would be called "Burden of Going Forward with the Evidence," and the hero would ultimately be saved by his lawyer's adept use of Fed.R.Evid. 301.

[15] In the words of Sir Isaac Newton, "[i]f I have seen further it is by standing on [the shoulders] of Giants." Letter to Robert Hooke, Feb. 5, 1675/1676.

Newton himself may have borrowed this phrase from Bernard of Chartres, who said something similar in the early twelfth century. Bernard in turn may have snatched it from Priscian, a sixth century grammarian. *See Lotus Dev. Corp. v. Paperback Software Int'l,* 740 F.Supp. 37, 77 n. 3 (D.Mass.1990).

[16] In fact, in the one California case raising the issue, the three state Supreme Court Justices who discussed this theory expressed serious doubts about it. *Guglielmi v. Spelling-Goldberg Prods.,* 25 Cal.3d 860, 864 n. 5, 160 Cal.Rptr. 352, 355 n. 5, 603 P.2d 454, 457 n. 5 (1979) (Bird, C.J., concurring) (expressing skepticism about finding a property right to a celebrity's "personality" because it is "difficult to discern any easily applied definition for this amorphous term").

Neither have we previously interpreted California law to cover pure "identity." *Midler v. Ford Motor Co.,* 849 F.2d 460 (9th Cir. 1988), and *Waits v. Frito-Lay, Inc.,* 978 F.2d 1093 (9th Cir. 1992), dealt with appropriation of a celebrity's voice. *See id.* at 1100-01 (imitation of singing style, rather than voice, doesn't violate the right of publicity). *Motschenbacher v. R.J. Reynolds Tobacco Co.,* 498 F.2d 821 (9th Cir. 1974), stressed that, though the plaintiff's likeness wasn't directly recognizable by itself, the surrounding circumstances would have made viewers think the likeness was the plaintiff's. *Id.* at 827; *see also Moore v. Regents of the Univ. of Cal.,* 51 Cal.3d 120, 138, 271 Cal.Rptr. 146, 157, 793 P.2d 479, 490 (1990) (construing *Motschenbacher* as "hold [ing] that every person has a proprietary interest in his own likeness").

[17] Some viewers might have inferred White was endorsing the product, but that's a different story. The right of publicity isn't aimed at or limited to false endorsements, *Eastwood v. Superior Court,* 149 Cal.App.3d 409, 419-20, 198 Cal.Rptr. 342, 348 (1983); that's what the Lanham Act is for.

Note also that the majority's rule applies even to advertisements that unintentionally remind people of someone. California law is crystal clear that the common-law right of publicity may be

766

[13] Consider how sweeping this new right is. What is it about the ad that makes people think of White? It's not the robot's wig, clothes or jewelry; there must be ten million blond women (many of them quasi-famous) who wear dresses and jewelry like White's. It's that the robot is posed near the "Wheel of Fortune" game board. Remove the game board from the ad, and no one would think of Vanna White. *See* Appendix. But once you include the game board, anybody standing beside it-a brunette woman, a man wearing women's clothes, a monkey in a wig and gown-would evoke White's image, precisely the way the robot did. It's the "Wheel of Fortune" set, not the robot's face or dress or jewelry that evokes White's image. The panel is giving White an exclusive right not in what she looks like or who she is, but in what she does for a living.[18]

[14] This is entirely the wrong place to strike the balance. Intellectual property rights aren't free: They're imposed at the expense of future creators and of the public at large. Where would we be if Charles Lindbergh had an exclusive right in the concept of a heroic solo aviator? If Arthur Conan Doyle had gotten a copyright in the idea of the detective story, or Albert Einstein had patented the theory of relativity? If every author and celebrity had been given the right to keep people from mocking them or their work? Surely this would have made the world poorer, not richer, culturally as well as economically.[19]

[15] This is why intellectual property law is full of careful balances between what's set aside for the owner and what's left in the public domain for the rest of us: The relatively short life of patents; the longer, but finite, life of copyrights; copyright's idea-expression dichotomy; the fair use doctrine; the prohibition on copyrighting facts; the compulsory license of television broadcasts and musical compositions; federal preemption of overbroad state intellectual property laws; the nominative use doctrine in trademark law; the right to make soundalike recordings.[20] All of these diminish an

---

violated even by unintentional appropriations. *Id.* at 417 n. 6, 198 Cal.Rptr. at 346 n. 6; *Fairfield v. American Photocopy Equipment Co.,* 138 Cal.App.2d 82, 87, 291 P.2d 194 (1955).

[18] Once the right of publicity is extended beyond specific physical characteristics, this will become a recurring problem: Outside name, likeness and voice, the things that most reliably remind the public of celebrities are the actions or roles they're famous for. A commercial with an astronaut setting foot on the moon would evoke the image of Neil Armstrong. Any masked man on horseback would remind people (over a certain age) of Clayton Moore. And any number of songs—"My Way," "Yellow Submarine," "Like a Virgin," "Beat It," "Michael, Row the Boat Ashore," to name only a few—instantly evoke an image of the person or group who made them famous, regardless of who is singing.

See also Carlos V. Lozano, *West Loses Lawsuit over Batman TV Commercial,* L.A. Times, Jan. 18, 1990, at B3 (Adam West sues over Batman-like character in commercial); *Nurmi v. Peterson,* 10 U.S.P.Q.2d 1775, 1989 WL 407484 (C.D.Cal.1989) (1950s TV movie hostess "Vampira" sues 1980s TV hostess "Elvira"); text accompanying notes 7-8 (lawsuits brought by Guy Lombardo, claiming big bands playing at New Year's Eve parties remind people of him, and by Uri Geller, claiming psychics who can bend metal remind people of him). *Cf. Motschenbacher,* where the claim was that viewers would think plaintiff was actually in the commercial, and not merely that the commercial reminded people of him.

[19] See generally Gordon, supra note 11; see also Michael Madow, Private Ownership of Public Image: Popular Culture and Publicity Rights, 81 Cal.L.Rev. 125, 201-03 (1993) (an excellent discussion).

[20] *See* 35 U.S.C. § 154 (duration of patent); 17 U.S.C. §§ 302-305 (duration of copyright); 17 U.S.C. § 102(b) (idea-expression dichotomy); 17 U.S.C. § 107 (fair use); *Feist Pubs., Inc. v. Rural Tel. Serv. Co.,* 499 U.S. 340, ----, 111 S.Ct. 1282, 1288, 113 L.Ed.2d 358 (1991) (no copyrighting facts); 17 U.S.C. §§ 115, 119(b) (compulsory licenses); *Bonito Boats, Inc. v. Thunder Craft Boats, Inc.,* 489 U.S. 141, 109 S.Ct. 971, 103 L.Ed.2d 118 (1989) (federal preemption); *New Kids on the Block v. News America Publishing, Inc.,* 971 F.2d 302, 306-308 (9th Cir. 1992) (nominative use); 17 U.S.C. § 114(b) (soundalikes); *accord G.S. Rasmussen & Assocs. v. Kalitta Flying Serv., Inc.,* 958 F.2d 896, 900 n. 7 (9th Cir. 1992); Daniel A. Saunders, Comment, *Copyright Law's Broken* Rear Window, 80 Cal.L.Rev. 179, 204-05 (1992). *But see Midler v. Ford Motor Co.,* 849 F.2d 460 (9th Cir. 1988).

intellectual property owner's rights. All let the public use something created by someone else. But all are necessary to maintain a free environment in which creative genius can flourish.

[16] The intellectual property right created by the panel here has none of these essential limitations: No fair use exception; no right to parody; no idea-expression dichotomy. It impoverishes the public domain, to the detriment of future creators and the public at large. Instead of well-defined, limited characteristics such as name, likeness or voice, advertisers will now have to cope with vague claims of "appropriation of identity," claims often made by people with a wholly exaggerated sense of their own fame and significance. *See* pp. 1512-13 & notes 1-10 *supra*. Future Vanna Whites might not get the chance to create their personae, because their employers may fear some celebrity will claim the persona is too similar to her own.[21] The public will be robbed of parodies of celebrities, and our culture will be deprived of the valuable safety valve that parody and mockery create.

[17] Moreover, consider the moral dimension, about which the panel majority seems to have gotten so exercised. Saying Samsung "appropriated" something of White's begs the question: *Should White have the exclusive right to something as broad and amorphous as her "identity"?* Samsung's ad didn't simply copy White's schtick—like all parody, it created something new.[22] True, Samsung did it to make money, but White does whatever she does to make money, too; the majority talks of "the difference between fun and profit," 971 F.2d at 1401, but in the entertainment industry fun *is* profit. Why is Vanna White's right to exclusive for-profit use of her persona—a persona that might not even be her own creation, but that of a writer, director or producer—superior to Samsung's right to profit by creating its own inventions? Why should she have such absolute rights to control the conduct of others, unlimited by the idea-expression dichotomy or by the fair use doctrine?

[18] To paraphrase only slightly *Feist Publications, Inc. v. Rural Telephone Service Co.*, 499 U.S. 340 (1991), it may seem unfair that much of the fruit of a creator's labor may be used by others without compensation. But this is not some unforeseen byproduct of our intellectual property system; it is the system's very essence. Intellectual property law assures authors the right to their original expression, but encourages others to build freely on the ideas that underlie it. This result is neither unfair nor unfortunate: It is the means by which intellectual property law advances the progress of science and art. We give authors certain exclusive rights, but in exchange we get a richer public domain. The majority ignores this wise teaching, and all of us are the poorer for it.[23]

---

[21] If Christian Slater, star of "Heathers," "Pump up the Volume," "Kuffs," and "Untamed Heart"—and alleged Jack Nicholson clone—appears in a commercial, can Nicholson sue? Of 54 stories on LEXIS that talk about Christian Slater, 26 talk about Slater's alleged similarities to Nicholson. Apparently it's his nasal wisecracks and killer smiles, St. Petersburg Times, Jan. 10, 1992, at 13, his eyebrows, Ottawa Citizen, Jan. 10, 1992, at E2, his sneers, Boston Globe, July 26, 1991, at 37, his menacing presence, USA Today, June 26, 1991, at 1D, and his sing-song voice, Gannett News Service, Aug. 27, 1990 (or, some say, his insinuating drawl, L.A. Times, Aug. 22, 1990, at F5). That's a whole lot more than White and the robot had in common.

[22] *Cf. New Kids on the Block v. News America Publishing, Inc.*, 971 F.2d 302, 307 n. 6 (9th Cir. 1992) ("Where the infringement is small in relation to the new work created, the fair user is profiting largely from his own creative efforts rather than free-riding on another's work.").

[23] The majority opinion has already earned some well-deserved criticisms on this score. Stephen R. Barnett, *In Hollywood's Wheel of Fortune, Free Speech Loses a Turn*, Wall St. J., Sept. 28, 1992, at A14; Stephen R. Barnett, *Wheel of Misfortune for Advertisers: Ninth Circuit Misreads the Law to Protect Vanna White's Image*, L.A. Daily J., Oct. 5, 1992, at 6; Felix H. Kent, *California Court Expands Celebrities' Rights*, N.Y.L.J., Oct. 30, 1992, at 3 ("To speak of the 'evisceration' of such a questionable common law right in a case that has probably gone the farthest of any case in any court in the United States of America is more than difficult to comprehend"); Shapiro, *supra* note 1 ("A fat chef? A blond robot in an evening

IV

[19] The panel, however, does more than misinterpret California law: By refusing to recognize a parody exception to the right of publicity, the panel directly contradicts the federal Copyright Act. Samsung didn't merely parody Vanna White. It parodied Vanna White appearing in "Wheel of Fortune," a copyrighted television show, and parodies of copyrighted works are governed by federal copyright law.

[20] Copyright law specifically gives the world at large the right to make "fair use" parodies, parodies that don't borrow too much of the original. *Fisher v. Dees,* 794 F.2d 432, 435 (9th Cir. 1986)....

VI

[21] Finally, I can't see how giving White the power to keep others from evoking her image in the public's mind can be squared with the First Amendment. Where does White get this right to control our thoughts? The majority's creation goes way beyond the protection given a trademark or a copyrighted work, or a person's name or likeness. All those things control one particular way of expressing an idea, one way of referring to an object or a person. But not allowing *any* means of reminding people of someone? That's a speech restriction unparalleled in First Amendment law.[28]

[22] What's more, I doubt even a name-and-likeness-only right of publicity can stand without a parody exception. The First Amendment isn't just about religion or politics—it's also about protecting the free development of our national culture. Parody, humor, irreverence are all vital components of the marketplace of ideas. The last thing we need, the last thing the First Amendment will tolerate, is a law that lets public figures keep people from mocking them, or from "evok[ing]" their images in the mind of the public. 971 F.2d at 1399.[29]

[23] The majority dismisses the First Amendment issue out of hand because Samsung's ad was commercial speech. *Id.* at 1401 & n. 3. So what? Commercial speech may be less protected by the First Amendment than noncommercial speech, but less protected means protected nonetheless.

---

gown? How far will this go?" (citing Douglas J. Wood, an advertising lawyer)). *See also* Mark Alan Stamaty, *Washingtoon,* Wash. Post, Apr. 5, 1993, at A21.

[28] Just compare the majority's holding to the intellectual property laws upheld by the Supreme Court. The Copyright Act is constitutional precisely because of the fair use doctrine and the idea-expression dichotomy, *Harper & Row v. Nation Enterprises,* 471 U.S. 539, 560, 105 S.Ct. 2218, 2230, 85 L.Ed.2d 588 (1985), two features conspicuously absent from the majority's doctrine. The right of publicity at issue in *Zacchini v. Scripps-Howard Broadcasting Co.,* 433 U.S. 562, 576, 97 S.Ct. 2849, 2857-58, 53 L.Ed.2d 965 (1977), was only the right to "broadcast of petitioner's entire performance," not "the unauthorized use of another's name for purposes of trade." *Id.* Even the statute upheld in *San Francisco Arts & Athletics, Inc. v. United States Olympic Comm.,* 483 U.S. 522, 530, 107 S.Ct. 2971, 2977, 97 L.Ed.2d 427 (1987), which gave the USOC sweeping rights to the word "Olympic," didn't purport to protect all expression that reminded people of the Olympics.

[29] The majority's failure to recognize a parody exception to the right of publicity would apply equally to parodies of politicians as of actresses. Consider the case of Wok Fast, a Los Angeles Chinese food delivery service, which put up a billboard with a picture of then-L.A. Police Chief Daryl Gates and the text "When you can't leave the office. Or won't." (This was an allusion to Chief Gates's refusal to retire despite pressure from Mayor Tom Bradley.) Gates forced the restaurant to take the billboard down by threatening a right of publicity lawsuit. Leslie Berger, *He Did Leave the Office-And Now Sign Will Go, Too,* L.A. Times, July 31, 1992, at B2.

See also Samsung Has Seen the Future: Brace Youself, Adweek, Oct. 3, 1988, at 26 (ER 72) (Samsung planned another ad that would show a dollar bill with Richard Nixon's face on it and the caption 'Dollar bill, 2025 A.D..,' but Nixon refused permission to use his likeness); Madow *supra* note 19, at 142-46 (discussing other politically and culturally charged parodies).

CentralHudson Gas & Elec. Corp. v. Public Serv. Comm'n, 447 U.S. 557, 100 S.Ct. 2343, 65 L.Ed.2d 341 (1980). And there are very good reasons for this. Commercial speech has a profound effect on our culture and our attitudes. Neutral-seeming ads influence people's social and political attitudes, and themselves arouse political controversy.[30] "Where's the Beef?" turned from an advertising catchphrase into the only really memorable thing about the 1984 presidential campaign.[31] Four years later, Michael Dukakis called George Bush "the Joe Isuzu of American politics."[32]

[24] In our pop culture, where salesmanship must be entertaining and entertainment must sell, the line between the commercial and noncommercial has not merely blurred; it has disappeared. Is the Samsung parody any different from a parody on Saturday Night Live or in Spy Magazine? Both are equally profit-motivated. Both use a celebrity's identity to sell things—one to sell VCRs, the other to sell advertising. Both mock their subjects. Both try to make people laugh. Both add something, perhaps something worthwhile and memorable, perhaps not, to our culture. Both are things that the people being portrayed might dearly want to suppress. *See* notes 1 & 29 *supra.*

[25] Commercial speech is a significant, valuable part of our national discourse. The Supreme Court has recognized as much, and has insisted that lower courts carefully scrutinize commercial speech restrictions, but the panel totally fails to do this. The panel majority doesn't even purport to apply the *Central Hudson* test, which the Supreme Court devised specifically for determining whether a commercial speech restriction is valid.[33] The majority doesn't ask, as *Central Hudson* requires, whether the speech restriction is justified by a substantial state interest. It doesn't ask whether the restriction directly advances the interest. It doesn't ask whether the restriction is narrowly tailored to the interest. *See id.* at 566.[34] These are all things the Supreme Court told us—in no uncertain terms—we must consider; the majority opinion doesn't even mention them.[35]

[26] Process matters. The Supreme Court didn't set out the *Central Hudson* test for its health. It devised the test because it saw lower courts were giving the First Amendment short shrift when confronted with commercial speech. *See Central Hudson,* 447 U.S. at 561-62, 567-68, 100 S.Ct. at 2348-

---

[30] *See, e.g.,* Bruce Horovitz, *Nike Does It Again; Firm Targets Blacks with a Spin on "Family Values",* L.A. Times, Aug. 25, 1992, at D1 ("The ad reinforces a stereotype about black fathers" (quoting Lawrence A. Johnson of Howard University)); Gaylord Fields, *Advertising Awards-Show Mania: CEBA Awards Honors Black-Oriented Advertising,* Back Stage, Nov. 17, 1989, at 1 (quoting the Rev. Jesse Jackson as emphasizing the importance of positive black images in advertising); Debra Kaufman, *Quality of Hispanic Production Rising to Meet Clients' Demands,* Back Stage, July 14, 1989, at 1 (Hispanic advertising professional stresses importance of positive Hispanic images in advertising); Marilyn Elias, *Medical Ads Often Are Sexist,* USA Today, May 18, 1989, at 1D ("There's lots of evidence that this kind of ad reinforces stereotypes" (quoting Julie Edell of Duke University)).

[31] See Wendy's Kind of Commercial; "Where's the Beef" Becomes National Craze, Broadcasting, Mar. 26, 1984, at 57.

[32] *See* Gregory Gordon, *Candidates Look for Feedback Today,* UPI, Sept. 26, 1988.

[33] Its only citation to *Central Hudson* is a seeming afterthought, buried in a footnote, and standing only for the proposition that commercial speech is less protected under the First Amendment. *See* 971 F.2d at 1401 n. 3.

[34] *See also Board of Trustees v. Fox,* 492 U.S. 469, 476-81, 109 S.Ct. 3028, 3032-35, 106 L.Ed.2d 388 (1989) (reaffirming "narrowly tailored" requirement, but making clear it's not a "least restrictive means" test).

The government has a freer hand in regulating false or misleading commercial speech, but this isn't such a regulation. Some "appropriations" of a person's "identity" might misleadingly suggest an endorsement, but the mere possibility that speech might mislead isn't enough to strip it of First Amendment protection. *See Zauderer v. Office of Disciplinary Counsel,* 471 U.S. 626, 644 (1985).

[35] Neither does it discuss whether the speech restriction is unconstitutionally vague. *Posadas de P.R. Assocs. v. Tourism Co.,* 478 U.S. 328, 347, 106 S.Ct. 2968, 2980, 92 L.Ed.2d 266 (1986).

49, 2352. The *Central Hudson* test was an attempt to constrain lower courts' discretion, to focus judges' thinking on the important issues—how strong the state interest is, how broad the regulation is, whether a narrower regulation would work just as well. If the Court wanted to leave these matters to judges' gut feelings, to nifty lines about "the difference between fun and profit," 971 F.2d at 1401, it could have done so with much less effort.

[27] Maybe applying the test would have convinced the majority to change its mind; maybe going through the factors would have shown that its rule was too broad, or the reasons for protecting White's "identity" too tenuous. Maybe not. But we shouldn't thumb our nose at the Supreme Court by just refusing to apply its test.

VII

[28] For better or worse, we *are* the Court of Appeals for the Hollywood Circuit. Millions of people toil in the shadow of the law we make, and much of their livelihood is made possible by the existence of intellectual property rights. But much of their livelihood—and much of the vibrancy of our culture— also depends on the existence of other intangible rights: The right to draw ideas from a rich and varied public domain, and the right to mock, for profit as well as fun, the cultural icons of our time.

[29] In the name of avoiding the "evisceration" of a celebrity's rights in her image, the majority diminishes the rights of copyright holders and the public at large. In the name of fostering creativity, the majority suppresses it. Vanna White and those like her have been given something they never had before, and they've been given it at our expense. I cannot agree.

In *In re NCAA Student–Athlete Name & Likeness Licensing Litigation*, the Ninth Circuit relies heavily on the transformative use test formulated by the Supreme Court of California in *Comedy III Productions, Inc. v. Gary Saderup, Inc.*, 25 Cal. 4th 387 (2001). Shown below on the right is the drawing of the Three Stooges at issue in that case. The Supreme Court of California found the drawing, as applied to various merchandise, not to be sufficiently transformative to avoid liability under Cal. Civ. Code. § 990 (now Cal. Civ. Code § 3344.1). (As indicated in brackets through the course of the opinion, images from certain of the other cases referenced in *In re NCAA Student–Athlete Name & Likeness Licensing Litigation* are shown for reference purposes after the opinion.)*

---

* All such images are taken from Wikipedia or Georgetown Law Intellectual Property Teaching Resources.

In *In re NCAA Student–Athlete Name & Likeness Licensing Litigation*, Judge Thomas issued a strong dissent from Judge Bybee's majority opinion. Which opinion do you find to be more persuasive, the majority or the dissent?

In re NCAA Student–Athlete Name & Likeness Licensing Litigation
724 F.3d 1268 (9th Cir. 2013)

BYBEE, Circuit Judge:

[1] Video games are entitled to the full protections of the First Amendment, because "[l]ike the protected books, plays, and movies that preceded them, video games communicate ideas—and even social messages—through many familiar literary devices (such as characters, dialogue, plot, and music) and through features distinctive to the medium (such as the player's interaction with the virtual world)." *Brown v. Entm't Merchs. Ass'n,* --- U.S. ----, 131 S.Ct. 2729 (2011).[1] Such rights are not absolute, and states may recognize the right of publicity to a degree consistent with the First Amendment. *Zacchini v. Scripps–Howard Broad. Co.,* 433 U.S. 562, 574–75, 97 S.Ct. 2849, 53 L.Ed.2d 965 (1977). In this case, we must balance the right of publicity of a former college football player against the asserted First Amendment right of a video game developer to use his likeness in its expressive works.

[2] The district court concluded that the game developer, Electronic Arts ("EA"), had no First Amendment defense against the right-of-publicity claims of the football player, Samuel Keller. We affirm. Under the "transformative use" test developed by the California Supreme Court, EA's use does not qualify for First Amendment protection as a matter of law because it literally recreates Keller in the very setting in which he has achieved renown. The other First Amendment defenses asserted by EA do not defeat Keller's claims either.

I

[3] Samuel Keller was the starting quarterback for Arizona State University in 2005 before he transferred to the University of Nebraska, where he played during the 2007 season. EA is the producer of the *NCAA Football* series of video games, which allow users to control avatars representing college football players as those avatars participate in simulated games. In *NCAA Football,* EA seeks to replicate each school's entire team as accurately as possible. Every real football player on each team included in the game has a corresponding avatar in the game with the player's actual jersey number and virtually identical height, weight, build, skin tone, hair color, and home state. EA attempts to match any unique, highly identifiable playing behaviors by sending detailed questionnaires to team equipment managers. Additionally, EA creates realistic virtual versions of actual stadiums; populates them with the virtual athletes, coaches, cheerleaders, and fans realistically rendered by EA's graphic artists; and incorporates realistic sounds such as the crunch of the players' pads and the roar of the crowd.

---

[1] In *Brown v. Electronic Arts, Inc.,* No. 09-56675, 724 F.3d 1235, 1241–42, 2013 WL 3927736, at *3 (9th Cir. July 31, 2013), we noted that "there may be some work referred to as a 'video game' (or referred to as a 'book,' 'play,' or 'movie' for that matter) that does not contain enough of the elements contemplated by the Supreme Court [in *Brown v. Entertainment Merchants Association*] to warrant First Amendment protection as an expressive work," but asserted that "[e]ven if there is a line to be drawn between expressive video games and non-expressive video games, and even if courts should at some point be drawing that line, we have no need to draw that line here." The same holds true in this case.

[4] EA's game differs from reality in that EA omits the players' names on their jerseys and assigns each player a home town that is different from the actual player's home town. However, users of the video game may upload rosters of names obtained from third parties so that the names do appear on the jerseys. In such cases, EA allows images from the game containing athletes' real names to be posted on its website by users. Users can further alter reality by entering "Dynasty" mode, where the user assumes a head coach's responsibilities for a college program for up to thirty seasons, including recruiting players from a randomly generated pool of high school athletes, or "Campus Legend" mode, where the user controls a virtual player from high school through college, making choices relating to practices, academics, and social life.

[5] In the 2005 edition of the game, the virtual starting quarterback for Arizona State wears number 9, as did Keller, and has the same height, weight, skin tone, hair color, hair style, handedness, home state, play style (pocket passer), visor preference, facial features, and school year as Keller. In the 2008 edition, the virtual quarterback for Nebraska has these same characteristics, though the jersey number does not match, presumably because Keller changed his number right before the season started.

[6] Objecting to this use of his likeness, Keller filed a putative class-action complaint in the Northern District of California asserting, as relevant on appeal, that EA violated his right of publicity under California Civil Code § 3344 and California common law.[2] EA moved to strike the complaint as a strategic lawsuit against public participation ("SLAPP") under California's anti-SLAPP statute, Cal.Civ.Proc.Code § 425.16, and the district court denied the motion. We have jurisdiction over EA's appeal pursuant to 28 U.S.C. § 1291. *See Batzel v. Smith*, 333 F.3d 1018, 1024–26 (9th Cir. 2003).[3]

II

[7] California's anti-SLAPP statute is designed to discourage suits that "masquerade as ordinary lawsuits but are brought to deter common citizens from exercising their political or legal rights or to punish them for doing so." *Batzel*, 333 F.3d at 1024 (internal quotation marks omitted). The statute provides:

> A cause of action against a person arising from any act of that person in furtherance of the person's right of petition or free speech under the United States Constitution or the California Constitution in connection with a public issue shall be subject to a special motion to strike, unless the court determines that the plaintiff has established that there is a probability that the plaintiff will prevail on the claim.

Cal.Civ.Proc.Code § 425.16(b)(1). We have determined that the anti-SLAPP statute is available in federal court. *Thomas v. Fry's Elecs., Inc.,* 400 F.3d 1206 (9th Cir. 2005) (per curiam).

[8] We evaluate an anti-SLAPP motion in two steps. First, the defendant must "make a prima facie showing that the plaintiff's suit arises from an act by the defendant made in connection with a public issue in furtherance of the defendant's right to free speech under the United States or California Constitution." *Batzel*, 333 F.3d at 1024. Keller does not contest that EA has made this threshold showing. Indeed, there is no question that "video games qualify for First Amendment protection,"

---

[2] There are actually nine named plaintiffs, all former National Collegiate Athletic Association ("NCAA") football or basketball players: Keller, Edward O'Bannon, Jr. (UCLA), Byron Bishop (University of North Carolina), Michael Anderson (University of Memphis), Danny Wimprine (University of Memphis), Ishmael Thrower (Arizona State University), Craig Newsome (Arizona State University), Damien Rhodes (Syracuse University), and Samuel Jacobson (University of Minnesota). EA's NCAA basketball games are also implicated in this appeal. Because the issues are the same for each plaintiff, all of the claims are addressed through our discussion of Keller and *NCAA Football.*

[3] We review *de novo* the district court's denial of a motion to strike under California's anti-SLAPP statute. *Mindys Cosmetics, Inc. v. Dakar,* 611 F.3d 590, 595 (9th Cir. 2010).

Entm't Merchs. Ass'n, 131 S.Ct. at 2733, or that Keller's suit arises from EA's production and distribution of *NCAA Football* in furtherance of EA's protected right to express itself through video games.

[9] Second, we must evaluate whether the plaintiff has "establish[ed] a reasonable probability that the plaintiff will prevail on his or her ... claim." *Batzel,* 333 F.3d at 1024. "The plaintiff must demonstrate that the complaint is legally sufficient and supported by a prima facie showing of facts to sustain a favorable judgment if the evidence submitted by plaintiff is credited." *Metabolife Int'l, Inc. v. Wornick,* 264 F.3d 832, 840 (9th Cir. 2001) (internal quotation marks omitted). The statute "subjects to potential dismissal only those actions in which the plaintiff cannot state and substantiate a legally sufficient claim." *Navellier v. Sletten,* 29 Cal.4th 82, 124 Cal.Rptr.2d 530, 52 P.3d 703, 711 (2002) (internal quotation marks omitted). EA did not contest before the district court and does not contest here that Keller has stated a right-of-publicity claim under California common and statutory law.[4] Instead, EA raises four affirmative defenses derived from the First Amendment: the "transformative use" test, the *Rogers* test, the "public interest" test, and the "public affairs" exemption. EA argues that, in light of these defenses, it is not reasonably probable that Keller will prevail on his right-of-publicity claim. This appeal therefore centers on the applicability of these defenses. We take each one in turn.[5]

A

[10] The California Supreme Court formulated the transformative use defense in *Comedy III Productions, Inc. v. Gary Saderup, Inc.,* 25 Cal.4th 387, 106 Cal.Rptr.2d 126, 21 P.3d 797 (2001). The defense is "a balancing test between the First Amendment and the right of publicity based on whether the work in question adds significant creative elements so as to be transformed into something more than a mere celebrity likeness or imitation." *Id.* 106 Cal.Rptr.2d 126, 21 P.3d at 799. The California Supreme Court explained that "when a work contains significant transformative elements, it is not only especially worthy of First Amendment protection, but it is also less likely to interfere with the economic interest protected by the right of publicity." *Id.* 106 Cal.Rptr.2d 126, 21 P.3d at 808. The court rejected the wholesale importation of the copyright "fair use" defense into right-of-publicity claims, but recognized that some aspects of that defense are "particularly pertinent." *Id.; see* 17 U.S.C. § 107; *see also SOFA Entm't, Inc. v. Dodger Prods., Inc.,* 709 F.3d 1273, 1277–78 (9th Cir. 2013) (discussing the "fair use" defense codified in 17 U.S.C. § 107).

[11] *Comedy III* gives us at least five factors to consider in determining whether a work is sufficiently transformative to obtain First Amendment protection. *See* J. Thomas McCarthy, *The Rights of Publicity and Privacy* § 8:72 (2d ed.2012). First, if "the celebrity likeness is one of the 'raw materials' from which an original work is synthesized," it is more likely to be transformative than if "the depiction or imitation of the celebrity is the very sum and substance of the work in question." *Comedy III,* 106 Cal.Rptr.2d 126, 21 P.3d at 809. Second, the work is protected if it is "primarily the defendant's own expression"—as long as that expression is "something other than the likeness of the celebrity." *Id.* This factor requires an examination of whether a likely purchaser's primary motivation is to buy a reproduction of the celebrity, or to buy the expressive work of that artist. McCarthy, *supra,* § 8:72.

---

[4] The elements of a right-of-publicity claim under California common law are: "(1) the defendant's use of the plaintiff's identity; (2) the appropriation of plaintiff's name or likeness to defendant's advantage, commercially or otherwise; (3) lack of consent; and (4) resulting injury." *Stewart v. Rolling Stone LLC,* 181 Cal.App.4th 664, 105 Cal.Rptr.3d 98, 111 (internal quotation marks omitted). The same claim under California Civil Code § 3344 requires a plaintiff to prove "all the elements of the common law cause of action" plus "a knowing use by the defendant as well as a direct connection between the alleged use and the commercial purpose." *Id.*

[5] Just as we did in *Hilton v. Hallmark Cards,* we reserve the question of whether the First Amendment furnishes a defense other than those the parties raise. 599 F.3d 894, 909 n. 11 (9th Cir. 2010).

Third, to avoid making judgments concerning "the quality of the artistic contribution," a court should conduct an inquiry "more quantitative than qualitative" and ask "whether the literal and imitative or the creative elements predominate in the work." *Comedy III,* 106 Cal.Rptr.2d 126, 21 P.3d at 809. Fourth, the California Supreme Court indicated that "a subsidiary inquiry" would be useful in close cases: whether "the marketability and economic value of the challenged work derive primarily from the fame of the celebrity depicted." *Id.* 106 Cal.Rptr.2d 126, 21 P.3d at 810. Lastly, the court indicated that "when an artist's skill and talent is manifestly subordinated to the overall goal of creating a conventional portrait of a celebrity so as to commercially exploit his or her fame," the work is not transformative. *Id.*

[12] We have explained that "[o]nly if [a defendant] is entitled to the [transformative] defense *as a matter of law* can it prevail on its motion to strike," because the California Supreme Court "envisioned the application of the defense as a question of fact." *Hilton,* 599 F.3d at 910. As a result, EA "is only entitled to the defense as a matter of law if no trier of fact could reasonably conclude that the [game] [i]s not transformative." *Id.*

[13] California courts have applied the transformative use test in relevant situations in four cases. First, in *Comedy III* itself, the California Supreme Court applied the test to T-shirts and lithographs bearing a likeness of The Three Stooges and concluded that it could "discern no significant transformative or creative contribution." *Id.* 106 Cal.Rptr.2d 126, 21 P.3d at 811. The court reasoned that the artist's "undeniable skill is manifestly subordinated to the overall goal of creating literal, conventional depictions of The Three Stooges so as to exploit their fame." *Id.* "[W]ere we to decide that [the artist's] depictions were protected by the First Amendment," the court continued, "we cannot perceive how the right of publicity would remain a viable right other than in cases of falsified celebrity endorsements." *Id.*

[14] Second, in *Winter v. DC Comics,* the California Supreme Court applied the test to comic books containing characters Johnny and Edgar Autumn, "depicted as villainous half-worm, half-human offspring" but evoking two famous brothers, rockers Johnny and Edgar Winter. 30 Cal.4th 881, 134 Cal.Rptr.2d 634, 69 P.3d 473, 476 (2003). [*See relevant images below*]. The court held that "the comic books are transformative and entitled to First Amendment protection." *Id.* 134 Cal.Rptr.2d 634, 69 P.3d at 480. It reasoned that the comic books "are not just conventional depictions of plaintiffs but contain significant expressive content other than plaintiffs' mere likenesses." *Id.* 134 Cal.Rptr.2d 634, 69 P.3d at 479. "To the extent the drawings of the Autumn brothers resemble plaintiffs at all, they are distorted for purposes of lampoon, parody, or caricature." *Id.* Importantly, the court relied on the fact that the brothers "are but cartoon characters . . . in a larger story, which is itself quite expressive." *Id.*

[15] Third, in *Kirby v. Sega of America, Inc.,* the California Court of Appeal applied the transformative use test to a video game in which the user controls the dancing of "Ulala," a reporter from outer space allegedly based on singer Kierin Kirby, whose "'signature' lyrical expression . . . is 'ooh la la.'" 144 Cal.App.4th 47, 50 Cal.Rptr.3d 607, 609–10 (2006). [*See relevant images below*]. The court held that "Ulala is more than a mere likeness or literal depiction of Kirby," pointing to Ulala's "extremely tall, slender computer-generated physique," her "hairstyle and primary costume," her dance moves, and her role as "a space-age reporter in the 25th century," all of which were "unlike any public depiction of Kirby." *Id.* at 616. "As in *Winter,* Ulala is a 'fanciful, creative character' who exists in the context of a unique and expressive video game." *Id.* at 618.

[16] Finally, in *No Doubt v. Activision Publishing, Inc.,* the California Court of Appeal addressed Activision's *Band Hero* video game. 192 Cal.App.4th 1018, 122 Cal.Rptr.3d 397, 400 (2011), *petition for review denied,* 2011 Cal. LEXIS 6100 (Cal. June 8, 2011) (No. B223996). [*See relevant images below*]. In *Band Hero,* users simulate performing in a rock band in time with popular songs. *Id.* at 401. Users choose from a number of avatars, some of which represent actual rock stars, including the members of the rock band No Doubt. *Id.* at 401. Activision licensed No Doubt's likeness, but allegedly exceeded the scope of the license by permitting users to manipulate the No Doubt avatars to play any song in the

game, solo or with members of other bands, and even to alter the avatars' voices. *Id.* at 402. The court held that No Doubt's right of publicity prevailed despite Activision's First Amendment defense because the game was not "transformative" under the *Comedy III* test. It reasoned that the video game characters were "literal recreations of the band members," doing "the same activity by which the band achieved and maintains its fame." *Id.* at 411. According to the court, the fact "that the avatars appear in the context of a videogame that contains many other creative elements[ ] does not transform the avatars into anything other than exact depictions of No Doubt's members doing exactly what they do as celebrities." *Id.* The court concluded that "the expressive elements of the game remain manifestly subordinated to the overall goal of creating a conventional portrait of No Doubt so as to commercially exploit its fame." *Id.* (internal quotation marks omitted).

[17] We have also had occasion to apply the transformative use test. In *Hilton v. Hallmark Cards,* we applied the test to a birthday card depicting Paris Hilton in a manner reminiscent of an episode of Hilton's reality show *The Simple Life.* 599 F.3d at 899. [*See relevant image below*]. We observed some differences between the episode and the card, but noted that "the basic setting is the same: we see Paris Hilton, born to privilege, working as a waitress." *Id.* at 911. We reasoned that "[w]hen we compare Hallmark's card to the video game in *Kirby,* which transported a 1990s singer (catchphrases and all) into the 25th century and transmogrified her into a space-age reporter, . . . the card falls far short of the level of new expression added in the video game." *Id.* As a result, we concluded that "there is enough doubt as to whether Hallmark's card is transformative under our case law that we cannot say Hallmark is entitled to the defense as a matter of law." *Id.*[6]

[18] With these cases in mind as guidance, we conclude that EA's use of Keller's likeness does not contain significant transformative elements such that EA is entitled to the defense as a matter of law. The facts of *No Doubt* are very similar to those here. EA is alleged to have replicated Keller's physical characteristics in *NCAA Football,* just as the members of No Doubt are realistically portrayed in *Band Hero.* Here, as in *Band Hero,* users manipulate the characters in the performance of the same activity for which they are known in real life—playing football in this case, and performing in a rock band in *Band Hero.* The context in which the activity occurs is also similarly realistic—real venues in *Band Hero* and realistic depictions of actual football stadiums in *NCAA Football.* As the district court found, Keller is represented as "what he was: the starting quarterback for Arizona State" and Nebraska, and "the game's setting is identical to where the public found [Keller] during his collegiate career: on the football field." *Keller v. Elec. Arts, Inc.,* No. C 09–1967 CW, 2010 WL 530108, at *5 (N.D.Cal. Feb. 8, 2010).

[19] EA argues that the district court erred in focusing primarily on Keller's likeness and ignoring the transformative elements of the game as a whole. Judge Thomas, our dissenting colleague, suggests the same. *See* Dissent at 1285. We are unable to say that there was any error, particularly in light of *No Doubt,* which reasoned much the same as the district court in this case: "that the avatars appear in the context of a videogame that contains many other creative elements[ ] does not transform the avatars into anything other than exact depictions of No Doubt's members doing exactly what they do as celebrities." *No Doubt,* 122 Cal.Rptr.3d at 411.[7] EA suggests that the fact that *NCAA Football* users can

---

[6] We also briefly addressed the transformative use test in a footnote in *Hoffman v. Capital Cities/ABC, Inc.,* 255 F.3d 1180 (9th Cir. 2001). We indicated that if we had considered the test, we would have concluded that an image of Dustin Hoffman from "Tootsie" that had been altered to make it appear like he was wearing fashions from a decade later "contained 'significant transformative elements.' " *Id.* at 1184 n. 2; 1182–83. "Hoffman's body was eliminated and a new, differently clothed body was substituted in its place. In fact, the entire theory of Hoffman's case rests on his allegation that the photograph is not a 'true' or 'literal' depiction of him, but a false portrayal." *Id.* at 1184 n. 2.

[7] Judge Thomas argues that the "sheer number of virtual actors," the absence of "any evidence as to the personal marketing power of Sam Keller," and the relative anonymity of each individual player

alter the characteristics of the avatars in the game is significant. Again, our dissenting colleague agrees. *See* Dissent at 1286–87. In *No Doubt,* the California Court of Appeal noted that *Band Hero* "d[id] not permit players to alter the No Doubt avatars in any respect." *Id.* at 410. The court went on to say that the No Doubt avatars "remain at all times immutable images of the real celebrity musicians, in stark contrast to the 'fanciful, creative characters' in *Winter* and *Kirby*." *Id.* The court explained further:

> [I]t is the differences between *Kirby* and the instant case … which are determinative. In *Kirby,* the pop singer was portrayed as an entirely new character—the space-age news reporter Ulala. In *Band Hero,* by contrast, no matter what else occurs in the game during the depiction of the No Doubt avatars, the avatars perform rock songs, the same activity by which the band achieved and maintains its fame. Moreover, the avatars perform those songs as literal recreations of the band members. That the avatars can be manipulated to perform at fanciful venues including outer space or to sing songs the real band would object to singing, or that the avatars appear in the context of a videogame that contains many other creative elements, does not transform the avatars into anything other than exact depictions of No Doubt's members doing exactly what they do as celebrities.

Id. at 410–11. Judge Thomas says that "[t]he Court of Appeal cited character immutability as a chief factor distinguishing [*No Doubt*] from *Winter* and *Kirby*." Dissent at 1287. Though No Doubt certainly mentioned the immutability of the avatars, we do not read the California Court of Appeal's decision as turning on the inability of users to alter the avatars. The key contrast with *Winter* and *Kirby* was that in those games the public figures were transformed into "fanciful, creative characters" or "portrayed as … entirely new character[s]." *No Doubt,* 122 Cal.Rptr.3d at 410. On this front, our case is clearly aligned with *No Doubt,* not with *Winter* and *Kirby*. We believe No Doubt offers a persuasive precedent that cannot be materially distinguished from Keller's case.[8],[9]

---

in *NCAA Football* as compared to the public figures in other California right-of-publicity cases all mitigate in favor of finding that the EA's First Amendment rights outweigh Keller's right of publicity. *See* Dissent at 1286–88. These facts are not irrelevant to the analysis—they all can be considered in the framework of the five considerations from *Comedy III* laid out above—but the fact is that EA elected to use avatars that mimic real college football players for a reason. If EA did not think there was value in having an avatar designed to mimic each individual player, it would not go to the lengths it does to achieve realism in this regard. Having chosen to use the players' likenesses, EA cannot now hide behind the numerosity of its potential offenses or the alleged unimportance of any one individual player.

[8] EA further argues that *No Doubt* is distinguishable because the video game company in that case entered into a license agreement which it allegedly breached. However, the California Court of Appeal did not rely on breach of contract in its analysis of whether the game was transformative. 122 Cal.Rptr.3d at 412 n. 7. Keller asserts here that EA contracted away its First Amendment rights in a licensing agreement with the NCAA that purportedly prohibited the use of athlete likenesses. However, in light of our conclusion that EA is not entitled to a First Amendment defense as a matter of law, we need not reach this issue and leave it for the district court to address in the first instance on remand should the finder of fact determine in post-SLAPP proceedings that EA's use is transformative.

[9] In dissent, Judge Thomas suggests that this case is distinguishable from other right-to-publicity cases because "an individual college athlete's right of publicity is extraordinarily circumscribed and, in practical reality, nonexistent" because "NCAA rules prohibit athletes from benefitting economically from any success on the field." Dissent at 1289. Judge Thomas commendably addresses the fairness of this structure, *see* Dissent at 1289 n. 5, but setting fairness aside, the fact is that college athletes are not indefinitely bound by NCAA rules. Once an athlete graduates from college, for instance, the athlete can capitalize on his success on the field during college in any number of ways. EA's use of a college athlete's likeness interferes with the athlete's right to capitalize on his athletic success once he is beyond the dominion of NCAA rule.

[20] The Third Circuit came to the same conclusion in *Hart v. Electronic Arts, Inc.,* 717 F. 3d 141 (3d Cir. 2013). In *Hart,* EA faced a materially identical challenge under New Jersey right-of-publicity law, brought by former Rutgers quarterback Ryan Hart. *See id.* at 163 n. 28 ("*Keller* is simply [*Hart*] incarnated in California."). Though the Third Circuit was tasked with interpreting New Jersey law, the court looked to the transformative use test developed in California. *See id.* at 158 n. 23 (noting that the right-of-publicity laws are "strikingly similar … and protect similar interests" in New Jersey and California, and that "consequently [there is] no issue in applying balancing tests developed in California to New Jersey"); *see also id.* at 165 (holding that "the Transformative Use Test is the proper analytical framework to apply to cases such as the one at bar"). Applying the test, the court held that "the *NCAA Football* … games at issue … do not sufficiently transform [Hart]'s identity to escape the right of publicity claim," reversing the district court's grant of summary judgment to EA. *Id.* at 170.

[21] As we have, the Third Circuit considered the potentially transformative nature of the game as a whole, *id.* at 166, 169, and the user's ability to alter avatar characteristics, *id.* at 166– 68. Asserting that "the lack of transformative context is even more pronounced here than in *No Doubt,*" *id.* at 166, and that "the ability to modify the avatar counts for little where the appeal of the game lies in users' ability to play as, or alongside [,] their preferred players or team," *id.* at 168 (internal quotation marks omitted), the Third Circuit agreed with us that these changes do not render the *NCAA Football* games sufficiently transformative to defeat a right-of-publicity claim.

[22] Judge Ambro dissented in *Hart,* concluding that "the creative components of *NCAA Football* contain sufficient expressive transformation to merit First Amendment protection." *Id.* at 175 (Ambro, J., dissenting). But in critiquing the majority opinion, Judge Ambro disregarded *No Doubt* and *Kirby* because "they were not decided by the architect of the Transformative Use Test, the Supreme Court of California." *Id.* at 172 n. 4. He thus "d[id] not attempt to explain or distinguish the[se cases'] holdings except to note that [he] believe[s] *No Doubt,* which focused on individual depictions rather than the work in its entirety, was wrongly decided in light of the prior precedent in *Comedy III* and *Winter.*" *Id.* We recognize that we are bound only by the decisions of a state's highest court and not by decisions of the state's intermediate appellate court when considering state law issues sitting in diversity jurisdiction. *See In re Kirkland,* 915 F.2d 1236, 1238–39 (9th Cir. 1990). Nonetheless, where there is no binding precedent from the state's highest court, we "must predict how the highest state court would decide the issue using *intermediate appellate court decisions,* decisions from other jurisdictions, statutes, treatises, and restatements as guidance." *Id.* at 1239 (emphasis added). As stated above, we believe *No Doubt* in particular provides persuasive guidance. We do not believe *No Doubt* to be inconsistent with the California Supreme Court's relevant decisions, and we will not disregard a well-reasoned decision from a state's intermediate appellate court in this context. Like the majority in *Hart,* we rely substantially on *No Doubt,* and believe we are correct to do so.

[23] Given that *NCAA Football* realistically portrays college football players in the context of college football games, the district court was correct in concluding that EA cannot prevail as a matter of law based on the transformative use defense at the anti-SLAPP stage. *Cf. Hilton,* 599 F.3d at 910–11.[10]

---

[10] Judge Thomas asserts that "[t]he logical consequence of the majority view is that all realistic depictions of actual persons, no matter how incidental, are protected by a state law right of publicity regardless of the creative context," "jeopardiz[ing] the creative use of historic figures in motion pictures, books, and sound recordings." Dissent at 1290. We reject the notion that our holding has such broad consequences. As discussed above, one of the factors identified in *Comedy III* "requires an examination of whether a likely purchaser's primary motivation is to buy a reproduction of the celebrity, or to buy the expressive work of that artist." McCarthy, *supra,* § 8:72; *see Comedy III,* 106 Cal.Rptr.2d 126, 21 P.3d at 809. Certainly this leaves room for distinguishing between this case—

B

[24] EA urges us to adopt for right-of-publicity claims the broader First Amendment defense that we have previously adopted in the context of false endorsement claims under the Lanham Act: the *Rogers* test.[11] *See Brown v. Elec. Arts*, 724 F.3d at 1239–41, 2013 WL 3927736, at *1–2 (applying the *Rogers* test to a Lanham Act claim brought by former NFL player Jim Brown relating to the use of his likeness in EA's *Madden NFL* video games).

. . . .

[25] In this case, EA argues that we should extend this test, created to evaluate Lanham Act claims, to apply to right-of-publicity claims because it is "less prone to misinterpretation" and "more protective of free expression" than the transformative use defense. Although we acknowledge that there is some overlap between the transformative use test formulated by the California Supreme Court and the *Rogers* test, we disagree that the *Rogers* test should be imported wholesale for right-of-publicity claims. Our conclusion on this point is consistent with the Third Circuit's rejection of EA's identical argument in *Hart. See Hart*, 717 F. 3d at 154– 58. As the history and development of the *Rogers* test makes clear, it was designed to protect consumers from the risk of consumer confusion—the hallmark element of a Lanham Act claim. *See Cairns v. Franklin Mint Co.*, 292 F.3d 1139, 1149 (9th Cir. 2002). The right of publicity, on the other hand, does not primarily seek to prevent consumer confusion. *See Hart*, 717 F. 3d at 158 ("[T]he right of publicity does not implicate the potential for consumer confusion . . . ."). Rather, it primarily "protects a form of intellectual property [in one's person] that society deems to have some social utility." *Comedy III*, 106 Cal.Rptr.2d 126, 21 P.3d at 804. As the California Supreme Court has explained:

> Often considerable money, time and energy are needed to develop one's prominence in a particular field. Years of labor may be required before one's skill, reputation, notoriety or virtues are sufficiently developed to permit an economic return through some medium of commercial promotion. For some, the investment may eventually create considerable commercial value in one's identity.

Id. 106 Cal.Rptr.2d 126, 21 P.3d at 804–05 (internal quotation marks and citations omitted).

[26] The right of publicity protects the *celebrity*, not the *consumer*. Keller's publicity claim is not founded on an allegation that consumers are being illegally misled into believing that he is endorsing EA or its products. Indeed, he would be hard-pressed to support such an allegation absent evidence that EA explicitly misled consumers into holding such a belief. *See Brown v. Elec. Arts*, 724 F.3d at 1242–43, 2013 WL 3927736, at *4 (holding under the *Rogers* test that, since "Brown's likeness is artistically relevant to the [*Madden NFL*] games and there are no alleged facts to support the claim that EA explicitly misled consumers as to Brown's involvement with the games," "the public interest in free expression outweighs the public interest in avoiding consumer confusion"). Instead, Keller's claim is that EA has appropriated, without permission and without providing compensation, his talent and years of hard work on the football field. The reasoning of the *Rogers* and *Mattel* courts—that artistic and literary works should be protected unless they explicitly mislead consumers—is simply not responsive to Keller's asserted interests here. *Cf. Hart*, 717 F. 3d at 157 ("Effectively, [EA] argues that [Hart] should be unable to assert a claim for appropriating his likeness as a football player precisely

---

where we have emphasized EA's primary emphasis on reproducing reality—and cases involving other kinds of expressive works.

[11] Keller argues that EA never asked the district court to apply *Rogers* and has therefore waived the issue on appeal. Although it could have been more explicit, EA's anti-SLAPP motion did cite *Rogers* and argue that Keller had not alleged that his likeness was "wholly unrelated" to the content of the video game or a "disguised commercial advertisement," the two prongs of the *Rogers* test.

because his likeness was used for a game about football. Adopting this line of reasoning threatens to turn the right of publicity on its head.").

. . . .

III

[27] Under California's transformative use defense, EA's use of the likenesses of college athletes like Samuel Keller in its video games is not, as a matter of law, protected by the First Amendment. We reject EA's suggestion to import the *Rogers* test into the right-of-publicity arena, and conclude that state law defenses for the reporting of information do not protect EA's use.

AFFIRMED.

THOMAS, Circuit Judge, dissenting:

[1] Because the creative and transformative elements of Electronic Arts' *NCAA Football* video game series predominate over the commercial use of the athletes' likenesses, the First Amendment protects EA from liability. Therefore, I respectfully dissent.

I

[2] As expressive works, video games are entitled to First Amendment protection. *Brown v. Entm't Merchs. Ass'n*, --- U.S. ----, 131 S.Ct. 2729 (2011). The First Amendment affords additional protection to *NCAA Football* because it involves a subject of substantial public interest: collegiate football. *Moore v. Univ. of Notre Dame*, 968 F.Supp. 1330, 1337 (N.D.Ind.1997). Because football is a matter of public interest, the use of the images of athletes is entitled to constitutional protection, even if profits are involved. *Montana v. San Jose Mercury News, Inc.*, 34 Cal.App.4th 790, 40 Cal.Rptr.2d 639, 643 n. 2 (1995); *see also* Cal. Civ.Code § 3344(d) (exempting from liability the "use of a name . . . or likeness in connection with any . . . public affairs, or sports broadcast or account").

[3] Where it is recognized, the tort of appropriation is a creature of common law or statute, depending on the jurisdiction. However, the right to compensation for the misappropriation for commercial use of one's image or celebrity is far from absolute. In every jurisdiction, any right of publicity must be balanced against the constitutional protection afforded by the First Amendment. Courts have employed a variety of methods in balancing the rights. *See, e.g., Doe v. TCI Cablevision*, 110 S.W.3d 363, 374 (Mo.2003) (en banc). The California Supreme Court applies a "transformative use" test it formulated in *Comedy III Productions, Inc. v. Gary Saderup, Inc.*, 25 Cal.4th 387, 106 Cal.Rptr.2d 126, 21 P.3d 797 (2001).[1]

[4] As the majority properly notes, the transformative use defense is "a balancing test between the First Amendment and the right of publicity based on whether the work in question adds significant creative elements so as to be transformed into something more than a mere celebrity likeness or imitation." *Comedy III*, 106 Cal.Rptr.2d 126, 21 P.3d at 799. The rationale for the test, as the majority notes, is that "when a work contains significant transformative elements, it is not only especially worthy of First Amendment protection, but it is also less likely to interfere with the economic interest protected by the right of publicity." *Id.* 106 Cal.Rptr.2d 126, 21 P.3d at 808.

---

[1] I agree with the majority that the test articulated in *Rogers v. Grimaldi*, 875 F.2d 994 (2d Cir. 1989), should not be employed in this context. The *Rogers* test is appropriately applied in Lanham Act cases, where the primary concern is with the danger of consumer confusion when a work is depicted as something it is not. 15 U.S.C. § 1125(a)(1). However, the right of publicity is an economic right to use the value of one own's celebrity. *Zacchini v. Scripps–Howard Broad. Co.*, 433 U.S. 562, 576–77, 97 S.Ct. 2849, 53 L.Ed.2d 965 (1977). Therefore, a more nuanced balancing is required. In our context, I believe the transformative use test—if correctly applied to the work as a whole—provides the proper analytical framework.

[5] The five considerations articulated in *Comedy III*, and cited by the majority, are whether: (1) the celebrity likeness is one of the raw materials from which an original work is synthesized; (2) the work is primarily the defendant's own expression if the expression is something other than the likeness of the celebrity; (3) the literal and imitative or creative elements predominate in the work; (4) the marketability and economic value of the challenged work derives primarily from the fame of the celebrity depicted; and (5) an artist's skill and talent has been manifestly subordinated to the overall goal of creating a conventional portrait of a celebrity so as to commercially exploit the celebrity's fame. *Id.* 106 Cal.Rptr.2d 126, 21 P.3d at 809–10.

[6] Although these considerations are often distilled as analytical factors, Justice Mosk was careful in *Comedy III* not to label them as such. Indeed, the focus of *Comedy III* is a more holistic examination of whether the transformative and creative elements of a particular work predominate over commercially based literal or imitative depictions. The distinction is critical, because excessive deconstruction of *Comedy III* can lead to misapplication of the test. And it is at this juncture that I must respectfully part ways with my colleagues in the majority.

[7] The majority confines its inquiry to how a single athlete's likeness is represented in the video game, rather than examining the transformative and creative elements in the video game as a whole. In my view, this approach contradicts the holistic analysis required by the transformative use test. *See Hart v. Elec. Arts, Inc.,* 717 F. 3d 141, 170– 76 (3d Cir. 2013) (Ambro, J., dissenting).[2] The salient question is whether the entire work is transformative, and whether the transformative elements predominate, rather than whether an individual persona or image has been altered.

[8] When EA's *NCAA Football* video game series is examined carefully, and put in proper context, I conclude that the creative and transformative elements of the games predominate over the commercial use of the likenesses of the athletes within the games.

A

[9] The first step in conducting a balancing is to examine the creative work at issue. At its essence, EA's *NCAA Football* is a work of interactive historical fiction. Although the game changes from year to year, its most popular features predominately involve role-playing by the gamer. For example, a player can create a virtual image of himself as a potential college football player. The virtual player decides which position he would like to play, then participates in a series of "tryouts" or competes in an entire high school season to gauge his skill. Based on his performance, the virtual player is ranked and available to play at select colleges. The player chooses among the colleges, then assumes the role of a college football player. He also selects a major, the amount of time he wishes to spend on social activities, and practice—all of which may affect the virtual player's performance. He then plays his position on the college team. In some versions of the game, in another mode, the virtual player can engage in a competition for the Heisman Trophy. In another popular mode, the gamer becomes a virtual coach. The coach scouts, recruits, and develops entirely fictional players for his team. The coach can then promote the team's evolution over decades of seasons.

[10] The college teams that are supplied in the game do replicate the actual college teams for that season, including virtual athletes who bear the statistical and physical dimensions of the actual college athletes. But, unlike their professional football counterparts in the *Madden NFL* series, the NCAA football players in these games are not identified.

[11] The gamers can also change their abilities, appearances, and physical characteristics at will. Keller's impressive physical likeness can be morphed by the gamer into an overweight and slow virtual athlete, with anemic passing ability. And the gamer can create new virtual players out of whole cloth.

---

[2] I agree fully with Judge Ambro's excellent dissent in *Hart,* which describes the analytic flaws of applying a transformative use test outside the context of the work as a whole.

Players can change teams. The gamer could pit Sam Keller against himself, or a stronger or weaker version of himself, on a different team. Or the gamer could play the game endlessly without ever encountering Keller's avatar. In the simulated games, the gamer controls not only the conduct of the game, but the weather, crowd noise, mascots, and other environmental factors. Of course, one may play the game leaving the players unaltered, pitting team against team. But, in this context as well, the work is one of historic fiction. The gamer controls the teams, players, and games.

[12] Applying the *Comedy III* considerations to *NCAA Football* in proper holistic context, the considerations favor First Amendment protection. The athletic likenesses are but one of the raw materials from which the broader game is constructed. The work, considered as a whole, is primarily one of EA's own expression. The creative and transformative elements predominate over the commercial use of likenesses. The marketability and economic value of the game comes from the creative elements within, not from the pure commercial exploitation of a celebrity image. The game is not a conventional portrait of a celebrity, but a work consisting of many creative and transformative elements.

[13] The video game at issue is much akin to the creations the California Supreme Court found protected in *Winter v. DC Comics,* 30 Cal.4th 881, 134 Cal.Rptr.2d 634, 69 P.3d 473, 476 (2003), where the two fabled guitarists Johnny and Edgar Winter were easily identifiable, but depicted as chimeras. It is also consistent with the California Court of Appeal's decision in *Kirby v. Sega of America, Inc.,* 144 Cal.App.4th 47, 50 Cal.Rptr.3d 607, 609–10 (2006), where a character easily identified as singer Kierin Kirby, more popularly known as Lady Miss Kier, was transformed into a "'fanciful, creative character' who exists in the context of a unique and expressive video game." *Id.* at 618. So, too, are the virtual players who populate the world of the *NCAA Football* series.

[14] *No Doubt v. Activision Publishing, Inc.,* 192 Cal.App.4th 1018, 122 Cal.Rptr.3d 397 (2011), is not to the contrary. The literal representations in *No Doubt* were not, and could not be, transformed in any way. Indeed, in *No Doubt,* the bandmembers posed for motion-capture photography to allow reproduction of their likenesses, *id.* at 402, and the Court of Appeal underscored the fact that the video game did not "permit players to alter the No Doubt avatars in any respect" and the avatars remained "at all times immutable images of the real celebrity musicians," *id.* at 410. The Court of Appeal cited character immutability as a chief factor distinguishing that case from *Winter* and *Kirby. Id.* Unlike the avatars in *No Doubt,* the virtual players in NCAA Football are completely mutable and changeable at the whim of the gamer. The majority places great reliance on *No Doubt* as support for its proposition that the initial placement of realistic avatars in the game overcomes the First Amendment's protection, but the Court of Appeal in *No Doubt* rejected such a cramped construction, noting that "even literal reproductions of celebrities may be 'transformed' into expressive works based on the context into which the celebrity image is placed." *Id.* at 410 (citing *Comedy III,* 106 Cal.Rptr.2d 126, 21 P.3d at 797).[3]

[15] Unlike the majority, I would not punish EA for the realism of its games and for the skill of the artists who created realistic settings for the football games. Majority op. at 1279 n. 10. That the lifelike roar of the crowd and the crunch of pads contribute to the gamer's experience demonstrates how little of *NCAA Football* is driven by the particular likeness of Sam Keller, or any of the other plaintiffs, rather than by the game's artistic elements.

[16] In short, considering the creative elements alone in this case satisfies the transformative use test in favor of First Amendment protection.

---

[3] Of course, to the extent that the Court of Appeal's opinion in *No Doubt* may be read to be in tension with the transformative use test as articulated by the California Supreme Court in *Comedy III* and *Winter,* it must yield.

B

[17] Although one could leave the analysis with an examination of the transformative and creative aspects of the game, a true balancing requires an inquiry as to the other side of the scales: the publicity right at stake. Here, as well, the *NCAA Football* video game series can be distinguished from the traditional right of publicity cases, both from a quantitative and a qualitative perspective.

[18] As a quantitative matter, *NCAA Football* is different from other right of publicity cases in the sheer number of virtual actors involved. Most right of publicity cases involve either one celebrity, or a finite and defined group of celebrities. *Comedy III* involved literal likenesses of the Three Stooges. *Hilton v. Hallmark Cards*, 599 F.3d 894, 909–12 (9th Cir. 2009), involved the literal likeness of Paris Hilton. *Winter* involved the images of the rock star brother duo. *Kirby* involved the likeness of one singer. *No Doubt* focused on the likenesses of the members of a specific legendary band.

[19] In contrast, *NCAA Football* includes not just Sam Keller, but thousands of virtual actors. This consideration is of particular significance when we examine, as instructed by *Comedy III*, whether the source of the product marketability comes from creative elements or from pure exploitation of a celebrity image. 106 Cal.Rptr.2d 126, 21 P.3d at 810. There is not, at this stage of the litigation, any evidence as to the personal marketing power of Sam Keller, as distinguished from the appeal of the creative aspects of the product. Regardless, the sheer number of athletes involved inevitably diminish the significance of the publicity right at issue. *Comedy III* involved literal depictions of the Three Stooges on lithographs and T-shirts. *Winter* involved characters depicted in a comic strip. *Kirby* and *No Doubt* involved pivotal characters in a video game. The commercial image of the celebrities in each case was central to the production, and its contact with the consumer was immediate and unavoidable. In contrast, one could play *NCAA Football* thousands of times without ever encountering a particular avatar. In context of the collective, an individual's publicity right is relatively insignificant. Put another way, if an anonymous virtual player is tackled in an imaginary video game and no one notices, is there any right of publicity infringed at all?

[20] The sheer quantity of the virtual players in the game underscores the inappropriateness of analyzing the right of publicity through the lens of one likeness only. Only when the creative work is considered in complete context can a proper analysis be conducted.

[21] As a qualitative matter, the essence of *NCAA Football* is founded on publicly available data, which is not protected by any individual publicity rights. It is true that EA solicits and receives information directly from colleges and universities. But the information is hardly proprietary. Personal vital statistics for players are found in college programs and media guides. Likewise, playing statistics are easily available. In this respect, the information used by EA is indistinguishable from the information used in fantasy athletic leagues, for which the First Amendment provides protection, *C.B.C. Distribution & Mktg., Inc. v. Major League Baseball Advanced Media, L.P.*, 505 F.3d 818, 823–24 (8th Cir. 2007), or much beloved statistical board games, such as Strat–O–Matic. An athlete's right of publicity simply does not encompass publicly available statistical data. *See, e.g., IMS Health Inc. v. Sorrell*, 630 F.3d 263, 271–72 (2d Cir. 2010) ("The First Amendment protects '[e]ven dry information, devoid of advocacy, political relevance, or artistic expression.'" (quoting *Universal City Studios, Inc. v. Corley*, 273 F.3d 429, 446 (2d Cir. 2001)) (alteration in original)).[4]

[22] Further, the structure of the game is not founded on exploitation of an individual's publicity rights. The players are unidentified and anonymous. It is true that third-party software is available to

---

[4] Contrary to the majority's suggestion, I do not claim that any use of a likeness founded on publicly available information is transformative. Majority op. 1283–84 n. 12. The majority's analogy to a commercial featuring Tom Brady is inapposite for at least two reasons: (1) a commercial is not interactive in the same way that *NCAA Football* is, and (2) Brady's marketing power is well established, while that of the plaintiffs is not.

quickly identify the players, but that is not part of the EA package. And the fact that the players can be identified by the knowledgeable user by their position, team, and statistics is somewhat beside the point. The issue is whether the marketability of the product is driven by an individual celebrity, or by the game itself. *Comedy III,* 106 Cal.Rptr.2d 126, 21 P.3d at 810. Player anonymity, while certainly not a complete defense, bears on the question of how we balance the right of publicity against the First Amendment. This feature of the game places it in stark contrast with *No Doubt,* where the whole point of the enterprise was the successful commercial exploitation of the specifically identified, world-famous musicians.

[23] Finally, as a qualitative matter, the publicity rights of college athletes are remarkably restricted. This consideration is critical because the "right to exploit commercially one's celebrity is primarily an economic right." *Gionfriddo v. Major League Baseball,* 94 Cal.App.4th 400, 114 Cal.Rptr.2d 307, 318 (2001). NCAA rules prohibit athletes from benefitting economically from any success on the field. NCAA Bylaw 12.5 specifically prohibits commercial licensing of an NCAA athlete's name or picture. NCAA, *2012–13 NCAA Division I Manual* § 12.5.2.1 (2012). Before being allowed to compete each year, all Division I NCAA athletes must sign a contract stating that they understand the prohibition on licensing and affirming that they have not violated any amateurism rules. In short, even if an athlete wished to license his image to EA, the athlete could not do so without destroying amateur status. Thus, an individual college athlete's right of publicity is extraordinarily circumscribed and, in practical reality, nonexistent.[5]

[24] In sum, even apart from consideration of transformative elements, examination of the right of publicity in question also resolves the balance in favor of the First Amendment. The quantity of players involved dilutes the commercial impact of any particular player and the scope of the publicity right is significantly reduced by the fact that: (1) a player cannot own the individual, publicly available statistics on which the game is based; (2) the players are not identified in the game; and (3) NCAA college athletes do not have the right to license their names and likenesses, even if they chose to do so.[6]

II

---

[5] The issue of whether this structure is fair to the student athlete is beyond the scope of this appeal, but forms a significant backdrop to the discussion. The NCAA received revenues of $871.6 million in fiscal year 2011–12, with 81% of the money coming from television and marketing fees. However, few college athletes will ever receive any professional compensation. The NCAA reports that in 2011, there were 67,887 college football players. Of those, 15,086 were senior players, and only 255 athletes were drafted for a professional team. Thus, only 1.7% of seniors received any subsequent professional economic compensation for their athletic endeavors. NCAA, *Estimated Probability of Competing in Athletics Beyond the High School Interscholastic Level* (2011), *available at* http:// www. ncaa. org/ wps/ wcm/ connect/ public/ ncaa/ pdfs/ 2011/ 2011+ probability+ of+ going+ pro.

And participation in college football can come at a terrible cost. The NCAA reports that, during a recent five-year period, college football players suffered 41,000 injuries, including 23 non-fatal catastrophic injuries and 11 fatalities from indirect catastrophic injuries. NCAA, *Football Injuries: Data From the 2004/05 to 2008/09 Seasons, available at* http:// www. ncaa. org/ wps/ wcm/ connect/ public/ ncaa/ health+ and+ safety/ sports+ injuries/ resources/ football+ injuries.

[6] While acknowledging that these considerations are relevant to the *Comedy III* analysis, the majority says EA's use of realistic likenesses demonstrates that it sees "value in having an avatar designed to mimic each individual player." Majority op. at 1276 n. 7. But the same is true of any right of publicity case. The defendants in *Winter* saw value in using comic book characters that resembled the Winter brothers. Andy Warhol—whose portraits were discussed in *Comedy III*—saw value in using images of celebrities such as Marilyn Monroe. In those cases, the products' marketability derives primarily from the creative elements, not from a pure commercial exploitation of a celebrity image. The same is true of *NCAA Football.*

[25] Given the proper application of the transformative use test, Keller is unlikely to prevail. The balance of interests falls squarely on the side of the First Amendment. The stakes are not small. The logical consequence of the majority view is that all realistic depictions of actual persons, no matter how incidental, are protected by a state law right of publicity regardless of the creative context. This logic jeopardizes the creative use of historic figures in motion pictures, books, and sound recordings. Absent the use of actual footage, the motion picture *Forrest Gump* might as well be just a box of chocolates. Without its historical characters, *Midnight in Paris* would be reduced to a pedestrian domestic squabble. The majority's holding that creative use of realistic images and personas does not satisfy the transformative use test cannot be reconciled with the many cases affording such works First Amendment protection.[7] I respectfully disagree with this potentially dangerous and out-of-context interpretation of the transformative use test.

[26] For these reasons, I respectfully dissent.

---

[7] *See, e.g., ETW Corp. v. Jireh Publ'g, Inc.,* 332 F.3d 915 (6th Cir. 2003) (affording First Amendment protection to an artist's use of photographs of Tiger Woods); J. Thomas McCarthy, *The Rights of Publicity and Privacy* § 8.65 (2013 ed.) (collecting cases); *Hart,* 717 F. 3d at 173 (Ambro, J., dissenting) (describing cases).

***Winter v. DC Comics,* 30 Cal.4th 881 (2003)**

Kirby v. Sega of America, Inc., 144 Cal.App.4th 47 (2006)

No Doubt v. Activision Publishing, Inc., 192 Cal.App.4th 1018 (2011)

Hilton v. Hallmark Cards, 599 F.3d 894 (9th Cir. 2010)

Comments and Questions

1. *Keller Settlement.* In June 2014, the NCAA announced a $20 million settlement with Samuel Keller, the lead plaintiff in *In re NCAA Student-Athlete Name & Likeness Licensing Litigation*. This is in addition to a previous $40,000,000 settlement Electronic Arts and Collegiate Licensing Company announced to settle a variety of lawsuits, including Keller's, over use of collegiate athletes' likenesses in video games. The total $60 million settlement fund was distributed among approximately 75,000 potentially eligible NCAA football and male basketball athletes with a cap of $5,000 per roster appearance per video game, with many athletes receiving significantly less than this amount. *See* Jon Solomon, *EA and NCAA Video Game Settlements Have a $5,000-a-Year Cap*, CBSSports.com, June 30, 2014, http://www.cbssports.com/collegefootball/writer/jon-solomon/24601765/ea-and-ncaa-video-game-settlements-have-5000-a-year-cap.

2. *The Fate of EA's* NCAA Football *Series.* In September 2013, EA announced that it would not produce a new NCAA Football video game in 2014, making *NCAA Football 2014* the final instalment in the series. EA did so after the NCAA and three major football conferences (the Big Ten, Pac-12, and SEC) cut ties with EA in light of the college players' intellectual property litigation against EA. *See* Steve Eder, *E.A. Sports Settles Lawsuit With College Athletes*, N.Y. TIMES, Sept. 26, 2013, http://www.nytimes.com/2013/09/27/sports/ncaafootball/ea-sports-wont-make-college-video-game-in-2014.html?_r=0.

3. *Using Right of Publicity to Evade* Rogers. Like the Keller case, Jim Brown's litigation against Electronic Arts provides a good example of the differences between trademark law's defendant-friendly approach to expressive uses and right of publicity law's plaintiff-friendly approach. In *Brown v. Electronic Arts*, 724 F.3d 1235 (9th Cir. 2013), involving EA's unauthorized use of Brown's likeness in a video game, the Ninth Circuit invoked *Rogers* to rule against Brown on his § 43(a) claim. But not all was lost for him. He subsequently amended his complaint to add a California state right of publicity claim. EA eventually settled the case for $600,000. *See* JENNIFER E. ROTHMAN, THE RIGHT OF PUBLICITY 159 (2018); Darren Rovell, *Jim Brown Receives $600,000 to Dismiss Lawsuit Against Electronic Arts*, ESPN, June 28, 2016, https://perma.cc/5DUZ-SA2B.

4. *Celebrities' Right of Publicity and Social Media.* In April 2014 American actress and celebrity Katherine Hegel sued the drugstore chain Duane Reade for posting the tweet and photograph shown below. She claimed violation of federal false advertising law under Lanham Act § 43(a), 15 U.S.C. § 1125(a), and New York state right of publicity law under N.Y. Civil Rights Law §§ 50 & 51. In August 2014, the parties announced a settlement in which Duane Reade agreed to make a contribution of an undisclosed amount to a Katherine Heigl charity. *See* Eriq Gardner, *Katherine Heigl Ends Lawsuit Over Duane Reade Tweet, Hollywood Reporter*, Aug. 27, 2014, http://www.hollywoodreporter.com/thresq/katherine-heigl-ends-lawsuit-duane-728552.

5. *Non-Celebrities Right of Publicity and Social Media.* In 2011, Facebook introduced its "Sponsored Stories" feature, which established as a default setting the insertion of advertisements into a user's newsfeed based on recent conduct by the user, such as Like-ing an advertiser's Facebook page or sharing location-based check-in information related to an advertiser. Distinguished only by the heading "Sponsored Story," these advertisements looked very similar to a user's status updates (see below). Facebook users brought a class action asserting violation of users' right of publicity under California Civil Code § 3344(a). After the Northern District of California rejected Facebook's motion to dismiss under § 3344(d)'s newsworthiness exception, *Fraley v. Facebook, Inc.*, 830 F. Supp. 2d 785 (N.D. Cal. 2011), Facebook ended its Sponsored Stories program and paid $20 million to settle the dispute. *See* Mike Wheatley, *Facebook Kills "Sponsored Stories" but Your Face Will Still Be Used in Ads*, SiliconANGLE.com, Jan. 13, 2014, http://siliconangle.com/blog/2014/01/13/facebook-kills-sponsored-stories-but-your-face-will-still-be-used-in-its-ads/. In a press release, Facebook announced a different approach: "Last year . . . [w]e also announced that marketers will no longer be able to purchase sponsored stories separately; instead, social context—stories about social actions your friends have taken, such as liking a page or checking in to a restaurant—is now eligible to appear next to all ads shown to friends on Facebook." *An Update to Facebook Ads*, Facebook.com Jan. 9, 2014, https://www.facebook.com/notes/facebook-and-privacy/an-update-to-facebook-ads/643198592396693.

---

1   From   http://siliconangle.com/blog/2014/01/13/facebook-kills-sponsored-stories-but-your-face-will-still-be-used-in-its-ads/.

VI. Remedies

A. Injunctive Relief

Lanham Act § 34(a), 15 U.S.C. § 1116(a)

> The several courts vested with jurisdiction of civil actions arising under this chapter shall have power to grant injunctions, according to the principles of equity and upon such terms as the court may deem reasonable, to prevent the violation of any right of the registrant of a mark registered in the Patent and Trademark Office or to prevent a violation under subsection (a), (c), or (d) of section 1125 of this title.

The primary remedy that most trademark and false advertising plaintiffs seek is injunctive relief, often in the form of a preliminary injunction. Though the circuits' criteria for a preliminary (or permanent) injunction vary somewhat, most circuits have traditionally required the plaintiff to show: (1) a likelihood of success on the merits, (2) a likelihood of irreparable harm in the absence of the injunction, (3) that the balance of the hardships tip in the movant's favor, and (4) that the injunction would not be adverse to the public interest. The Second Circuit, by contrast, has formulated a different test: "A party seeking a preliminary injunction must establish (1) irreparable harm and (2) either (a) a likelihood of success on the merits or (b) a sufficiently serious question going to the merits and a balance of hardships tipping decidedly in the moving party's favor." *Brennan's, Inc. v. Brennan's Rest., L.L.C.*, 360 F.3d 125, 129 (2d Cir. 2004).

Most circuits have traditionally held that a showing of a likelihood of confusion triggers a presumption of irreparable harm. *See, e.g., Federal Exp. Corp. v. Federal Espresso, Inc.*, 201 F.3d 168, 174 (2d Cir. 2000) ("[P]roof of a likelihood of confusion would create a presumption of irreparable harm, and thus a plaintiff would not need to prove such harm independently"); *GoTo.com, Inc. v. Walt Disney Co.*, 202 F.3d 1199, 1209 (9th Cir. 2000) ("From our analysis of the *Sleekcraft* factors, we conclude that GoTo has demonstrated a likelihood of success on its claim that Disney's use of its logo violates the Lanham Act. From this showing of likelihood of success on the merits in this trademark infringement claim, we may presume irreparable injury.").

However, as the following two opinions show, the Supreme Court's decision in *eBay Inc. v. MercExchange, LLC*, 547 U.S. 388 (2006), has significantly complicated this line of doctrine. *eBay* was a patent case. Do you accept the application of its reasoning and holding to trademark law, and in particular, the precise manner in which the Ninth Circuit applies *eBay* in *Herb Reed*?

Herb Reed (1928-2012) is at the 3 o'clock position.

Herb Reed Enterprises, LLC v. Florida Entertainment Management, Inc.
736 F.3d 1239 (9th Cir. 2013)

McKeown, Circuit Judge:

[1] "The Platters"—the legendary name of one of the most successful vocal performing groups of the 1950s—lives on. With 40 singles on the Billboard Hot 100 List, the names of The Platters' hits ironically foreshadowed decades of litigation—"Great Pretender," "Smoke Gets In Your Eyes," "Only You," and "To Each His Own." Larry Marshak and his company Florida Entertainment Management, Inc. (collectively "Marshak") challenge the district court's preliminary injunction in favor of Herb Reed Enterprises ("HRE"), enjoining Marshak from using the "The Platters" mark in connection with any vocal group with narrow exceptions. We consider an issue of first impression in our circuit: whether the likelihood of irreparable harm must be established—rather than presumed, as under prior Ninth Circuit precedent—by a plaintiff seeking injunctive relief in the trademark context. In light of Supreme Court precedent, the answer is yes, and we reverse the district court's order granting the preliminary injunction.

Background

[2] The Platters vocal group was formed in 1953, with Herb Reed as one of its founders. Paul Robi, David Lynch, Zola Taylor, and Tony Williams, though not founders, have come to be recognized as the other "original" band members. The group became a "global sensation" during the latter half of the 1950s, then broke up in the 1960s as the original members left one by one. After the break up, each member continued to perform under some derivation of the name "The Platters."

[3] Litigation has been the byproduct of the band's dissolution; there have been multiple legal disputes among the original members and their current and former managers over ownership of "The Platters" mark. Much of the litigation stemmed from employment contracts executed in 1956 between the original members and Five Platters, Inc. ("FPI"), the company belonging to Buck Ram, who became the group's manager in 1954. As part of the contracts, each member assigned to FPI any rights in the name "The Platters" in exchange for shares of FPI stock. According to Marshak, FPI later transferred its rights to the mark to Live Gold, Inc., which in turn transferred the rights to Marshak in 2009. Litigation over the validity of the contracts and ownership of the mark left a trail of conflicting decisions in various jurisdictions, which provide the backdrop for the present controversy.

. . . .

[4] Last year brought yet another lawsuit. HRE commenced the present litigation in 2012 against Marshak in the District of Nevada, alleging trademark infringement and seeking a preliminary injunction against Marshak's continued use of "The Platters" mark . . . . The district court found that HRE had established a likelihood of success on the merits, a likelihood of irreparable harm, a balance of hardships in its favor, and that a preliminary injunction would serve public interest. Accordingly, the district court granted the preliminary injunction and set the bond at $10,000. Marshak now appeals from the preliminary injunction.

. . . .

III. Preliminary Injunction

[5] To obtain a preliminary injunction, HRE "must establish that [it] is likely to succeed on the merits, that [it] is likely to suffer irreparable harm in the absence of preliminary relief, that the balance of equities tips in [its] favor, and that an injunction is in the public interest." *Winter v. Natural Res. Def. Council, Inc.*, 555 U.S. 7, 20 (2008) . . . .

B. Likelihood of Irreparable Harm

[6] We next address the likelihood of irreparable harm. As the district court acknowledged, two recent Supreme Court cases have cast doubt on the validity of this court's previous rule that the likelihood of "irreparable injury may be *presumed* from a showing of likelihood of success on the

merits of a trademark infringement claim." *Brookfield Commc'ns, Inc. v. W. Coast Entm't Corp.*, 174 F.3d 1036, 1066 (9th Cir. 1999) (emphasis added). Since *Brookfield,* the landscape for benchmarking irreparable harm has changed with the Supreme Court's decisions in *eBay Inc. v. MercExchange, L.L.C.,* 547 U.S. 388, in 2006, and *Winter* in 2008.

[7] In *eBay,* the Court held that the traditional four-factor test employed by courts of equity, including the requirement that the plaintiff must establish irreparable injury in seeking a permanent injunction, applies in the patent context. 547 U.S. at 391. Likening injunctions in patent cases to injunctions under the Copyright Act, the Court explained that it "has consistently rejected . . . a rule that an injunction automatically follows a determination that a copyright has been infringed," and emphasized that a departure from the traditional principles of equity "should not be lightly implied." *Id.* at 391–93 (citations omitted). The same principle applies to trademark infringement under the Lanham Act. Just as "[n]othing in the Patent Act indicates that Congress intended such a departure," so too nothing in the Lanham Act indicates that Congress intended a departure for trademark infringement cases. *Id.* at 391–92. Both statutes provide that injunctions may be granted in accordance with "the principles of equity." 35 U.S.C. § 283; 15 U.S.C. § 1116(a).

[8] In *Winter,* the Court underscored the requirement that the plaintiff seeking a preliminary injunction "demonstrate that irreparable injury is *likely* in the absence of an injunction." 555 U.S. at 22 (emphasis in original) (citations omitted). The Court reversed a preliminary injunction because it was based only on a "possibility" of irreparable harm, a standard that is "too lenient." *Id. Winter's* admonition that irreparable harm must be shown to be likely in the absence of a preliminary injunction also forecloses the presumption of irreparable harm here.

[9] Following *eBay* and *Winter,* we held that likely irreparable harm must be demonstrated to obtain a preliminary injunction in a copyright infringement case and that actual irreparable harm must be demonstrated to obtain a permanent injunction in a trademark infringement action. *Flexible Lifeline Sys. v. Precision Lift, Inc.,* 654 F.3d 989, 998 (9th Cir. 2011); *Reno Air Racing Ass'n, Inc., v. McCord,* 452 F.3d 1126, 1137–38 (9th Cir. 2006). Our imposition of the irreparable harm requirement for a permanent injunction in a trademark case applies with equal force in the preliminary injunction context. *Amoco Prod. Co. v. Village of Gambell, AK,* 480 U.S. 531, 546 n. 12 (1987) (explaining that the standard for a preliminary injunction is essentially the same as for a permanent injunction except that "likelihood of" is replaced with "actual"). We now join other circuits in holding that the *eBay* principle—that a plaintiff must establish irreparable harm—applies to a preliminary injunction in a trademark infringement case. *See N. Am. Med. Corp. v. Axiom Worldwide, Inc.,* 522 F.3d 1211, 1228–29 (11th Cir. 2008); *Audi AG v. D'Amato,* 469 F.3d 534, 550 (6th Cir. 2006) (applying the requirement to a permanent injunction in a trademark infringement action).

[10] Having anticipated that the Supreme Court's decisions in *eBay* and *Winter* signaled a shift away from the presumption of irreparable harm, the district court examined irreparable harm in its own right, explaining that HRE must "establish that remedies available at law, such as monetary damages, are inadequate to compensate" for the injury arising from Marshak's continuing allegedly infringing use of the mark. *Herb Reed Enters., LLC v. Fla. Entm't Mgmt., Inc.,* No. 2:12–cv–00560–MMD–GWF, 2012 WL 3020039, at *15 (D.Nev. Jul. 24, 2012). Although the district court identified the correct legal principle, we conclude that the record does not support a determination of the likelihood of irreparable harm.

[11] Marshak asserts that the district court abused its discretion by relying on "unsupported and conclusory statements regarding harm [HRE] *might* suffer." We agree.

[12] The district court's analysis of irreparable harm is cursory and conclusory, rather than being grounded in any evidence or showing offered by HRE. To begin, the court noted that it "cannot condone trademark infringement simply because it has been occurring for a long time and may continue to occur." The court went on to note that to do so "could encourage wide-scale infringement

794

on the part of persons hoping to tread on the goodwill and fame of vintage music groups." Fair enough. Evidence of loss of control over business reputation and damage to goodwill could constitute irreparable harm. *See, e.g., Stuhlbarg Int'l Sales Co., Inc. v. John D. Brush and Co., Inc.*, 240 F.3d 832, 841 (9th Cir. 2001) (holding that evidence of loss of customer goodwill supports finding of irreparable harm). Here, however, the court's pronouncements are grounded in platitudes rather than evidence, and relate neither to whether "irreparable injury is *likely* in the absence of an injunction," *Winter*, 555 U.S. at 22, nor to whether legal remedies, such as money damages, are inadequate in this case. It may be that HRE could establish the likelihood of irreparable harm. But missing from this record is any such evidence.

[13] In concluding its analysis, the district court simply cited to another district court case in Nevada "with a substantially similar claim" in which the court found that "the harm to Reed's reputation caused by a different unauthorized Platters group warranted a preliminary injunction." *HRE*, 2012 WL 3020039, at *15–16. As with its speculation on future harm, citation to a different case with a different record does not meet the standard of showing "likely" irreparable harm.

[14] Even if we comb the record for support or inferences of irreparable harm, the strongest evidence, albeit evidence not cited by the district court, is an email from a potential customer complaining to Marshak's booking agent that the customer wanted Herb Reed's band rather than another tribute band. This evidence, however, simply underscores customer confusion, not irreparable harm.[5]

[15] The practical effect of the district court's conclusions, which included no factual findings, is to reinsert the now-rejected presumption of irreparable harm based solely on a strong case of trademark infringement. Gone are the days when "[o]nce the plaintiff in an infringement action has established a likelihood of confusion, it is ordinarily presumed that the plaintiff will suffer irreparable harm if injunctive relief does not issue." *Rodeo Collection, Ltd. v. W. Seventh*, 812 F.2d 1215, 1220 (9th Cir. 1987) (citing *Apple Computer, Inc. v. Formula International Inc.*, 725 F.2d 521, 526 (9th Cir. 1984)). This approach collapses the likelihood of success and the irreparable harm factors. Those seeking injunctive relief must proffer evidence sufficient to establish a likelihood of irreparable harm. As in *Flexible Lifeline*, 654 F.3d at 1000, the fact that the "district court made no factual findings that would support a likelihood of irreparable harm," while not necessarily establishing a lack of irreparable harm, leads us to reverse the preliminary injunction and remand to the district court.

[16] In light of our determination that the record fails to support a finding of likely irreparable harm, we need not address the balance of equities and public interest factors.

REVERSED and REMANDED.

{On March 31, 2014, on cross-motions for summary judgment, the district court granted summary judgment to HRE. *See* Herb Reed Enterprises, LLC v. Florida Entm't Mgmt., Inc., No. 12 Civ. 00560, 2014 WL 1305144 (D. Nev. Mar. 31, 2014).}

---

[5] In assessing the evidence with respect to irreparable harm, we reject Marshak's assertion that the district court may rely only on admissible evidence to support its finding of irreparable harm. Not so. Due to the urgency of obtaining a preliminary injunction at a point when there has been limited factual development, the rules of evidence do not apply strictly to preliminary injunction proceedings. *See Republic of the Philippines v. Marcos*, 862 F.2d 1355, 1363 (9th Cir. 1988) ("It was within the discretion of the district court to accept . . . hearsay for purposes of deciding whether to issue the preliminary injunction.").

adidas Am., Inc. v. Skechers USA, Inc.
890 F.3d 747 (9th Cir. 2018)

Nguyen, Circuit Judge:

[1] Skechers USA, Inc. appeals the district court's issuance of a preliminary injunction prohibiting it from selling shoes that allegedly infringe and dilute adidas America, Inc.'s Stan Smith trade dress and Three–Stripe trademark. We hold that the district court did not abuse its discretion in issuing the preliminary injunction as to adidas's claim that Skechers's Onix shoe infringes on adidas's unregistered trade dress of its Stan Smith shoe. We conclude, however, that the district court erred in issuing a preliminary injunction as to adidas's claim that Skechers's Cross Court shoe infringes and dilutes its Three–Stripe mark. Accordingly, we affirm in part and reverse in part.

I. FACTUAL BACKGROUND

[2] adidas is a leading manufacturer of athletic apparel and footwear. Skechers is a footwear company that competes with adidas in the active footwear and apparel market. Skechers has grown to become the second largest footwear company in the United States, ahead of adidas and behind only Nike.

[3] The Stan Smith has become one of adidas's most successful shoes in terms of sales and influence since its release in the 1970s. Deemed "[t]he favorite shoe of [fashion industry] insiders like designer Raf Simons and Marc Jacobs" by *The Wall Street Journal* and the "ultimate fashion shoe" by *i-D* magazine, the Stan Smith has received extensive media coverage and been featured in such print and online publications as *Time*, *Elle*, *InStyle*, and *Vogue*. The Stan Smith also has frequently appeared on lists of the most important or influential sneakers of all time and has earned industry accolades such as *Footwear News*'s 2014 "Shoe of the Year." That same year, adidas announced that the Stan Smith had become its top-selling shoe of all time, selling more than 40 million pairs worldwide.

[4] adidas is also known for its Three–Stripe mark, which has been featured on its products for many years as part of its branding strategy and for which it owns federal trademark registrations. adidas claims to earn several hundred million dollars in annual domestic sales of products bearing the Three–Stripe mark. adidas advertises the Three–Stripe mark in print publications, on television, and in digital media and promotes it through celebrity endorsements, sporting events sponsorships, and athletic partnerships.

[5] The parties have a history of trademark litigation that has previously resulted in Skechers acknowledging that "adidas is the exclusive owner" of the Three–Stripe mark and agreeing not to use it or any other protected mark "confusingly similar thereto." Despite the agreement, adidas has sued Skechers several times in the last twenty years for infringement of its Three–Stripe trademark.

[6] adidas filed the present lawsuit against Skechers on September 14, 2015, alleging, among other things, that Skechers's Onix shoe infringes on and dilutes the unregistered trade dress of adidas's Stan Smith shoe (both pictured below).

The Stan Smith Trade Dress   The Skechers "Onix"

adidas further alleges that Skechers's Relaxed Fit Cross Court TR (pictured below) infringes and dilutes adidas's Three–Stripe trademark, in violation of 15 U.S.C. § 1125(a), (c).

[7] adidas filed a motion for preliminary injunction to prohibit Skechers from manufacturing, distributing, advertising, selling, or offering for sale the Onix and Cross Court. The district court granted adidas's motion and issued the preliminary injunction, finding that adidas established all the *Winter* factors. *See Winter v. Nat. Res. Def. Council, Inc.*, 555 U.S. 7, 20, 129 S.Ct. 365, 172 L.Ed.2d 249 (2008) ("A plaintiff seeking a preliminary injunction must establish that he is likely to succeed on the merits, that he is likely to suffer irreparable harm in the absence of preliminary relief, that the balance of equities tips in his favor, and that an injunction is in the public interest.").

[8] Skechers timely appealed.

II. STANDARD OF REVIEW

[9] We review the district court's issuance of a preliminary injunction for an abuse of discretion. . . .

III. ANALYSIS

[10] Skechers contests only two of the factors under *Winter*, specifically, the district court's findings that adidas showed a likelihood of success on the merits and irreparable harm. Because the analysis for Skechers's Onix and Cross Court shoes differ, we take them each in turn.

A. Skechers's Onix and adidas's Stan Smith

i. Likelihood of Success on the Merits

{The Ninth Circuit found no clear error in the district court's determination that adidas demonstrated a likelihood of success on its claim that Skechers's Onix shoe infringes and dilutes adidas's Stan Smith trade dress.}

ii. Likelihood of Irreparable Harm

[11] Skechers also argues that the district court's finding of a likelihood of irreparable harm to the Stan Smith was erroneous.

[12] In *Herb Reed Enterprises, LLC v. Florida Entertainment Management, Inc.*, we reaffirmed that "[e]vidence of loss of control over business reputation and damage to goodwill [can] constitute irreparable harm," so long as there is concrete evidence in the record of those things. 736 F.3d 1239, 1250 (9th Cir. 2013). Consistent with *Herb Reed*, the district court here based its finding of irreparable harm from the Onix shoe on evidence that adidas was likely to suffer irreparable harm to its brand reputation and goodwill if the preliminary injunction did not issue. adidas's Director of Sport Style Brand Marketing testified to the significant efforts his team invested in promoting the Stan Smith through specific and controlled avenues such as social media campaigns and product placement, and he stated that the Stan Smith earned significant media from various sources that was not initiated or solicited by adidas. adidas also presented evidence regarding its efforts to carefully control the supply of Stan Smith shoes and its concerns about damage to the Stan Smith's reputation if the marketplace were flooded with similar shoes. Finally, adidas produced customer surveys showing that

approximately twenty percent of surveyed consumers believed Skechers's Onix was made by, approved by, or affiliated with adidas.[4]

[13] The extensive and targeted advertising and unsolicited media, along with tight control of the supply of Stan Smiths, demonstrate that adidas has built a specific reputation around the Stan Smith with "intangible benefits." *See Regents of Univ. of Cal. v. Am. Broad. Cos.*, 747 F.2d 511, 519 (9th Cir. 1984) (internal quotation marks omitted). And, the customer surveys demonstrate that those intangible benefits will be harmed if the Onix stays on the market because consumers will be confused about the source of the shoes. We find that the district court's finding of irreparable harm is not clearly erroneous. *See Herb Reed*, 736 F.3d at 1250; *Rent–A–Ctr., Inc. v. Canyon Television & Appliance Rental, Inc.*, 944 F.2d 597, 603 (9th Cir. 1991) (noting that harm to advertising efforts and goodwill constitute "intangible injuries" that warrant injunctive protection).

B. Skechers's Cross Court and adidas's Three–Stripe Mark

i. Likelihood of Success on the Merits

{The Ninth Circuit found no clear error in the district court's determination that adidas showed a likelihood of success on the merits as to its claims that Skecher's Cross Court shoe infringes and dilutes adidas's Three-Stripe mark.}

ii. Likelihood of Irreparable Harm

[14] Skechers next argues that the district court abused its discretion in issuing the preliminary injunction because under *Winter*, adidas has not shown that it will be irreparably harmed from sale of the Cross Court. We agree.

[15] Both below and on appeal, adidas advanced only a narrow argument of irreparable harm as to the Cross Court: that Skechers harmed adidas's ability to control its brand image because consumers who see others wearing Cross Court shoes associate the allegedly lesser-quality Cross Courts with adidas and its Three–Stripe mark.[6] Yet we find no evidence in the record that could support a finding of irreparable harm based on this loss of control theory.

[16] First, adidas's theory of harm relies on the notion that adidas is viewed by consumers as a premium brand while Skechers is viewed as a lower-quality, discount brand. But even if adidas presented evidence sufficient to show its efforts to cultivate a supposedly premium brand image for itself, adidas did not set forth evidence probative of Skechers's allegedly less favorable reputation. The only evidence in the record regarding Skechers's reputation was testimony from adidas employees.[7] First, adidas claimed that "Skechers generally sells its footwear at prices lower than adidas's"—how much lower, and for what of any number of possible reasons other than the quality of its products, we

---

[4] Skechers's intent to foment and capitalize on such confusion is evident from its use of the terms "adidas" and "Stan Smith" in its source code for the Onix shoe webpage.

[6] While there are other ways post-sale confusion could hypothetically harm a trademark holder, *see, e.g., Gen. Motors Corp. v. Keystone Auto. Indus., Inc.*, 453 F.3d 351, 358 (6th Cir. 2006); 4 J. Thomas McCarthy, *McCarthy on Trademarks and Unfair Competition* § 23:7 (5th ed. 2017), adidas has not raised any other theories of harm here. Unlike the dissent, we hold adidas to its burden of showing a likelihood of irreparable harm on the theory that it actually raised. *See* Dissent at 762–64 & n.2 (outlining how adidas *could have* suffered post-sale harm if the Skechers buyer could benefit from others believing she was wearing adidas shoes).

[7] Such employee testimony is hardly the most reliable evidence of the reputation of a competitor.... However, we need not (and do not) rely on the diminished reliability of employee testimony here, where the testimony did not demonstrate that Skechers is a lower-value brand—one of the tenets of adidas's theory of irreparable harm—anyway. Nor do we "disregard" it, as the dissent suggests, Dissent at 766–67; we merely disagree with the dissent about what the testimony actually shows.

do not know. This generalized statement regarding Skechers's price point does not indicate that consumers view Skechers as a value brand. Second, one adidas employee noted that within adidas, Skechers is viewed as inferior to adidas. Again, Skechers's reputation among the ranks of adidas employees does not indicate how the general consumer views it. Thus, the district court's finding that Skechers is viewed as a "value brand" is an "unsupported and conclusory statement[ ]" that is not "grounded in any evidence or showing offered by [adidas]." *See Herb Reed*, 736 F.3d at 1250 (internal quotation marks omitted).[8]

[17] Second, adidas's theory of harm is in tension with the theory of customer confusion that adidas has advanced to establish a likelihood of success on the merits. adidas did not argue in the district court, and has not argued on appeal, that a Cross Court purchaser would mistakenly believe he had bought adidas shoes at the time of sale. Indeed, this argument would be implausible because the Cross Court contains numerous Skechers logos and identifying features. Instead, adidas argues only that *after* the sale, *someone else* looking at a Cross Court shoe from afar or in passing might not notice the Skechers logos and thus might mistake it for an adidas.

[18] The tension between adidas's consumer confusion and irreparable harm theories, then, boils down to this: How would consumers who confused Cross Courts for adidas shoes be able to surmise, from afar, that those shoes were low quality? If the "misled" consumers could not assess the quality of the shoe from afar, why would they think any differently about adidas's products? How could adidas's "premium" brand possibly be hurt by any confusion?

[19] Indeed, such a claim is counterintuitive. If a consumer viewed a shoe from such a distance that she could not notice its Skechers logos, it is unlikely she would be able to reasonably assess the quality of the shoes. And the consumer could not conflate adidas's brand with Skechers's supposedly "discount" reputation if she did not know the price of the shoe and was too far away to tell whether the shoe might be a Skechers to begin with. In short, even if Skechers does make inferior products (or even if consumers tend to think so), there is no evidence that adidas's theory of post-sale confusion would cause consumers to associate such lesser-quality products with adidas. And, even if we agree with the district court that some consumers are likely to be confused as to the maker of the Cross Court shoe, we cannot simply assume that such confusion will cause adidas irreparable harm where, as here, adidas has failed to provide concrete evidence that it will. *See Herb Reed*, 736 F.3d at 1250–51.

[20] As discussed above, adidas presented specific evidence that its reputation and goodwill were likely to be irreparably harmed by Skechers's Onix shoe based on adidas's extensive marketing efforts for the Stan Smith and its careful control of the supply of Stan Smiths available for purchase. Thus, even post-sale confusion of consumers from afar threatens to harm the value adidas derives from the scarcity and exclusivity of the Stan Smith brand. But there was no comparable argument or evidence for the Cross Court.

---

[8] The dissent criticizes our reliance on *Herb Reed*. Dissent at 765–66. True, there are more facts in the record here that adidas *claims* support a finding of likelihood of irreparable harm than there were in *Herb Reed*. *See* 736 F.3d at 1250 (noting there was only one email in the record that might support an inference of irreparable harm). The problem is that none of those facts *actually* support such a finding. *Herb Reed* makes clear that it is the plaintiff's burden to put forth specific evidence from which the court can infer irreparable harm. *See id.* ("The district court's analysis of irreparable harm is cursory and conclusory, rather than being grounded in any evidence or showing offered by [the plaintiff]."). Regardless of our deferential review, there must actually be such evidence in the record before we can uphold the district court's factual findings. *Id.* (overturning the district court where its "pronouncements [were] grounded in platitudes rather than evidence"). We simply disagree with the dissent that there is any such evidence supporting adidas's theory of irreparable harm on this record.

[21] Because adidas failed to produce evidence that it will suffer irreparable harm due to the Cross Court, we conclude that the district court abused its discretion by issuing a preliminary injunction for the Cross Court. *See Herb Reed*, 736 F.3d at 1250.

* * *

[22] We affirm the district court's preliminary injunction order as to the Onix shoe as likely infringing on, and causing irreparable harm to, adidas's Stan Smith trade dress. However, because we find that there was no evidence in the record that met the standard outlined in *Herb Reed* for likelihood of irreparable harm to adidas's Three–Stripe mark, we reverse the preliminary injunction as to the Cross Court shoe. The parties should bear their own costs on appeal.

CLIFTON, Circuit Judge, concurring in part and dissenting in part:

[1] The preliminary injunction entered by the district court should be affirmed in full. I join with my colleagues in affirming the preliminary injunction regarding Skechers's Onix shoe based on its infringement on the trade dress of adidas's Stan Smith shoe and concur in that part of the majority opinion.

[2] Where I part ways with the majority concerns the infringement by Skechers with its Cross Court shoe of the Three–Stripe mark owned by adidas. The majority holds that adidas has demonstrated a likelihood of success on the merits of that claim, sufficiently demonstrating both trademark infringement and trademark dilution, and I agree. Nonetheless, the majority reverses the preliminary injunction as to the Cross Court shoe on the ground that there was not evidence to support the district court's determination that adidas was likely to suffer irreparable injury. As to that, I disagree. In my view, the majority opinion misunderstands our precedent, misperceives the means by which adidas will suffer irreparable injury, and mischaracterizes the evidence before the district court. As a result, I must, in part, respectfully dissent.

I. Herb Reed

[3] The precedent relied upon by the part of the majority decision in question comes down essentially to a single case, *Herb Reed Enterprises, LLC v. Florida Entertainment Management, Inc.*, 736 F.3d 1239 (9th Cir. 2013) . . . .

[4] Our decision in *Herb Reed* did not disclaim the logic that led to the creation of the now-discarded legal presumption {that irreparable injury may be presumed from a showing of likelihood of success on the merits of a trademark infringement claim}. It is not hard to understand how the presumption arose. If a plaintiff can demonstrate a likelihood that it will succeed on the merits of its trademark claim—as adidas succeeded in establishing that Skechers's Cross Court shoe infringed and diluted adidas's famous Three–Stripe mark, a conclusion we affirm—it is not a big leap to conclude that adidas would be injured by that action. The inference might not always follow, as the facts in *Herb Reed* illustrate. That one Platters tribute band might be mistaken for another did not necessarily establish that the band that had a legal right to the name suffered an injury to its reputation. But in other circumstances, including those here, the inference of injury is logical. As the Third Circuit observed in affirming a similar preliminary injunction: "Although we no longer apply a presumption, the logic underlying the presumption can, and does, inform how we exercise our equitable discretion in this particular case." *Groupe SEB USA, Inc. v. Euro–Pro Operating LLC*, 774 F.3d 192, 205 n.8 (3d Cir. 2014). Our decision in *Herb Reed* did not change that.

II. Irreparable Injury

[5] The district court found that adidas likely suffered harm as the result of post-sale confusion. The theory of post-sale confusion in the trademark context provides that "consumers could acquire the prestige value of the senior user's product by buying the copier's cheap imitation," and that, "[e]ven though the knowledgeable buyer knew that it was getting an imitation, viewers would be confused." 4

J. Thomas McCarthy, *McCarthy on Trademarks and Unfair Competition* § 23:7 (5th ed. 2018). "Thus, the senior user suffers a loss of sales diverted to the junior user, the same as if the actual buyer were confused." *Id.* In other words, sale of the Cross Court, which infringed and diluted adidas's Three-Stripe trademark, would result in post-sale confusion and harm adidas, the trademark holder, by threatening to divert potential customers who can obtain the prestige of its goods without paying its normal prices.[2] *See Rolls–Royce Motors Ltd. v. A & A Fiberglass, Inc.*, 428 F.Supp. 689, 694 n.10 (N.D. Ga. 1976) (regarding grill and hood ornament kit meant to make a Volkswagon look like a Rolls–Royce).

[6] Post-sale confusion accounts for consumers who buy imitations of a prestigious senior holder's brand at lower prices in the very hope that others will confuse their products as being manufactured by the senior holder. About thirty years ago, when I was in private practice, my law firm was retained by Louis Vuitton to combat the sale of cheaper imitations. Some were counterfeits, reproducing the distinctive "LV" mark and pattern on bags similar to those actually sold by Louis Vuitton. Others were knock-offs, such as bags with a similar looking "LW" mark or products that Louis Vuitton probably wouldn't dream of making, such as baseball caps covered with dozens of "LV" marks. Many of the items were sold at locations, like swap meets and flea markets, where few would expect to find real Louis Vuitton products. Prices were often a tiny fraction of what the real thing cost, and it was unlikely that the purchasers thought that they were walking away with genuine Louis Vuitton merchandise. Leaving the legal arguments aside, it wasn't a surprise to me (and still isn't) that Louis Vuitton was concerned and was willing to expend considerable effort to protect its trademark. As Professor McCarthy described, if the prestige of carrying a bag with the Louis Vuitton trademark could be obtained at a fraction of the price, and if viewers could not tell the difference, the value of the trademark would be in jeopardy. And, if someone did confuse the cheap imitation for the real thing, the lesser quality of the imitator could further imperil the perceived value of the Louis Vuitton products and trademark.

[7] The Three–Stripe mark owned by adidas is one of the most famous marks in the world. There is evidence in the record that it has been heavily advertised and promoted by adidas for many years, at the cost of millions of dollars each year. adidas sells several hundred million dollars worth of products bearing the Three–Stripe mark each year in the United States and billions of dollars globally. The Three–Stripe mark is the subject of multiple trademark registrations, in this country and others. adidas has worked to protect its mark, including through litigation against Skechers, and Skechers has acknowledged, as the majority opinion notes, that adidas is the exclusive owner of the Three–Stripe mark and agreed not to use it or any confusingly similar mark.

[8] That adidas is concerned about the impact of trademark infringement and dilution on the Three–Stripe mark, like Louis Vuitton was, is obvious. The reasons seem pretty obvious to me as well. If a shoe bearing a mark that looks like the Three Stripes cannot reliably be identified as being an adidas shoe, available at adidas prices, and made to satisfy the quality standards of adidas, then that Three–Stripe mark will lose some of its value and adidas will be harmed.

[9] The majority opinion describes this as "counterintuitive." Maj. Op. at 760. It seems logical to me, and it is well established in the law as a basis for a claim of dilution.

[10] The majority opinion attempts to justify its constrained consideration of the post-sale confusion harm suffered by adidas on the premise that adidas "advanced only a narrow argument of irreparable harm" as to the Skechers shoe that infringed on the Three–Stripe mark, the Cross Court shoe. The majority describes the argument as follows: "that Skechers harmed adidas's ability to control

---

[2] Diversion of customers is a form of irreparable harm. *See* McCarthy, *supra*, § 30:47 ("confusion may cause purchasers to refrain from buying either product and to turn to those of other competitors. Yet to prove the loss of sales due to infringement is also notoriously difficult"); *see also, e.g., China Cent. Television v. Create New Tech. (HK) Ltd.*, 2015 WL 12732432, at *20 (C.D. Cal. Dec. 7, 2015).

its brand image because consumers who see others wearing Cross Court shoes associate the allegedly lesser-quality Cross Courts with adidas and its Three–Stripe mark." *Id.*[3]

[11] That argument is actually not so narrow. It is remarkably similar to the explanation provided by Professor McCarthy, as quoted above, at 763, that the majority opinion claims that adidas did not make: that "consumers could acquire the prestige value of the senior user's product by buying the copier's cheap imitation," and that, "[e]ven though the knowledgeable buyer knew that it was getting an imitation, viewers would be confused." McCarthy, *supra*, § 23:7. It is also consistent with the definition of "dilution" applied by the district court in its preliminary injunction order: "'the lessening of the capacity of a famous mark to identify and distinguish goods or services' of the owner of the famous mark such that the strong identification value of the owner's trademark whittles away or is gradually attenuated as a result of its use by another." (Quoting *adidas-Am., Inc. v. Payless Shoesource, Inc.*, 546 F.Supp.2d 1029, 1060 (D. Or. 2008) (quoting *Horphag Research Ltd. v. Garcia*, 475 F.3d 1029, 1035 (9th Cir. 2007) (quoting 15 U.S.C. § 1127)).)

[12] The district court went on to observe that "[t]here are two types of dilution: by blurring and by tarnishment." Tarnishment appears to be the only argument the majority considers. The district court described that form of dilution: "a famous mark is considered diluted by tarnishment when the reputation of the famous mark is harmed by the association resulting from the use of the similar mark." But the district court's order described the blurring form of dilution as well, recognizing it as part of adidas's claim, and defining it as "association arising from the similarity between a mark or trade name and a famous mark that impairs the distinctiveness of the famous mark." The district court found that adidas has offered sufficient proof to support a blurring claim. It specifically found that "Skechers' infringement undermines adidas's substantial investment in building its brand and the reputation of its trademarks and trade dress" and that "Skechers' attempts to 'piggy back' off of adidas's efforts by copying or closely imitating adidas's marks means adidas loses control over its trademarks, reputation, and goodwill." There was nothing counterintuitive or narrow about the dilution claim presented by adidas and found persuasive by the district court.

    . . . .

{Judge Clifton went on to argue in detail that the majority violated the clear error standard of review in discounting adidas's evidence of harm from Skechers's sale of the Cross Court shoe.}

    . . . .

V. Conclusion

[13] In reviewing a preliminary injunction, the scope of our review "is limited and deferential." *Guzman v. Shewry*, 552 F.3d 941, 948 (9th Cir. 2009) (citation omitted). *Herb Reed* reiterated that "limited and deferential" standard. 736 F.3d at 1247 (citation omitted). Moreover, *Herb Reed* instructed us to afford district courts wide discretion to make a finding when there is supporting evidence, and acknowledged that, "we will reverse only if the court's decision resulted from a factual finding that was illogical, implausible, or without support in inferences that may be drawn from the facts in the record." *Id.* (internal quotation marks omitted). Based upon the record and adidas's unrebutted evidence, it is clear to me that the district court did not abuse its discretion, and that the preliminary injunction should be affirmed in full. I respectfully dissent.

---

[3] As discussed below, at 768–69, the majority is wrong in concluding that adidas's dilution claim depends upon establishing that Skechers is perceived as a lesser-quality brand.

Comments and Questions

1. *Second Circuit treatment of* eBay. The Second Circuit has not yet explicitly embraced *eBay* in the trademark context, though it came close to doing so. In *Guthrie Healthcare Sys. v. ContextMedia, Inc.*, 826 F.3d 27 (2d Cir. 2016), the Second Circuit stated:

> We recognize further that the competing equities do not always favor a senior user that has shown infringement. Cases frequently arise in which imposition of a broad injunction on an innocent infringer, which had no realistic way of knowing that its mark was subject to a prior claim, would cause the junior user a catastrophic loss of goodwill acquired through investment of years of toil and large amounts of money. In such cases, notwithstanding that the legal right unquestionably belongs to the senior user, competing equities can complicate the issue of the breadth of injunctive relief. In our case, in contrast, a number of equitable considerations appear to favor Plaintiff.

Id. at 49–50. *Cf. Salinger v. Colting*, 607 F.3d 68, 77-78 (2d Cir. 2010) (in analyzing remedies for copyright infringement, stating that "nothing in the text or the logic of *eBay* suggests that its rule is limited to patent cases. On the contrary, *eBay* strongly indicates that the traditional principles of equity it employed are the presumptive standard for injunctions in any context."); *Juicy Couture, Inc. v. Bella Int'l, Ltd.*, 2013 U.S. Dist. LEXIS 34846 (S.D.N.Y. 2013) (in analyzing remedies for trademark infringement, stating that "irreparable harm may not be presumed upon a showing of likelihood of success on the merits").

2. *How should* eBay *apply to trademark law?* Mark Lemley has criticized the manner in which courts have applied *eBay* to trademark law:

> I think *eBay* was a good—indeed, great—development in patent law and copyright law.
>
> Trademark, however, is different. The purposes of trademark law—and whom it benefits—should lead us to treat trademark injunctions differently than patent and copyright injunctions. Further, trademark courts have misinterpreted *eBay*, treating each of the four factors as a requirement rather than a consideration. That is a particular problem in trademark law, where proof of future injury can be elusive. And perhaps most remarkably, courts have expanded *eBay* in trademark cases at the same time they have denied damages relief, with the result that trademark owners can and do win their case only to receive no remedy at all. The result is a very real risk that courts will hurt rather than help consumers by allowing confusion to continue.

Mark A. Lemley, *Did eBay Irreparably Injure Trademark Law?*, 92 NOTRE DAME L. REV. 1795, 1796 (2017). Lemley notes in particular that due to trademark courts' strict application of *eBay* and trademark law's heightened requirements for the award of monetary damages or defendant's profits, "[t]he result is that sometimes plaintiffs win their cases but are awarded exactly nothing—no damages and no injunction." *Id.* at 1808.

3. *Law school casebook law versus the reality of the daily life of trademark litigation in the federal courts.* In summarizing a thorough review of the case law, Gilson notes that

> Even a decade after *eBay*, the lower courts, in fact *most* of them, are *still* relying on the presumption of irreparable harm in trademark cases without analysis. What's more, a few district courts in circuits that have expressly rejected the presumption have unexpectedly followed it. Why? Because they are simply unaware of the *eBay* game changer. Judges or their law clerks and counsel, possibly new to trademark litigation, are simply pulling up outdated boilerplate and citing reflexively to the obsolete presumption.

3 GILSON ON TRADEMARKS § 14.02 (2019). 山高皇帝远 ("The mountains are high and the emperor is far away").

4. *Injunctive relief and the right to a trial by jury.* If only injunctive relief is sought, then the case is purely equitable and neither party has the right to a jury trial. For this reason, plaintiffs may sometimes seek only an injunction (and not damages or defendant's profits) so that the defendant cannot demand a jury trial. *See, e.g., Toyota Motor Sales, U.S.A., Inc. v. Tabari*, 610 F.3d 1171, 1183–84 (9th Cir. 2010) ("Finally, we consider the Tabaris' claim that the district court deprived them of their right to a trial by jury when it failed to empanel a jury to decide Toyota's trademark claims. Because Toyota only sought an injunction, the district court did not err by resolving its claims in a bench trial. Nor were the Tabaris entitled to a jury trial on their equitable defenses to those claims, or their counterclaims seeking declarations of trademark invalidity and non-infringement." (citations omitted)).

B. Plaintiff's Damages and Defendant's Profits

Lanham Act § 35, 15 U.S.C. § 1117

(a) Profits; damages and costs; attorney fees

When a violation of any right of the registrant of a mark registered in the Patent and Trademark Office, a violation under section 1125(a) or (d) of this title, or a willful violation under section 1125(c) of this title, shall have been established in any civil action arising under this chapter, the plaintiff shall be entitled, subject to the provisions of sections 1111[1] and 1114[2] of this title, and subject to the principles of equity, to recover (1) defendant's profits, (2) any damages sustained by the plaintiff, and (3) the costs of the action. The court shall assess such profits and damages or cause the same to be assessed under its direction. In assessing profits the plaintiff shall be required to prove defendant's sales only; defendant must prove all elements of cost or deduction claimed. In assessing damages the court may enter judgment, according to the circumstances of the case, for any sum above the amount found as actual damages, not exceeding three times such amount. If the court shall find that the amount of the recovery based on profits is either inadequate or excessive the court may in its discretion enter judgment for such sum as the court shall find to be just, according to the circumstances of the case. Such sum in either of the above circumstances shall constitute compensation and not a penalty. The court in exceptional cases may award reasonable attorney fees to the prevailing party.

. . . .

(d) Statutory damages for violation of section 1125(d)(1)

In a case involving a violation of section 1125(d)(1) of this title, the plaintiff may elect, at any time before final judgment is rendered by the trial court, to recover, instead of actual damages and profits, an award of statutory damages in the amount of not less than $1,000 and not more than $100,000 per domain name, as the court considers just.

---

[1] {15 U.S.C. § 1111 reads as follows: "Notwithstanding the provisions of section 1072 of this title, a registrant of a mark registered in the Patent and Trademark Office, may give notice that his mark is registered by displaying with the mark the words "Registered in U.S. Patent and Trademark Office" or "Reg. U.S. Pat. & Tm. Off." or the letter R enclosed within a circle, thus ®; and in any suit for infringement under this chapter by such a registrant failing to give such notice of registration, no profits and no damages shall be recovered under the provisions of this chapter unless the defendant had actual notice of the registration."}

[2] {15 U.S.C. § 1114 provides safe harbors for publishers and distributors of physical and electronic media, including those in which infringing advertisements appear, when they qualify as "innocent infringers".}

1. **Recovery of Defendant's Profits**

   a. **Willful Intent and Profits**

Romag Fasteners, Inc. v. Fossil, Inc.
590 U.S. __, 140 S.Ct. 1492 (2020)

Justice GORSUCH delivered the opinion of the Court.

[1] When it comes to remedies for trademark infringement, the Lanham Act authorizes many. A district court may award a winning plaintiff injunctive relief, damages, or the defendant's ill-gotten profits. Without question, a defendant's state of mind may have a bearing on what relief a plaintiff should receive. An innocent trademark violator often stands in very different shoes than an intentional one. But some circuits have gone further. These courts hold a plaintiff can win a profits remedy, in particular, only after showing the defendant *willfully* infringed its trademark. The question before us is whether that categorical rule can be reconciled with the statute's plain language.

[2] The question comes to us in a case involving handbag fasteners. Romag sells magnetic snap fasteners for use in leather goods. Fossil designs, markets, and distributes a wide range of fashion accessories. Years ago, the pair signed an agreement allowing Fossil to use Romag's fasteners in Fossil's handbags and other products. Initially, both sides seemed content with the arrangement. But in time Romag discovered that the factories Fossil hired in China to make its products were using counterfeit Romag fasteners—and that Fossil was doing little to guard against the practice. Unable to resolve its concerns amicably, Romag sued. The company alleged that Fossil had infringed its trademark and falsely represented that its fasteners came from Romag. After trial, a jury agreed with Romag, and found that Fossil had acted "in callous disregard" of Romag's rights. At the same time, however, the jury rejected Romag's accusation that Fossil had acted willfully, as that term was defined by the district court.

[3] For our purposes, the last finding is the important one. By way of relief for Fossil's trademark violation, Romag sought (among other things) an order requiring Fossil to hand over the profits it had earned thanks to its trademark violation. But the district court refused this request. The court pointed out that controlling Second Circuit precedent requires a plaintiff seeking a profits award to prove that the defendant's violation was willful. Not all circuits, however, agree with the Second Circuit's rule. We took this case to resolve that dispute over the law's demands. 139 S.Ct. 2778 (2019).

[4] Where does Fossil's proposed willfulness rule come from? The relevant section of the Lanham Act governing remedies for trademark violations, § 35, 60 Stat. 439–440, as amended, 15 U.S.C. § 1117(a), says this:

> "When a violation of any right of the registrant of a mark registered in the Patent and Trademark Office, a violation under section 1125(a) or (d) of this title, or a willful violation under section 1125(c) of this title, shall have been established ..., the plaintiff shall be entitled, subject to the provisions of sections 1111 and 1114 of this title, and subject to the principles of equity, to recover (1) defendant's profits, (2) any damages sustained by the plaintiff, and (3) the costs of the action."

Immediately, this language spells trouble for Fossil and the circuit precedent on which it relies. The statute does make a showing of willfulness a precondition to a profits award when the plaintiff proceeds under § 1125(c). That section, added to the Lanham Act some years after its initial adoption, creates a cause of action for trademark dilution—conduct that lessens the association consumers have with a trademark. But Romag alleged and proved a violation of § 1125(a), a provision establishing a cause of action for the false or misleading use of trademarks. And in cases like that, the statutory language has *never* required a showing of willfulness to win a defendant's profits. Yes, the law tells us that a profits award is subject to limitations found in §§ 1111 and 1114. But no one suggests those cross-referenced sections contain the rule Fossil seeks. Nor does this Court usually read into statutes words that aren't there. It's a temptation we are doubly careful to avoid when Congress has (as here) included the term in question elsewhere in the very same statutory provision.

[5] A wider look at the statute's structure gives us even more reason for pause. The Lanham Act speaks often and expressly about mental states. Section 1117(b) requires courts to treble profits or damages and award attorney's fees when a defendant engages in certain acts *intentionally* and with specified *knowledge*. Section 1117(c) increases the cap on statutory damages from $200,000 to $2,000,000 for certain *willful* violations. Section 1118 permits courts to order the infringing items be destroyed if a plaintiff proves any violation of § 1125(a) or a *willful* violation of § 1125(c). Section 1114 makes certain *innocent* infringers subject only to injunctions. Elsewhere, the statute specifies certain *mens rea* standards needed to establish liability, before even getting to the question of remedies. See, *e.g.*, §§ 1125(d)(1)(A)(i), (B)(i) (prohibiting certain conduct only if undertaken with "bad faith intent" and listing nine factors relevant to ascertaining bad faith intent). Without doubt, the Lanham Act exhibits considerable care with *mens rea* standards. The absence of any such standard in the provision before us, thus, seems all the more telling.

[6] So how exactly does Fossil seek to conjure a willfulness requirement out of § 1117(a)? Lacking any more obvious statutory hook, the company points to the language indicating that a violation under § 1125(a) can trigger an award of the defendant's profits "subject to the principles of equity." In Fossil's telling, equity courts historically required a showing of willfulness before authorizing a profits remedy in trademark disputes. Admittedly, equity courts didn't require so much in patent infringement cases and other arguably analogous suits. See, *e.g.*, *Dowagiac Mfg. Co. v. Minnesota Moline Plow Co.*, 235 U.S. 641, 644, 650–651 (1915). But, Fossil says, trademark is different. There alone, a willfulness requirement was so long and universally recognized that today it rises to the level of a "principle of equity" the Lanham Act carries forward.

[7] It's a curious suggestion. Fossil's contention that the term "principles of equity" includes a willfulness requirement would not directly contradict the statute's other, express *mens rea* provisions or render them wholly superfluous. But it would require us to assume that Congress intended to incorporate a willfulness requirement here obliquely while it prescribed *mens rea* conditions expressly elsewhere throughout the Lanham Act. That might be possible, but on first blush it isn't exactly an obvious construction of the statute.

[8] Nor do matters improve with a second look. The phrase "principles of equity" doesn't readily bring to mind a substantive rule about *mens rea* from a discrete domain like trademark law. In the context of this statute, it more naturally suggests fundamental rules that apply more systematically across claims and practice areas. A principle is a "fundamental truth or doctrine, as of law; a comprehensive rule or doctrine which furnishes a basis or origin for others." Black's Law Dictionary 1417 (3d ed. 1933); Black's Law Dictionary 1357 (4th ed. 1951). And treatises and handbooks on the "principles of equity" generally contain transsubstantive guidance on broad and fundamental questions about matters like parties, modes of proof, defenses, and remedies.... Our precedent, too, has used the term "principles of equity" to refer to just such transsubstantive topics. See, *e.g., eBay Inc. v. MercExchange, L. L. C.*, 547 U.S. 388, 391 (2006).... Congress itself has elsewhere used "equitable principles" in just this way: An amendment to a different section of the Lanham Act lists "laches, estoppel, and acquiescence" as examples of "equitable principles." 15 U.S.C. § 1069. Given all this, it seems a little unlikely Congress meant "principles of equity" to direct us to a narrow rule about a profits remedy within trademark law.

[9] But even if we were to spot Fossil that first essential premise of its argument, the next has problems too. From the record the parties have put before us, it's far from clear whether trademark law historically required a showing of willfulness before allowing a profits remedy. The Trademark Act of 1905—the Lanham Act's statutory predecessor which many earlier cases interpreted and applied— did not mention such a requirement. It's true, as Fossil notes, that some courts proceeding before the 1905 Act, and even some later cases following that Act, did treat willfulness or something like it as a

prerequisite for a profits award and rarely authorized profits for purely good-faith infringement. See, *e.g., Horlick's Malted Milk Corp. v. Horluck's, Inc.*, 51 F.2d 357, 359 (W.D. Wash. 1931) (explaining that the plaintiff "cannot recover defendant's profits unless it has been shown beyond a reasonable doubt that defendant was guilty of willful fraud in the use of the enjoined trade-name"); see also *Saxlehner v. Siegel-Cooper Co.*, 179 U.S. 42, 42–43 (1900) (holding that one defendant "should not be required to account for gains and profits" when it "appear[ed] to have acted in good faith"). But Romag cites other cases that expressly rejected any such rule. See, *e.g., Oakes v. Tonsmierre*, 49 F. 447, 453 (C.C.S.D. Ala. 1883); see also *Stonebraker v. Stonebraker*, 33 Md. 252, 268 (1870); *Lawrence-Williams Co. v. Societe Enfants Gombault et Cie*, 52 F.2d 774, 778 (C.A.6 1931).

[10] The confusion doesn't end there. Other authorities advanced still different understandings about the relationship between *mens rea* and profits awards in trademark cases. See, *e.g.,* H. Nims, Law of Unfair Competition and Trade-Marks § 424 (2d ed. 1917) ("An accounting will not be ordered where the infringing party acted innocently and in ignorance of the plaintiff's rights"); N. Hesseltine, Digest of the Law of Trade-Marks and Unfair Trade 305 (1906) (contrasting a case holding "[n]o account as to profits allowed except as to user after *knowledge* of plaintiff's right to trademark" and one permitting profits "although defendant did not know of infringement" (emphasis added)). And the vast majority of the cases both Romag and Fossil cite simply failed to speak clearly to the issue one way or another. See, *e.g., Hostetter v. Vowinkle*, 12 F.Cas. 546, 547 (No. 6,714) (C.C.D. Neb. 1871); *Graham v. Plate*, 40 Cal. 593, 597–599 (1871); *Hemmeter Cigar Co. v. Congress Cigar Co.*, 118 F.2d 64, 71–72 (C.A.6 1941).

[11] At the end of it all, the most we can say with certainty is this. *Mens rea* figured as an important consideration in awarding profits in pre-Lanham Act cases. This reflects the ordinary, transsubstantive principle that a defendant's mental state is relevant to assigning an appropriate remedy. That principle arises not only in equity, but across many legal contexts. See, *e.g., Smith v. Wade*, 461 U.S. 30, 38–51 (1983) (42 U.S.C. § 1983); *Morissette v. United States*, 342 U.S. 246, 250–263 (1952) (criminal law); *Wooden-Ware Co. v. United States*, 106 U.S. 432, 434–435 (1882) (common law trespass). It's a principle reflected in the Lanham Act's text, too, which permits greater statutory damages for certain willful violations than for other violations. 15 U.S.C. § 1117(c). And it is a principle long reflected in equity practice where district courts have often considered a defendant's mental state, among other factors, when exercising their discretion in choosing a fitting remedy... Given these traditional principles, we do not doubt that a trademark defendant's mental state is a highly important consideration in determining whether an award of profits is appropriate. But acknowledging that much is a far cry from insisting on the inflexible precondition to recovery Fossil advances.

[12] With little to work with in the statute's language, structure, and history, Fossil ultimately rests on an appeal to policy. The company tells us that stouter restraints on profits awards are needed to deter "baseless" trademark suits. Meanwhile, Romag insists that its reading of the statute will promote greater respect for trademarks in the "modern global economy." As these things go, *amici* amplify both sides' policy arguments. Maybe, too, each side has a point. But the place for reconciling competing and incommensurable policy goals like these is before policymakers. This Court's limited role is to read and apply the law those policymakers have ordained, and here our task is clear. The judgment of the court of appeals is vacated, and the case is remanded for further proceedings consistent with this opinion.

It is so ordered.

Justice ALITO, with whom Justice BREYER and Justice KAGAN join, concurring.

[13] We took this case to decide whether willful infringement is a prerequisite to an award of profits under 15 U.S.C. § 1117(a). The decision below held that willfulness is such a prerequisite. App. to Pet. for Cert. 32a. That is incorrect. The relevant authorities, particularly pre-Lanham Act case law,

show that willfulness is a highly important consideration in awarding profits under § 1117(a), but not an absolute precondition. I would so hold and concur on that ground.

Justice SOTOMAYOR, concurring in the judgment.

[14] I agree that 15 U.S.C. § 1117(a) does not impose a "willfulness" prerequisite for awarding profits in trademark infringement actions. Courts of equity, however, defined "willfulness" to encompass a range of culpable mental states—including the equivalent of recklessness, but excluding "good faith" or negligence. See 5 McCarthy on Trademarks and Unfair Competition § 30:62 (5th ed. 2019) (explaining that "willfulness" ranged from fraudulent and knowing to reckless and indifferent behavior); see also, *e.g., Lawrence-Williams Co. v. Societe Enfants Gombault et Cie*, 52 F.2d 774, 778 (C.A.6 1931); *Regis v. Jaynes*, 191 Mass. 245, 248–249, 77 N.E. 774, 776 (1906).

[15] The majority suggests that courts of equity were just as likely to award profits for such "willful" infringement as they were for "innocent" infringement. *Ante*, at 1496 – 1497. But that does not reflect the weight of authority, which indicates that profits were hardly, if ever, awarded for innocent infringement. See, *e.g., Wood v. Peffer*, 55 Cal.App.2d 116, 125, 130 P.2d 220 (1942) (explaining that "equity constantly refuses, for want of fraudulent intent, the prayer for an accounting of profits"); *Globe-Wernicke Co. v. Safe-Cabinet Co.*, 110 Ohio St. 609, 617, 144 N.E. 711, 713 (1924) ("By the great weight of authority, particularly where the infringement ... was deliberate and willful, it is held that the wrongdoer is required to account for all profits realized by him as a result of his wrongful acts"); *Dickey v. Mutual Film Corp.*, 186 A.D. 701, 702, 174 N.Y.S. 784 (1919) (declining to award profits because there was "no proof of any fraudulent intent upon the part of the defendant"); *Standard Cigar Co. v. Goldsmith*, 58 Pa.Super. 33, 37 (1914) (reasoning that a defendant "should be compelled to account for ... profits" where "the infringement complained of was not the result of mistake or ignorance of the plaintiff 's right"). Nor would doing so seem to be consistent with longstanding equitable principles which, after all, seek to deprive only wrongdoers of their gains from misconduct. Cf. *Duplate Corp. v. Triplex Safety Glass Co.*, 298 U.S. 448, 456–457, 56 S.Ct. 792, 80 L.Ed. 1274 (1936). Thus, a district court's award of profits for innocent or good-faith trademark infringement would not be consonant with the "principles of equity" referenced in § 1117(a) and reflected in the cases the majority cites. *Ante* at 1496 – 1497.

[16] Because the majority is agnostic about awarding profits for both "willful" and innocent infringement as those terms have been understood, I concur in the judgment only.

b. Actual Confusion and Profits

Most circuits do not require a showing of actual confusion to trigger a disgorgement of defendant's profits. *See, e.g., Web Printing Controls Co., Inc. v. Oxy-Dry Corp.*, 906 F.2d 1202, 1205 (7th Cir. 1990) ("These remedies [including a recovery of defendant's profits] flow not from the plaintiff's proof of its injury or damage, but from its proof of the defendant's unjust enrichment or the need for deterrence, for example . . . . To collapse the two inquiries of violation and remedy into one which asks only of the plaintiff's injury, as did the district court, is to read out of the Lanham Act the remedies that do not rely on proof of 'injury caused by actual confusion.' And this, of course, is improper."); *Gracie v. Gracie*, 217 F.3d 1060, 1068 (9th Cir. 2000) ("[A] showing of actual confusion is not necessary to obtain a recovery of profits.").

There has been considerable uncertainty over whether the Second Circuit requires a showing of actual confusion to support an award of profits. In *4 Pillar Dynasty LLC v. New York & Co., Inc.*, 933 F.3d 202, 212 (2d Cir. 2019), however, it explained: "To dispel any doubts as to this question, we write to clarify that, in our Circuit, a plaintiff need not establish actual consumer confusion to recover lost profits under the Lanham Act." *Id.* at 212.

Note that Lanham Act § 35(a) provides: "In assessing profits the plaintiff shall be required to prove defendant's sales only; defendant must prove all elements of cost or deduction claimed."

2. Recovery of Plaintiff's Damages

a. Willful Intent and Damages

Court typically do not require a showing of defendant's willful intent for damages to be awarded. *See, e.g., Gen. Elec. Co. v. Speicher*, 877 F.2d 531, 535 (7th Cir. 1989) ("[E]ven if he is an innocent infringer he ought at least reimburse the plaintiff's losses.").

b. Actual Confusion and Damages

Courts typically require a showing of actual confusion for damages to be awarded. *See, e.g., Brunswick Corp. v. Spinit Reel Co.*, 832 F.2d 513, 523 (10th Cir. 1987) ("Likelihood of confusion is insufficient; to recover damages plaintiff must prove it has been damaged by actual consumer confusion or deception resulting from the violation . . . . Actual consumer confusion may be shown by direct evidence, a diversion of sales or direct testimony from the public, or by circumstantial evidence such as consumer surveys."); *Int'l Star Class Yacht Racing Ass'n v. Tommy Hilfiger, U.S.A., Inc.*, 80 F.3d 749, 753 (2d Cir. 1996) ("Proof of actual confusion is ordinarily required for recovery of damages for pecuniary loss sustained by the plaintiff."). "Such damages may include compensation for (1) lost sales or revenue; (2) sales at lower prices; (3) harm to market reputation; or (4) expenditures to prevent, correct, or mitigate consumer confusion." *Id.* "The apparent justification for making actual confusion a threshold requirement is that it is a proxy for actual marketplace damage that can be difficult to prove." 3 GILSON ON TRADEMARKS § 14.03 (2019).

3. Enhanced Damages

Lanham Act § 35(a), 15 U.S.C. 1117(a), empowers the court to award an amount up to three times the plaintiff's actual damages: ""In assessing damages the court may enter judgment, according to the circumstances of the case, for any sum above the amount found as actual damages, not exceeding three times such amount." Enhanced damages cannot be punitive in nature. *See Fifty-Six Hope Rd. Music, Ltd. v. A.V.E.L.A., Inc.*, 778 F.3d 1059, 1077 (9th Cir. 2015) ("The district court ought to tread lightly when deciding whether to award increased profits, because granting an increase could easily transfigure an otherwise-acceptable compensatory award into an impermissible punitive measure. Generally, actual, proven profits will adequately compensate the plaintiff. Because the profit disgorgement remedy is measured by the defendant's gain, the district court should award actual, proven profits unless the defendant infringer gained more from the infringement than the defendant's profits reflect." (citation omitted)).

4. The Notice Requirement for Registered Marks

Lanham Act § 29, 15 U.S.C. § 1111, makes clear that the owner of a registered mark must provide statutorily-prescribed notice of the mark's registered status (typically in the form of the circle-R) in order to recover profits and damages for infringement of the mark. In the event that the owner fails to provide statutorily-prescribed notice, then the owner can recover profits and damages only for infringing conduct that occurred after the owner provided the infringer with actual notice of the mark's registered status.

What about *unregistered* marks protected under Lanham Act § 43(a), 15 U.S.C. § 1125(a)? McCarthy summarizes the strange state of affairs: "[T]he statutory notice requirement is not a limitation on recovery of damages under a § 43(a) count for infringement of an unregistered mark. . . . This means that a trademark owner can sue under Lanham Act § 43(a) for damages from infringing acts occurring prior to registration unaffected by the notice requirement and under Lanham Act § 32(1) for damages for acts post-registration so long as the notice requirement is met." 3 McCARTHY ON

TRADEMARKS AND UNFAIR COMPETITION § 19:144 (5th ed. 2019). *See also GTFM, Inc. v. Solid Clothing, Inc.*, 215 F. Supp. 2d 273, 306 (S.D.N.Y. 2002).

Finally, can a registrant who fails to provide notice nevertheless claim all of its profits and damages under Lanham Act § 43(a) rather than Lanham Act § 32, thus avoiding the limitation on recovery set out in Lanham Act § 29? Probably not. *See Audemars Piguet Holding S.A. v. Swiss Watch Int'l, Inc.*, 46 F. Supp. 3d 255, 290 (S.D.N.Y. 2014) ("[A]fter a mark has been registered, Section 1111 limits Plaintiffs' recovery under Section 1117(a) for both Section 32 and Section 43(a) violations.").

C. Corrective Advertising

Corrective advertising by defendant. Courts may order defendants to engage in corrective advertising to mitigate the consumer confusion that their conduct has caused. Corrective advertising orders are especially common in false advertising cases. *See, e.g., Merck Eprova AG v. Gnosis S.p.A.*, 760 F.3d 247, 264 (2d Cir. 2014) (affirming a corrective advertising injunction ordering defendant to advertise on its homepage and various other websites and magazines that it had been ordered by the court to explain the difference between its products and plaintiff's products, and finding that the corrective advertising order paired with recovery of defendant's profits did not constitute unfair double recovery).

Corrective advertising by plaintiff. Courts may also take into account in their award of damages the cost to a plaintiff of running corrective advertising to mitigate confusion caused by the defendant and to restore the plaintiff to the position it would have been in had defendant not infringed. See, *e.g., Big O Tire Dealers, Inc. v. Goodyear Tire & Rubber Co.*, 561 F.2d 1365, 1375-76 (10th Cir. 1977) (following FTC practices, awarding plaintiff 25% of defendant's advertising budget, or $678,302, to cover the cost of plaintiff's corrective advertising).

D. Attorney's Fees

In *Fleischmann Distilling Corp. v. Maier Brewing Co.*, 386 U.S. 714 (1967), the Supreme Court held that the Lanham Act did not provide for the award of attorney's fees to the prevailing party. In 1975, Congress amended Lanham Act § 35(a), 15 U.S.C. 1117(a), by adding the sentence: "The court in exceptional cases may award reasonable attorney fees to the prevailing party."

Up until the Supreme Court decision in *Octane Fitness, LLC v. ICON Health & Fitness, Inc.*, 134 S. Ct. 1749 (2014), the doctrine relating to what makes a trademark case "exceptional" for purposes of recovery of attorney's fees varied randomly across the circuits. *See Nightingale Home Healthcare, Inc. v. Anodyne Therapy, LLC*, 626 F.3d 958 (7th Cir. 2010) (Posner, J.) (reviewing the "jumble" of the circuits' tests for an award of attorney's fees); *Yankee Candle Co. v. Bridgewater Candle Co., LLC*, 140 F. Supp. 2d 111, 120 (D. Mass. 2001) (discussing the "rainbow of standards" among the circuits). The circuits generally required (i) bad faith by the defendant, (ii) willful infringement, or (iii) bad faith, vexatious, or "oppressive" litigation. *See Eagles, Ltd. v. American Eagle Foundation*, 356 F.3d 724, 728 (6th Cir. 2004) (defining "oppressive" litigation). Some circuits applied different evidentiary and substantive standards depending on whether the prevailing party was the plaintiff or the defendant. *See Nightingale Home Healthcare*, 626 F.3d at 961.

Octane Fitness has since begun to exert some discipline on the circuits' approaches. In *Octane Fitness*, the Supreme Court interpreted the meaning of the Patent Act's fee-shifting provision, 35 U.S.C. § 285, which is identical to Lanham Act § 35(a).[3] The effect of the Court's interpretation was to relax

---

[3] The *Octane Fitness* standard is not itself especially clear. *See Octane Fitness, LLC v. ICON Health & Fitness, Inc.*, 572 U.S. 545, 554 (2014) ("We hold, then, that an 'exceptional' case is simply one that stands out from others with respect to the substantive strength of a party's litigating position (considering both the governing law and the facts of the case) or the unreasonable manner in which

significantly the standard for fee-shifting in the patent context. In light of the identity of 35 U.S.C. § 285 and Lanham Act § 35(a), the circuits have begun to apply *Octane Fitness* in the trademark context as well. *See, e.g., Sleepy's LLC v. Select Comfort Wholesale Corp.*, 909 F.3d 519, 531 (2d Cir. 2018); *SunEarth, Inc. v. Sun Earth Solar Power Co.*, 839 F.3d 1179, 1181 (9th Cir. 2016); *Georgia–Pac. Consumer Prods. LP v. von Drehle Corp.*, 781 F.3d 710 (4th Cir. 2015), as amended (Apr. 15, 2015); *Slep–Tone Entm't Corp. v. Karaoke Kandy Store, Inc.*, 782 F.3d 313, 317–18 (6th Cir. 2015); *Fair Wind Sailing, Inc. v. Dempster*, 764 F.3d 303 (3d Cir. 2014). Those circuits that have not yet incorporated *Octane Fitness* will very likely do so when given the opportunity.

In *Baker v. DeShong*, 821 F.3d 620, 625 (5th Cir. 2016), the Fifth Circuit spelled out the new standards that courts should apply to determine if the case before it is an "exceptional case" under Lanham Act § 35(a):

> We merge *Octane Fitness*'s definition of "exceptional" into our interpretation of § 1117(a) and construe its meaning as follows: an exceptional case is one where (1) in considering both governing law and the facts of the case, the case stands out from others with respect to the substantive strength of a party's litigating position; or (2) the unsuccessful party has litigated the case in an "unreasonable manner." *See Octane Fitness*, 134 S.Ct. at 1756. The district court must address this issue "in the case-by-case exercise of their discretion, considering the totality of the circumstances." *See id.*

Id. at 625. It remains to be seen how courts will apply these standards to the facts before them, and what role defendant's bad faith or willful infringement might continue to play.

E. Counterfeiting Remedies

In essence, for the defendant's conduct to constitute counterfeiting, (1) the plaintiff's mark must be registered and in use at the time of the defendant's conduct, (2) the defendant's mark must be identical with or substantially indistinguishable from the plaintiff's mark, (3) the defendant must be using its mark in connection with goods or services for which the plaintiff's mark is registered, and (4) the defendant must be using its mark without authorization from the plaintiff.

Lanham Act § 34(d)(1)(B), 15 U.S.C. § 1116(d)(1)(B), defines the term "counterfeit mark":

(B) As used in this subsection the term "counterfeit mark" means--

(i) a counterfeit of a mark that is registered on the principal register in the United States Patent and Trademark Office for such goods or services sold, offered for sale, or distributed and that is in use, whether or not the person against whom relief is sought knew such mark was so registered; or

(ii) a spurious designation that is identical with, or substantially indistinguishable from, a designation as to which the remedies of this chapter are made available by reason of section 220506 of Title 36 {relating to Olympics designations};

but such term does not include any mark or designation used on or in connection with goods or services of which the manufacture or producer was, at the time of the manufacture or production in question authorized to use the mark or designation for the type of goods or services so manufactured or produced, by the holder of the right to use such mark or designation.

---

the case was litigated. District courts may determine whether a case is 'exceptional' in the case-by-case exercise of their discretion, considering the totality of the circumstances."). While *Octane Fitness* addressed whether a defendant could obtain attorney's fees for defending against a plaintiff's allegedly meritless claim, the case is understood in trademark law to apply to fee-shifting in either direction.

Lanham Act § 45, 15 U.S.C. § 1127, additionally provides a definition of "counterfeit": "A 'counterfeit' is a spurious mark which is identical with, or substantially indistinguishable from, a registered mark." The Lanham Act § 45 definition of "counterfeit" is largely subsumed under the Lanham Act § 34 definition of "counterfeit mark," but § 45 adds the important detail that the similarity standard for purposes of determining counterfeiting is identity or near identity ("substantially indistinguishable from").

The remedies for counterfeiting are severe. They may consist primarily of (1) mandatory treble damages or, at the plaintiff's election, statutory damages, (2) ex parte seizure of the counterfeit goods, (3) attorney's fees, (4) prejudgment interest, and (5) civil destruction orders. The statutory provisions relating to treble damages and statutory damages appear in Lanham Act § 35(b) & (c), 15 U.S.C. § 1117(b) & (c):

(b) Treble damages for use of counterfeit mark

In assessing damages under subsection (a) for any violation of section 1114(1)(a) of this title or section 220506 of Title 36, in a case involving use of a counterfeit mark or designation (as defined in section 1116(d) of this title), the court shall, unless the court finds extenuating circumstances, enter judgment for three times such profits or damages, whichever amount is greater, together with a reasonable attorney's fee, if the violation consists of

(1) intentionally using a mark or designation, knowing such mark or designation is a counterfeit mark (as defined in section 1116(d) of this title), in connection with the sale, offering for sale, or distribution of goods or services; or

(2) providing goods or services necessary to the commission of a violation specified in paragraph (1), with the intent that the recipient of the goods or services would put the goods or services to use in committing the violation.

In such a case, the court may award prejudgment interest on such amount at an annual interest rate established under section 6621(a)(2) of Title 26, beginning on the date of the service of the claimant's pleadings setting forth the claim for such entry of judgment and ending on the date such entry is made, or for such shorter time as the court considers appropriate.

(c) Statutory damages for use of counterfeit marks

In a case involving the use of a counterfeit mark (as defined in section 1116(d) of this title) in connection with the sale, offering for sale, or distribution of goods or services, the plaintiff may elect, at any time before final judgment is rendered by the trial court, to recover, instead of actual damages and profits under subsection (a) of this section, an award of statutory damages for any such use in connection with the sale, offering for sale, or distribution of goods or services in the amount of--

(1) not less than $1,000 or more than $200,000 per counterfeit mark per type of goods or services sold, offered for sale, or distributed, as the court considers just; or

(2) if the court finds that the use of the counterfeit mark was willful, not more than $2,000,000 per counterfeit mark per type of goods or services sold, offered for sale, or distributed, as the court considers just.

Note that Lanham Act § 35(b)(1) limits treble damages only to intentional counterfeiting. When would counterfeiting not be intentional? Retailers may not be aware that they are selling counterfeit goods. *See* 2 GILSON ON TRADEMARKS § 5.19 (2019). *See also, e.g., Lorillard Tobacco Co. v. J.J. Shell Food Mart, Inc.*, 2005 U.S. Dist. LEXIS 26626 (N.D. Ill. 2005) (finding defendant retail store did not act willfully or with willful blindness under Lanham Act § 35(b)(1) in selling counterfeit cigarettes, and awarding a modest $7500 in damages).

812

Courts have not hesitated to grant substantial statutory damages awards. *See, e.g., Louis Vuitton Malletier, S.A. v. Akanoc Solutions, Inc.*, 658 F.3d 936, 946 (9th Cir. 2011) (affirming jury award of $10.5 million in statutory damages for contributory trademark infringement); *State of Idaho Potato Com'n v. G & T Terminal Packaging, Inc.*, 425 F.3d 708 (9th Cir. 2005) ($100,000 in statutory damages against ex-licensee of certification mark whose continued use was deemed to be counterfeit use); *Nike Inc. v. Variety Wholesalers, Inc.*, 274 F. Supp. 2d 1352, 1373 (S.D. Ga. 2003) ($900,000 in statutory damages; $100,000 for nine categories of counterfeit goods; awarded instead of $1,350,392 profits).

F. Federal Criminal Penalties for Counterfeiting

In 1984, Congress for the first time made trademark counterfeiting a federal crime. Congress has enhanced criminal penalties for counterfeiting with amendments in 1996, 2006, and 2008. *See* McCarthy § 30:116. The criminal penalty regime is set forth in 18 U.S.C. § 2320. The first offense by an individual may result in a fine of not more than $2,000,000 and/or imprisonment of not more than 10 years (for corporations, which are unimprisonable persons, the fine may not exceed $5,000,000). *See, e.g.,* Dorothy Atkins, *5-Hour Energy Scheme Nets Husband 7 Years, Wife 2 Years*, Law360, June 20, 2017, https://www.law360.com/articles/936408/5-hour-energy-scheme-nets-husband-7-years-wife-2-years (reporting criminal sentencing of ring leaders behind massive scheme to sell counterfeit 5-HOUR ENERGY drinks). A second offense by an individual may result in a fine of not more than $5,000,000 (for corporation, $15,000,000) and imprisonment of not more than 20 years. Individuals whose counterfeiting conduct results in "serious bodily injury or death" face significantly enhanced penalties. "Whoever knowingly or recklessly causes or attempts to cause serious bodily injury" from counterfeiting conduct faces up to 20 years in prison. "Whoever knowingly or recklessly causes or attempts to cause death" from counterfeiting conduct faces up to life in prison. Finally, individuals who engage in counterfeiting of "military goods or services" and pharmaceuticals also face enhanced penalties—for a first offense, not more than 20 years in prison and a fine of not more than $15,000,000; for a second offense, not more than 30 years in prison and a fine of not more than $30,000,000.

Made in the USA
Middletown, DE
12 January 2021